Jew, Nomad or Pariah

JEW, NOMAD OR PARIAH

studies on Hannah Arendt's Choice

HANS DERKS

Aksant
Amsterdam
2004

isbn 90 5260 157 7

Cover design: Bert Heesen Produkties, Utrecht
Printed in the Netherlands by: A-D Druk BV, Zeist

Aksant Academic Publishers, Cruquiusweg 31, 1019 AT Amsterdam, The Netherlands

'The Jews are the secret gypsies of history.'

Theodor Adorno in a letter to Max Horkheimer (18-9-1940)

''No assimilation could be achieved merely by surrendering one's own past, but ignoring the alien past. In a society on the whole hostile to the Jews – and that situation obtained in all countries in which Jews lived, down to the twentieth century – it is possible to assimilate only by assimilating to antisemitism also. If one wishes to be a normal person precisely like everybody else, there is scarcely any alternative to exchanging old prejudices for new ones. If that is not done, one involuntarily becomes a rebel ... and remains a Jew. And if one really assimilates, taking all the consequences of denial of one's own origin and cutting oneself off from those who have not or have not yet done it, one becomes a scoundrel.'

Hannah Arendt, *Rahel Varnhagen. The Life of a Jewess.* (1938/1957/97)

'If it is not race, what then makes a Jew? Religion? I am an atheist. Jewish Nationalism? I am an internationalist. In neither sense am I, therefore, a Jew. I am, however, a Jew by force of my unconditional solidarity with the persecuted and exterminated; because I feel the pulse of Jewish history ...'

Isaac Deutscher, *The Non-Jewish Jew* (1968)

'Unless, argues Rosenzweig, the Zionist Jew feels himself to be a nomad, a wanderer even in Zion, he will have betrayed the mission of Judaism, which is, precisely, one of unfulfilment, of the "not yet". Assimilation threatens the Diaspora; a premature "domesticity" and nationalism put Israel in danger. Is there any resting place?'

George Steiner, *Zion's shadows* (TLS, 27-2-2004)

TABLE OF CONTENTS

LIST OF ABBREVIATIONS

ABB   H. Arendt, H. Blücher, *Briefe 1936 – 1968*, Ed. L. Köhler (München: Piper, 1996);

ABK   H. Arendt, K. Blumenfeld, '*... in keinem Besitz verwurzelt' Die Korrespondenz.* Ed. I. Nordmann, I. Pilling (Hamburg: Rotbuch, 1995);

AJC   H. Arendt, K. Jaspers, *Correspondence 1926 – 1969*, Ed. L. Köhler, H. Saner (New York: Harcourt, 1993);

BF   *Between Friends. The Correspondence of Hannah Arendt and Mary McCarthy 1949-1975*, Ed. C. Brightman (New York: Harcourt, 1995);

BHH   B. Reicke, L. Rost (Ed.), *Bijbels-Historisch Woordenboek* (Utrecht: Het Spectrum, 1969/70) Vol. I-VI;

EC   M. Weber, *Economy and Society* (Berkeley: University of California Press, 1978);

EK   H. Arendt, *Essays und Kommentare. Vol. I. Nach Auschwitz; Vol. II. Die Krise des Zionismus.* Ed. E. Geisel, K. Bittermann (Berlin: Tiamat, 1989);

ENS   W. Benz, H. Gramml, H. Weiß (Ed.), *Enzyklopädie des Nationalsozialismus* (Stuttgart: Klett-Cotta, 1997);

GAR   M. Weber, *Gesammelte Aufsätze zur Religionssoziologie* (Tübingen: Mohr, 1923-1934), Vol. I-III;

GPS   M. Weber, *Gesammelte Politische Schriften* (Tübingen: Mohr, 1971);

HAB   H. Arendt, H. Broch, *Briefwechsel 1946 bis 1951.* Ed. P.M.Lützeler (Frankfurt a/M: Jüdischer Verlag, 1996);

HH   M. Berenbaum, A. Peck (Ed.), *The Holocaust and History. The Known, the Unknown, the Disputed and the Reexamined.* (Bloomington: Indiana University Press, 1998);

JP   H. Arendt, *The Jew as Pariah: Jewish identity and politics in the modern age*, Ed. Ron H. Feldman (New York: Grove Press, 1978);

OT   H. Arendt, *The Origins of Totalitarianism*, (New York: Harcourt, n.d.); new edition of the three parts in one volume with added prefaces [1979];

RV   H. Arendt, *Rahel Varnhagen. The Life of a Jewess.* Ed. L. Weissberg (Baltimore: Johns Hopkins, 1997);

TOT   H. Arendt, *The Origins of Totalitarianism* (New York: Harcourt, n.d.); new edition (1980) with added prefaces;

VEJ   R. Hilberg, *Die Vernichtung der europäischen Juden.* (Frankfurt a/M.: Fischer, 1991);

WG   M. Weber, *Wirtschaft und Gesellschaft* (Tübingen: Mohr, 1972).

PREFACE

Theodor Adorno's confession that Jews are the '*secret gypsies of history*' brought many pieces together for me from unrelated studies like analyses of Max Weber's social theory, the sad German history of the 20th century or the importance of nomadism in ancient Greek life. The last seems the strangest one in this combination. Yet nomadism is not confined to gypsies in their caravans, the deserts and their age-old political fata morgana's so well-known since Ibn Khaldûn (1332-1406) or the orientalisms of the 19th century. Today, one can find genuine nomadism in large parts of Asia and Africa, while a nomadic way of life can be found in the poorest corners of the world's megalopoleis and in a typical quality of the (richest) globalizing elites as well. Nomadism was and will be a phenomenon of all times from which we sedentarians still know too little as is shown so bitterly in the present Asian, Near Eastern and African adventures of USA, European or Soviet governments.

Whereas the basis of the following texts is formed by analyses of the relationship between '*nomads*' and '*sedentarians*', the main aim of the book is the *reflection* on Theodor Adorno's confession by means of this basic antagonism. I hope in this way to contribute to the present debate about the identity of the *relationship* between Jews, 'non-Jewish Jews', non-Jews and anti-Jews in their historical and present settings. The debate about this relationship is of the utmost importance not only for Jews as Shoah and Holocaust victims which receives most of the publicity, but also for the highly necessary emancipation of Germans and other Europeans as perpetrators and for the serious difficulties national minorities suffer in a globalizing world in which new perpetrators exercise the old power play.

We all know that for many reasons this relationship is now caught in the deepest crisis since 1945 and that it seems as if several separate, long-standing discussions have become entangled in an unexpected and unpleasant way. This cannot lead to a loud silence but only to an open debate in which political propaganda like, for instance, the blatant identifications of 'Israel' and 'Holocaust' or 'Palestine' and 'Liberation' should be excluded. It is also inevitable that the debate about these matters cannot be done in a hypocritical value-free way but in a sharp and intellectual way. That is also the case in this book and its essays, given that here we can deal with (counter)arguments and proofs better than in direct media debates. What are the general contours of our discussions?

Adorno did not disclose the sources of his knowledge about the (ancient) Jews, which were – in all probability – Max Weber and/ or Werner Sombart. Hannah Arendt, however, had a specific relationship with Max Weber and with 'the Jew' through her extensive reflections on what was called the *pariah* status of Jews. Through her writings the complicated background of Weber's world historical and theological thoughts can be combined with her own political, historical and other analyses. Moreover, she stands anew in the limelight of international scientific publicity, not the least because she drove many intelligent people mad with her controversial opinions about Zionism, Jewry or the Holocaust. Or seriously disappointed people with her Heidegger relationship, as recently George Steiner was: 'It is in a Jacob's bout with the dark angel of *Sein und Zeit* that Jewish thinkers from Hermann Cohen to Derrida and beyond hammer out their own identity and are, sometimes, left lame. The case of Hannah Arendt is only the saddest.' (TLS, 27-2-2004). However, till now her "nomadic view" or the "nomadic view" in general are not considered as in this book, although it will be shown how they serve to re-stimulate deadlockeddebates.

Whoever wants to uncover the fundamental characteristics of the nomad-sedentarian relationship as circumscribed in the four leitmotifs of this book is confronted with a 'Holocaust framework' and a series of specific debates. Today, these are pretty rough, as shown in Peter Novick's *The Holocaust and Collective Memory*; Tim Cole's *Images of the Holocaust. The myth of the 'Shoah Business'*; and in particular, Norman Finkelstein's *The Holocaust Industry: Reflections on the Exploitation of Jewish Suffering*, Daniel Goldhagen's *A Moral Reckoning* or the recent Dutch controversial study of Hajo Meyer *Het Einde van het Jodendom (The End of Judaism)*. Also controversies between Jewish groups about the division of the money received from European banks or governments open many old wounds and demonstrate the serious difficulties of defining a Jew, a Shoah or even a Holocaust victim. Last but not least there is the case of Israel. The ascent of Netanyahu, Barak and Sharon and the outbreak of the next 'Intifadah', have not only resulted in the deepest Israeli crisis ever, but also in mixing up a terrorism and anti-Americanism debate with all possible old and future world problems.

Only in a few notes and passages will some of these problems be discussed. Through the various analyses of 'Jews as nomads and/or pariah', however, I hope to contribute to a genuine *European* alternative for the serious difficulty of 'being Jew in this world' relative to 'being a minority in this world'. It is, therefore, a highly sensitive discussion in which I will not support any theological position. I am a historian and sociologist, which is also a relevant statement vis-à-vis my criticism of Weber's theological stand. Another a priori confession is equally important here.

Inherent in much American-Jewish anxiety is the real fear that strong assimilating tendencies are detrimental for the religious and Israeli support among American Jewry. Because of the peculiar course of this study (see, for exemple, Hannah Arendt's quotation above), it is right to state here that I personally respect the individual's decision to assimilate with all consequences. It is also this American-Jewish anxiety which was a major drive to use "The Holocaust" in support of a religious battle for Israel as, for instance, Goldhagen is raging anew in his recent assault on Roman Catholicism. Indeed, in my book much can be found in support of such a battle and much against it, and not only because my heroine, Hannah Arendt, is one of Goldhagen's or radical Zionists' *bêtes noires*. The main point here is that I am not writing a political pamphlet about Roman Catholic guilt and desire to pay its debt. Although I sympathize with this aim and acknowledge how incontestable much of what he writes about the dubious Catholic hierarchy is, it seems to me not the best strategy to send a lightweight like Goldhagen into this old Roman arena full of professional gladiators, whatever his mediamatic value.

Anyway, new questions and answers on the Holocaust phenomenon (in the first and last resort an European matter!) are urgently needed, but can be given here in a limited sense only. My much debated last book, *Deutsche Westforschung. Ideologie und Praxis im 20.Jahrhundert*, opened up a whole new field of research related to these questions. The present book analyses *preconditions* of the 20th century Holocaust, *reactions* on this disaster with its world-wide impact, and *understanding* (definitions) of the many kinds of victims during the Holocaust and Shoah.

In the large political and ideological discussions which started to rage after 1945, the writings of Hannah Arendt and Max Weber played a pivotal role. They disclose here how their 'mutual concept', *Jew as nomad and pariah*, stand at the very centre of their controversial thoughts and how reflections on it can contribute to necessary political solutions. Therefore, this book is addressed not only to a readership interested in a critical reception of Arendt's and Weber's work or in broadly historical information about the relationship between nomads and sedentarians but also to a readership involved in some 'Jewish case' if one is tolerant enough to discuss challenging perspectives.

This book went through a long gestation, and, therefore, many people should be thanked for encouraging me during the thinking and writing or for reading the whole or parts of it. I mention here only the following. I thank the editors of *Archive européenne de sociologie/ European Journal of Sociology* for refusing according to them 'a very important,... rich' article just because Max Weber was criticized sharply for his antisemitic or anti-Judaistic thoughts. It is published here as the third chapter. Ezra and Sascha Talmor (Haifa) are thanked for demonstrating their intellectual independence by publishing this text in a slightly revised form as 'Nomads, Jews and Pariahs' in their famous journal *The European Legacy*, 4 (1999), p. 24-48.

Furthermore, I was also pleased by the highly inspired 'answer' of bestseller author Harry Mulisch after sending him the draft of the eighth chapter in which he appears as the controversial author of among others a book on the Eichmann trial; as a possible reaction on my analysis he immediately published the essay *Het zevende Land/ The Seventh Country*, an evocation of his living in and wandering through seven earthly and spiritual 'spaces'.

It was a consolation that my nearly 100 year old friend, the sociologist Wim Wertheim (died November 1998), could still be inspired by our discussions to alter some of his lifelong and strongly defended theses. We specifically discussed my analysis of Max Weber's controversial views on China which appears here in a revised form as chapter two. It was published as 'Nomads in Chinese and Central Asian History' in: *Oriens Extremus*, 41 (1999), p. 7-34. The historian Gabriel Kolko was so kind to discuss an earlier draft of the whole manuscript in a highly stimulating temper. I also thank Marti Huetink for his confidence in this project, Kim Hershorn and, in particular, Alison Fisher who helped with editing and correcting the English.

Some neologisms are used and explained as they are introduced (see, for instance, Introduction, note 4). First is 'antisemitism', which I prefer to 'anti-Semitism' because 99% of the anti-Jewish attitudes and thoughts do not refer to 'Semites' and I do not want to constantly repeat this typical nonsensical racist concept: in 'antisemitism' I strike a balance between a historical phenomenon and actual practice. 'Holocaust' is taken as an overall concept incorporating the attempts to destroy and the destruction of all humans deemed by the Nazis and their supporters as 'inferior' or 'sub-human' (*Minderwertig; Untermensch*); consequently, the *Shoah* is seen as the destruction of Jews, whatever the definition of these peoples, while it would be worthwhile to make comparable concepts for the fate of the Gypsies, homosexuals, Poles, etc. Confusion around the 'Holocaust' could be avoided in this way.

Amsterdam, July 2004
www.hderks.dds.nl

INTRODUCTION

A radio program[1] broadcast on the 50th anniversary of the Second World War testified to children yelling in the streets of the Dutch government seat, The Hague, where Jews were rounded up in 1943. The children shouted: '*Woestijnnomaden! Woestijnnomaden!*' ('Desert nomads! Desert nomads!'). Strangely enough, it was also a common Dutch practice to talk about the invading Germans as 'The Huns', one of the most famous examples of the alleged (Mongolian) *nomadic menace*. Here, in a most dramatic context, the interrelations looked for in this book can be felt, and a bewildering number of questions arise immediately. Two of the least strange ones are: How is it possible that both perpetrators and victims were abused as 'nomads'? Why on earth is 'nomad' abusive at all? Is "The East" the home of all menaces for Westerners?

During the second World War the Germans tried and failed to erect the only Jewish ghetto in Dutch history; apparently they needed a ghetto in Amsterdam to facilitate the capture of their victims. Of course, that was a very different constellation to the former Jewish quarter in this city which was in 1941 only for 50 per cent populated by 'Israelites'.

The German sociologist Max Weber (1864-1920), among others discoverer of the 'pariah/ guest' concept, knew all about it. During a holiday trip to Holland (August 1907), he, like every tourist, visited the fisher tribe of Marken Island in the Zuiderzee not very far from Amsterdam. Here, the blond people, clothed in strange costumes, lived in humble houses concentrated on sandbanks. From Amsterdam Weber wrote the following postcard to his wife about another visit: 'Yesterday I was in the library, and then, in the evening, I went into the Jewish quarter [*Judenviertel*] – fantastic faces [*tolle Physiognomien*] and a horrible screaming and market mess, till at about six o'clock the sabbath [*Schabbes*] starts and silence descends.'[2] Elsewhere in the Netherlands about 30 per cent of the Jews did not live in some quarter, which meant that all of them had to be caught *as neighbours*. Thus, the yelling playmates and the adults who indoctrinated these

---

1. VPRO radio 4-5-1995.
2. Max Weber, *Briefe 1906-1908* Ed. M. Rainer Lepsius, W. Mommsen (Tübingen: Mohr, 1990), p. 371.

kids said good-bye to their disappearing neighbours wholeheartedly. What does this mean subjectively? In a German Jewish paper Joachim Prinz related the following impression (17 April 1935):

> 'Now we become conscious of the fact that we live in a ghetto. This ghetto, however, differs in many things from what we understood till this moment about its meaning and reality ... it has a sign. This sign is: neighbourless. The fate of the Jews is to be without neighbours. Probably, this shall happen only once in the world and, who knows, how long one can bear this: life without neighbours ...'[3]

The image of Holland is of a place that had always shown the highest degree of hospitality to foreigners. However, – relatively speaking – almost nowhere else in Europe were more Jews caught and transported to concentration camps. In the dangerously hypocritical country that Holland still is today, practically no-one wishes to address the background of this remarkable contradiction, let alone initiate measures to avoid a recurrence. Now, against all possible international agreements and without any principal necessity, the Christian government decided in 2004 to expel no fewer than 20,000 foreigners and introduced vignettes to mark those who can remain for a while! Relatively few people protested.

Did Dutch Jews have (and still do) the status of foreigners in a social or juridical sense? Certainly not! They were (and are) more or less integrated in Dutch society, and at the time, most of them had a Dutch passport and had almost nothing to do with a Jewish religion. Why, then, 'desert nomads'? What were the similarities and differences between those strange fishermen and Jews, except that they were both touristic attractions? Were these people similar to Weber's 'guests/pariahs' notwithstanding their citizenship?

Whoever tries to answer these questions, inevitably, will be confronted with the intriguing work of the political philosopher Hannah Arendt (1906-1975). In her life she made a specific choice in order to jump over history, the history of *The Jew as Pariah*, the title of one of her many books. The leading theme running through the third and last part of the present book will be the character, motives and consequences of her choice in order to fulfil the aims described in the preface. Seeking for an understanding of Hannah's choice confronts us in the preceding chapters with a specific history from Adam to Adolf which Arendt wanted to negate.

Certainly, at a purely emotional level, her choice originates from the conclusion given in the Varnhagen citation above and finds a definite formulation in Adorno's dictum: a man who is accused by Arendt of attempted cooperation with the Nazis in 1933. Both of them were also highly skilled in incorporating subjective elements

---

3. Cited in G.Schwarz, *Die nationalsozialistischen Lager* (Frankfurt a/M. : Fischer, 1996), p. 41.

into broad historical or sociological argumentations, and it is these which will concern us here, in particular because the substance of both citations form our main thesis: the decision not to assimilate into a (sedentary) society has to be followed by the acceptance of a nomadic way of social life in which an individual intellectual and material fulfilment has the better chance. In my view, Hannah Arendt made this specific choice, which is of paramount intellectual and political importance.

Whatever study of historical experiences in remote or contemporary times I am obliged to provide below, we cannot forget that Hannah's choice shall always remain an existential one forced in this case by experiences subsumed under the heading *Auschwitz*. Another of Adorno's dictums, that writing poems 'after Auschwitz' is barbaric, is well known but receives a curious significance through Hannah's almost mysterious other choice to exchange poems even after 1945 with her former lover, the highly compromised word – conjurer and dubious philosopher Martin Heidegger. It is again Adorno who is one of the main antagonists of this man, who displays behaviour typical of those who do not want to take any responsibility for crimes they (in)directly supported or, in more general terms, for those who deny the intimate relationship between their social and thinking behaviour and consider themselves as gods.

The fundamental historical and socio-anthropological contradictions signalled here in passing (*Täter versus Opfer*, perpetrator versus victim; sedentarians versus nomads; barbarism versus civilization) as well as the conspiracy-like relationships, interdependencies or love – hate connections between these antipodes and the often strong animosities between the victims (Adorno versus Arendt, vice versa) foreshadow the complexities we have to master in this book. Reliable guides in this exploratory activity are difficult to find, which is also true for the much studied heroine of the study, Hannah Arendt. It is another thesis of this study, that she borrowed a pariah/guest theory from Max Weber which she expanded without knowing what Weber really wanted to express. In her search for a way out of the many dilemmas of her life and times, this was not the least of the reasons why she could not see the dark in which she walked for so long.

A statement like this presupposes that Max Weber and his pariah theory must receive important attention. However, Weber in his turn develops this theory in his sociology of religion as an offshoot of or closely related to his more general views of the role of nomads in world history. This makes it necessary that the fundamental elements of a nomadic way of life have to be shown once in their historical and present, sociological or political contexts.

In the battlefield of this book is the division of labour of a traditional simplicity: the man Max Weber acts as the arch-perpetrator and defender of the oikoidal stronghold;[4] the woman Hannah Arendt, very unsatisfied with the predetermined role of women, has chosen not even to act as a kind of Florence Nightingale but as a fully armed Jeanne d'Arc without a nation. My role could be circumscribed as her unarmed adviser showing in the end a way out of this battle.

*

Because this book has to tell a complicated and highly problematic story in only a few pages, I have chosen a prudent strategy. In *A First Round* a short exposé of *pariah* definitions leads to two sketches of situations or contexts in which the main elements of the pariah *complex* are revealed. Together they serve as the problem-definition of the following study from which sequence and subject of the argumentation can be derived in a reasonable way.

The first sketch is related to the famous biblical story of Ishmael, first son of the nomad Abraham; the other tells the story of a traditional Jewish intellectual – in this case the historian Arnaldo Momigliano – who is objectively as a scholar and subjectively as an Italian Jew confronted with Weber's pariah concept and the practice of a pariah. Chapter 1 opens up a specific, vast, world historical panorama and at the same time provides an impression of the complicated individual reactions to the European drama of the Holocaust and Shoah. The former is detailed in the next two chapters, and the latter are placed in perspective in chapters 4, 5 and 6.

The steppes, lowlands or highlands of China, Mongolia and Central Asia form such a vast panorama; certainly, here can be found the longest and most profound nomadic traditions of all sorts. If one wants to know something about nomads, one has to study their history, economy, ecology, anthropology, etc. Herodotos

---

4. The meaning of 'oikoidal' which will be used throughout this book can be explained as follows. The Aristotelian use of the Greek *oikos* (house, family, household), which stresses, among other things, the absolute power of the *pater familias* over the life and death of wives and children or the virtues of an autarkic, agricultural-based economy, became the model for the monarchical or aristocratic household and state from the early modern period. The political as well as the economic aspects of this *oikos* were the subject of the most powerful European theories of society (from Bodin to Roman Catholicism, from mercantilism to nineteenth-century cameralism). In some way or other, they all stressed princely autocracy or paternalism, strong state influence over the economy, etc. Political and economic freedoms, as they developed in urban commercial and industrial centres, were always viewed with great suspicion by this state-centred thinking. In the 19th century a real and effective bourgeois counter-concept developed, the market with its 'laws' of supply and demand. The real battle of *Oikos gegen Markt*, as Max Weber would say, started with the rise of industrial and financial capitalism, a specific way of manipulating the market. Therefore, below I use the adjective *oikoidal* to refer not only to its literal meaning ('of or representing the *oikos*, house, etc.') but first and foremost to an autocratic state-centred concept with a long European tradition. A good introduction to the relevant 'oikoidal theory' has recently been given by D. Lindenfeld, *The Practical Imagination. The German Sciences of State in the Nineteenth Century* (Chicago/London : University of Chicago Press, 1997).

had already discovered this and provided extensive descriptions of the Scythians, after which he turned to stories about the North African nomads.

Chapter 2 has the same aim: it informs the reader about the main elements of the complex and controversial relations between nomadic and sedentary societies from past to present. We shall be looking at these relations through the eyes of Max Weber. This scholar with his vast and encyclopaedic knowledge about the non-Western world was strangely ignorant about this Asian nomadism. Therefore, the chapter provides the most important elements of 'theory and practice of anti-nomadism in sedentary societies' as well. Apart from this, it introduces Weber's world historical theory.

In the most profound way this theory is exploited in his in-depth analysis of the Near Eastern nomadic scene of the Old Testament, *Das antike Judentum*. Here, Weber demonstrates also more practical knowledge about his subject. From time immemorial (Adam – Eve and Cain – Abel onwards), nomads and pastoralists combined the valuable production and professional marketing of labour, basic foodstuffs and animal products with commercial and money transactions. Their market behaviour, anti – governmentism and way of life became a pretext and starting point for many metaphoric and real contradictions. The Bible, however, is first and foremost a battleground of highly contradictory theories and belief systems. Weber informs us about them and takes sides.

His anti – Judaism (if not antisemitism) is matched by his oikoidal ideology and anti – nomadism. This work can be seen as a *traite d'union* within the learned German generation of people like Wellhausen, Harnack, Sombart, Troeltsch or Eduard Meyer. They belong to the high-priests who are mostly left out of all Holocaust or Shoah discussions except to deliver an obligatory quotation. Not only is their work highly influential in the European intellectual traditions, it supported a strong state-power, expansionism and stringent nationalism as well. Their contribution to the ascent of Nazism is still in need of an explanation. In any case, after this analysis of an always topical Biblical theme, we perceive the tricky concept on which Hannah Arendt based her political theories.

In the next part the perspective is narrowed to the European scene 'where it all happened'. Three main characteristics come to the fore in the following chapters. One aspect of the pariah complex concerns the *guest-position* of the stranger; for Weber 'guest' and 'pariah' sometimes seem to be identical. Question: If such a guest is put into a ghetto as happened only with 'Jewish guests' in Europe, what does it mean except that you have to replace the world historical scene directly with an European one if you seek an explanation? Is a ghetto an unorthodox means to sedentarize nomads? Or place to control the exploitation of a useful labour force? In any respects, central elements of the *Jewish Question* as related to the *Nomadic Question* can be discovered in the theory and practice of the European ghettos. What did it mean before the war to be a 'Jewish guest' in a country? Prinz showed how in Nazi Germany the binding to a ghetto became the logo of the Jew in a spiritual as well as a practical and historical sense.

Max Weber firmly roots the ghetto elements in Jewish nature itself and transcends time and place as if he supported current racial theories. His famous colleague, Werner Sombart, was the first who connected the Jewish and the Nomadic Questions in a controversial theory about the place and influence of Jews in European economic life. Weber and Sombart and their unexpected supporters will be confronted in chapter 4 with ghetto practices past and present.

Chapter 5 is concerned with the astonishing focus in European history on seeing *Jews as scapegoats*. Another thesis of this book is, that it would be a great mistake to see anti – Judaism as the only reason for the Shoah, let alone the Holocaust. Therefore, priority must be given in the debate to making fundamental distinctions between this anti-Judaism, antisemitism and the actions of states (governments) against Jews as one of the many *non-conformist* elements in society. These three distinctions have their own history in Europe and *coalesce only* in the beginning of the violent 20th century with disastrous effects unforeseen by any of the 'parts'. This chapter retells the story of what is erroneously called 'The First Holocaust' (the expulsion of Jews from Spain in 1492) to demonstrate the validity of this threefold distinction.

With this information we have not yet discovered enough basic elements of the relationship at stake to start the discussion about the present (post- 1945) situation. After 'the Jew as guest' and as 'scapegoat', the most dramatic element consists of the 'Jew as victim', as usual in this study 'related to the Nomadic Question'. As a mass-phenomenon it is typical of the first part of the 20th century: why and how people could become 'Jewish victims'. In chapter 6 we have to discuss a most painful problem: what does it mean if your identity is defined by your worst enemy, a fate followed, certainly for the proletarians among these subjects, by a terrible death. In the past there had mostly been a realistic oppor-tunity to choose. Now, in the 20th century this chance was too small or too often non-existent. A quite new analysis of the fate of the Dutch Jews (1900-1940) will not provide us with all the answers we are looking for, but it will give us a solid basis with which to understand the very different situation after 1945 and to judge the theories produced by Arendt, Weber and so on.

The analysis of Arnaldo Momigliano's criticism of Weber's pariah concept enabled us to see how a high degree of assimilation blocks understanding of the (alleged) pariah position. In this light it is an intriguing question as to why so many Jewish intellectuals and scholars, including Hannah Arendt, accepted the pariah concept as politically correct. In *The Present Context* we, first, have to cope with the ever increasing uneasiness with the concept 'Jew' as the object of inquiry 'Jew as pariah, guest, nomad'. Therefore, the first chapter of this part of the study is devoted to this question: who or what is a Jew? The strange fact remains that even nowadays there is no satisfactory answer. Different authorities come up with their conflicting definitions. This is not as disturbing as the fact that the Nazis introduced a definition which soon after led to the murder of about 6 million people who had specific qualities mentioned in *their* definition. Long ago the Christians created their own 'Jew' which sometimes led to serious persecution as well.

Unsatisfied with the results of this chapter, one of the aims of the subsequent chapters is to provide a sound answer with the help of Hannah Arendt, herself a staunch defender of Weber's pariah concept, her former husband, Günther Anders, 'secret gypsies' like Harry Mulisch or Alan Bloom (Saul Bellow's new hero, Ravelstein) as an ambiguous user of the pariah concept. Together they produce in fact the arguments to liberate us of the concept and its consequences.

It is inevitable that as we approach the end of the book, it becomes clearer that we are dealing with the fallacies of the nation-state and something like 'the winning of the world as home' in the future. This quite new perspective is opened up thanks to Hannah Arendt's 'nomadic choice', which brings us back into the orbit of a world historical development starting with the strange adventures of Adam, Eve and Co. and, therefore, with my reflections on an old world historical context. Assistance to overcome a certain 'jet-lag' in this trip will be received from a rather unexpected quarter, the famous Arab historian Ibn Khaldûn. He knew many interesting things about the behaviour of Jews, but he is primarily one of the best sources in 'nomadic matters'. What was his advice to a non-Arab neighbour? This is not only of interest regarding the present situation in Israel. It gives us a clue in our problem-analysis which will start now with the most basic stories and analyses about the interrelations between the *Jewish* and *Nomadic Questions*. Although the 'eternal' and serious effects of the '*Cain-Abel complex*' can always rear their ugly heads again, the possibilities to heal the cleavages seem to be more interesting than could be concluded from a *Genesis* text.

In the city of The Hague, where Jews were rounded up in 1943 and children abused them with their cries: 'Desert nomads!', there is an unobtrusive monument near the Gedempte Gracht with the text: '*Remember what Amalek did to you. Never forget it.*' Whether we like it or not, after reading the following chapters, this warning will become a different one.

Moses stream near Petra in Edom. Source: M. Soloweitschik, *Die Welt der Bibel* (Berlin: Jüdischer Verlag, 1926), p. 12.

1. A FIRST ROUND

'I am a pariah and I know not out of what elements to rebuild myself a dignity and personality.'

Bernard – Lazare, Dreyfusard (1896)

From outcasts to 'pariah states'

A brief review of the different meanings and (Jewish) usages of *pariah* is appropriate to clarify boundaries of the debate. 'Pariah' in the OED has an early imperialistic background because it originated from the Tamil language in 1613 (*paraiyar* meaning literally 'hereditary drummer') and is related, in particular, to the domestics in European service coming from the lowest caste in Southern India. Probably these domestics damaged too many tea cups and tea pots of the English ladies, because a hundred years later all members of low Hindu castes were called 'pariah'. Again a century later, at the time when a whole sociopolitical colonial hierarchy had overloaded the Indian societies, 'pariah' received the abstract meaning of 'social outcast'.

From a very honourable meaning the concept became increasingly more negative and more general. From a domestic servant of the most prestigious households, it evolved into social scum which must be kept as far away from those households as possible. Apparently, 'caste' in 'outcast(e)' meant nothing more than the *white* overlords. 'Outcast-Pariah' was one of the counter-concepts of the white colonial *oikos*. Therefore, it cannot be accidental that in the 19th century this general meaning also became popular within the father- or motherlands and in typical European discourses. In addition, the *Britannica CD* (1997) states that in the old colony exactly the reverse happened: Mahatma Gandhi liberated not only his country from the whites, but renamed their pariahs into Harijans, i.e. children of God.

In 19th century Europe, several Jewish desiderata were formulated in the wake of their emancipation. Already in 1823 a Jewish-German playwright, Michael Beer, thought of supporting Jewish emancipation by writing a play called *Der Paria*. This reproduced the concept's history, as sketched above, in a most perfect way. Here a Hindu outcast, Gadhi (not yet Gandhi), complained of 'being born to an unfortunate tribe"[1] which, in the name of Brahma, is denied civil and human dignity.

Beer's definition of this dignity is given in the passage in which Gadhi explains to his German audience how eager he is to fight for his fatherland: 'I have a fatherland and I wish to protect it. Give me a life and I shall repay with interest.' Very uneconomical, the man is prepared to pay the highest possible interest in advance because he wants to sacrifice his life and the life of his son on the bloody altar of (monarchical and imperialistic) war games: 'Do you see this boy who stands beside me? This is my child – my child. He fought for you. His father fell for you.' Alas, 'I am only a pariah, I cannot be permitted to fight for my fatherland.'

You can hear the laughter after the curtain fell: applause for this foreigner who wants to die for *our* fatherland; it spares the lives of our own children and men. It is not certain whether Jews have learned their lesson in this respect: there were numerous cases during the Shoah in which they pleaded for mercy on the grounds that they had fought for the Germans in World War I. But, was there an alternative for these sacrifices for the 'oikoidal case'? Or, wasn't it precisely the most relevant preview of things to come? To be cannon-fodder for the big powers?

At the end of the 19th century in Germany[2] as well as in France, *pariah* was often used in connection with Jews, particularly during and after the Dreyfus Affair. Not only antisemites but also Dreyfusards, like the left-wing journalist Bernard-Lazare (1865-1903), or Zionists thought of it as an appropriate concept. Thus, the father of Zionism, Theodor Herzl, was rather categorical in writing to influential Jews: 'You are pariahs. You have to live on tenterhooks lest anyone deprive you of your rights of property.' Apart from his declaration cited at the beginning of this chapter, Bernard-Lazare described the position of a pariah as follows:

'No longer are Jews cloistered in the West, no longer are chains stretched at the ends of the streets on which they dwell, but around them has been created a hostile atmosphere, an atmosphere of distrust, of latent hatred, of unavowed –

1. See E. Shmueli, The 'Pariah-People' and its 'Charismatic Leadership', in: *Proceedings American Academy for Jewish Research*, New York, 1968 p. 167-247. This article is one of the very few criticizing Weber (from a religious point of view), which is largely reproduced by Arnaldo Momigliano. See below. For the citations on Beer, Lazare and Herzl see p. 170, 171. Strindberg also wrote a play *Paria(h)* in 1889, as did the very influential British diplomat and extreme Germaniphobe, Baron Vansittart (1881-1957), with *Les Pariahs* (1902). For a comparable approach as Shmueli see at present the 'secular Judaist' D. Nirenberg, The birth of the pariah: Jews, Christian dualism, and social science, an article which I found on www.looksmart.com (Spring 2003) who knows already good sources for his analysis: Max Weber, Werner Sombart, Hannah Arendt and Arnaldo Momigliano. A comparison with my arguments in this book demonstrates clearly who is the "secular analyst".

2. So, for instance, in J. Bluntschli's famous *Deutsches Staats-Wörterbuch* (Stuttgart: Expedition des Staats-Wörterbuchs, 1860), Vol.5, p. 444 one can read: 'Nur in dem Kirchenstaate, der in allen Dingen die mittelalterlichen Zustände festzuhalten sich zuletzt vergeblich abmüht, sind die Juden noch in dem Ghetto als eine Kaste europäischer Parias eingeschlossen.' Regarding the emancipation of Jews in Germany Bluntschli's article is quite interesting, but I have not seen it used yet.

and thus all the more powerful – prejudices, a ghetto more terrible than one whence you might escape by rebellion or exile. Even when this animosity is dissembled, the intelligent Jew is aware of it, henceforward he feels a resistance, he has the impression of a wall erected between him and those in whose midst he lives.'

Bernard-Lazare called the (non-)emancipated Jew, '*the (un)conscious pariah*'. However, there was another side to this coin. This left-wing journalist made other distinctions as well, such as between honest, hard-working *israélites* and dishonest, mean, rich, orthodox *juifs* who were 'voluntary pariahs' as well. In this way Bernard-Lazare erected a high wall 'between him and those in whose midst he lived' and the many Jewish immigrants from the East, who flooded Paris in those days:

> 'And what should I care, me, an *israélite* of France, about these Russian usurers, these Galician taverners and moneylenders, these Polish horse-traders ... [T]hanks to these hordes, with whom we are confounded, it is forgotten that we have lived in France for almost 2,000 years ... We should abandon them.'[3]

Similar opinions, although less harsh, could be found for *Ostjuden* in Holland and elsewhere. So, paradoxically, the thesis becomes provable that (established) pariahs create (foreign) pariahs! We will have the opportunity to comment later on these embarrassing statements. Let us first finish our 'archaeological survey' of the pariah concept.

It is easy to find examples that fit the present situation. In an expert dictionary P.L. van den Berghe substitutes 'pariah' by the category *underclass*, recently coined by William Wilson: 'Near synonyms for underclass are Lumpenproletariat, sub-proletariat, pariahs, and outcaste groups.'[4] The author explains how each of these

---

3. N.L.Green, *The Pletzl of Paris. Jewish immigrant workers in the Belle Epoque* (New York: Holmes&Meier, 1986), p. 59. Later Lazare had contacts with the emigrants states Nancy Green, trying to pardon Lazare for his remarks. But at the moment she lifts the veil over these contacts (p. 180, 181) she shows, in fact, the foundations of the wall. First, Lazare writes that antisemitism was directed, in particular, at the Jewish immigrants. How this is to be understood is clear: a Parisian shopkeeper complained in a left-wing paper that he had lost the competition with the Jewish immigrants and that he now should vote for an antisemitic party. From the lowest party-member to Jean Jaurès himself they started directly attacking the Jewish immigrant. Jaurès: '*We protest against the invasion of foreign workers ...(and).. cheap wages ... we who are internationalists ... but what we do not want is that international capital seeks out labor on the market where it is most debased ... to cast it onto the French market ...*' Here is the twist which made the Jewish immigrant the victim of all parties, left and right, sedentary Jews or two-faced socialists. For Lazare's antisemitism see N. Wilson, *Bernard-Lazare. Antisemitism and the problem of Jewish identity in late nineteenth-century France* (Cambridge: Cambridge University Press, 1978), p. 66-109.
4. E.Cashmore (Ed.), *Dictionary of Race and Ethnic Relations* (London: Routledge, 1994), p. 334. See from the same author the lemma 'Caste' (p. 56ff.) and 'Segregation' (p. 307 ff.).

terms has special connotations and is used by scholars of different ideological backgrounds. *Lumpenproletariat* is favoured by Marxists and by those who want to stress economic dimensions of status; *pariah* refers to the 'moral devaluation of the status group and is used more by liberal scholars.' It is not explained whether the word has a historical or empirical value, nor that it could be related only to a perception of a devaluation. This is not unimportant since the *Britannica CD 97* talks in its Judaism lemma about nothing less than 'the Jews, even as a pariah people' which should be 'both a challenge and a warning'.

Another example concerns the perception of Israel in Stephen Green's *Living by the Sword.*[5] As is well known, on September 22, 1979, Israel and South Africa tested a nuclear bomb or device in the sea between South Africa and Antarctica. Nine years later and after scrutinizing the evidence, Green concluded: 'Two pariah states had now tested a credible, usable tactical nuclear device.'[6] Green did not define pariah, but apartheid morally and politically isolated South Africa from the whole world. By implication 'pariah' means 'outcast' in a general sense; in this case 'somebody' is 'cast out of the community of civilized nations' or something like that. This must be the case with Israel as well, thanks to its anti-Palestinian, anti-Arabian, etc. policies. That the USA from the beginning of the Cold War considered Israel as its personal hireling and guardian of its oil interests did not stop Green from using 'pariah' to describe this country.

Green might have been reminiscing about the situation the playwright Beer

5. S.Green, *Living by the Sword. America and Israel in the Middle East 1968-1987* (London: Faber&Faber, 1988) which was preceded by *Taking Sides. America's Secret Relations with a Militant Israel 1948-1967* (1984).

6. S. Green, *Living by the Sword* , p. 133 written in a chapter entitled 'Pariahs with Bombs'. Green made a correct prediction in 1988 as he wrote in the book's concluding chapter refering to the war raging between Iraq and Iran: 'But even the concerted efforts of the Reagan Administration and the Government of Israel will not be able to keep that war going for ever and, when it is over, one or both of the adversaries will turn their attention to Jerusalem.' (p. 232) What about his other profetic conclusion: 'By now it should be apparent to all that no amount of land, no amount of arms will assure a safe future for Israel.'? Now, a quarter of a century later Israel is still a pariah country as is told by a Rabbi Wein: 'There are two countries in the world that are international pariahs ... One is Saddam Hussein's Iraq. This lawless regime has been a menace ... The other pariah country is naturally the State of Israel. There is no country that has been the subject of so many UN resolutions ...' ! See http://rabbiwein.com for the rest of this brilliant political analysis. He is not alone. See Rabbi Schulweis, "Creating Pariahs in the Jewish Community" (March 10, 2003) on www.jewishjournal.com or Rabbi Greenberg who in his sharp attack on Christianity tells among others: 'The "nice guy" Christian version was to ghettoize Jews, treat them like pariahs, make them suffer but keep them alive, until the Jews finally repented and became Christians.' See www.beliefnet.com. These rabbi's could be reassured to a certain extent if they had read the philosopher Karl Jaspers' afterthoughts in 1946. At least, they could have learned a rather relevant definition of a ''Pariavolk'': 'Es ist die Frage, ob es politisch sinnvoll, zweckmäßig, gefahrlos, gerecht sei, ein ganzes Volk zum Pariavolk zu machen, es hinabzudrücken unter den Rang der anderen Völker, es, nachdem es selber seine Würde preisgegeben hatte, weiter zu entwürdigen.' K. Jaspers, *Die Schuldfrage. Ein Beitrag zur deutschen Frage.* (Zürich: Artemis, 1946), p. 26. For Jaspers see chapter 9.

constructed for his hero, Gadhi. His identification is of considerable importance since now, at 'the end of history' (Fukuyama), at least of the 20th century, and of an apocalyptic 'clash of civilizations' (Huntington), every scenario forecasts some attacks 'from pariah states ... (with their) ... nuclear and missile technology' and 'organized criminals in the former USSR' (*Britannica CD 97* 'The world at the end of the 20th century') Israel and South Africa are placed in the corner with criminals, militant Islamic fanatics, North Korea and so on. They are all pariah states. Unfortunately, this has nothing to do with the archaeology of a concept, but only with the present day's nightmares.

ABRAHAM AND HIS FIRST SON

In the previous impressionistic overview of definitions and identifications, a world historical panorama of severe contradictions unfolds itself. It is worthwhile looking at a specific story in more detail because it anticipates many claims on and references to *Genesis*-old traditions in this book.

Roget's Thesaurus directs attention to the much more general connotations of *pariah* to 'unsociability' and 'seclusion' to which an 'outcast(e)' is related in some way or other. Interestingly, the following topics are also mentioned in connection with 'pariah': outsider, leper, expatriate, foreigner, exile, deportee, refugee, stateless person, wanderer, outlaw, bandit, vagabond, Ishmael, and many more. Only the last connotation brings us to Jewish history and immediately into its origins as well as in the very beginning of the 20th century Shoah drama.

According to the OED 'Ishmael' *in the meaning of outcast* was introduced in 1899 by reference to a *Genesis* text cited as '*whose hand is against every man, and every man's hand against him*' (16:12). Now, the outcast receives a highly aggressive character (OED: 'one at war with society') and at the same time the method is produced to eliminate him, as sanctioned by the Bible. Those were the first heydays of the new antisemitism and anti-Judaism, in which one was eager to use dubious Bible texts against the Jews. Still, it is a Bible text which is, for some, synonymous with truth. So, let us accept this for a moment and look into the Ishmael question and the meaning of the *Genesis* quotation given above.

First, one has to know that there is a fundamental difference between 'Ishmael' and 'Ismael'.[7] The former refers to the son of patriarch Abraham and Hagar (see below). The latter is the son of the sixth Imam whose name is used by a Shiite-like sect (the Ismaelites, literally 'the Seventh') which was highly influential from the 8th to about the 13th century in India, Persia, Syria and, in particular,

---

7. See OED, but also S. and N. Ronart (Eds.), *Lexikon der Arabischen Welt* (Zürich: Artemis, 1972),p.546-548. A. Hourani, *A History of the Arab Peoples*; Dutch translation (Amsterdam: Contact, 1992), p. 58 ff.; H. Ben-Sasson, *Geschichte des jüdischen Volkes. Von den Anfängen bis zur Gegenwart* (München: Beck, 1995), p. 80 ff.

North Africa (Fatimids dynasty). Sometimes Jews used this name as a general term for Arabs, because they are supposedly descended from Ishmael. This is probably the reason for the confusion. For us, only Ishmael is of interest here.[8] This son of Abraham (Abram) and the Egyptian maiden of Sarah (Sarai), Hagar, is celebrated in all important sources as one who 'shall be the father of twelve princes, and I will make him a great nation' (*Gen.* 17:20); both he and his pregnant mother were protected by a special angel (*Gen.* 21:15-21), etc.

Apart from Hagar, Abraham had two other wives, the Aramaean 'princess' Sarah and 'a free and independent Arabian nomadic woman', Keturah. According to the myth Sarah herself urged Abraham to make love to Hagar until a child was born, the first son, Ishmael. The story did not mention whether the same procedure was followed with Keturah, who also bore many children to old Abraham. Knowing how angry Sarah could be, this must be the case. According to existing Hebrew customs, Sarah's reactions were rather strange because all these relations were illegal; this was certainly not the case according to normal nomadic customs. However, in myths everything is possible. Here, they represent the three ways of life for Yahweh-worshipping peoples now 'at the beginning of history': between the Nile and the Euphrates there were 'Hebrew rulers, Hebrew slaves, and free Hebrews' (according to the ruler).

The sons of Ishmael lived to the east of Egypt, in the Negev, the Biblical Edom, etc. They were sheep and camel Bedouin, merchants, robbers; like the tribes which settled later in 'Palestine', they had already formed a covenant of twelve tribes. The six Keturah sons occupied a vast area to the east of Canaan, and they were Bedouin as well. Inbetween lived the nomadic Aramaean Hebrews in Canaan. Their areas of influence (borders is a 19th century AD custom) remained rather stable if the marriage practices did not change.[9] The only remark to be made is that Abraham proved how irrelevant were ethnic criteria and a 'law of the blood': heirs of the land are those who are born in it, irrespective of their mother or father. It is the

---

8. See P. Achtemeier (Ed.), *Bible Dictionary* (New York: HarperCollins, 1996), p. 464 ff.; BHH, II, p. 415. Highly provocative and interesting is G. Hoekveld-Meijer, *Esau, Salvation in disguise. Genesis 36; a hidden polemic… about Edom's role in post-exilic Israel…* (Kampen: Kok, 1996), p. 166-182. Hoekveld made a geographical-theological analysis of the long list of names in Genesis 36 in order to reconstruct the history of Edom (a regional power south of Judah) which suffered most of the time from repression by Judah because of its favorable place in the gold trade (control of the Shechem defile). Hoekveld fully exploits the Hebrew use of word- and sound-play to discover interrelations between place- and other names and concludes, for instance, that around 520-480 BC not one but three peoples wanted to invade 'Israel'; that there is a theological conflict between several Yahweh interpretations and conflicts about the (temporary) leadership of Edom or the acceptance of Jersalem as capital city; that according to one interpretation Canaan is not the promised country but a much larger area (from the Nile to the Euphrates) in which the descendants of Isaac and Ishmael live in peace and marry each other; etc. I did not study her book long enough to see whether it could be more useful for our discussion.

9. See my article: Myth and Reality in the Archaeology of Ancient Israel, in: *Tijdschrift voor Mediterrane Archeologie* 9 (1996), p. 23-32.

consequence of the nomadic way of life in which the management, quality, etc. of the animal stock determines to a large degree how human policies shall be shaped. It is, therefore, no accident that all men in the three areas were circumcised.

For the religious analyst no other conclusion remains than that only Yahweh's law is important[10] because it is stated in *Genesis* over and over. Still, he could ask himself which Yahweh and which 'laws' are at stake, or what is a 'law' in these cases. A normal scholar, however, does not stop thinking and reading: the story of Ishmael proves that Yahweh also accepts different rules for different groups, as he accepts Sarah's rejection of Ishmael (including her curse); he protects Ishmael in the wildernis and gives him an immense territory, much gold, etc. Furthermore Yahweh accepts that Sarah, notwithstanding Abraham's example, seemed to introduce a racial argument: Ishmael is not allowed to inherit Abraham's heritage, because he is of mixed blood. The case is even more complicated, but that does not matter here.[11]

My conclusion has to be: if one looks for some unifying principle, this cannot be religion but simply the fact that we are dealing here with nomadic tribes or families who are determined to listen to 'the laws of the animals' and not much else. However, what is important is that the three basic nomadic groups with their rather complicated differences formed the start of the Holy History first of Jews and Arabs and, after the robbing of this tradition, also of Christians. But in this first myth it is crystal clear: it is the combination of similarities and conflicts between 'equal groups' which gave the individual the chance to become responsible for certain results. The consequences could be felt millennia later.

Concerning the pariah concept, it is now possible to answer the question why in *Roget's Thesaurus* and the OED 'Ishmael' appears in relation with 'pariah/-outcast'. In the end, and therefore in mythology, it is the greedy Sarah's jealousy, curse and racism and Abraham's consent to the harsh treatment of Hagar by Sarah which directed dear Roget's pen. Its impact is of a truly universal mythological nature. The Sarah-Abraham act is not just reproduced in the actions of Rebecca – Isaac who send the nomad Esau into the hands of Ishmael. In my view, this myth also refers to earthly history as well as the original myth of Eve's seduction of Adam in the Garden of Eden and the fundamental division between settled and nomadic peoples (Cain-Abel): it is told from the Sarah-Isaac-Jacob group, the middle part of the 'Abramites' Bedouin, that they settled and suddenly became immobile peasants.

---

10. G. Hoekveld-Meijer, p. 168, 169.

11. See, for instance, the interesting P. Vidal-Naquet, *The Jews. History, Memory, and the Present* (New York: Columbia University Press, 1996), p. 13, 14. Disappointing is G. van Ginniken's feministic interpretation in M. Bal et al., *En Sara in haar tent lachte ... Patriarchaat en verzet in bijbelverhalen* (Utrecht: Hes, 1984), p. 27-47. Although bewildering see also A. Momigliano, *Alien Wisdom. The Limits of Hellenization* (Cambridge: Cambridge University Press, 1993), p. 93 ff., 117 ff. for the invention of an Abraham tradition.

This fundamental deviation from the original nomadic way of life and its norms and values is in need of a harsh legitimation. Because it is a 180 degree shift, this real sin must first be committed and, second, be pardoned through an 'Umwertung aller Werte'; the trick is, of course, to start perceiving the sin as the highest form of goodness. The breathtaking actions of the sinners (Eve, Cain, Sarah, Abraham, Rebecca, Jacob, etc.) are accompanied by a fundamental transformation of Yahweh into a settled and terrible war-god who constantly proclaims one wholesale slaughter of so-called enemies after another as the ultimate goodness. All kinds of frauds and cruelties are allowed to reach and contain the Settlement (from, for example, the brother-sister game of Abraham-Sarah in *Genesis* 20, repeated by Isaac-Rebecca in Genesis 26 to the highly degrading brutalities from Judges 19-21[12]). In the most absolute sense, all thoughts became polarised in the strongest black-white fashion: who is not pro is con; the enemy of my enemy is my best friend, etc.

The middle part of Abraham's 'nomadic empire' became, one (mythical) day, a real Israel/Palestine for Israelites/Palestinians, whereupon two fundamental cleavages gradually became institutionalised. First, from now on these 'middle people' could refer to the eastern Keturah descendants and the southern Ishmael group living in Edom, the Negev, etc. as the *eternal enemies*. There is no evidence for the reverse. In addition, the latter were perceived as the origin of the Arabs, who were in this myth synonymous with 'Hebrew slaves' (still Thora translation). Somewhere in this constellation the phenomenon of Amalek must be found studied through Max Weber's Bible interpretation. The continuation of this story can be discovered elsewhere as well (chapter 5) in, for example, the words of Abravanel: Edom ' inimical Christians; Ishmael ' inimical Islam/Arabs. From the Jewish perspective the *eternal enmity* was projected upon the Christians (vice versa). This is the only proposition of its kind which can be proved empirically to contain a large degree of truth.

It seems, furthermore, as if we are confronted here with the archaeology of the deepest intra-Jewish conflict between diaspora and settled/'Jerusalemites'. For the latter the diaspora is the ultimate negation, the absolute deviation from the right track, a sentiment strongly aggravated in the 20th century AD by the Zionist creed.

---

12. Stil today this story is used in an ambiguous way for accusing 'tribal mores ... evolved in the context of nomadic desert life ... violence becomes an important tactic of acquisition as well as a response to the acquisitiveness of others. A family punishes attempts at competition as brutally as possible in order to signal to other families to beware. Powerful individuals and families ... carry out brutal threats. A seemingly endless cycle of violence ...' See L. Duhan Kaplan, The Parable of the Levite's Concubine, in: L. Bove, L.Duhan Kaplan (Ed.), *From the Eye of the Storm. Regional Conflicts and the philosophy of Peace* (Amsterdam, Atlanta: Rhodopi, 1995), p. 250. Duhan Kaplan quotes Th. Friedman who accuses in this way 'nomadic Mideastern leaders' like Assad or Saddam Hussein! She herself discovers that 'the Mideast is no longer an uncultivated desert and the vast majority of the population are no longer nomads'. Next, she derives from this alleged 'nomadic violence' a plea for a strong central government, the sedentarian logo *par excellence!*

'Sarah's curse' threatened not only her own people, family and heirs until 'after Auschwitz' but the two other, directly related people, as well. They became gradually more other than brother, because, even today, they have been a constant target of the 'middle people' who became in their turn the pariahs for 'foreigners'.

The most threatening foreigners for Jews were (and are!) Christians. I think it is highly significant that the one who is considered the legitimizer of the theft of the Jewish tradition, the apostle Paul, produced the Hagar-Sarah story in a crucial moment.[13] In the letter from Paul to the Galatians, the difficult question of the interrelationship between pagans, Christians and Jews is aggravated by the circumcision issue. Paul did not like this operation and was determined to attack even the Christian Galatians to convince them to abandon not only this important issue in Jewish law but also the whole law of *present Jerusalem*. This reveals the existence of several factions among Christians, contradictions between Peter and Paul, etc. What concerns us here is Paul's use of the Hagar story, which he retold in an allegorical way, a Hellenistic method to make things more interesting than they really or literally are. About Hagar and Sarah he writes:

> 'For it is written that Abraham had two sons, one by a slave and one by a free woman. But the son of the slave was born according to the flesh, the son of the free woman through promise. Now this is an allegory: these women are two covenants. One is from Mount Sinai, bearing children in slavery; she is Hagar. Now Hagar is Mount Sinai in Arabia; she corresponds to the present Jerusalem, for she is in slavery with her children. ... Now we brethren, like Isaac, are children of promise ... But what does the scripture say? 'Cast out the slave and her son; for the son of the slave shall not inherit with the son of the free woman'. So, brethren, we are not children of the slave but of the free woman.' (*Gal.* 4: 22-31)

Paul, a good example of a fanatical convert, provides a classic example of the conversion of truth/myth in order to create a new truth/myth. It is a major phase in the theft of the Jewish tradition by the Christians because, historically speaking, Paul was successful: his 'new truth' became 'newspeak'. The new truth says that both Jews and Arabs are the slaves, belong to 'the old system' (Mount Sinai) and, finally, are sexually perverted (both circumcised); subsequently, the Christians are the 'free' men/women, the real heirs of Yahweh's promise to Abraham. Jews and Arabs are no longer guardians of the law, but slaves of this law as well as outlaws, true Ishmaels, for the Christians. From now on, a whole tradition of lies is invented (euphemistically called 'allegorical constructions') which are not based on the original Biblical texts. By necessity, a parallel tradition had to be invented of

---

13. For the following see K.Smelik, *Hagar en Sara. De verhouding tussen Jodendom en Christendom in de eerste eeuwen* (Baarn: Ten Have, 1979), p. 47 ff.

so-called Jewish arguments against Christianity or, if you wish, so-called Islamic arguments against Judaism which could not rely on any evidence.

So far the complications and implications of the Hagar-Abraham myth, which is nothing more than the creation myth of a true *pariah triangle*, the mutual and fundamental discrimination of the monotheists, Muslims, Jews and Christians. How until today this mutual relationship has kept its deadly character can be read daily in the papers.

This was the story but not yet the real or the entire history, the practice of how and why 'Ishmael' became a pariah. In any respects, its consequence was/is that the one who claimed this to be their own, exclusive (expert) knowledge introduced another, fundamental cleavage within Jewish lives, lifestyles, history and theories/religions: the one between the *'insiders'* and the *'outsiders'*.

We also learn how women in nomadic society can 'make history' in their own right: Rebecca and Sarah were real insiders who knew perfectly well how to play the power game in creating (by definition) outsiders like Ishmael or Esau. Apparently, Keturah was even able to give her name to six tribes, creating a kind of common identity.

'Later', when all these mythical veils were woven by more or less institutionalised ideology-makers, the insider-outsider antagonisms became much more differentiated. Priests or rabbis with their expert language created outsiders as the non-experts, the uncritical believers in and outside 'Jerusalem', but also outsiders as enemies, the (critical) unbelievers.

Below (chapter 3) we examine whether settlements in the 'middle area', at least in the first phase of their existence, had strong positive relationships with nomads. Much later, it was the nomads who became the worst outsiders, the eternal enemies, and so on. This was the outcome of the serious struggles raging about the fundamental issue of whether the *nomadic ideal* could remain the social and spiritual basis of the 'middle peoples'. This 'mechanism' is the most intriguing and paradoxical part of (this) history. At the same time, it provides the solution to Adorno's problem definition or the sources for the debate about Jewish identity.

AN ITALIAN JEW FROM PIEDMONT

To study the pariah question in its present form, we can use two intelligent but contradictory perceptions of Weber's pariah theory from Jewish scholars. The first comes from an Italian critical historian and controversial man; the other is from a German controversial philosopher and critical woman. The latter, Hannah Arendt (1906-1975), occupied an important place in the post-war international elite and its public debates. The influence of the former, Arnaldo Momigliano (1908-1987), was confined to learned journals and the usual academic networks of a specialist field, ancient history. Here he can show us the intricacies of the pariah problem at a personal level for the first time as a prelude to the Arendt and Weber discussions elsewhere.

Momigliano was a religious orthodox Italian Jew from Piedmont, a heritage which dominated his scholarly work. The Jewishness of Arendt is difficult to define and only popped up in specific writings and in debates about specific questions like Zionism or the Holocaust. She is certainly not religious; her German-American academic habitus as such is not Jewish either; her family history and education are highly liberal and 'assimilated'. Because Momigliano is a strong critic of Weber's pariah concept and Arendt as strong a supporter, together they can demonstrate how the previous discovered 'mechanism' works. Both his biography and pariah criticism are described by Momigliano himself in his last book, a collection of essays on ancient and modern Judaism.[14]

During the last centuries very few Jews lived in Italy. At most, there were perhaps 30,000 in 1800 (including Triest and Nice), while in 1939 there were about 50,000. This simple fact seems not unimportant as an explanation for the so-called Italian-Catholic-Mussolini tolerance for Jews. Still, this contrasts with the 25 per cent killed by the Mussolini regime, including the father and mother and nine other members of Momigliano's family. Arnaldo himself went into exile in England in 1938. Through the eyes of Arnaldo and in his autobiographical remarks, this embarrassing fate receives special dimensions.

Arnaldo's father was one of the first officials of the Fascist party; at least three other family members had personal contacts with Mussolini, which Arnaldo perceived as 'flexible' in 1987. He himself was a party member from 1928 onwards and did not follow the refusal of his own professor, Gaetano de Sanctis, to take an oath of loyalty to the regime in 1931. Of course, Arnaldo was full of anger about the fate of his family, but it is not known to me whether he protested after 1945, for example, against a growing neo-Fascist influence in Italy (under the leadership of Mussolini's daughter), whether he analysed the fascist historical theory or aesthetics so substantially influenced by the Roman past, his special subject. In the autobiographical texts known to me, he did not elaborate on his own role during the regime till 1938, nor on why so many Italian Jews supported Fascism (about 25 per cent), nor on why many Jewish women (Arnaldo names them) had affairs with Mussolini. He only mentioned that this was the case (but see below). After his death, the problem created thanks to these 'facts' was touched on in a review and

---

14. The short article in which Max Weber is directly attacked is A. Momigliano, A Note on Max Weber's Definition of Judaism as a Pariah Religion, in: Idem, *Essays on Ancient and Modern Judaism* (Chicago: University of Chicago Press, 1994), p. 171-178. Many essays contain autobiographical data, but Silvia Berti's introduction (p. vii-xxiv) was quite helpful in this respect. Biographical data of M. are discussed in K.Christ, *Neue Profile der Alten Geschichte* (Darmstadt: Wissenschaftliche Buchgesellschaft, 1990), p. 248-295.

several letters in *The Times Literary Supplement*,[15] but it was neither defined nor analysed. That is not possible here either, but some hints can be given.

First, the character of Italian Jews as described by Momigliano gives some important clues.[16] It does not seem very appropriate for the understanding of his personality to know that Italian Jews are a mixture of Jews from nearly all corners of Europe, but this reality partly constituted his religious and cultural education. Piedmontese Jews were quite different from, for example, those of Ferrara: 'The explanation is partly in the agrarian situation of the region, which helped to form the pro-Fascist attitudes of the Jews of Ferrara centuries later.' In Arnaldo's youth all Italian Jews spoke the dialect of their region (sometimes interspersed with some Hebrew words), and it was the exceptional child who had a reasonable knowledge of Italian. Where Jews had to live in ghettos for centuries as in Rome, their Roman dialect was more archaic than that of the Roman Christians. Together with the small number of Jews, this regional constellation made them strongly family-oriented in a (regional) network fashion. This must have moulded his scholarly work quite considerably, as it is loaded with biographical details from historians.

Arnaldo, of course, studied his own family history and traced it back to a fourteenth century village and the capital of Savoy, Chambéry. From here his ancestors followed the expansion of the Dukedom of Savoy into Piedmont as traders and moneylenders while they also held rabbinical services for the small Jewish communities in other places. 'There they remained for centuries, terribly poor, pious, and scholarly, until Napoleon brought new ideas, and ... new delusions to the Italian Jews.' The family on his mother's side lived as industrialists in Turin; on his father's side he was related to the opposite extreme, the landowners.

From this linguistic and regional analysis, so far, one receives the impression that for him town-country relationships were rather decisive in moulding a person's way of acting and thinking, which he connected with a left-right division in politics. In this constellation Arnaldo seems to locate his family history in the urban and in the left sections of society: it was 'a family that has a permanent place in the history of the Italian socialist movement', whatever relation that may have to his own behaviour and the nationalist and mystical characteristics of his beloved socialist uncle Felice.

The famous European year 1848 also gave Jews in the kingdom Piedmont-Sardinia the equality they needed, and then they all got patriotism 'in their blood'. This was most apparent with the (voluntary) heros in World War I: the most spectacular 'were all Jews' and in the 'disgraceful Abyssinian and Spanish wars of

---

15. *Times Literary Supplement* 10-5-1996 (T.Cornell); 24-5-1996 (W.Harris); 14-6-1996 (C.Dionisotti); 28-6-1996 (R.Ridley). These reactions were triggered by a fair review of some of Momigliano's publications in TLS, 12-4-1996 from W. Harris entitled 'The silences of Momigliano'.
16. For the following quotations see his *Essays*, p. 121 ff.

1936' Jews again were heroic Italians. The freedom they obtained after 1848 was used by them in a peculiar way. A new direction to their lives 'was the possibility of becoming farmers and landowners ... especially (in) Piedmont, Veneto, Emilia and Tuscany ... strongly inclined to buy land and settle on it ... This ... explains the strong conservative bias of many Italian Jews.' When Jews industrialized, they remained medium-sized entrepreneurs. The Momiglianos 'stuck to the traditional Italo-Jewish combination of banking and silk mills', which were crushed under a mortal competition and the invention of artificial silk.

In 20th century secularizing Italy, Jews exploited the opportunities of modern education. Although they often excelled in academic life, most characteristic is 'that ... they came to play a very important part in the state administration as civil servants, judges, and above all soldiers.' Jews played the most important roles in saving Triest for Italy, and (Jewish) university professors often became 'ministers of the crown'.

This whole picture reveals the very small Jewish minority, including the Momiglianos, to be ideal-typical oikoidalists: if they were socialist, it meant that they were first and foremost nationalists; they were mostly bound to the soil as well, and militant defenders of the monarchy or the state and its culture whatever its 'disgraceful' policies. No wonder that Italian Jews mostly remained loyal to Mussolini and his regime. Momigliano explains that during his whole career, Mussolini 'had been helped by Jews, both men and women. He had exploited them ruthlessly, above all the women – and he had betrayed them.' I think that here we find the very reason why Momigliano and so many other Italian Jews (except for a few) are practically silent about the Nazi or Fascist period. Their problem: it is beyond any (ir)rationality that such a deep loyalty to the Italian oikoidal case and a nearly one hundred per cent assimilation could be rewarded with genocidal actions.[17]

In 1938 there came an end to Momigliano's Italian oikoidal world, and he has remained in exile since that date, clinging with time more and more to his Jewish belief which became 'alien wisdom'. From the point of view of *general* develop-

---

17. Because their Fascist alignment was such a remarkable element of Italian Jewry, the argument also arose 'that the Jews would have become Nazis as easily as their German fellow-citizen if only they had been permitted to join the movement ...' H. Arendt, OT, p. 21. Arendt rightly argues that this may be true on an individual level but that the German Jews developed in an exceptional way (p.22). In my view, the Italian situation is comparable to the world of the *Hofjuden* (court Jews) and their successors, the Jewish bankers and notables including their typical oikoidal family life. In 19th century Germany, however, the Jewish notables 'ruled the Jewish community' and 'they had a vested interest in the poverty and even backwardness' of the Jewish masses (p. 62). In Italy there was no real Jewish proletariat which could be used as a token of the elite's security. Therefore, the dependence of the 'indigenous ruler' was much larger in Italy. See for Jewish Fascism in Italy A. Stille, *Benevolence and Betrayal. Five Italian Jewish Families under Fascism* (New York: Summit Books, 1991) and J. Petersen, W. Schieder (Hrsg.), *Faschismus und Gesellschaft in Italien* (Köln: SH-Verlag, 1998). Not very revealing is S. Zuccotti, *The Italians and the Holocaust* (New York: Basic Books, 1987), p. 12-28.

ments, however, there is no longer a place for religious interference with (scientific) work, daily life or moral judgements. Although he is sometimes a fascinating scholar, he is also alienated from most trends in modern historiography: positivism, marxism, structuralism, etc. and from nearly all historical disciplines: economic, political, sociological, ecological, etc., apart from some name-dropping. Also remarkable is the absence of a 'real book' publication, i.e. any systematically researched period/subject laid down in a profound publication. Momigliano masterly manipulated the pieces of a puzzle from which he, apparently, did not know and, anyway, did not reveal the (whole) picture. Also, within his own isolated corner, he did not develop some new 'metahistorical faith'[18] but stuck to traditional models.

Momigliano seems to be a brilliant teacher, but the absence of a main systematic study about his speciality, the Jewish-Christian relationship in Roman times, is a serious regret. Probably in 1938 he was not ready for this task, and his existence in exile was too restless, while the digestion of the Auschwitz drama and its consequences must have taken too much of his energy. Instead, he recently came up with the deeply erroneous opinion that

> 'the fusion of Greek, Latin and Jewish tradition is Christian. The Jews (and the Arabs) continued to face Greek thought in isolation. They were never deeply concerned with Latin ways of living or thinking.'[19]

This seems to be Momigliano's declaration of faith in which he proves that he, in the end, is more Italian and Catholic than Jew. For him the so-called *collegium trilingue* is the essence of civilization, which is formed by the fusion of Jews and Latins in particular and by the Greeks, notwithstanding the latter's isolationism. However, there are only a few reasons why the 'fusion' of the Jewish and Latin traditions cannot be seen as a continuous attempt to steal and eliminate the former by the latter tradition, starting with the apostle Paul.

A second point concerns Momigliano's disqualification of the Greek tradition, which shows in the clearest way how he sticks to his (Latin/Italian) oikoidal point of view. Thanks to his cooperation with S. Humphreys, he became tightly connected to the oikoidal Finley school, which is responsible for another distortion of Greek history.[20] Are we also confronted here with a revenge on the very bad pogrom record of the Greek Orthodox culture (see Benzion Netanyahu's attack on Hellenism; chapter 5)?

---

18. S. Berti in her introduction to M.'s *Essays*, p. xx.
19. Idem, p. xiv. The substantiation of my criticism cannot only be found in my Ishmael analysis above, etc. but in the very argument of my book which is, among others, to be seen as a defense of a *sound* Jewish identity and a critical analysis of the ways Christianity undermined this identity.
20. See among others H. Derks, The "Ancient Economy": the problem and the fraud, in: *The European Legacy*, 7 (2002), 597 – 620.

His last and, in fact, most dramatic point concerns his opinion that a 'fusion' with Big Brother should be the best for the Jews. I guess that he made an 'ideal type' of his personal Italian history up to 1938 which was, indeed, for him a period of a happy youth and education and of a brilliant career wholly embedded in a liberal and secular Italian elite culture. He was a Jew with the Italians, and an Italian with the Jews. I cannot imagine another reason than nostalgia for his last text. It is one of the few he directly addressed to 'Auschwitz'. Momigliano's explanations for this drama are astonishingly simplistic but understandable against the background sketched above. He states: Whatever one can say about Fascists or Nazis, the fundamental reason for this drama is

'a centuries-old indifference on the part of the peoples of (Italy, France and Germany) toward their Jewish fellow citizens. This indifference was the ultimate result of the hostility of the churches, which viewed 'conversion' as the only solution to the Jewish problem. I solemnly repeat that Jews have a right to their religion, the first monotheistic and ethical religion in history ...'[21]

What Momigliano repeated was nothing more or less than the 1848 bourgeois codification concerning freedom of religion initiated by the French Revolution and today common knowledge and practice in nearly all codifications. After 'Auschwitz' it was far too easy to come up with an old Risorgimento anti-Christian view as an explanation for the 20th century genocide. This can only be true, in particular, where the differences between religious and scientific guidelines are seriously blurred, as in Momigliano's case.[22] Besides this, his own recapitulation of the (recent) history of the Italian Jews proves everything except 'indifference': what is indifference for somebody who remembers at the end of his life how he loved the Catholic nuns as his 'ideal teachers'?;[23] was it not the reason the churches were in a deadly way hostile because they were interested to the utmost in the Jewish tradition, so that they even came to steal its tradition?; was it caused by indifference or a very special interest in Jews that kept only Italian Jews in real ghettos thanks to the Pope? All this leads us to question Momigliano's self-esteem, which seems the same as asking: why didn't Momigliano accept Weber's qualification of the Jews as pariahs?

Momigliano used a specific strategy in attacking Weber's position.[24] First, he

---

21. S. Berti, p. xxvii, xxviii.

22. Exaggeration is part of the academic network communication, but if several historians who should know better write about Momigliano 'as one of the greatest scholars of his time, probably of all times' then the standards in ancient history must have sunk far below acceptable levels. Cited by K. Christ in the introduction to Momigliano's *Wege in die Alte Welt* (Frankfurt a.M.: Fischer,1995), p. 7.

23. S. Berti, p. xxvi.

24. Momigliano must have been very fond of his Weber criticism because he reprinted it time and again. A Jewish Weber supporter is H. Liebeschütz, Max Weber's Historical Interpretation of Judaism, in: *Leo Baeck Yearbook* IX (1964), p. 4-68 which is a direct contribution to the making of

obviously did not (want to) read texts like Weber's 'Patriarch analysis' which will be discussed in chapter 3. It is a kind of third-party remark when Momigliano says: 'At one point he seems to imply that even the Patriarchs had been pariahs ...' However, there cannot be the slightest doubt about Weber's qualification of the Patriarchs as pariahs and about the far-reaching consequences of this. Why didn't Momigliano criticize this fact, and why did he neglect Weber's Patriarch analysis? And what about the status of Abraham as the acknowledged father of two religions?

The answer suggests that Momigliano does not argue as a historian nor, in my opinion, as a scholar. He comes up with the thesis:

> 'Hebrew historical tradition (as distinct from certain rabbinic speculation) has always maintained that the Patriarchs lived before the Hebrews received their God-given law and God-given land. The status of the Patriarchs cannot be used to define the status which the Jews subjectively attributed to themselves as a consequence of the revelation on Sinai and of the conquest of the Promised Land.'[25]

In other words, for Momigliano the Patriarchs are cut out of the picture in referring to 'the whole Jewish religious tradition' or what 'believing Jews' are supposed to believe. It's a remarkable comment on the previous Abraham/Ishmael-story.

Even Jewish historians do not dare to act in such an irrational way. They tell their readers: 'The relationship between Israel and the Holy Land is fixed after God ordered Abraham, the first Patriarch: 'Go forth from your native land and from your father's house to the land that I will show you. I will make of you a great nation' (*Genesis* 12:1). The obedience of Abraham is a fundamental change in the history of Mankind and the beginning of a historical process which, as yet, did not arrive at its zenith.'[26] Of course, this is a religious statement, but far from Momigliano's dogmatic theological reasoning which, *expressis verbis*, makes an appeal to 'Talmudic reasoning ... notorious for not taking any notice of faits accomplis'.

Here we come across the real Momigliano as well as the highly tragic one. It is the end of all historical reflection and, in my view at least, of all more or less

---

Saint Max ('..*Weber's third volume confirms the importance of the Hebrew contribution to the structure of Western civilisation.*' p. 67, is repeated several times; Weber received the role of criticizing the villain Sombart; etc.). The most honorable historian in this respect is Moses Finley who is also the most frenetic Weber fan. Never in his substantial oeuvre did he make a remark about Weber's pariah concept. The 'Patriarch passage' is not considered in F. Raphael, nor in the important article of E. Fleischmann (see chapter 3, note 5). All these authors rely on Weber's GAR III, p. 281-400, and I do not intend to repeat discussions about that part of the Weber text.

25. A. Momigliano, *Essays*, p. 175.
26. H. Ben-Sasson, p. 4.

realistic ways of life if one does not take any notice of the forces which influence you, your kin and surroundings. In this case, it seems impossible to resist a course of events, and the only possibility left is to accept the fate largely constructed by the actions of others. History is even reduced further than to the zero-sum option of the religious historians as cited: it becomes no option at all. Or, in other words: one surrenders all of the godly power which is supposed to steer our fate from some 'outside'. This perception of the god-world relationship (inspired by Maimonides' writings, to whom Momigliano refers) must be responsible, among others, for Arnaldo's 'unworldly' behaviour before, during and after the Mussolini dictatorship: Mussolini or the state in the role of god-in-this-world and Jews unable or unwilling to resist. But what about the Jew as pariah?

'Believing Jews,' Momigliano states, believe that under any circumstances, whatever the inimical environment, they had 'their sovereign rights and never admitted to being without political institutions of their own'. With nothing but this conviction or theological 'fact', Momigliano concludes that it is impossible that Jews could be as inferior as a pariah: 'This excludes that subjective acceptance of an inferior, nonpolitical status which seems to be essential to Weber's definition of the Jews as pariahs.' In this way, life becomes rather easy and uncomplicated, while historical facts like ghettos, expulsions or a Shoah belong to another world.

It is significant that Momigliano also had to rely on the ambiguous strategy of distorting Weber's aim in order to prove 'Weber's distortion'. He writes that the only way of saving Weber's identification of the Jews 'with a pariah *nation*' (italics added, D.) is to say that they were treated as 'a landless nation without rights'. His conclusion is correct: in this case, Weber's thesis would have been in need of 'a complete transformation'. However, Momigliano knew perfectly well that Weber did not talk at all about a pariah nation (see Green above) and that it was not the lack of 'territoriality' which made Jews pariahs in Weber's view. As explained in chapter 3, Weber saw Jewish pariahs as if they were guest people in a guest country ('*von der sozialen Umwelt geschiedenes Gastvolk*'). To connect Jews to 'a (landless) nation' is for many reasons highly ambivalent and purely a theological question. However, it was not Weber's subject.

Probably Momigliano abstained from discussing the Patriarchs for other reasons. The second part of Weber's *Das antike Judentum* is headed *Die Entstehung des jüdischen Pariavolkes* ('The origin of the Jewish pariah-people'). It concerns the *post*-exilic period in which, according to Weber, the Jews became a '*Gastvolk*' (guest of another people) ritually separated from their social environment. All commentators accepted this chronology before giving their affirmative or negative comments. This allows the opportunity for some to play hide-and-seek with (Weber's) biblical history, i.e. to substitute a clean non-pariah period and to criticize the second period in order to liberate the whole history from a pariah stigma.

If it should be accepted that the *pre*-exilic period is also stigmatized (which is the consequence of Weber's 'Patriarch legend'), the pariah problem becomes a general instead of a particular problem. In this case, 'Weber' becomes a general problem too, which is unacceptable for most if not all of his supporters. For many, it must also be unacceptable that the classical distinctions between a pre- and post-exilic period should be undermined. This is nearly as important as the clear distinction between an Old and New Testament for the controversy between Christianity and Judaism.

OUTLINE OF A JEWISH-NOMADIC PARIAH COMPLEX AND ITS CONTEXTS
At the end of this *first round,* let's try to produce an outline of the pariah complex. Some elements of it have become already clear enough, but most are in need of special attention in the following chapters.

A.   The first two paragraphs superficially showed how the deeper penetration of 'The West' in 'The East' during the imperialistic actions of the 19th century also created a worldwide, underlying pariah complex as a specific mixture of 'Western' exploitative discriminations, superiority *and* guilt feelings and 'Eastern' excessively subservient behaviour, unobtrusiveness, unaccomplished expectations *and* vindictive feelings. From exclamations by Bernard-Lazare, Gadhi and others, it follows that pariahs are all kinds of people who for some reason or other want to be accepted in 'The West' to find a new identity there. This implies, for instance, that they have to strip off their old identity or to find ways of combining the two. Anyway, there is an 'entrance price' to pay . Whether this price has to be paid once or becomes a longterm sacrifice for some 'infight period', or even permanently, depends on the rate of discrimination in the guest land, the foreign background of the newcomers, and so on. As shown, once *arrivé*, even people like Bernard-Lazare easily forget their own history and start discriminating towards the next groups of pariahs.

These latter derive from something which is indicated as 'The East': from China, India or the so-called *Pale of Settlement,* the land of the *Ostjuden* in Eastern Europe. In this way 'The West' becomes identical with "good", and it seems equally unavoidable that 'The East' is designated as "bad". The road between the pariah's 'East' and the desired destination in the pariah's 'West' is normally long, but also difficult and dangerous; the chance that one will become an *arrivé* is not very large, and the chance that one remains a wanderer or nomad is considerable. Probably it is a consolation that the Christmas story tells us that 'wise men' came from the East as well. On camels!

B.   In the second paragraph we arrived in a quiet different way at a world historical context. It concerned the intricacies of how the Ishmael nomads could transform into pariahs while others who try to settle in a 'middle country' do not. The latter, however, became pariahs much later thanks to the action of some Jewish renegade, a convert to a competing belief system, and for different reasons. We also learned how women in nomadic society can 'make history' in their own right: the insiders Rebecca and Sarah created (by definition) outsiders like Ishmael or Esau; apparently, Keturah provided six tribes with a 'common identity'.

The pariah complex, however, concerns not only 'a nomadic problem', a 'problem of nomads or people who left their home on a dangerous trip to utopia'. It is also related to the mechanism by which the three monotheistic religions are caught in an eternal and deadly battle trying to belittle, discriminate or destroy each other. In short: a real *pariah triangle*. As we know, the religion from real sedentarians from 'the West' ultimately won the competition with the two from 'the East'.

To the pariah complex also belong cleavages inside 'parties' which follow well-known patterns. The conflicts arise where people claim to possess their own, exclusive (expert) knowledge, lifestyle, history or theories: the battles between the *'insiders'* and the *'outsiders'* start. Thus, "Jerusalem" versus "the Diaspora" is a metaphor for the settled versus the nomads.

The insider – outsider histories are not static but change constantly according to existing power positions and the use of countless forgeries and tricks. Again and again, they reproduce Sarah's *'coup d'état'*, the nomad Abraham's sacrifice of his son Isaac, the nomad Jacob's foul play with his father and brother, etc. It is certain that within the insider-outsider relationship a *pariah* must be first an insider before becoming an outsider. Or: he/she must first be an 'incast', a parasite, before becoming an outcast. And: the very antagonism between 'in' and 'out' is not possible without an 'in'; before (permanent) settlement it seems difficult to create one.

These histories from the patriarch's life provide us with the background for the next step in the pariah analysis. The coordinates of the discussion could be tightened up within a constellation marked by the main images of *pariah*: insiders (expert-insiders versus laymen-insiders) versus outsiders; outcasts versus 'incasts'. The basic question of this book remains: what have Jews to do with Jews as pariahs and/ or Jews as nomads *and vice versa*? The *Nomadic Question* is omnipresent, so we have to look first much closer into its basic elements, but from outside a mythical context.

C.   With Momigliano we arrived in a typical European context, and we were able to study the pariah complex at an individual insider's level. His criticism of Weber's pariah concept is, first, a consequence of his religious belief: even his last published sentence refers to a 'pact between God and the Jewish nation' which should have saved Jews 'from whatever self-abasement [is] associated with the word *pariah*'.

However, his Italian background seems to be of greater importance. In Italy and in 19th century history, Jews became assimilated to such a degree that they simply perceived themselves as 'the best Italians', the heroes and primary defenders of oikoidal regimes as top-bureaucrats. Jews belonged to the very defenders of the *national* juridical system or of the *national* military force doing the dirty imperialistic jobs. They all converted to Catholicism, but Momigliano suggests that he stuck to a Jewish belief system notwithstanding a basic education by Catholic nuns.

Until 1938 Momigliano, his family and the members of their privileged class lived as the classic *Hofjuden* (court Jews), first and foremost dedicated and appreciated servicemen of the most powerful in the state. Their freedom, (in)-dependence, intellectual skills and wealth hinged on that position including the associated networks. It was just as incomprehensible that such a status belonged to a pariah as that so many members of this status group had to perish through the hands of their very masters.

Of course, all this refers to the substantially wealthy part of the tiny Jewish minority in Italy and not to the Jewish proletarians living still, for instance, in the (old) Roman ghetto. They were never Momigliano's subject; neither he nor apparently his ancestors lived in a ghetto. It is more revealing of his class position that he never discussed (let alone opposed) the aims or deeds of his political or cultural Italian 'superiors'. The most remarkable aspect is his nearly absolute silence about the heirs of his lifelong object of study, the Roman empire, the Catholic Church and its doctrines. The very centre of all his ancient studies is religion; that is to say: 'the triangle Greece-Rome-Judea' remains this centre 'as long as Christianity remains the religion of the West'.[27] In this way Judaism fully depends on the belief system which is (jointly) responsible for the ghettoïzation and worst repression of Jews and Judaism.

If the terms of the 'mechanism' described in the second story are employed directly, one obtains the following result. After 1945 Momigliano did not want to reflect on the profound changes the Italian Jews went through. It should be clear that they were first *incasts* within the Italian oikoidal power system and, subsequently, *outcasts* and, eventually, *pariahs* in Weber's sense. Instead he stuck to his perception of the first position. As we will see, Hannah Arendt, whose cultural outlook had many similarities to that of the historian, succeeded in coming up with a highly interesting and rather realistic theory about the social, political and cultural transformation from pariahs into parvenu's.

How remote the Italian Momigliano was from German-educated scholars like Benjamin, Scholem and Arendt is revealed by the few and rather derogatory and largely unjustified remarks about their attention to a 'mixture of Jewish guilt feelings and German metaphysical "Sehnsucht" ... Esotericism .. [and] .. Stefan

---

27. Cited in K. Christ in his introduction to A.Momigliano, *Wege in die Alte Welt*, p. 12.

George.'[28] Elsewhere he only mentions the title of Arendt's *The Jew as Pariah* and some subtitles as a demonstration of this typically German spiritual constellation. Arendt's anti-Zionist writings or her Eichmann book did the rest.[29]

Therefore, not only the post-1945 'pariah positions' must be elucidated in the following chapters (in particular ch. 7-9), the pre-1900 'pariah positions', in particular those from the 'formative years' around 1500, must also be discussed. At that time the first European ghetto was erected in Italy and Jews were expelled from Spain as part of a general new policy of the Catholic state/church and its supporters (ch. 4 and 5). And in between both periods two world wars triggered a *Zivilisationsbruch* in Europe and the rest of the world culminating in new phenomena, a Shoah and a Holocaust, which are often aggressively misunderstood in politics and scholarship by its perpetrators and victims, or neglected through the execution of comparable actions, so that its study must be constantly renewed (ch. 6) in combination with the question of how to liberate the pariahs (ch. 10). Hannah Arendt wrote about this short period, in which killing was not only allowed but became a moral duty: 'In the Thirties and Forties we experienced a total collapse of all existing moral norms in public and private life ... Without much fuss, it all collapsed nearly overnight ... a system of *mores* and customs could be exchanged for another system with no more difficulties than changing the eating habits of an individual or a people.'[30]

D.   From this first round the relevancy of Max Weber's writings for the Jewish pariah discussions must be clear. As far as I know, Momigliano never looked into the nomadic aspect of the Jewish problem to which Weber devoted highly interesting thoughts, as we will see in the following two chapters. Before doing so, it is necessary to make a remark of an educational nature which is important for the following debate with Weber.

The historian Momigliano did not realize that one has to read and use the sociologist Weber in a specific way. As a rule, his concepts are abstracted from any sociological and historical context and related to individual behaviour 'in its own right'. One can see this, as I do, as Weber's main methodological weakness. But he gave enough hints about this method. Therefore, forewarned is forearmed.[31]

---

28. A. Momigliano, *Essays*, p. 194.
29. Idem, p. 142.
30. Quoted by R. Bernstein, Verantwortlichkeiten, Urteilen und das Böse, in: G. Smith (Ed.), *Hannah Arendt Revisited: "Eichmann in Jerusalem" und die Folgen* (Frankfurt a.M.: Suhrkamp, 2000), p. 303.
31. For the pariah case see, for instance, the following remark: 'The 'caste' is, indeed, the normal form in which ethnic communities usually live side by side in a 'societalized' manner ... Such a caste situation is part of the phenomenon of 'pariah' peoples and is found all over the world. ... The Jews are the most impressive historical example.' H.H. Gerth, C. Wright Mills (Ed.), *From Max Weber. Essays in sociology* (London: Routledge & Kegan Paul, 1977), p. 189. As a confession related to the whole project of his religion studies, see GAR, I, p. 267. Here he claims the freedom to be 'unhistorisch' and to establish a large 'logischen Geschlossenheit und Entwicklungslosigkeit'. Of

In Weber's view, 'polis', 'feudalism', 'capitalism' or 'bureaucracy' and, indeed, 'castes' or 'pariahs' can be developed with data from all periods of history and all places on the map. Later on, one can try to connect these concepts to 'real historical behaviour/situations'. Their definitions are as abstract as possible; they try to fix universal or transhistorical meanings *a priori* as ideal types far beyond time and place. This explains why Weber received so much support from theologians and conservatives and so much criticism from empirically oriented historians, sociologists and the like.

To accept Weber, generally or specifically, these historians have to deny, for instance, that pariahs and castes can only be regarded as immanent phenomena from Hindu-Indian history and society. Using these concepts out of their context, they then have to accept them as highly scientific instead of fiction. A dictum 'as if somebody belonged to pariahs' is certainly nonsensical for empirically oriented historians. And, of course, they have to see real pariahs as 'guest people' instead of people integrated within Indian society.[32]

Not only is the historicity of Weberian concepts highly problematic, the other side of the problem has serious implications as well. At the *abstract level* of the concepts, one never deals with one concept alone but with some conceptual 'constellation'. Accepting or denying only one concept in the 'constellation' becomes a rather difficult matter. It seems, in my view at least, an act of bad faith if Momigliano ends his critical article with: 'Much of what Weber said on ancient Judaism remains valid even if we eliminate his definition of it as a pariah-religion.' There always seem to be scholars who believe that one can be just a little bit

<hr />

course, the problem is also that Weber himself sinned time and again in writing about 'real' historical and sociological situations! These passages, however, are nearly all outdated, false, in need of serious criticism, etc. A good lesson about the degree to which this is the case for Hinduism is provided in the section *Critiques* in C. Loomis, Z. Loomis (Ed.), *Socio-Economic Change and the Religious Factor in India. An Indian Symposium of Views on Max Weber* (New Delhi/ New York: Affiliated East-West Press/Van Nostrand, 1969). Although selected to support American modernization programs, the Indian participants at this symposium sponsored by the Ford Foundation were highly critical of Weber's use of Hinduistic concepts, his judgments on the real situation of the caste system, the pariahs, etc.

32. In this matter Momigliano (like Weber) acts and thinks as a believer-theologian, but he still cannot resist the historian's temptation to ask whether Weber's analysis would bring 'us nearer to the Indian model that was Weber's starting point?' This undermines the integrity of the scholar. A better example is provided by a Weberian sociologist like G.R. Madan, *Western Sociologists on Indian Society. Marx, Spencer, Weber, Durkheim, Pareto* (London: Rotledge & Kegan Paul, 1979), p. 123 who admits: 'With the increasing stabilization of economic conditions, the ritually segregated guest and pariah tribes were more and more integrated into the expanding caste order which thus became the dominant system. For a thousand years, from the second century AD to the beginning of Islamic rule ... expansion ... As a closed system, the caste order is a product of consistent brahmanical thought.' A critical evaluation of Weber's Hinduism studies is given by H. Kulke, Orthodoxe Restauration und hinduistische Sektenreligiosität im Werk Max Webers, in: W. Schluchter (Ed.), *Studie über Hinduismus und Buddhismus* (Frankfurt a./M.: Suhrkamp, 1984), p. 293-333. See also other contributions in this interesting reader like J. Heesterman's 'Kaste und Karma' (p.72-87); S. Tambiah's analysis of early Buddhism (p. 202-247) or G. Obeyesekere's essay on the same subject (p.247-274).

pregnant: it is impossible to deny the validity of a pariah concept without regarding '*the pariah complex*', and the rabbi Momigliano case is part of it.

It's certainly my aim to tell a realistic story of the development of a pariah complex and analyse its main characteristics in a non-abstract way. That will be demonstrated now in the first part of the study about the world historical context of an 'eastern' *nomadic question* and its connection with an 'eastern' *Jewish question.*

Mongol horsemen, from Reichsführer SS, *Der Untermensch* (1992). Source: R.J. van Pelt, D. Dwork, *Auschwitz, 1270 to the present* (New Haven/London: Yale University Press, 1996), p. 260.

A WORLD – HISTORICAL CONTEXT

'Humanity in the form of fraternity invariably appears historically among persecuted peoples and enslaved groups. ... This kind of humanity is the great privilege of pariah peoples; it is the advantage that the pariahs of this world always and in all circumstances can have over others. The privilege is dearly bought; it is often accompanied by so radical a loss of the world, so fearful an atropy of all the organs with which we respond to it ... that in extreme cases, in which pariahdom has persisted for centuries, we can speak of real worldlessness. And worldlessness, alas, is always a form of barbarism.'

Hannah Arendt, *Men in Dark Times* (1968)

2. WEBER AND THE NOMADS IN CHINESE AND CENTRAL ASIAN HISTORY

'Persian, I have never yet run from any man in fear and I am not doing so from you now. There is, for me, nothing unusual in what I have been doing: it is precisely the kind of life I always lead, even in times of peace. If you want to know why I will not fight, I will tell you. In our country there are no towns and no cultivated land; fear of losing which, or seeing it ravaged, might indeed provoke us to hasty battle. If however you are determined upon bloodshed ... one thing there is for which we will fight – the tombs of our forefathers. Find those tombs and try to wreck them, and you will soon know whether or not we are willing to stand up to you.'

The Scythian chieftain Idanthyrsus to Darius, king of Persia.
Herodotos, *The Histories*. IV, 125.

WEBER'S COMPARATIVE WORLD HISTORY

Soon after the legendary Scythian chief informed the king of kings, Darius, about basic social and anthropological elements of nomadic life, this Persian conqueror like so many of his predecessors and imitators saw his Waterloo. Herodotos learned us another thing. Most important reasons also for this failed clash of life-styles was the substantial ignorance about 'the enemy' and the inability to cope in a practical and peaceful way with alternative ways of life. In our century there seems to be no change in these circumstances and attitudes as will be substantiated in this chapter.

The first part is devoted to the subject of the sociological ignorance about nomadism in the highly influential work of Max Weber; the main part sketches the practical difficulties Chinese and Russian states met in coping with their nomadic populations. Both parts together display the most important elements of theory and practice of anti-nomadism in sedentary societies. It's not only basic knowledge for understanding the next chapters. If one looks at the substantial clashes between Chinese and nomads in Sinkiang nowadays or at the implications of the far from secret war about Central Asian gas- and oil reserves for traditional nomadic areas or at the long-lasting Afghan drama, one knows how the chapter still concerns a topic of the day. However, here not the present but the past problems between sedentary and nomadic societies have to come to the fore. In Max Weber's writings one can find a perception of the complexities of this subject in a world – historical context from which we can derive a specific part to discuss.

Interest in Max Weber increasingly shifts to his sociology of religion only[1], but the Weber-literature remains historically an interesting part of sociological and other discourses. Weber's own writings – sometimes *nolens volens* – still help tracing complicated historical and sociological problems. Even so, it is difficult to find articles or books about at least two important and mutually connected subjects however extensive the Weber-literature may be. First, there are the (inter-relations between) market and *oikos,* which cover formally only a very few pages of *Economy and Society* (*Wirtschaft und Gesellschaft*).[2] Second, there is the subject of the nomads or, in general, of mobile as opposed to sedentary peoples.

The relationship between the two subjects can be found rather easily. Not only the words of the Scythian chieftain above show the connections and contradic-tions. Also opinions relating mobile behaviour to markets and a sedentary way of life to the agriculturally oriented *oikos* (another word for a patriarchally ruled *latifundium,* household, manor, family, an estate as well as a state) demonstrate the relationship. Superficially, it looks as if Weber dealt with both subjects only spora-dically. However, one can argue that they belong to the very heart of his thinking and oeuvre and, more important, that they belong to the centre of intriguing and complex problems such as town – country contradictions.[3]

In this chapter I deal with the second theme as a consequence of the book's subject.[4] Inevitably, the first subject will also be touched but analyses of *oikos* – market relations remain in the background. In the mean time, it is far from easy to discover Weber's opinions about nomads and related groups.[5] The EC – index does not help find traces of nomads or pastoralist people; in WG there is already one entry on Bedouins. In the essays on the sociology of religion there is a bit more and in the so-called *Wirtschaftsgeschichte* one can find also some interesting material.[6] If the subject should be extended to all kinds of animal-breeding ('*Viehaltung*', '*Viehwirtschaft*' etc.) the yield on Weberian thoughts on the subject

---

1. H. Derks, Das Ende eines einmaligen Phänomens? Die Max Weber-Literatur 1920-1988, in: *Zeitschrift für Soziologie* 18,4 (1989), p. 282-297.

2. M. Weber, *EC*, p. 370-385, 635-641 and Idem, *WG*, p. 230-234, 382-385. Furthermore one can find many remarks related to the *oikos-market* relationships throughout his works.

3. H. Derks, *Stad en Land, Markt en Oikos* (Amsterdam: hab. Un. of Amsterdam, 1986), p. 456-507 (*Town and Country, Market and Oikos*).

4. Idem, *De Koe van Troje. De mythe van de Griekse Oudheid* (Hilversum: Verloren, 1995) (*The Trojan Cow. The Myth of Greek Antiquity*); Idem, A Note on 'homogalaktes' in Aristotle's POLITIKA, in: *Dialogues d'Histoire Ancienne* 21,2 (1995), p. 27-40.

5. See first the excellent T. Ingold (Ed.), *Companion Encyclopedia of Anthropology* (London: Routledge, 1997) with many relevant articles.

6. S. Hellmann, M. Palyi (Ed.), *Wirtschaftsgeschichte von Max Weber. Abriss der universalen Sozial- und Wirtschafts -Geschichte* (München/ Leipzig: Duncker & Humblot, 1924) [hereafter: WGe].

is again a bit larger.[7] So, all in all the result is rather meager. The same conclusion holds for the extensive Weber-literature: you will search in vain for an article on Weber and nomadism!

However, the following quotations will give a very different view of the priority Weber gave to the subject. We can also gain perspective of the problems that must be discussed. The following remarks are derived from the second version of his *Agrarverhältnisse im Altertum (1898)*. In the introduction Weber states:

'The settlements of the West have in common a transition from nomadic animal-husbandry to sedentary agriculture; East-Asian peoples, however, have in common a transition from shifting cultivation to sedentary agriculture. ... The consequences are ... that in oriental villages, in so far they are not from modern origin, the western concepts of mark and allmende are absent. ... Also the "individualism" inherent in the property of herds and flocks with its sharp economic and social differentiation – in the West the primitive basis of feodalism – is absent in Asian cultures. ... The East-Asians as well as the old American cultures seem to know feodalism in principle as group- or caste- feodalism: a strongly closed and locally organised warrior-group, often living in fortified settlements, is maintained in a *naturalwirtschaftlich* way by a population who are considered as state-slaves or -serves. Also the Egyptian and Asian Orient is in their whole development determined by the preponderance of a colossal Pharaohnic or imperial "Oikos", i.e. the state-economy based on *Naturalwirtschaft*.'[8]

So, here we deal with one of the broadest themes in comparative world history as well as a subject that can be tested in regional and local environments. This is also one of the most hotly debated subjects complicated by the changing opinions of participants during their lifetime. Weber, for instance, altered eleven years later the first part of this fundamental statement in the following way:

---

7. In this case in WGe more text is available and one can also consult M. Weber, *Gesammelte Aufsätze zur Sozial- und Wirtschaftsgeschichte* (Tübingen: Mohr, 1924) [hereafter: GASW] p. 1 ff. i.e. the article, Agrarverhältnisse im Altertum.

8. M. Weber, Agrarverhältnisse im Altertum, in: *Handwörterbuch der Staatswissenschaften*, J. Conrad, et al. Ed. (Jena: Fischer, 1898), second ed., p. 57, 58. Like the first edition Idem (1897), *Zweiter Supplementband*, p. 1-18 this second draft of Weber's *Agrarverhältnisse* is also never consulted. This is a serious mistake. One always uses the article in the third edition of the *Handwörterbuch* (1909). The English translator, R.I. Frank, does not know of their existence as is shown in M. Weber, *The Agrarian Sociology of Ancient Civilizations* (London: New Left Books, 1976), p. 29 ff. Widow Marianne Weber, notorious for her dubious information about her Saint Max, did not mention the previous drafts either (See GASW, p. 1 note). In the '*Vorwort*' of GASW, a much repeated remark is made about the short time Weber needed to write the lengthy third version. No wonder, the model was finished in the previous editions. Weber only had to fill in the details. The first version consisted only of chapters on Greece and Rome; the second added a chapter on Near Eastern developments and extended the Greek chapter considerably; as a new item, the third edition also contained a short (3% of the text) analysis of the Old Israelite situation.

'The settlements of the European West have in common ... the transition ... from a dominant milk cattle-husbandry plus some agriculture to a dominant agriculture plus some cattle-husbandry in the definite sedentary constellation; the East-Asian peoples, however, have in common ... a transition from a shifting cultivation to a horticultural use of fields without any milk cattle-husbandry.'[9]

Which questions arise from these sweeping statements and what will be the 'problem-definition' of this chapter?

First, there is the geographical expansion of Weber's argument. In the new edition Weber adds to the former that the given Northern European type of transition is also suitable for Southern Europe and the Near East. 'East Asia' remains what it was: similar to 'old American cultures', to Pharaohnic and other colossal imperial *Oikoi* with state-slaves and all the rest. Interesting is that here 'Near East' spearheads the North European type of development right into a vast area with only 'Eastern Despotism'. In this way, the classic Greek and hellenistic cultures get their space in time, let alone the Judaist phenomenon.

Next, it follows from both citations that Weber sees all histories ending in sedentary agriculture. Is this wishful thinking, already a reality or, for my part, a desirable perspective? These questions have to be posed against the background of the near impossibility to settle nomads. Only recently, after about 1870, nomads of the worlds *Nomads Belt* were 'settled' by force. Too often this kind of settlement meant nothing more than an attempted genocide. In other cases world market prices in wool and other 'nomadic' products were too low during a long period. Together with the usual hazzards of nomadic life such as droughts and animal-pests, this depression meant starvation of North African nomads at a large scale. Governments and development agencies experienced that their energetic efforts to 'peasantizise' nomads largely failed.[10] So, what is meant by Weber with '*a transition from nomadic animal-husbandry to sedentary agriculture*'?

Furthermore, the '*milk-question*' as well as the '*cattle-husbandry*' phenomenon received pivotal importance. This problem is partly related to the farreaching differences between a population's dominant milk-consumption and a dominant

---

9. GASW, p. 1. To understand Weber's opinions, in my view, it is necessary to 'translate' the content and not the form. I am, therefore, not fond of most of the available English translations, although they might demonstrate much better English! For example, Weber used the rather ambiguous '*nomadisierender Ackernutzung*' translated by R. Frank as '*nomadic agriculture*'. Perhaps Weber wanted to use a concept expressing a wandering way of collecting or growing fruits or grains by peasants. Wim Wertheim rightly proposed to substitute for this the technical term '*shifting cultivation*' (*ladang*-cultivation) which was widely spread in Asian countries for a very long time. Western imperialists and developers wrongly opposed the burning of the (old) forest-land while looking elsewhere for new cultivation opportunities as a very primitive and damaging way of food-production. If Wertheim's next proposition should be true that the typical western *three field system* is in principle a similar cultivation-technique, then already at the start Weber's thesis has to fall apart.
10. P. Salzman (Ed.), *When Nomads settle. Processes of Sedentarization as Adaptation and Response* (New York: Praeger, 1980) provides an interesting introduction to the problem.

meat-consumption. Partly it is related to the antagonism between the use of the animal's milk/meat and the use of animal-energy ('horse-power', oxen, donkeys, etc.). At present, in industrial urban society *milk* seems to be one of the million consumer-products in a super-market. Sometimes, at the moment the so-called '*milk-oceans*' float the EEC again, people awake but only for as long as headlines in the papers reach. Sometimes we are surprised by interesting anthropological studies about strange tribes, their bonds of blood and milk, their symbolic and medical use of milk, etc.[11]

Weber, however, even used the milk-item in a comparative world-historical perspective. But did he rightly understood that as nearly no other product milk is a metaphor for specific kinds of societies? Why gave he, for instance, East-Asian peoples no access to milk cattle-husbandry? Is't not remarkable as well that, in fact, *nomadism* remains only a feature in 'Western' history, whereas the Asian history seems wholly occupied by peasants who became later horticulturalists?

The last element of this problem-definition concerns ideology. In all respects, one can say: Dealing with nomads is never value-free. 'Nomad-ideological problems' concern, first, well-known discrimination-patterns which could lead us to question their origin and to compare relevant histories. Brent Shaw, for instance, began an important Herodotos-article, *Eaters of Flesh, Drinkers of Milk*, by offending the reader's 'civilized sensibilities' to illustrate that nomads, whether ancient or modern, have never had a 'good press'.[12] He quotes Hunter Thompson as follows:

'... The Menace is loose again, the Hell's Angels, the hundred carat headline, running fast and loud on the early morning freeway, low in the saddle, nobody smiles, jamming crazy through traffic and ninety miles an hour down the centre stripe, missing by inches ... like Genghis Khan on an iron horse, a monster steed with fiery anus, flat out through the eye of a beer can and up your daughter's leg with no quarter asked and none given ...'

Here Shaw appeals to a string of prejudices commonly associated with mobile people. Immediately, he directs the reader's attention to the general effects of the 'nomadic challenge'. Shaw rightly complains about the 'complete shortfall in recorded history of an entire sector of human community'. In Classical antiquity it is due to the little sympathy with the (pastoral) nomad in written accounts of historians, military men or administrators. Their perception of the world, their sedentarist outlook, determined to a large extent existing prejudices.

The ideological problems concerning nomadic peoples and societies can be

11. M. Creyghton, *Bad Milk. Perceptions and Healing of a Children's illness in a North African Society* (Amsterdam: Univ. of Amsterdam habil., 1981).
12. B. Shaw, Eaters of Flesh, Drinkers of Milk: the ancient mediterranean ideology of the pastoral nomad,in: *Ancient Society* 13/14 (1982/'83), p. 5-31.

also studied in all the three parts of Weber's sociology of religion. Indeed, it seems almost self-evident to develop the general argumentation of this chapter on the basis of these '*wirtschaftsethische*' texts. Within his very incomplete *oeuvre*, they not only form a rather complete corpus but they also deal in a comparative way with regions most suitable for the study of nomadism i.e. the Chinese, Hinduistic or Palestinian societies/ histories. It is well known that these analyses were of paramount importance for Weber to answer questions raised with the rise of modern capitalism in the West and the role of religion in that process. I cannot deal with that part of the problem here but by implication my analysis of Weber's view on nomadism etc. will affirm or criticize his capitalism-theory.

It is clear, then, that the given problem-definition displays a vast and complex field of research which must be kept in mind when looking into a specific corner of that field: Max Weber's views on the East-Asian, in particular Chinese, se-dentarism-nomadism contradictions. I put to the test, first, the Chinese and other Asian 'milk and meat evidence' as a direct consequence of Weber's writings. It not only gives the opportunity to dive into Weber's thought but also to highlight some specific nomadic features. The second part of the chapter concerns the general characteristics of the sedentarism/ agriculture versus nomadism/ animal-hus-bandry relationships. Much misunderstandings concerning nomadism in history can be discussed by means of a broad historical analysis so that a relevant insight is reached into a highly complex phenomenon as 'the (chance of) a transition from nomadic animal-husbandry to sedentary agriculture'. I hope to show, at least, the main elements of this transition-problem in a Chinese and Central Asian context. In the end I can come back on characteristics of Weber's 'nomadism-theory' to be used as a stepping- stone for the next chapters.

A MILK AND MEAT IDEOLOGY

When Weber talked about the social basis of Chinese development in the 18th century, he pointed to the extraordinary intensity of the Chinese 'acquisitive drive'.[13] Commercial organizations were very powerful as well as autonomous and the Chinese were very eager to work and perform well. In this respect nearly no one could compete with them. Weber supposed that the fast population-growth of the 18th century combined with an ever increasing stock of strategic metals should have given China the best opportunity to become a capitalist country. But this did not happen. Why?

Weber summed up the following reasons: The large increase of the peasant population instead of a strong decrease as in England; the small-scale peasant-

---

13. See GAR, I, p. 349 ff. Weber used here '*Erwerbstrieb*' which is translated according WG, p. 371 and EC, p. 617 although 'aquisitive drive', at least, does not remind to '*Haushalten*' as the unavoidable counter-concept to Weber's '*Erwerbstrieb*'.

holdings instead of the agricultural large enterprises as in Prussia[14]; cattle-breeding was largely undeveloped and, subsequently, milk-drinking was absent and meat-consumption 'something for the rich'. This last item is even seen as a *'Hauptgegensatz'* between Europe and Asia. This could be expected given what was cited in the first paragraph.[15]

In trying to answer the question anew, Why all this?, Weber apologised for *not* dealing with the case of the nomadic past of the Chinese. In a long note, however, he compensated this with a fundamental statement.[16] He argued that nomadic invaders from Inner-Asia, who suppressed the population of the main Chinese valley's, showed up repeatedly. Weber went on to say that

'From time to time only the nomadic Mongols did serious efforts of sustaining their power-positions against the higher farm-culture (by means of a prohibition to grow crops in a certain distance of the capital). However, the Chinese never drink milk and this fact is clearly more important than all histories about the continuity of the centuries old field- and horticulture. Besides this the rituals of the Emperor prescribed the ceremonial use of the plow. Compared with these facts the nomadic descent of (part of) the old ruler-elite seems insignificant. The existence of "Man-houses" ... has nothing to do with "nomadism", but it shows that war and game is cared for by these communities, but the agriculture by the women. The absence of milk-consumption in China is clearly very old and it contradicts the "Nomad" – Hypothesis. Large animals were used for work or sacrifice and small animals were used to satisfy the normal need for meat.'

14. M. Elvin, *The Pattern of the Chinese Past* (Stanford, Cal.: Stanford Univ. Pr., 1973), p. 268 gives the modern view. In the eighteenth and nineteenth centuries there was a fast increase of market towns: '...they grew up around temples, around the manors of great landlords and the country residences of important merchants, and even around industrial undertakings such as pottery works ...' One development which can certainly be compared to the Prussian situation (this occured at the same time but on a much larger scale!), was the penetration of the large agro-monasteries into the plains of Mongolia. In around 1825 'some 30% of the male population had taken vows. Monasteries increased in size and towns grew round them.' J. Gray, *Rebellions and Revolutions. China from the 1800s to the 1980s* (Oxford: Oxford Univ. Press, 1990), p. 94. Later, one got as much trouble with these monks as with the Junkers! But it is true, the small peasant economy prevailed, although their political-economy is hardly comparable to the European peasant economy which was Weber's frame of reference (see, for instance, Gray, p. 8 ff.).

15. WGe, p. 39 note 1. In relation to his capitalism-thesis, he later (GAR, I, 373 ff.) made the differentiation between the '*political capitalism*' of money-lenders and suppliers of patrimonial courts and '*modern capitalism*'. The first kind earned high profit-rates in their money-business and one knew how to exploit mines and commerce to accumulate wealth. 'The development of the capitalism oriented to the market proper and free exchange remained, however, in statu nascendi.' What developed in Western medieval cities was absent in China till nowadays: there were 'no legal and sociological bases for capitalist "enterprises" with their rational *Versachlichung* of the economy ... the liability of the clans for their members' was rudimentary developed ... 'commercial gains were invested immediately in land ...(it was) in particular an internal and political booty-capitalism which dominated the capital gains and ... land-accumulation.' (p. 374/ 375).

16. Ebd. p. 350, 351. The causal relationship in this note is highly blurred but that shall not be my first worry here.

This view rests first and foremost on the typical European (sedentary!) prejudices about the always war-making and 'barbaric' nomads; they not only kill and enslave poor peasants and threaten peaceful, godfearing rulers, but they never accept any control or the authority of the State. As will be shown, the Weberian prejudices fit perfectly well with views within the Chinese *oikoidal* (court) elite.

But let me first give a short and rather unsystematic answer to the question of meat- and milk-consumption in Chinese history, which presupposes animal-breeding, pastures and so on. It is told that the idea of the Chinese non-consumption of milk comes from Alexander von Humboldt (1769-1859).[17] If he has stated this, his words must be hidden beyond his *Gesammelte Werke*. It should be interesting to know which sources, except his learned thumb, Humboldt used. In any case, the milk-statement must have been part of his general social evolution-theory in which everywhere sedentary agriculture had to come before nomadism and 'hunterism'. Most scholars in the 19th century, however, adhered to the opposite theory, the so called *'Dreistufentheorie'* in which hunters are followed first by nomads and later by 'agriculturalists' (*Ackerbauer*). Some even dared to expand this theory with 'industrialism'.

At the moment one can easily find supporters of both opinions but, in my view, they are both wrong starting-points. Apart from the fallacy of every *prime mover* thinking, at least, one has to consider all kinds of ecological, climatical or economical circumstances before posing relevant transitions. If this is done, one conclusion seems unavoidable: there have to be several developments for different regions thanks to combinations of possibilities. Second, the knowledge about the *mutual relations* or dependencies of agriculture, nomadism and the other forms has to be taken in serious consideration. So far, so good.

In Weber's Heidelberg the economic-geographer Eduard Hahn published numerous influential studies about this social evolution.[18] He is a rather agressive

---

17. E. Hahn, *Die Entstehung der Pflugkultur (unsres Ackerbaus)* (Heidelberg: Carl Winter's Univ. Buchhandl., 1909), p. 4, 5, 24.

18. In 1908 Hahn published here *Die Entstehung der wirtschaftlichen Arbeit* and in 1905 *Das Alter der wirtschaftlichen Kultur der Menschheit*, etc. The renewal of Humboldt's thesis was arrived by stating, for instance, the following stupidities: 'Die Frau muß im wesentlichen dauernd die Nahrung beschaffen, und da sie fast nie zur Jägerin und selten zur Fischerin geworden ist ..., so ist fast immer die wirtschaftliche Basis der Urstämme pflanzliche Nahrung.' (Ebd. p. 5). Hahn became one of those forerunners of Fascism and Nazism with his opinion that 'man's biological type was determined by domestication, which influences him in much the same manner as it influences animals.' See W. Mühlmann, Eduard Hahn (1856-1928), in: *Encyclopaedia of the Social Sciences*, Ed. E. Seligman (New York: Macmillan, 1949), Vol. VII, p. 244 ff.; see also F. Ratzel, *Anthropogeographie* (Stuttgart: Engelhorn Verlag, 1909), Vol. I, p. 322-325 (orig. 1882). More important is the originally in 1897 written third chapter in Ratzel's *Politische Geographie* (München/ Berlin: Oldenbourg, 1923), p. 33-59 about 'Property and Domination' [*Besitz und Herrschaft*]. Here Ratzel formulated, in fact, the foundation for the influential and notorious *Deutsche Geopolitik* embedded in his description of the basic war between agriculture [*Ackerbau/ Boden 'Kultur*] and nomadism. He used Hahn's *Ackerbau* – point of view (Ebd., p. 49 ff.). For the very influential geographers 'scene' see G. Sandner, In Search

conservative defender of 'our agriculture' in science as well as in politics. Hahn renewed not only Humboldt's agricultural evolution-thesis but also his opinion about the Chinese milk-consumption. According to him, Humboldt told 'that the consumption of milk – for us a selfevident matter – is detested by the Chinese as a people and that they do this already for thousands of years.' Hahn adds to this that Chinese at present never eat cheese: 'From this food we received our bad smell, they think.'[19] Milk is a beloved subject of Hahn's book. Strange enough, he does not mention any reason why 'the Chinese as a people' (!) should abhor this healthy white drink. Also in other respects Hahn used an equal development model as Weber: Exactly the milk consumption and animal husbandry in our culture is strictly embedded within the agriculture [*Ackerbau* or *Pflugkultur* for Hahn] and by this fact we received major elements of our identity. It is not difficult to prove whether Weber is directly influenced by Hahn who does not discuss an anti- 'Chinese meat-case' or a pro- 'Chinese vegetarianism'.[20]

Although early in the century Chinese restaurants were not widespread, it remains strange how unfamiliar Weber was with Chinese food. At least, he would have known that pork always was (and is happily) a normal part of the common Chinese family-diet. By 5000 BC., the Neolithic villagers' main meat animals were pigs and chickens. They also raised and ate sheep and dogs. Soon afterwards the cow, waterbuffalo and duck were added 'and the Chinese meat roster was essentially complete'.[21] Since Weber thinks that the absence of milk-consumption in

---

of Identity: German Nationalism and Geography 1871-1910, in: *Geography and National Identity*, Ed. D. Hooson (Oxford: Blackwell, 1994), p. 71-92. Lewis Mumford also accepted Hahn's perspective and at present feminists like Badinter still support his thesis! See E. Badinter, *L'un est l'autre* (Dutch transl., Amsterdam: Contact, 1988), p. 54 ff., p. 277.

19. E. Hahn, *Die Entstehung*, p. 24 (as a source he mentions E. Parker's *China, history..* , London, 1901), see also p. 28.

20. In GASW, p. 508-556 within a very principal discussion about some hot issues of the German historiography in his days (*Der Streit um den Charakter der altgermanischen Sozialverfassung ...*) Weber very positively referred to Hahn (p. 524). Weber's affirmation is given although he strongly doubts Hahn's scholarship (note 1): in his perception Hahn has the '*überlieferten Vorstellungen über die "Wirtschaftsstufen" zuerst einen eingehender begründeten Widerspruch entgegengesetzt ...*' (H. criticized old-fashioned ideas about economic development in a highly appropriate way). It is very informative how Weber here took the reverse position as in the Chinese case: here the old West-Germans as alleged nomads are not seen as consumers of milk, cheese and meat but first as '*Ackerbauer*', whereas the more eastern German tribes were (still) milk etc. consumers (p. 524 ff.). It is not possible to discuss this position which must be seen in relation to Weber's 'East Asian' view.

21. E. Anderson, *The Food of China* (New Haven/London: Yale Univ. Press, 1988), p. 143, 144. See also Ebd., p. 164 ff., 177. He also reports: In Sung China, as the 'golden age of Chinese *sushi* making ... pork was the main meat eaten, but sheep, goat and even donkey were common...' (p.68). For the earliest milk and meat consumption in Central Asia now see the excellent A. Dani; V. Masson (Ed.), *History of civilizations of Central Asia* (Paris: Unesco, 1992), vol.I for example p. 39 ff., 225 ff., 272 ff. (pre-Indus cultures), 432 ff.; D. Christian, *A History of Russia, Central Asia and Mongolia* (Oxford: Blackwell, 1998), Vol. I with numerous data on milk and meat consumption. Anderson tells about the traveller Robert Fortune who wrote in 1847: 'The food of the people is of the simplest kind ... rice,

China is very old, then in the third century AD it was not necessary to come up with proposals for large-scale changes of pastures into arable lands. That occurred in specific parts of China, whereas elsewhere the extraordinary richness of many large estates could be reported where, for instance, 'their horses, cattle, sheep and swine' were so numerous that 'the upland valleys cannot hold' them.[22] In around 644, the emperor T'ai-tsung of the T'ang complained about the difficult food-situation and ordered:

'The situation is especially bad in the San-Wei, and yet grazing lands for pigs, sheep and horses are spread throughout this region. All of these should be done away with ... All the pasturages should be removed, so that the horses, cattle, pigs and sheep feed on the grass of the empty plains.'[23]

One of Mark Elvin's relevant answers to the question also addressed by Weber as to why (Western) industrial capitalism did not develop in China from the 18th century onwards was: 'There was a shortage of draught-animals, and possibly therefore of animal manures, as northern grazing-lands were turned into fields.'[24] Elvin's remark could mean that the government still failed to take announced

vegetables, and a small portion of animal food, such as fish and pork.' (Ebd. p. 96). Hsiao-Tung Fei, *Peasant Life in China. A Field Study of Country Life in the Yangtze Valley* (London: Routledge & Kegan Paul, 1980), p. 126-128 tells about the relative poor peasants diet in the thirties of the 20th century: 'The only kind of meat eaten is pork...' and 'During the period of agricultural work, the dinner is comparatively rich. They have meat and fish. But in ordinary times meat is not very often served. Pure vegetarianism is rare except for a few widows.' In Kwantung there was even a tax on slaughtered animals in 1908. Such a tax is only appropriate if there is a large amount of meat-eaters. W. Yeh-chien, *Land Taxation in Imperial China, 1750-1911* (Cambridge, Mass.: Harvard Univ. Press, 1973), p. 79.

22. M. Elvin, p. 33. In about 1100 when the Southern Sung introduced paper money a source reported that the bills were paid half in paper and half in cash: 'A similar practice was followed among the common people for the mortgaging or sale of fields, houses, horses, cattle ....' (Ebd., p. 160).

23. See also Ebd., p. 39 about the same time: 'The importance of livestock in the farm economy of north-eastern China at this time is in marked contrast with the predominance of cereal crop cultivation, ... in the late traditional period and at the present.' Other aspects of milk-drinking are given in Wolfgang Bauer's brilliant book *China und die Hoffnung auf Glück.* (München: DTV, 1989). It is an analysis and description of most of the utopian visions and ideas about the best possible world in Chinese history from the beginning up to Mao Zedong's political-economical experiments. Bauer often reports about a most beautiful world 'of milk and honey', a subterranean world with milk-resources (ca. AD 825; Ebd., p. 275-277); a vision of a new world, Uttarakuru, still used in about 1650 in which there grew lotus-flowers with juice 'which looks like milk, tastes sweet and delicious, smells like honey ... large, heavy clouds as big as the whole country ... wonderful rain ... like cow milk ... There is no egoism (wu wo), nor a ruler (wu chu) or police ...' (Ebd., p. 235), etc. Another comment about Weber's meat-verdict can be seen in a Confucian story from the 13th century which shows the opposite: members of the sect of 'Satans-friends and Vegetable-eaters' are forbidden to eat meat and to drink wine. Some of them became rich. This inspired the story-teller to complain about the naivety of the people 'because it is selfevident that one becomes rich if one does not eat meat and drink wine...' (Ebd., p. 312).

24. M. Elvin, p. 301.

measures, but also that over a very long period well into modern times there were large areas with animal-husbandry and, subsequently, milk-consumption. Elvin shows as well that, apart from milk, the *manure*-problem is of the utmost importance for the peasants and, in general, for the interdependence of agriculture and animal-breeding. The large agricultural potential could only be exploited given an abundance of water and animal manure (see below).

In 1847 the traveller Robert Fortune 'was surprised to find that in Foochow beef and milk were widely eaten'.[25] At the end of the nineteenth century, Arthur H. Smith writes: 'In the northern parts of China the horse, the mule, the ox, and the donkey are in universal use, and in large districts the camel is made to do full duty. ... it is the general practice to eat all of these animals as soon as they expire, no matter whether the cause of death be an accident, old age, or disease. ... and this truth is recognized in the lower scale of prices asked for it, but it is all sold, and is all eaten.'[26] It is no surprise to read nowadays: 'The consumption of dairy products has increased markedly since World War II, but only in the northwestern pastoral regions are cattle widely used for meat or milk products.'[27] A comment to this very quick overview over the 'milk-centuries' seems unnecessary.

This brings us to the following related 'practical' points. If Weber looked into the matter of milk- and meat-consumption, he must have considered the densely populated eastern parts of China, the coastal-areas or the river-valleys (together about 50% of China's surface and 75% of the population). The real Chinese pasture – provinces in the North, interior and (South)West are neglected. This must have seriously influenced his perception and from many other scholars. For all these people, the facts must come as a surprise: 'Not only the Mongols, nomadic Turkic groups ... and Tibetans, but also the western Chinese eat yogurt, cheese, kumys ... and other fermented products.'[28] But also elsewhere in China there were and are many opportunities for several kinds of pastoralism and animal breeding. A few statistics are sufficient to explain this point further.

---

25. Op cit. E. Anderson, p. 96. Foochow or F(o)uchou is located at the coast opposite Taiwan; a very remote place in relation to the pasture heartlands!

26. A.H. Smith, *Chinese Characteristics* (New York: Revell Company, 1894,orig. 1890), p. 21. The reverend Smith lived and worked for twenty-two years in China and also wrote books on Chinese village life.

27. Chiao-min Hsieh, *Atlas of China* (New York: McGraw Hill, 1973), p. 87, 88. This atlas is very helpful in discovering the many pitfalls and possibilities of the present Chinese climate, hydrology etc. and the resulting land use, crops, etc. I don't know if this atlas may be accurate about the historical record. In that case Mongolia (and many parts of Central Asia as Kazakhstan, Uzbekistan etc.) an area nearly as great as Western Europe with 80% pastures, must also be considered.

28. E. Anderson, p. 145. For the present situation in Central Asia see C. van Leeuwen et. al., *Nomads in Central Asia. Animal husbandry and culture in transition, 19th- 20th century* (Amsterdam: Royal Tropical Institute, 1994).

In the thirties a remarkable inquiry appeared from J. Lossing Buck c.s.[29] This gave the first reliable possibility to compare 'Western' and 'Eastern' agricultural practices. Although Lossing Buck c.s. mainly studied the hard core agricultural areas, he could estimate that approximately one-fourth of all land is cultivated which is an average in the world (between 12 to 45 per cent). One-half is in some kind of productive use consisting out of trees, grass and reeds for fuel. One-fifth is occupied by forest and twelve per cent is real pasture. At the moment thirty-one per cent of the Chinese surface is qualified as 'pasture'; it is an area as large as eighty per cent of Europe (excl. Russia) with a population of, at least, 200 million people![30] If Lossing Buck only looks into the twenty-five per cent of cultivated land, he estimates that nearly ninety per cent is used for crops and about two per cent for pasture. In the United States this relation is forty-two per cent against forty-seven (and at the time in Europe – excl. Russia – it had to be about sixty-five and thirty per cent). Therefore, Lossing Buck concludes that there is a small animal industry in China and a consequent low food consumption of animal products, as compared with a large animal industry and a high consumption of animal products in many of the Western countries. In an optimistic mood, this could be seen as a first substantiation of Weber's thesis.

However, the conclusion is drawn at the basis of only a *quarter* of the total Chinese surface. Notwithstanding this fact, Lossing Buck c.s. conclude next: 'The density of animal population is, however, surprisingly high in China: 0.34 animal units per crop acre, as compared with 0.70 in Great Britain ... (it) means that over a large part of the country the farms are moderately to well-stocked. This is true in spite of the fact that 10 per cent of the farms have no animals. This degree of animal density is a large factor in the maintenance of the fertility of the land.'[31]

---

29. J. Lossing Buck, *Land Utilization in China* (Shanghai: 1937/38). In the three volumes of this study the report is given from an eight years' field investigation of 17,000 farms involving 46,601 farm families in twenty-two out of China's twenty-eight provinces by over 3000 experts.

30. This is not as remarkable as it seems because in scrutinizing Lossing Buck's data the gap can be diminished. Furthermore, one must always control the vital data used by the scholars at stake. Lossing Buck used, for instance, a total Chinese surface of about 1.400.000 sqare miles; the *Times Atlas of the World* gives a surface of 3.900.000 square miles (1959); the *Third World Guide* ('89/'90) uses 9.596.961 square kilometres, and so on.

31. The American agriculturalist Lossing Buck c.s. did a great job. It is, however, undeniable that he made only a typical agricultural investigation in the northern wheat- and southern rice-regions. Animal husbandry and its products in the broadest sense of the word got too less attention. Other sources like eye-witness accounts must be consulted awaiting new and relevant studies. See, for instance, Lossing Buck's colleague the important Frederick King, *Farmers of Forty Centuries or permanent agriculture in China, Korea and Japan* (London: Cape, 1949, orig. 1911). I thank Wim Wertheim for pointing to this study. This American agriculturalist made the following comparison about the animal density in Shantung (p. 206). Well-to-do farmers in this city are able to provide for eight people, two cows, two donkeys and about eight pigs. If taking the same density 'an area of farm land equal to the state of Wisconsin would have 86,000,000 people; 21,500,000 cows; 21,500,000 donkeys and 86,000,000 swine ... It is clear, therefore, that either very effective agricultural methods

The myths of 'a vegetarian China' or of 'China, the country of only small peasants' should come to an end. The same must happen with the related myth of 'the Chinese or East Asian abstinence from dairy products'. The classic Chinese explanation for this last myth is clear enough: '..prejudice against Central Asians and desire to avoid economic dependence on them.'[32] Here we arrive at the hard core of the 'Nomadic Challenge'. The given prejudice enlightens a most typical oikoidal argument inspired by autarkic state-policies. 'The Chinese State' (whatever this may be in Chinese history) had already become dependent on horse-imports from Central Asia: another dependence would have been 'too costly and too humiliating'!

After solving these fundamental practical problems, we can look into the Chinese Weber-case in more detail.

THE MUTUAL RELATIONSHIPS

For a period of at least two thousand years (200 BC – AD 1700), 'trade was the chief determinant of peace and war between the nomadic and Chinese peoples along China's northern borders'.[33] The Turkic and Mongolian nomads needed and

---

are practiced or else extreme economy is exercised. Both are true'! Elsewhere (p. 132) he tells about a cattle farm in Shanghai (!) with 40 cows, fed with a.o. cotton seed cakes, which produced milk 'far better than the Danish and New Zealand products served at the hotels.' Still, even King cannot fully free himself from the vegetarian-myth in quoting an American colleague instead of looking around (p. 121 ff.).

32. E. Anderson, p. 145, 146. Of course, it is true that at the moment the majority of East Asians are poor milk- or dairy consumers. Certainly Buddhism, as another oikoidal power, is effective by declaring cows as holy animals. It is also a typical oikoidal argument to come up with a *biological* explanation for the alleged milk-abstinence in East Asia. Also in the case of milk-consumption one must be exact as possible because most nomads of Central Asia never drink *fresh* milk. It is first boiled and then fermented; butter and various kinds of cheese are made from fermented milk. Furthermore one has to understand the pecularities of the various kinds of milk and their popularity for different reasons. Sheep and cow-milk are consumed the most but for special occasions the beestings (the first milk of cows, sheep and goats) or the fermented mare's milk (koumiss or kumys) are more popular. Camels do have a large milk production; it is said, however, that pregnant women do not drink this milk. See C. van Leeuwen et all., p. 65.

33. For the following is most important S. Jagchid; V.J. Symons, *Peace, War, and Trade along the Great Wall. Nomadic – Chinese Interaction through two Millennia* (Bloomington: Indiana Univ. Press, 1989), hereafter: Jagchid. A general devastating critic of Weber's writings on China is M. Elvin, Warum hat das vormoderne China keinen industriellen Kapitalismus entwickelt? Eine Auseinandersetzung mit Max Webers Ansatz, in: *Max Webers Studie über Konfuzianismus und Taoismus*, Ed. W. Schluchter (Frankfurt a/M.: Suhrkamp, 1983), p. 114-134. However, I can imagine that some think of Schluchter's very weak defence of Weber in this volume (p. 11-55) as even more devastating for Weber's 'impressionistic' (Elvin) view. From both Elvin's article and Schluchter's defence, one can learn that Weber might have known better. First, the 18th century French writings (see ebd. p. 122) gave more differentiated information. Furthermore, the sinologist Arthur von Rosthorn (see ebd. p. 48 note 13 and 24), a Weber-'club colleague' from Heidelberg, gave lectures on the subject. He could easily have informed Weber much better. Later he criticized Weber heavily in: Religion und Wirtschaft in China,

got particularly large quantities of rice, cloth, silk and lacquer wares for themselves and for trade with other (Near)Asian peoples. The grain was partly used as a supplement to their daily diet of milk and meat. The Chinese agriculturalists needed and sometimes got slaves, but always got horses, cattle, sheep, wool, furs (sable and fox in particular), hides, tendons and horns, the famous jade or strategic metals as copper and iron in large quantities. From the Sung Chinese, nomads bought rice etc. for large quantities of silver money, whereas already in the Han-period the Chinese gave substantial amounts of money and gold as gifts.

In the 19th century, from a Centralasian perspective, the picture looks as follows.[34] In all nomadic societies along the Western Chinese borders there existed many bazars. Here livestock (sheep, camels, horses, etc.) and handicrafts (skins, leather, footwear, wool, carpets, etc.) are sold by nomads but nearly no food. Dairy products normally were not used for trade or barter. The nomads bought agricultural products and products of city craftsmen like cotton, silk and pottery. But now also copperware, iron pots and so on are bought from city-merchants. Fundamental changes, however, did not occur before the collectivisation-programmes from the thirties of the twentieth century onwards. Below I shall deal with that subject.

It would be an error to suppose that only pure nomadic products came to the Chinese farmers or that agricultural products went to the nomads. The Uighur people (about AD 1000), for instance, also traded white wheat, Tibetan wheat, yellow hemp, green onions and other vegetables to T'ang and later courts. In AD 48 the Han court offered the Southern Hsiung-nu even 36.000 cattle, because they had to flee for the Northern Hsiung-nu without being able to save their herds. In the following years the court continued with these deliveries. Also in later sources, cattle and other animals appeared to be sold to nomads.

In the 19th century nomadic people in the West exchanged flour and other food products with Afghan and Arab wool. Also carpets and bags went from Arab countries into all the nomadic carpet-producing countries. In spring the Afghans and Arabs even drove their rams through the southern regions of Tajikistan as far as Kokand near the Chinese border. No wonder that Emeljanenko could conclude: 'The existence of these economic connections testified that the peoples and ethnic groups of Central Asia did not live an isolated life, limited within the framework of their natural economy.'[35] In this century agriculture got also a somewhat larger share in the total economic and production activities of Central Asian countries. Several forms of sedentary life became more popular as urbanization increased.

in: *Erinnerungsgabe für Max Weber*, Ed. M. Palyi (München: Duncker & Humblot, 1923), Vol. II, p. 221-239.

34. T. Emeljanenko, Nomadic year cycles and cultural life of Central Asian livestock-breeders before the 20th century, in: C. van Leeuwen et al., p. 67 ff.

35. Ebd., p. 68. This implies a critique on Weber's ideas about *Naturalwirtschaft* (see quotations in the first paragraph of this chapter).

This kind of mutual relations grew more intens as well. For some regions it seemed a reproduction of what happened in the past.

From the earliest records of the Ch'in and Han periods until the seventeenth century mostly both 'parties' accepted all the benefits of their mutual dependency. As such, this is a later development from the oldest records, the most famous Anyang oracle texts from the Shang society (14th – 12th century BC). Here in the middle and lower reaches of the Huang Ho emerged from 2000 BC onwards proto-urban, rather democratical and women-friendly communities. They had well-developed agriculture as well as a prominent 'animal-economy' (cattle, sheep, horses); the interdependence between the two economies, therefore, was an internal matter.

Conflicts with equally organized neighbours, however, were often caused by quarrels about grazing grounds.[36] In the Ch'in and Han periods, their peaceful relations with nomads was ensured through certain ritualistic customs like inter-marriages, bestowals etc. A market-urbanisation along the frontiers and a market-infrastructure came into existence. There were nucleï of all sorts of economic or cultural interferences with effects felt deep into the hinterlands. During the sixteenth century there seems to have been a large-scale employment of Chinese peasants on Mongolian land, demanded by Mongolian leaders to supplement their normal diet.[37] Still they needed grain shipped from the south of China, which demonstrates the extensiveness of their communication-lines.

Even this superficial profile shows the large degree of interdependence of nomads (pastoralists and other animal breeders) and agriculturalists. The very fact of this interdependence counteracts thoughts and policies exploiting in some way or other animosities and antagonisms between peoples.[38] What then can be said about the strongest form of animosity, war, between nomads and Chinese?

The *peacefulness* of the relations between the areas *was the norm and war the deviation or exception.* For historians etc. familiar with the very bloody 19th and 20th century Chinese history, this might be a rather utopian exclamation. But the very existence of the 'Chinese or Great Wall', the main logo of the older Chinese society for all foreigners, also seems to be the main proof of the heavy antagonism between 'barbarians' and 'highly cultured' Chinese. (Contrary to popular belief, the Great Wall was not there in Mongol times).

---

36. T.V. Stepugina, The First States in China, in: I. Diakonoff (Ed.), *Early Antiquity* (Chicago: Univ. of Chicago Press, 1991), p. 387-420.

37. That is a bit different from Weber's opinion that Mongolians prohibited the grows of crops.

38. Jagchid, p. 191 note 37 in which Lattimore is quoted saying that the exchange of goods was important, but that 'the steppe nomad can withdraw into the steppe, if he needs to, and remain completely out of contact with other societies.' Jagchid also remarks that Lattimore did not study 'the completely self-sufficient nomad, isolated in the remote vastness of the Central Eurasian steppe...' very well. Here the same complex problem arises as in the case of the autarkic peasant who has haunted ideological discussions in history, economy, sociology and philosophy for so long. See my, Autarkeia in Greek theory and practice, in: *The European Legacy* 1,6 (1996) p. 1915-1933.

The first question is, therefore, why the peace was often violated, because the consequences were always rather far-reaching: no trade for years, poverty, devastation, cruelties and, nearly always, the nomads gained the victories. For the Chinese 'party', therefore, there was the near certainty that they had to loose everything with conflicts. They often knew this perfectly well.[39] Why then was war made against 'the other'?

THE RULERS AND THEIR WARS

First, we have to remember what the Scythian nomadic chieftain Idanthyrsus told to the 'ideal-typical Chinese emperor', the Persian king Darius. From this speech one could derive the following thesis: The aggressive way 'Western' ruling elites (who nearly always act on their own behalf) think about war is fundamentally different from the defensive attitudes of 'indigenous' leaders. To support this thesis, it is not necessary to rely on the *good savage* ideology but only (!) on the practices of democratic or non-oikoidal leadership. It is not possible here to elaborate on this thesis but it is necessary to keep it in mind. Below some support for this view will be given.[40]

In the end Jagchid and Symons answer the question, why rulers made war in East Asia, as follows:

'(1) the prejudice and mistrust felt by nomad and also sedentarist toward the other; (2) the ineffectiveness of Chinese dynasties in implementing frontier trading policies and regulating unscrupulous frontier officials; and (3) the chaotic nature of the frontier, rife with unsavory characters and illicit trading activities.'[41]

There could be more reasons to invade the land of 'the other': famines, floods and other natural disasters made whole populations move in the 'wrong' direction; rinder- and other animal-pests were for nomads the worst dangers in life and

---

39. See the discussion at the court of the Chin dynasty, Jagchid, p. 53, 54.

40. For the problem-definition of this part of the argumentation it should be appropriate to reproduce (part of) the famous debate about the so called *primitive warfare* (including Turney-High's dictum 'True warfare is not primitive' written in 1942 !) started a.o. by the social-darwinist S.R.Steinmetz with his *Der Krieg als sociologisches Problem* (Amsterdam: Versluys, 1899), his articles, Die Bedeutung des Krieges bei den Kulturvölkern, in: *Zeitschrift für Socialwissenschaft*, NF,5 (1914), p. 295 ff. and 386 ff. Before World War II Steinmetz received the strongest opposition in the Netherlands from the ethnologist T. van der Bij, *Ontstaan en eerste ontwikkeling van den oorlog* (Groningen: Wolters, 1929). Nowadays sociobiologists renewed Steinmetz' perspective; see for example D. Baer, D. McEachron, A review of selected Sociobiological principles: application to hominid evolution: I. The development of group social structure, in: *Journal of Social and Biological Structures* 5,I (1982), p. 69-90; W. Divale, *Warfare in Primitive Societies: A Bibliography* (Santa Barbara: Clio Press, 1983).

41. Jagchid, p. 165.

certainly much worse than Chinese armies; adventurous warlords or court-officials who wanted to gamble when in 'the other' land impelled internal conflicts or raged civil war.[42]

What about the three points Jagchid and Symons raised? The last is clear enough. Smugglers, bandits, illicit trade in iron weapons etc. made the frontier-regions unsafe areas, apart from the fact, that the whole corridor was a *melting-pot of non-conformists* from both sides. It seems to me, however, exceptional that such groups should provoke 'parties' to make war (probably the case of the Hsien-pei[43] in the Han-period). More important are the first two points.

The Chinese disdain for their northern and western neighbours in the first place originates from the court-located part of the Chinese elite. From here spread the stereotypical qualities assigned to all 'barbarians' regardless where they came from. One Chinese source qualifies the Hsiung-nu (about 50 BC) as follows:

> 'The barbarians (*i ti*) are covetous for grain, they have long hair, they button their [clothes] on the left side, and are human faced [but] bestial hearted.'[44]

This racism too frequently led Chinese rulers to see relations with nomads as deleterious to 'the Chinese state'. Friendship or affection must be unknown to nomads, they supposed, and nomads know only greed; it is, therefore, wise to take aggressive measures against them. Also in this case, imperialism and racism were part and parcel of an (Super)oikoidal constellation (see below). This is a consequence of or legitimated by the ideological and abstract doctrine of the universal Chinese right of empire which is only comparable to the same doctrine of the Roman Catholic Church.

The nomadic rulers in their turn never accepted any kind of Chinese assertion of (cultural) superiority, which could be interpreted as an acceptance of a subordinate position. As the reason for this behaviour Jagchid/ Symons mention the preponderance of military power most frequently held by the nomadic peoples. More important to me is, that nomadic people do have a totally different way of

---

42. A typical example is also given in Jagchid, p. 63 were court officials advised: '...the barbarians, both humans and animals, suffer disease and death. Drought and locusts have made their land turn red, and with their strength sapped by drought and disease they cannot even match a commandery ... How can we hang onto literary virtue and neglect military affairs?'

43. Under one of their tribal leaders, P'ien-ho, the Hsien-pei could be bribed to attack the other arch-enemy of the Han, the Wu-huan (ca. 50 AD). The initiative to render this service to the Han came from P'ien-ho c.s. in exchange for the vast sum of money of no less then 270 million coins each year. In the same period the Han also paid about 100 million coins to the Southern Hsiung-nu for the same kind of services. To '*divide-and-rule*' costed a lot of money those days. See Jagchid, p. 32 ff.

44. Cited in Jagchid, p. 174.

treating rulers (including their own) as sedentary people.[45] This is seldom understood by sedentaries. They too easily believe in and accept hierarchies which are by definition based on (strong), often hereditary, forms of top-down discriminations.

The nomadic treatment of rulers and the general decision-making process rested, however, on a firm and basic kind of *practical democracy*. To put it bluntly: this was not a 'top-down hierarchy' but a 'bottom-up' constellation based on a strong mistrust against authority. For squinting outsiders it seems difficult to discover the differences. In many cases that decision-making process consisted out of (and often still has) following elements.

Those who are powerful rulers in the eyes of outsiders do have internally (very) weak, non-hereditary more or less ceremonial positions. For instance, the initiation-rituals for shamans often equalize the 'enthronement ceremonies' of the *qayan* (first Türk 'State', 552-630) or whatever other leader. A Turkish ancestral legend also points to the blacksmith as head, while in Shamanism there is a close relation between the shaman and the blacksmith. If the *qayan* comes from clan A., a consort is chosen from clan B as countervailing power (compare the two so-called 'kings' in old Sparta, etc.). These figures have to display for the outer world the might and glory of the confederation of clans or of the tribe, consisting of many clans. Clan elders (always *plural*) are, in fact, the first institutionalized rulers with real power. However, they too have to share this power with (extended) family-heads, who have to listen first and foremost to the meeting of experienced adult men and women of the families.

Most important is the even less known circumstance that the objects of the public decision-making processes in nomad circles are very different from those in sedentarist environments. Here the complex *work* which is to be done through the year to breed, move and cater for animals is the main object of political deliberations. In sedentary circles, however, the political deliberations nearly never concern work (of agriculturalists or other professions) or work organization. First and foremost, one deals with orders that heads of state or high ranked persons (fail to) give to lower echelons, the norms/ laws involved or the status inside the hierarchy. Derived from these questions one probably worries about work proper and its organization.

Nomadic attitudes against foreigners were (and are) guided by the nearly unshakeable rules and rituals of hospitality. Sympathetic as this may be, this hospitality was also the 'weak belly' in external relations of nomads and pastoral-

45. H. Derks, *De Koe van Troje*, ch. I.1. For the following see M. Mori, Political Structure of the Ancient Nomadic State in Mongolia, in: *Proceedings 13ᵗʰ Int. Congres Hist. Sciences*. Moscow (1973), Vol.I, p. 268-275. This is a good example of the desperation of fitting nomadic ruler-systems in 'western' (in this case marxist class-) categories. Another example is L. Krader, *The Asiatic Mode of Production* (Assen: Gorkum, 1975).

ists. If they were confronted with foreigners or foreign institutions with hidden agendas, this hospitality was the open gate for all kinds of 'Trojan Horses'. Generally speaking: People starting relationships with cheaters in an open mood of trust and friendship are, at least, one step behind. In the frontier-zones, in peace- and war-time, it became clear how frustrating mutual relations could be.

IMPERIAL OIKOIDAL COURT RULES.

The failure of the Chinese dynasties to implement effective frontier trading policies, 'left nomads vulnerable to unscrupulous Chinese officials and merchants, who often bilked them of their possessions.'[46] Because these Chinese could cheat nomads rather easily (gadgets-for-worthwile products, etc.), they regarded them as foolish. In their turn nomads learned by bitter experience to see Chinese as mendacious and shrewd. Things went from bad to worse, when Chinese frontier-officials started all kinds of actions against nomads in the expectation to gain credits at the capital-courts.

An activist and provocative military approach – for instance by bribing Mongolian bandits – became part and parcel of a *courtly* career planning. In their turn, the high ranking court-militaries suffered from the typical oikoidal high rewards – heavy punishment policies. Their successes were proved 'by counting the collected number of heads of enemy soldiers. This lead generals to order the slaying of non-belligerent to meet established quotas.'[47] (These massacres of nomadic peoples in the market-places often lead to counter-measures of the same cruel kind). The court-rule for failure was demotion or robbing of privileges, properties etc. and sometimes execution. The inconsistencies of the rewards-punishment mechanism are seen where officials got rewards even if wars were lost, which was normally the case. A striking example of alternative behaviour is the famous nomad-leader Mao-tun (about 200BC) who once encircled a large Han-army. Instead of starting a slaughter as Chinese usually did, he opened the encirclement: 'Fortunately, Mao-tun was more interested in economic than political or territorial gain.'[48]

So, the general mental climate at the Chinese courts was, to say the least, not in favour of reasonable relations with nomads, their markets and cultures. This inevitably became one of the most important vehicles for anti-nomadic sentiments in the centre as well as in the frontier-zones. It is worthwile to consider these relations in more (historical and theoretical) detail, because they demonstrate in an extraordinarily clear way the contents of *oikos-market contradictions*.

Let's take the above mentioned complaint about the greed of nomads as a

---

46. Jagchid p. 176.
47. Ebd., p. 178, 62.
48. Ebd., p. 57.

kind of excuse to take action against them. 'Greed' for the Chinese must be an effect of the ineradicable attitude of nomads to make deals about everything and nothing and to get what they want for – what they consider – the lowest possible price. They are experts in selling and buying animals and related products. This market depends, to a large degree, on individual action and on the principle of *honesty is the best quality*.[49] Every participant learns this rather quickly through the given price-mechanisms ('best quality, highest price') for which the norms are rather fixed.

Why exist this rule? Because the price standard consists of animals from which already a nomad child knows the many (dis)qualities. During a long period also in European history it is well known that cows were widely valued as 'legal means of payment' and as 'walking wealth'.[50] The source for the nomadic incessant drive to trade, in fact, is the (ecological) necessity to look constantly for opportunities to get rid of more or less large parts of their flocks and flock-products. Further-more, within nomad and pastoral ways of life stress is laid on *individual achieve-ment in their work and on the individual performance of work-skills*. The permanent struggle to strike a balance between the drive for wealth and the crude 'laws of animal-health' belongs to the very basis of nomadic or pastoralist life. All factors discussed so far (in a schematic way) are favorable for *open external relations*.

One of the consequences of these characteristics is, that nomads did not treat the Chinese in a racist and/or disdaining way. They did not rush to accept Chinese culture either and viewed the Chinese as impolite and improperly raised. Typical nomadic advice from the eighth century after warning of the seduction of the bitter-sweet voices of the Chinese says:

'Thus, O Turk, when you go into that country you come to the edge of death, but when, on the other hand, you stay in your Otukan fastnesses, and only send caravans [for trade or tribute] you have no woes at all.'[51]

It is not by accident that the Mongolian word for 'merchant' was synonymous for a Chinese verb 'to lie'.

MARKET-BEHAVIOUR.
The resulting market-behaviour could become or be interpreted as naive if it is confronted with an alternative market-behaviour from quite different origin. The

---

49. For a quite different use of this creed see WG, 383 and 723 or EC, 637 and 1206. It is quite revealing to study the oikoidal way Weber perceives 'the market' here in this unfinished text about the *Marktvergesellschaftung* (translated with '*The Market: Its Impersonality and Ethic*').
50. H. Derks, *De Koe van Troje*, p. 62 ff.
51. Cited in Jagchid, p. 175.

frontier – zones gave this opportunity. The first is the confrontation with 'smugglers and illicit traders'. Who receives these qualifications is decided by both nomadic and sedentary norms which can seriously differ in this matter. Other alternatives that become apparent result from trade relations of common men/ wives in both cultures. As usual, sources are almost silent about the grassroots levels. The third kind of alternative comes here from sources which try to dominate fully, namely from the Chinese courts and related circles.

Their sedentary attitudes are first and foremost functional to a fixed hierarchical order based on giving orders by a few, fulfilling them by the (large) majority of a given population and neglecting them by a (small) minority. (The hierarchy falls apart if the last two categories mutually alter their position). Market behaviour of (high ranked) sedentarists compared to the normal sedentarist way of life is nonconformist. Compared to the normal nomadic way of market behaviour it is also non-conformist. The 'grey area' in a socio-economic sense which arises corresponds to the frontier-area between two cultures. It goes without saying that both nonconformist positions have to be valued by the norms in their resp. cultures or lifestyles.

The nomads were (and still are!) very proud of their mobility and freedom and 'their land was not denuded by the plow ... They disdained those who worked on their knees in mud and dirt ...'[52] The Chinese autocratic leadership and government, however, derived their wealth mostly from immobile agricultural sources and showed little interest in mercantile activities. Also the agro-ideology it developed, thanks to many Confucian philosophers, stressed the high esteem of agriculture and, subsequently, the low esteem of merchants. They warned the governments, when they became involved in marketing activities that

'entered into financial competition with the people, dissipating primordial candor and simplicity and sanctioning propensities to selfishness and greed. As a result, few among our people take up the fundamental pursuits of life, while many flock to the non-essential ...'[53]

This Confucian anti-marketing prejudice often led emperors to ignore or evade their responsibilities to regulate frontier markets. Those who took the initiative to open markets to all nomadic people were the exception to the rule;[54] too many

52. Jagchid, p. 175.
53. Cited in ebd. p. 177.
54. In around 1577, a large debate started about the need to continue the long peace and favorable market relations between Ming China and the Mongols (Jagchid, p. 106 ff.). In defence of the markets, Fang Feng-shih, also gave a political argument: 'When there are markets and tribute there is no war...' The relationship between war and agriculture, however, was set for the next centuries (or even millennia !?) by Shih Huang-ti (r. 247-210 BC). He was a radical anti-market ruler and even hated 'merchants who did not have any binding to the land and moved from town to town'. J. Duyvendak, *Wegen en gestalten der Chineesche geschiedenis* (Amsterdam: Elsevier, 1948), p. 64. This

even viewed trade with nomads as economically disadvantageous and in this way nurtured isolationism. Therefore, military action or the threat of attack was often the only vehicle open to nomads to force Chinese rulers to open markets. Normalization in an economic sense, however, never meant a substantial abolishment of ideological barriers on the side of the Chinese.

The nature of the Chinese bureaucracy also disfavoured market-normalizations. The hierarchy at the top was small and too disciplined by the courtly and imperial ritualistic rules. Active debate about market-frontier policies was restricted to a limited number of members of key ministries and a few individuals having direct access to the emperor. It is striking that court-officials who were in favour of peace and good commercial relations had to discuss their stand in terms of 'peace to gain time to prepare the next military confrontation with the "barbarians".'[55] It is also striking that high Chinese court-officials thought to impress nomad leaders with the same kind of corruption as was usual at the court itself.

The case of the Mongolian leader Esen and the Ming court (about 1450) is remarkable in this respect. Some high court officials suddenly reduced prices offered nomads for horses and that was the reason for invading China. This was not understood at the court because they gave Esen personally so much bestowals (silk rolls etc.). They looked at the highest person with which they made the deals as an absolute ruler, the type they knew the best. In other words, these Chinese court-negotiators did not understand the nature of horse-prices (usually related to the income of at least all horse-breeders) nor the nature of honest trading (in this case even with a large part of a whole people), nor the true nature of the nomad decision-making process. This occurred despite the fact that Esen's bestowals were mistreated (cut, disfigured). This was (only!) a personal affront for a tribal leader but as such an insult of the whole tribe.

Jagchid and Symons did not stop after they helped so well to undermine the myth of the barbarian nomads who constantly plundered, massacred or destroyed that beautiful, 'agro-peaceful' imperial culture. The basic tenets of their thesis, in their view, fits perfectly well for the 19th and 20th century as nomads eventually were replaced by 'white, mainly British barbarians'.[56] Like the nomads, the British also failed to persuade the Ch'ing court to grant them political and economic concessions during the first two centuries of their relationship. The British 'discovered that the Chinese, and their Manchu overlords, were chauvinistic, arrogant, self-centered, and condescending towards them ... As was the case with the Turks and Mongols, the British also found it difficult to find goods to trade which the Chi-

---

author also wrote 'Sje Hwang-ti strongly favoured agriculture. In imposing heavy demands on manpower and services on the people, he tried to intensify agriculture in order to establish sufficient corn-supplies in wartime ... he gave peasants property rights on land and levied a tax related to the size of the plot.' (Ebd., p. 64).

55. Jagchid, p. 178.
56. Ebd., p. 185 ff.

nese desired.' They had to pay for silk and tea with hard currency (silver and gold bullion).

In the 19th century, however, the British started illegal trade to China (opium), which enabled them to purchase tea and silk without paying in bullion. The rest of this story is well known (the British-Chinese Opium War): ' ...as was the case with nomadic peoples throughout Chinese history, war with China was undertaken to better secure goods the British felt were essential to the well-being of their country.'[57] In a bold futuristic forecasting, the authors could have envisaged a new trade-war between a strong market-oriented outer-world, which can use anew a typical wild-west frontier zone to do their Hongkong-like business, and still bureaucratized, old-fashioned courtlike centralized CP- headquarters. If China should loose (a) new war(s), would it not change their oikoidal structures again?

IDEOLOGICAL HISTORIOGRAPHY.

Of course, in the scholarly literature used nowadays the strong reliance on court-sources makes sure that the 'barbarians' are blamed for all anger and misery.[58] Unfounded are the suggestions that there is a permanent state of war at the (northern) borders during these 2000 years. The most negative consideration in this case is: Most of the time the Chinese power-elites may be willing to destroy the 'barbarians', but did not have the resources to do this in such a vast area against such a powerful enemy. Their military activities, in fact, were restricted in all respects: in space, in time, in effect. Sometimes one gets the impression of being confronted with fake-wars to sustain anti-nomadic sentiments and anti-market ideologies. It is an oikoidal syndrome *par excellence* which got too much attention.[59]

The historians and sinologists seldom tried to reverse this 'central perspective' to what happened in its own right elsewhere in that very vast territory. Too often many scholars[60] tried to establish the false impression of an unchangeable China

---

57. Ebd., p. 186.

58. For the ideological interpretation of Chinese-Mongol history see O. Lattimore, Herdsmen, farmers, urban culture, in: *Pastoral Production and Society/ Production pastorale et société* (London/ Paris: Cambridge Univ. Press, 1979), p. 479-491. Ten years later, David Morgan still writes about even the heyday of Asian nomadic history, Khubilai Khan's long hegemony (1260-1294): 'Historians of China had previously tended to shun this period, preferring not to concern themselves with barbarian rule, but now their views on the impact of Mongol rule are shifting, and shifting in the Mongols favour.' From the Chinese side another aspect of the ideological historiography is important whereas Morgan quotes: ' ...a biography [of Khubilai Khan] based merely on the Chinese records could not be written ... (because he is) portrayed ... as a typical Confucian ruler, not as a real human being.' in: *Times Literary Supplement*, 5/8, (1988), p. 849.

59. In its most abstract way this happenend in L. Krader, The origin of the state among the nomads of Asia, in: *Pastoral Production and Society*, p. 221-235.

60. A relevant overview provides Wim Wertheim, The Contribution of Weberian Sociology to Studies of Southeast Asia, in: *Journal of Southeast Asian Studies* 26,1 (1995) p. 17-29. Idem: *Emancipation in Asia: positive and negative lessons from China* (Rotterdam: CASP, 1983), p. 57-133. H. Derks, *Karl Marx*

as an 'Oriental (Palace) Despotism' which always sought to pose an 'Asiatic Mode of Production' onto the most remote corners of this territory. One of the results is a very schematic 'centrally guided' historiography, sociology, etc. One could better suppose as a rule a very differentiated development in time and in space.

Chinese old and new cities as 'clear Western bourgeois' will be discovered along with purely residential/ oikoidal cities and indigenous market-places; within the 'real Chinese countries', there lived not only small peasants as the image prescribes, but also nomads, pastoralists or merchants; there were extensive trade-networks almost uninterrupted by 'state'-influences. Furthermore it is necessary to point to the substantial revolutionary potentials in large parts of the population in all periods of Chinese history. The target is directly or indirectly nearly without exception the imperial authority and its representatives in some capital.[61] The result is a.o. that the allmighty emperor must be seen as a restricted power. In short: one could come nearer to the 'Chinese truth' by supposing *normal* towns and countries with *normally reacting people* instead of imperial/ Confucian constructions and marionets.

From the first Weber quotation in this chapter one has to conclude that in the Weberian construction a 'Chinese State' is seen as an 'Oriental Despotism'. His Oikos is 'colossal', all-embracing with subjects as 'state-slaves'. Wertheim rightly points to the fact that Weber in *Economy and Society* came up with the more specific perspective of the so-called 'patrimonial-bureaucratic state'.[62] This, however, cannot be seen as a kind of defence of Weber who rooted this kind of state in the princely *domain* (' oikos) managed by means of the *Oikenwirtschaft*. This last domain-economy is based in the *manor*.

In this context Weber referred again to Pharaohnic Egypt, the Roman imperial domain, the Inca state, the Jesuit state in Paraguay, the Carolingian villas, the Near Eastern and Hellenistic states, etc. For instance: '.. the actual political power of the Oriental sultans, the medieval princes and the Far Eastern rulers centered in these great patrimonial domains. In these latter cases the political realm as a whole is approximately identical with a huge princely manor.'

It is important to understand the distinction Weber made here between the political ('juridical and military) and economic realm of the prince. It seems nearly a matter of geography: 'We shall speak of a patrimonial state when the prince organizes his political power over extrapatrimonial areas and political subjects ...'.[63] About the economic impact of this state Weber did not talk, apart from the fun-

---

and Lawrence Krader over de zgn. Aziatische Productiewijze: van externe theorie tot intern probleem (Amsterdam: Univ. of Amsterdam, 1978).

61. H. Derks, De Taiping-opstand in China (1850-1864), in: Idem (Ed.), *Kroniek van drie eeuwen revoluties* (Groningen: Wolters, 1989), p. 153-159.

62. EC., p. 1013 ff.; WG, p. 585 ff.; W. Wertheim, *East-West Parallels. Sociological Approaches to Modern Asia* (The Hague: Mouton, 1964), p. 106 ff.

63. EC., p. 1013.

damental obligation of the subjects to maintain the ruler in a material sense 'just as is the case in a patrimonial household.' Only for Pharaohnic Egypt Weber postulates the extension of *both* the political and economic authority over the whole country. For this case one can easily substitute the 'Oriental Despotism' concept, apart from the question whether Weber is right or wrong in the Egyptian case. In the Chinese case, however, in my view we have to do with an isolated and rather autonomous Super-Oikos which was and probably is in an economic sense of little or only negative value to the (rest of) Chinese society. In other words: here we cannot discover an 'Oriental Despotism' but there existed a marked contradiction between the (imperial) Oikos and the market (' the 'extrapatrimonial economy'). Through the nomadic part of this economy one can demonstrate the antagonisms at stake almost ideal-typically.

Which example could be more interesting than the recent collectivisations of the herding economies in Central and East Asia (Mongolia)?[64] As is well known, in these unique phenomena the Soviet (inspired) Super-Oikoi ruthlessly tried to interfere into all aspects of agricultural and herding life. In my view, however, these very powerful state-bureaucracies (inclusive the armies) did not succeed very well in their objective to eradicate (or industrialize) the nomadic way of life and all immanent market and mobile elements. Without going into much detail some of the main characteristics and effects of these collectivisations are the following.[65]

NOMADS AND OIKOIDAL COLLECTIVISATIONS

The imperialism of Tsarist Russia from the late 1500s to 1917 brought about an exceptionally broad contact among the peoples of Central Asia and newcomers. In the 19th century Russians introduced new agricultural techniques (iron plough) and settled peasants in 'Nomad's Land' from many countries including Poles, Germans and Koreans. At the end of the century 'Nomad's Land' of the cattle, camel and sheep breeders still existed. However, it was clear that in some area's

---

64. For Central Asia see L. Popova, Modern animal husbandry in Central Asia: a call for research, in: C. van Leeuwen et al., p. 69-83. For Mao's China see V. Veit, Die Mongolen: Von der Clanföderation zur Volksrepublik, in: M. Weiers (Ed.), *Die Mongolen. Beiträge zu ihrer Geschichte und Kultur* (Darmstadt: Wissenschaft. Buchgesellschaft, 1986), p. 155-183. O. Lattimore, The collectivization of the Mongolian herding economy, in: *Marxist Perspectives*, 3,1 (1980), p. 116-127.

65. For the general problem I only mention P. Nolan, Collectivization in China: Some Comparisons with the USSR, in: *Journal of Peasant Studies*, 3,2 (1976), p. 192-219; R. Davies, *The Industrialisation of Soviet Russia* (Cambridge. Mass.: Harvard Univ. Press, 1980); M. Broekmeyer, *De Russische Landbouw. Boeren, dorpen, platteland* (Utrecht: Aula, 1983); S. Merl, *Bauern unter Stalin. Die Formierung des sowjetischen Kolchossystems 1930-1941* (Berlin: Duncker & Humblot, 1990); G. Rittersporn, Modernisierung durch Vernichtung? Über einige Folgen der Kollektivierung der sowjetischen Landwirtschaft, in: *Zeitschrift für Geschichtswissenschaft*, 43,9 (1995), p. 809-821; L. Viola, *Peasant Rebels under Stalin. Collectivization and the Culture of Peasant Resistance* (New York: Oxford Univ. Press, 1996).

seasonal pastures, especially the winter ones, were reduced and that farmlands cut of nomadic routes and access to water reservoirs. Central Asia became gradually a grain and cotton belt for the Russians. Thirty years later it should become Krushchev's 'virgin and long-fallow lands' which provided the first substantial increase in Soviet grain production above the pre-revolutionary level (Davies). Everywhere the urbanization was enhanced with its usual effects on the adjacent lands. These were serious but within those vast lands still regional effects of Western imperialism. It seemed that in 1914 almost a quarter of the Kyrghyz were leading some settled life.

According to Lattimore, the Russian militaries and traders received relatively much sympathy among the Siberian and Central Asian peoples during the 19th century. Usually Russian traders learned the indigenous languages. This good relationship is generally reproduced with Mongols who traditionally disliked Chinese with their economic monopolies. At Urga, the later Mongolian capital Ulan Bator ('Red Hero'), a substantial Russian and foreign population settled. From here the ideas of the October Revolution spread over the *yurtas* (nomadic tent-houses) and *auls* (nomadic villages). New Russian military technology (machine guns and artillery) and discipline was introduced. The preconditions for an own proletarian revolution *à la russe* from Mongolian and Central Asian herdsmen against real class-enemies seemed fulfilled. The enemies were the Chinese bourgeoisie, the high priests, monasteries and some hereditary Mongolian 'feudal nobles'. In the tsarist Central Asian countries the class enemies were different: the oikoidal Tsarist bureaucracy inclusive its Greek-Orthodox offshoot and the Russian backed Central Asian elite.

Peasants from all classes suffered the most from the atrocities accompanying the Russian collectivisations. There was never a comparable movement against the urban laborers or population although they suffered as well by the side-effects of the collectivisations. Only one thing seemed clear for all levels of Soviet decision making: from 1929 onwards the Country, as opposed to the City, definitely has to be re-modelled from the ground in order to adjust to a rather unclear idea about a centralized, industrial urban society. In all corners of social and economic life a deep crisis undermined every possibility to have even a minimum existence in town and country. The chaos, panic, wild massacres and deportations and the sharp contradictions between all levels of decision makers which reigned for years made the start of the collectivisations a nightmare. In my view, the most serious failure was that the power-interests of the Super-Oikos always had to prevail over the technical, economical, agronomical etc. rationalities of country-life. In particular, the reproduction of the political idea of centralized decision making into the technical, economical, etc. realities created unsolvable disparities in the whole Soviet Union.

In the Central Asian republics, the peasants settled in the 19th century by the Tsarist administration, had to pay the highest prize. But a large amount of nomads used an effective weapon unknown to their immobile 'colleagues'. In hindsight one can say that they demonstrated the irrationalities of the centralisation-policies the first and make these abandonned the quickest. Many administrators in the new Soviet republics practiced centralization and concentration even in a much more vulgar and primitive way as in the West. Central Asia still had the image of a colony. Their first ideal objective was cristal-clear: *peasantization* and settlement of these wild, uncivilized and uncontrolable peoples.

In the same time these peoples had to cater for the enormous meat and wool needs of the fast growing Western urban population. Sometimes hundreds of nomadic communities scattered in an enormous area were forcefully concentrated in only one place. Others interpreted the objective in the sense that all *yurtas* had to be arranged within the grid of an ideal square. Orders were given from behind the bureaucratic desks to shear millions of sheep in winter cold. The animals could not stand the weather and died.

Indeed, the breeders were faced with unprecedented casualties on the animal population while many lost their own lives in bitter fights. After the collectivisation – campaigns and the terrible famine in 1931-33 in Kazakhstan only 1.3 out of 18.5 million sheep were left; the number of horses was reduced from 3.5 million to 855.000 in 1941; only 63.000 camels stayed alive of 1.04 million in 1935 (Popova). Also the population was decimated but not in the first place by the harsh repression and its by-effects. The nomads were not immune for certain diseases which came with the famine (typhoid). The nomads had a weapon which they used effectively: they knew how to flee with their animals and where to go. At least a million people from Kazakhstan (with 6.5 million people in 1920) and countless animals went to China, Mongolia, Afghanistan, Iran and Turkey. Later half of them came back.

After 1945 a certain *modus vivendi* between nomads and regime was found and between the indigenous livestock-breeding and the centralized *kolkhoz*- or *sovkhoz*-breeding which was often too large to handle. That was the sign the Soviets could not gain control over the Central Asian area's and had to stick to the approved methods of the Tsars to create and influence a dependent elite. As usual, in practice this 'colonial elite' had only a restricted and relative influence in the country. In the seventies and eighties the restrictions on establishing private farms etc. were weakened and they recently disappeared. A typical result of this process was the following: in 1989 a Kyrgyzstanian *sovkhoz* state flock numbered 4,500 sheep, whereas 20,000 were privately owned. The same accounts for horned cattle. Another pecularity is that the nomads, contrary to the peasants, still do not pay taxes which is the metaphor for their position *vis à vis* the state, the Super-Oikos. Unchanged remained the hard herding life as well.

So, generally speaking, one has to affirm the question whether the collectivisations in the Soviet nomadic countries were in vain. The effects of these collectivisations are, again metaphorically, that nowadays nomads even use helicopters for herding camels, cattle and sheep as well as the latest medical techniques for breeding and selection purposes. But still they favour living in the *yurtas* and *auls* although their kids show the limits of these houses by buying gettoblasters and house-music during their city-trips. Town-country contradictions take all kinds of forms!

The Mongolian collectivisations followed the Soviet model. After the Mongols gained their independence from China (1921), the state bureaucracy could come 'closer' to the nomads as in the Soviet example. This resulted in some not in-significant differences from the Soviet *kolkhoz*-model. Still the most important economic activity in Mongolia remains the animal-breeding. The total amount of animals is about 24 million (with 21 animals per head of the population the highest animal concentration in the world); 70% of the land surface is occupied by pasture and only 0.2% for agriculture (Veit). The camels, cattle, goats, horses and sheep still are herded all year long in a nomadic manner. The organizational framework, however, became after 1948 gradually the *cooperative* of herding-families (for 77% of all animals). In principle, this is a hierarchical way of organizing work which is alien to the nomadic ways of work organizations. The latter are based on the needs of the work to be done and not on status and power of decision makers.

Probably, the practice corresponds still to the traditional and more democratic mode of organization but, at the moment, I do not have any information about this possibility. In any case, what was left from an oikoidal state-organization (outside the cities never more than 15%) is privatized in 1992. In short, also in the animal country *par excellence* the (Soviet) collectivisations did not work out as in peasant regions. Many Mongolians today – whether living within China's neighbourhood or in the former Soviet Union – 'look to Ghenghis Khan as their national hero ... Buddhist monasteries are being restored and reoccupied, the traditional Mongol script is replacing Cyrillic ... and statues of Lenin and Stalin are being torn down and replaced by those of Ghenghis Khan.'[66] Old oikoidal forces of Mongolia are trying again to occupy the rooms at the top and showed that they did not forget the most classical oikoidal tricks: To start a separation-movement in neighbouring China's Inner Mongolia (with more Mongols than in the own country!) in order to gather 'the whole Mongolian people' behind their ticket.

An evaluation.

In this chapter many details about the nomadic way of life in Central and East Asia are revealed. Even today in large parts of Asian countries, this way of life prevails. Usually, the history of this corner of the world is told in terms of the *Yellow Menace* of great nomadic conquerors or of barbarian nomadic Manchus who even

---

66. L. Husman, 'National Unity' and National Identities in the People's Republic of China, in: D. Hooson (Ed.), *Geography*, p. 149.

became emperors of China. In my view, compared with the economic or cultural contradictions, continuities and interdependencies of nomads and sedentaries, these are mere political incidents which hardly affected everyone outside a small elite. It is noteworthy that in the Mongolian history books, the 'world-conquering' activities of some nomadic chieftains are not given much attention, while a 'real political history' of these regions is still in its infancy.[67]

It is, therefore, a bit difficult to blame even famous scholars for a lack of knowledge. It may be that Max Weber was right in delineating the pivotal importance in history of the contradictions between sedentaries and nomads of different kinds and between agriculture and animal-husbandry. It is, however, crystal clear that he failed to understand even the basic characteristics of the nomadic way of life and, consequently, failed to make the proper comparisons with his own sedentary way of life. He could have known from available sources that milk and meat in Central and East Asia were common consumer products and in many regions even the main ingredients of the daily diet. Also, within his own 'Ackerbau'-stand, Weber could not differentiate between rice and wheat cultivation. By neglecting these large differences, some clues to a capitalism discussion within a Chinese context remained hidden for him. In his time. much of that knowledge was available.

Weber, however, was highly biased by a complicated set of thoughts and norms which avoided the necessary change of paradigm. Therefore, the question of whether there is any empirical basis for Weber's Asian nomadic (pastoralist, non-sedentary, etc.) ideal type must be denied. Next, one can seriously question his broader approach to the theory of civilizations as stipulated in the first paragraph.

The highly complex problem of the transition from nomadic animal-husbandry to sedentary agriculture is a very basic feature in world history. It cannot be reduced to a practical affair, i.e. the eradication of tribal and other resources in the hope that nomads (a collective concept for many kinds of mobile people and groups) would disappear 'automatically'. First, it is necessary to start a fresh series of studies into the history of these social, economic or cultural transitions.

The above discussion will be extended now by studying Weber's perception of the Near Eastern nomads relative to the practicalities of the highly important role Bedouins, etc. have played in this part of the world and its dramatic history. With them we meet the most western nomads in Central Asia, trading partners along the Silk Route, the oldest and longest trading and cultural communication line. We also meet Jews, for some the ultimate merchants – nomads, who oriented themselves towards the West and almost never eastwards. Their most precious

---

67. See the preface of the excellent D. Sinor (Ed.), *The Cambridge History of Early Inner Asia* (Cambridge: Cambridge Univ. Press, 1990).

merchandise for western authorities is a collection of strange texts, which are deemed to form a holy book. Once this was accepted, these same authorities obliged 'the rest of the world' to believe its content. Was Max Weber still a defender of this world historical decision, and what did he believe from the content of this Book at the beginning of the twentieth century?

3. MAX WEBER AND HIS 'SECRET GYPSIES'

'The Jews are the secret gypsies of history'.
Th. W. Adorno (18-9-1940).

The Problem

When this chapter was nearly finished, I glanced at the recently published correspondence of Max Horkheimer. I was struck dumb by the word 'Nomaden-tum' and the passage in which it appeared: After an intensive study, I had come to conclusions which seemed quite similar to opinions written nearly 60 years ago! Although my astonishment partly faded away after studying the whole letter and its context, the content is perfectly suitable for circumscribing the problems to be discussed in this chapter.[1]

On the 18th of September 1940, 'Teddie' Adorno wrote a letter to Max Horkheimer who was on a business tour in Hollywood. Both were coping with the problem of how to get money for new scientific projects. An unsuccessful *German Project* on German history from 1900-1933 had been proposed in which they had invested a lot of time and money. In this letter Adorno wrote about another project, the *Antisemitismusprojekt*, which had to result in a new 'antisemitism theory' and not in a 'commentary of a law-sociological nature'. In a postscriptum to the short letter, he confidentially formulated provisional thoughts on this theory. With these, Adorno felt, he should arrive at a 'unified and non-rationalistic explanation of antisemitism'. Therefore, he proposed Horkheimer to direct activities along those lines. This never happened. In fact, the start was made with what later became the famous *Studies in Prejudice ('the Authoritarian Personality'*, etc.). But what did Adorno propose in vain about nine years earlier?

Antisemitism, he stated, dates back far beyond the period in which liberalism and capitalism triumphed. It has certain archaic traits and relies on motives 'which are very old and already second nature'. According to Adorno, we are in need of an 'Urgeschichte des Antisemitismus'. 'This *Urgeschichte* cannot be understood as a psychological one as Freud supposed but has to search for the origin within

---

1. M. Horkheimer, *Gesammelte Schriften. Briefwechsel 1937-1940* (Frankfurt a/M.: Fischer, 1995), Vol.16, p. 760-765. See also p. 748.

archaic but real social movements.' That was a clear statement which obviously could not earn Horkheimer's approval.

Like the historian Geremek later,[2] Adorno points to specific connotations for Jews in the German folklore: their old age and *'Wanderschaft'* (roaming around) or their perception as *'Schnorrer'* (beggar). Probably, this last image is related to 'a rich beggar's shoulder-bag filled with *taler'*. For Adorno, this situation could not be explained from the history of the Jewish diaspora, let alone from a Jewish character.

> 'I, however, want to point to the following explanation. In a very early stage of the history of mankind, the Jews despised the transition from nomadism to sedentarity and remained nomads, or they only made an incomplete and fake transition, a kind of pseudomorphosis.'

Biblical history should be analysed from this perspective. In contrast with Momigliano (chapter 1) Adorno stresses that the period of the Patriarchs, the history of the 'promised land from milk and honey' and the short period of the weak monarchy should be studied. The specific idea of the old age of the Jewish people, according to Adorno, must be related to 'the archaic nomadic way of life within a sedentary world. The Jews are the secret gypsies of history'.

Also monotheism has to be seen in the light of this fixation to nomadism. In Adorno's view, Jews are *'prämatriarchal'*. This made Jewish patriarchalism so fully incompatible with modern society and the developed society in antiquity. 'The reasons why the Jews refused to accept some partial or local gods could be discovered in connection with their refusal to accept a single and isolated home.' The editor of the correspondence remarks that Horkheimer wrote at this place in the margin: 'very true'. Political miscalculations of the Jews could be explained, according to Adorno, to this fixation of their prehistorical past.

> 'In any case, this explains that typical ex-territoriality of the Jews vis-à-vis the whole European [*abendländischen*] history. In both antisemitism and in Jewish reactions to this, one can find it expressed nowadays. The revival of nomadism among the Jews cannot be the explanation for only the Jewish condition but also, and even more, for antisemitisrn. It seems as if in history the abandonment of nomadism was one of the severest sacrifices imposed on humanity. The European [*abendländischen*] concept of labor and all the instinctual negations [*Triebverzicht*] connected to it must have precisely coincided with sedentari-sation. The image of the Jews represents a condition of humanity without labor, and all the later attacks on the parasitic, greedy Jewish character are only rationalizations. The Jews are those who did not want to be 'civilized' or sub-

---

2. B. Geremek, *La Stirpe di Caino. L'immagine dei vagabondi e dei poveri nella letterature europee dal xv al xvii secolo* (Milano: Mondadori, 1988).

mitted to the primacy of labor ... They did not want to be kicked out of the Paradise or wanted to leave it only against their will. Moses' description of the 'promised land of milk and honey' is still a sketch of Paradise. This clinging to the oldest image of happiness is the Jewish utopia. Here, it is unimportant whether the nomadic way of life was indeed the condition of ultimate happiness. In all probability, it was not. But the longer the world reproduced sedentarity as repressing labor, the more the older condition had to appear like the ultimate happiness. It was a forbidden longing; even thinking about it must be forbidden as well. This prohibition is the origin of antisemitism... '

In this way Theodor Adorno provided a historical and socio-economical framework for a highly topical and complicated problem. In the end, we can only guess why this promising perspective disappeared from his agenda. Horkheimer's quick reaction (24th of September) is reserved in two ways.

Of course, Adorno's analysis is to the point but only as far as antisemitism is concerned and not so much for the 'explanation ... of *Judentum*'. At present, this *Judentum* is only to be understood in a negative sense, 'from the negation of its God [*aus dem Abfall von seinem God*] ... they are lost for the false Gods ... Even in England they are thrown in concentration camps.' Furthermore, Horkheimer wanted to use the Antisemitismusprojekt as a 'discussion with Freud, the maker of the latest antisemitism theory'.[3] This was the far-reaching decision which paved the way for the famous post-war 'Authoritarian Personality' studies. In the same time, however, Horkheimer rejected, in my view, a more relevant historical and socio-economical study.

Another reasonable guess seems to be that the financier of the *Prejudice* project, the American Jewish Committee, was not victim- but offender-directed.

The question of how to avoid new right-wing racial crimes brought about a strong interest in oikoidal strata within the American population. This project pragmatically focused on 'the socialisation practices of the middle-class patriarchal family ... in which the father's authority could not rely anymore on an independent civil existence'.[4] In fact, one was interested in a socio-psychology of (the most sedentarized!) white middle-class city-dwellers, the so-called potential future enemies. At the same time, Horkheimer's psychological and philosophical approach almost guaranteed an inoffensive attitude against (American) govern-

---

3. M. Horkheimer, *Idem*, p. 765: letter of the 24th of September 1940. He added: 'Ich bin davon überzeugt, daß die Judenfrage die Frage der gegenwärtigen Gesellschaft ist – da sind wir mit Marx und Hitler einig, sonst aber hierin so wenig wie mit Freud.' As far as I know, Adorno or Horkheimer did not use Adorno's socio-historical thoughts elsewhere. Not in their 'Elemente des Antisemitismus' in their *Dialektik der Aufklärung* (Amsterdam: Querido, 1944), p. 199-245, nor in the chapter on antisemitism in Th. Adorno, *Kritik. Kleine Schriften zur Gesellschaft* (Frankfurt a/M.: Suhrkamp, 1971), p. 105-134. In the last text, it seems as if antisemitism is reduced to a matter of educational and psychological concern.

4. Th. Adorno, *Studien zum autoritären Charakter* (Frankfurt a/M.: Suhrkamp, 1976), p. XI.

ment agencies and private interests. In particular, Adorno's stress on the labour side of the problem must have worried Horkheimer and later members of the *Prejudice* project like Löwenthal. It is not necessary to fear social consequences or fundamental policy changes from a psychological project, apart from the fact that the political temperature had already decreased substantially in the first years of the Cold War.

Concerning the definition of my problem, however, Adorno pointed to important elements. First, nomadism and Judaism are mutually related, but the characteristics of this relationship must be analysed. Second, a historical and socio-economical study of 'biblical circumstances' is preferable in order to find the data about the former relationship. Next, the antagonisms between sedentarism and nomadism are highly responsible for phenomena as different as antisemitism and the utopia of a happy paradise. Finally, then the Jews are typified as '*the secret gypsies of history*' who made a '*fake transition*' from nomadism to a sedentary way of life. These qualifications tell as much about Jews as about gypsies and their position *vis-à-vis* tensions from a sedentary lifestyle. At the same time, they question the real meaning of a transition between these two antagonistic social, economic, etc. ways of existence.

The unexpected acquaintance with Adorno's view on the 'Jewish Question' led to a renewed confrontation with my own search for a historical definition of the 'Nomadic Question' in Max Weber's relevant studies. Using Weber's sociology of religion for the sake of the study of nomadism, some serious ideological problems arose. Those, concerning the alleged *nomadic menace*, are discussed in the former chapter. Other are elucidated by the following essential statements.

In the first sentences of *Das antike Judentum*, Weber uses the concept which hints at the main characteristics of his ideological position, his sociological theory as well as his stand on the Nomadic Question:

'From a standpoint of the history and sociology of religion, the best way of understanding the original problem of Judaism is to compare it with the Indian caste system. In fact, what were Jews in a sociological sense? A pariah people. This means as we know from India: a guest-people which is formally or factually separated from the social environment but also in a ritual sense ... one can derive from this the essence of the dualism between an internal and external morale and its way of life in the ghetto, voluntarily chosen long before it existed as an enforced internment.'[5]

---

5. GAR, III, p. 1-5. The difficulties with this pariah-concept are legion. See for a good introduction W. Schluchter (Ed.), *Max Webers Studie über das antike Judentum* (Frankfurt a./M.: Suhrkamp, 1981) with the excellent essays by E. Fleischmann (p.263-289) and F. Raphaël (p. 224-263). My way of analysing the whole question is so different that I want to develop my argumentation first instead of debating the problematic opinions of Schluchter, etc.

In a historical perspective, Weber's choice to look into Indian social relations, is rather obvious as is demonstrated in the first paragraph of chapter 1. However, the background for Weber's pariah concept must be grasped from the following part of Weber's Hinduism analysis. I quote extensively to show how Weber developed his concept, because there are many, even dangerous misunderstandings (see end of the chapter) about it:

> 'Everywhere there existed (and still exists) within the hinduistic communities the social phenomenon of 'guest-peoples'. We know these still today... only as the Gypsies, a typical old Indian ... guest-people.... This phenomenon does not exist only in the form of a wandering people living completely without any dwelling place. More often one can see it in tribes with their own village settlements, but which interlocally sell their own homemade products ... or their casual labor... or who monopolize the interlocal trade in a specific product ... or a service which is considered as religiously unclean by the sedentary population ... in its most developed form, sedentary guest-work of a specific and very skilled nature is in the hands of people who are considered as 'Ungenossen' ... and who have to live outside the settlement without any rights ... but only a guest-right partly religiously sanctioned and partly by a king ... Where a guest-people is liable to such ritual limits, we want to speak ... of a pariah-people. A pariah people ... is not everybody which is considered from a local-community as an 'alien', 'barbaric' or 'magical unclean' group of workers [Arbeiterstamm]. (It can get this qualification only) 'if it is for a substantial part or wholly a guest-people. This type is shown in the clearest way if it has lost completely its own binding to the land [Bodenständigkeit] and is fully incorporated within the satisfaction of economic needs [Bedarfsdeckung] of other sedentary people. This is the case with the Gypsies or ... with the Jews in the Middle Ages.'[6]

Here I conclude, first, that this concept is or became a kind of *trait d'union* between the EastAsian, Near Eastern and European world. Most important, the pariah concept seems to be a universal concept directly related to nomadic peoples. Furthermore, Weber first and foremost tries to circumscribe and classify what is going on in the non-sedentary sectors of societies strictly from the *sedentary point of view*. This is the main antagonism from which negative valuations of specific Jews or Jews in general could be derived. Here the Jewish Question becomes a real

---

6. GAR, II, p. 11, 12. Other misunderstandings are created by the master in this profession. In a note to this last page, Weber rightly announces that his pariah concept has nothing to do with the Hinduistic realities. He adds to this announcement (and, for many, to the confusion): 'We use the expression 'pariah' here just as there it is in the usual European way, comparable to the expression 'Kadi' in 'Kadi-Law''!. See also WG, p. 300; EC, p. 493. The problem is, of course, that Weber perceives the concept in a pejorative and European-Christian way while trying to explain it by means of a largely positive and Indian-Hinduistic way. The inevitable next series of problems is the subject of the following and many other analyses!

'*Nomadic Challenge*' in receiving the very nasty undertones referred to even by Schluchter as he stated: 'Between Weber and us existed the National Socialism'.[7]

In between, in 1940, Adorno also conquered his *locus operandi* as he connected in one stroke the unbearable fate of the Jews in World War II with nomadism.

Along with Adorno and Weber, I define a highly complex problem, the interrelations between a Jewish and a Nomadic Question. Indeed, both Adorno's suggestions and Weber's option urge the need for a comparative world historical analysis of these interrelations, but we have to know first what we have to look for in history. Adorno seems to have a positive idea about the relationship nomads-Jews as a result of a victim-oriented point of view. Thanks to the development of his pariah concept, one can expect that Weber had a negative perception of the nomads-Jews relationship. If true, one could deduce that Weber's point of view implies an offenders' orientation as well, whereas it certainly is part of a classical oikoidal defense mechanism against (alleged) enemies from the outside.

My thesis concerning Weber's point of view is that he defends not only a radical anti-Judaistic position (for many peoples synonymous with antisemitism) but also a radical sedentarist stand. Both are mutually related. If true, this outcome is a relevant substantiation of Adorno's argument. This leads to the following procedure in this chapter. First, we need a better understanding of the Near Eastern setting of Adorno's 'secret gypsy' or Weber's nomadic (pastoralist, non-sedentary, etc.) 'ideal type'. Second, we have to analyse both Adorno's and Weber's ideological position concerning the 'Nomadic Question', which both point to the need of an analysis of Old Testament sources. Adorno's case, however, remained too abstract to derive other guidelines for this chapter. Therefore, I shall mainly concentrate on Weber's 'biblical performance' and confrontation with the nomadic way of life in the Near Eastern region. At the end we can see how this fits with the outcome of the former chapter.

THE NEAR EASTERN CHALLENGE

Only the first question is obvious: What does Weber's nomadic ideal type look like in the Near Eastern context? In *Das antike Judentum*, Weber starts with a description of the Palestinian geography. He describes old Egyptian, Mesopotamian, etc. political developments in the area.[8] In about the 8th century Palestine became independent. At the time, her neighbors were Phoenician cities and Philistines in the South, Aramaeans in Lebanon, and the Bedouin tribes in the eastern desert. From the earliest times one could find corn in the central and northern plains along with cattle husbandry. In the desert oases dates were grown. The peasants

---

7. W. Schluchter (Ed.), p. 9.
8. GAR, III, p. 8 ff. Here he discovers in old Babylon already 'frühkapitalistischen Geschäftsformen' (p. 8).

and pastoralists did not like the 'sterile desert' in the south and east where the demons lived. In the steppe regions one could find camel, sheep, etc. husbandry and shifting cultivation [*nomadisierenden Gelegenheidsanbau*] and in particular camel, sheep, etc. husbandry by steppe-nomads [*Hirten*]. In fact, Weber sketches a highly mobile situation with all forms of animal culture including the so-called *transhumance* (in the winter with the flocks at the coast; in summertime in the mountains). He also notes 'that times of sedentarization in villages changed with times of nomadism ... peasants in their mountain-villages of Juda live in tents during ... half the year ... The strictest binding at the soil and the tent-nomadism are connected by all possible transitions...'.[9] Especially for the steppe-nomads, Palestine is mostly no 'land of milk and honey', Weber remarks.

After this geographical description, he constructed a 'scale' to give some order to the main elements of Palestinian life. A few strategic citations are necessary to understand his position on the Nomadic Question:

> 'At one end of the scale stood and stand the Bedouin of the desert. The original bedu, who differed strongly from the sedentary Arab also in North Arabia, always detested agriculture and living in houses or castles; nourished himself with camel milk and dates; had no knowledge about wine; did not need or accept some form of state organization.'[10] 'At the other end of the scale stood and stand the city (*gir*). ... Its early forms were ... castles of military leaders with their personal followers [*Gefolgschaft*] or refuges for animals and peoples ... The city was quite different in an economical and political sense: a small market town with ramparts inhabited by peasants [*Ackerbürgergemeinde mit Markt*]. ... In a fully developed stage, the city was not only a marketplace, but, in particular, a fortress and as such the habitation of the armed forces [*Wehrverband*], of the local diety with its priests, and of the monarchical, subsequently oligarchical, power. This equals clearly ... the polis in the Mediterranean area.'[11] In between City and Bedouin Weber placed two other elements on his scale: 'Against the city-patricians and the Bedouin stood both the peasants and pastoralists [*Hirten*] in the same kind of opposition. For this reason they had the same interests [*Interessengemeinschaft*].'[12]

---

9. Idem, p. 11 ff. He bases this rather flexible opinion on present descriptions found in the *Zeitschrift* and *Mitteilungen* of the (political) influential *Deutsche Palästina Verein*. Idem, note p. 10 etc.

10. GAR, III, p. 13 ff. For nearly the same text see also WG, p. 519 and EC, p. 909, 910. A remarkable difference between GAR and WG/ EC is that Weber talks about Arabs ('*heidnischen Zeit der Araber*'/'Arabs during their "pagan" age') in WG/ EC. Apart from the fact that this indication does not fit very well with the Bedouin, Weber refers in both publications to his main source in Judaism questions, the theologist Wellhausen.

11. Idem, p. 16, 17. In this chapter I do not analyse or criticize Weber's 'Stadt' -ideal-type. This is already done in Chr. Schäfer, Stadtstaat und Eidgenossenschaft ... in: W. Schluchter (Ed.), *Max Webers Studie über das antike Judentum* ,p. 78-110. More detailed Ch. Schäfer-Lichtenberger, *Stadt und Eidgenossenschaft im Alten Testament. Eine Auseinandersetzung mit Max Webers Studie 'Das Antike Judentum'* (Berlin/ New York: de Gruyter, 1983) and in H. Derks, *De Koe van Troje*, p. 168-199.

12. GAR, III, p. 62, 63.

For our discussion Weber's profile of the Bedouin is most interesting. After listing the characteristics, he continued to describe these nomads in an almost aggressively negative way. This description is dominated by strong language like "adventurous', 'blood vengeance', 'war', '(street)robbing', etc. Their political organization is highly unstable [*höchst labil*] because they usually do not have strong top leaders. 'From an economic point of view, the present Bedouin is seen as a traditionalist without any creativity and as someone who is not in for peaceful work.'[13]

For Weber, there is only one reason not to generalize this judgment, namely, the Bedouin's interests in trade relations. Still, for him there is no difference between '*Zwischenhandel und Straßenraub*': 'The foreign merchant was and will be robbed' if he is not protected by militaries. His conclusion concerning the relationship nomads versus 'Israel' is not unexpected after these hostile judgments. Still, it is an astonishing verdict, a Biblical ordeal:

'...traditionally the Bedouin is the mortal enemy of Israel. Eternal struggle exists between Jahweh and Amalek. The ancestor of the Kenites tribe, Cain, marked with "Cain's sign", the tribal tatoo, is the murderer of God and as such he is damned to be on the move forever. The terrible harshness of the blood vengeance is his only privilege. Also in other respects, traces of the Bedouin within Israeli customs are missing nearly completely. Only one important trace is known: the painting of doorposts with blood to keep off the demons ...'[14]

Understanding and explaining Weber's Near Eastern nomadic ideal type, a remarkable mixture of ideology and historical 'fact', is a complex affair; a step-by-step strategy seems most appropriate here.

'Weber's Challenge' can be defined as '*Weber's provocation by the nomadic phenomenon*'. The question then is how he handled this 'attack' from reality on his

---

13. Idem, p. 15. For the interpretation of Weber's point of view see my *Stad en Land, Markt en Oikos*, p. 531-533 note 20, p. 546/ 547 note 123.

14. GAR, III, p. 16. See also p. 46 for the same text. A transformation into present language is, for example, W. Keller's description of Abraham's Palestine: 'The nomads are there suddenly and without any warning, they kill everybody, capture the cattle and steal the harvest. Just as suddenly they disappear, and it is impossibile to find them in the wide deserts of the South and the East. The struggle of the sedentary peasants and stock-farmers rages permanently with the robbing tribes who does not know a fixed house, which is only a tent from goat-hair somewhere outside in the wide deserts' in his *Und die Bibel hat doch recht* (Hamburg: Rowohlt, 1964), p. 83; see also p. 168. To demonstrate from the beginning the typical use of 'Amalek' which will be commented throughout the whole text of my book, I refer already here to the famous Shoah-historian Raul Hilberg who wrote having seen a book about the Shoah-perpetrators named *Out of the Whirlwind*: 'In the last resort this attitude is a consequence of a warning in the *Second Book Moses*: ' .. I will utterly blot out the remembrance of Amalek from under heaven.' [text from *Exodus* 17-14] ... As their ancestors the present Jews know of the danger to provide the perpetrators with a face ...'. See R. Hilberg, *Unerbetene Erinnerung. Der Weg eines Holocaust-Forschers* (Frankfurt a.M.: Fischer, 1994), p. 114.

theoretical model? If I can provide a reasonable answer to this question, the second can be answered as well: Why did he 'attack' reality with his harsh ideological point of view? He answered the first question in his conclusion given in the last quotation.

Weber, like many others before and after him, confronts us here with the single most important myth, legitimating legend, ancestor-history (etc.) in our culture. As is suggested above and will be substantiated below, it also became a decisive story in the case of the *Nomadic Challenge*. A 'Weber case' is rather unimportant compared to that. In addition, I shall take the opportunity to develop, step by step, an alternative way of thinking about the subject. Therefore, a close reading of these few lines is worthwile. This is necessary but not very pleasant reading.

THE MANY 'SIGNS OF CAIN'

The wording of the last citation is rather similar to a passage in Meyer's *Israeliten*[15], but there are important differences. Whereas Weber speaks about an 'eternal' enmity, Meyer quotes *Exodus* 17:16, 'war with Amalek from generation to generation', and 1 *Samuel* 30:26 which talks about Amalekites as 'enemies of Jahweh'; not more, nor less. Since in the Bible nearly everybody and everything seems inimical to Jahweh (and vice versa), this is not a very disturbing announcement. Apart from this, the 'Israelites', whoever they were, fought holy wars against many other tribes. And in the end, Meyer showed how there are different Jahwehs for several landscapes.

Weber, however, tells the story to stigmatise the Bedouin ('Amalek'; 'Kenites'; etc.), a *general* name for – say – camel driving nomads in the Near East, whereas Meyer does not exaggerate and points at the Bedouin as an 'older brothership'. This can refer positively to a love relation between biological brothers as, for instance, Cain (Qain, for Meyer) and Abel. Weber, however, wants to create nasty phenomena such as blood vengeance. He forgets that this is nearly as common as addressing people as 'brother'!

In principle, this activity is not a Bedouin prerogative but a 'privilege' for everybody and every culture in the Near East or Mediterranean region. Weber should have known as well how the Bible favored blood vengeance. In *Deuteronomium* (19:11-13) one can read:

> 'But if any man hates his neighbor, and lies in wait for him, and attacks him, and wounds him mortally so that he dies, and the man flees into one of these cities, then the elders of his city shall send and fetch him from there, and hand him over to the avenger of blood, so that he may die. Your eye shall not pity him ...'

---

15. E. Meyer, B. Luther, *Die Israeliten und ihre Nachbarstämme. Alttestamentliche Untersuchungen* (Halle: Niemeyer, 1906), p. 391 and p. 394. See also R. de Vaux, *Ancient Israel. Its Life and Institutions* (London: Darton/ Longman, 1961), ch. 5.

Weber even forgot another well-known fact because, for some reason or other, he denied the existence of a Bedouin law. In, for instance, the wording of De Vaux: 'In contrast with Bedouin law, however, Israelite legislation does not allow compensation in money, alleging for this a religious motive: blood which is shed defiles the land in which Yaweh dwells, and must be expiated by the blood of him who shed it (Nb 35: 31-34).'[16] Nowadays, it is still the case that premeditated murder in Bedouin and rural Arab societies may be settled through payment of *diyya* (blood money) or through mediation rather than through revenge.[17] Depending on the membership of some co-liable group, cases can become rather complicated. 'It is customary, however, for every male member of the group who is not of the co-liable group to give the family of the murdered man a camel or its value in money. This payment is called *be'ir al-nom* ('camel of sleep') and once it is accepted the giver can sleep in his tent without fear. The payment is really an 'insurance policy', a wise precaution ...'[18]

Remarkable conclusions could be drawn from this. First, blood vengeance is for settled (Christian) peoples and, obviously, for peasants in particular a much harsher affair than for the most 'savage, demonic,' etc. nomad. Weber's 'terrible harshness of the blood vengeance', therefore, seems pure sedentary prejudice. Furthermore, in the acceptance or not of money compensation in matters of life and death, one can detect a specific characteristic of the *oikos-market* contradictions. But it is, in particular, the common character of blood vengeance which

---

16. R. de Vaux, p. 12. Weber's omission is rather serious. Eduard Westermarck's (1862-1939) famous encyclopaedical socio-anthropological works like *The Origin and Development of Moral Ideas* (1906-1908) were available in Germany. In *Ursprung und Entwicklung der Moralbegriffe* (Leipzig: Verlag Klinkhardt, 1907), Bnd. I, übers. Leopold Katscher, chapter 16 provides many interesting facts about blood-vengeance (p. 397-411). Due to a four-year stay in Morocco to study Bedouin/ Berber life, Westermarck was one of the few scholars with first-hand knowledge about nomadic life. Nowadays, nobody will support his theory on the importance of emotions, but there is no reason to reject his wide-ranging research. In the case of blood-vengeance, he sometimes referred to Biblical sources but more often to other customs. Among the Algerian Kabyles the dialectic of vengeance/ indemnification is even solved by replacing the son-victim with the murderer as a new son (p. 402). Moroccan Berber tribes also have several kinds of peaceful indemnification rules. For Bedouin Law see F.H. Stewart; H. Blanc (Ed.), *Texts in Sinai Bedouin Law* (Wiesbaden: Harrassowitz, 1988-1990), two volumes.

17. J. Ginat, *Blood Disputes among Bedouin and Rural Arabs in Israel. Revenge, Mediation, Outcasting and Family Honor* (London/ Tel Aviv: Un. of Pittsburgh Press, 1987), p. 22 ff. Differences between unintentional and premeditated killing are not always clear. In some Arab countries there are legal rates for *diyya*; in Oman, a person who unintentionally kills somebody has to pay $14,500 to the injured family (half of this for a woman !). If family honor is violated (through illicit sexual relations, for instance) the judge prescribes a penalty for murder of between six months to two years in Jordan. In Lebanon, however, with its strong Christian influences, in cases of illicit sexual relations of wives or daughters, the husband-murderer will not be punished.

18. Idem, p. 41. These affairs are always managed through mediators who will receive a share in the payments. This 'market-situation' makes it interesting for all kinds of persons to become involved in settling activities. The effect is, of course, that the chances for peace are larger.

worries me, as Weber uses an expression like '*Cain-murderer-of-God*' which cries for vengeance! And who was accused of the same crime? Exactly – the Jews. Are these victims of the largest act of theologically legitimated blood vengeance, indeed, comparable to nomads? In the last paragraph, I will try to answer this question.

As Bible theologians in Weber's time and 'normal' historians like Redford nowadays have stated: Jahweh is a *nomadic* god.[19] I am not familiar with theological concepts, but it seems to me that Weber's expression '*Cain-murderer-of-God*' is ambiguous, to say the least. The only possible option I can imagine in this case is: If this is true, then God and Abel, a true nomad, are 'equal'. That is not Weber's intention but near to a 'historical truth' *if it is assumed that only Abel is a nomad*.

This brings me immediately to the next bloody practice, *fratricide*. The prelude to such an act could be Jacob's cheating his brother Esau, Judah's selling of his brother Joseph as an Egyptian slave and other noble deeds. Not only the Bible has 'the privilege' of repeatedly reporting about brother murder. Pierre Oberling talks proudly about the subject of his studies, the influential Iranian Qashqa'i nomadic tribe with its long history lasting into the last century. There were sometimes violent quarrels between brothers, but they never resulted 'in the death of any member of the Quasqa'i ruling family. This is in sharp contrast to the practices of other tribal ruling families in Persia, where fratricide was a common occurrence.'[20] Fratricide was not uncommon but still an exception among, for instance, the Greek Sarakatsani (pastoral nomads).[21] This was *not* a consequence of inheritance rules. After the dowries were spent, in principle, parents and children had an equal share of the flock, but the youngest brother got an extra portion because of his duty to look after the aging parents. No, fratricide occurred in relation to the competition between brothers (and do not forget the sisters) for all kinds of external favours, e.g. the praise of the world outside the family. If in large constellations like the Iranian Quasqa'i (in Weber's time about 300,000 members and ca. 5 million animals) or Khamsé[22] the social differentiation was great enough to give rise to 'ruling families', the external favors and praise weighed much heavier on the shoulders of its brothers. Only in these families can fratricide become a rather common phenomenon.

In the case of Cain and Abel, there was an external force/praise with a divine status. Suppose: *both* biological brothers *were nomads* (in fact, the most self-evident situation). They made antagonistic decisions in a crucial situation. Young Abel wanted to remain a nomad, while older brother Cain decided to quit the nomadic way of life in favour of a peasant existence. The end is known: the no-

19. D. Redford, *Egypt, Canaan, and Israel in Ancient Times* (Princeton: Princeton Un. Press, 1993), p. 272, 273 on the basis of Egyptian sources from the 19th and 20th dynasties. See also BHH, II, p. 300.
20. P. Oberling, *The Qashq'i Nomads of Fars* (The Hague/ Paris: Mouton, 1974), p. 217.
21. J.K. Campbell, *Honour, Family and Patronage* (Oxford: Oxford Un. Press, 1964), p. 172-179.
22. V. Monteil, *Les tribus du Fârs et la sédentarisation des nomades* (Paris: Mouton, 1956), p. 15 ff.

madic God Jahweh did not applaud this last idea whereupon Cain, immediately losing his honor and *raison d'etre*, killed his brother. He got the usual nomadic punishment: if he had killed somebody of another tribe or family, he would have been killed also by blood vengeance if he could not pay compensation. In this case, which was an internal family affair, he was sent into the desert in the expectation that he would die. As everybody knows, the man survived, and by this 'act' he received a new identity. This interpretation has the *dis*advantage of its logical consistency within a nomadic context. In concentrating on the reasons why a Cain-Abel story is told in the Bible, Weber's position can also be seen in another light, because a second interpretation can be offered.

The Cain problem, located directly at the start of all histories, concerns what can be called '*the sin of the second stage*'. It is a really serious case with a highly symbolic meaning. Only one thing seems to be equal to real homicide cases: nobody cares about the victim![23] Many different groups had an interest in rewriting (biblical) history and accused their alleged enemies, of course, of 'rewriting history'.[24] Furthermore, it is assumed that the Hebrew *qain*, the word from which 'Cain' is derived, equals 'blacksmith'.[25] Probably in very vulgar Marxist writings this laborer can be found at the very beginning of human history. There also seems to be a contradiction between this most sedentary profession and Cain's status as nomad. In another context, however, things become clearer.

In Paradise, Adam and Eve were collectors of what was available. When they wanted more than this (or when the plenty was over), they had *no other choice* (a good definition for a divine ordeal) than to leave and *collect* new opportunities and products. With Abel and Cain, the second stage came in which an answer had to be given to the more fundamental question: now that we clearly have *to produce* food ourselves, how should we continue? There were only two options (otherwise more brothers would have been introduced!): we fundamentally improve our way of roaming around (Abel), or we stay in a place, build a house and grow food (Cain). Both answers were judged by Yahweh, and he, without any hesitation and in the clearest possible way, decided in favor of the nomad Abel and a mobile way of life. Cain was a digger of the soil, the first peasant and sedentary because he was the one who sacrificed to Yahweh the first fruits of the fields. In Yahwist tradition

---

23. The exception to the rule is the article 'Abel' from R. Hess in: *The Anchor Bible Dictionary* (New York: Anchor, 1992), Vol. 1, p. 9 ff. and subsequently his article 'Cain', in idem, p. 806 ff.

24. Weber, for instance, accused a 'politische Tendenzlegende' which 'redigierte die Überlieferung um' (GAR, III, p. 123). In this case Weber decided that Goliath was not killed by David, but by 'einer der Ritter Davids' and the 'Tendenzlegende' came up with a 'unbekannten und ungepanzerten Hirtenknaben David' who killed the colossus 'nach Bauernart'. BHH, I, p. 500 did not want to decide on the question of whether Elchanan, Weber's 'Ritter Davids', was the same as David. In BHH, II, p. 207-208, however, the identity of the oldest and youngest 'tradition' is implied. R. de Vaux, p. 108, clearly states that 'Elhanan' was the birthname of David and, therefore, the 'original killer of Goliath'.

25. See, for instance, N. Gottwald, *The Tribes of Jahweh. A Sociology of the Religion of Liberated Israel, 1250-1050 BCE* (New York: Orbis Books, 1979), p. 578, 579.

there is also this picture of Cain: 'The building of the first cities and the invention of the first arts are attributed to the cursed race of Cain.'[26] Therefore, he seems to be the 'ideal-typical' sedentarist.

Cain, the metaphor, also happened to have very nasty and jealous qualities: for 'the first time in history', aggressiveness against a nomad was expressed in an act of killing. The story continues with Yahweh's remarkable verdict: as the most serious punishment for an aggressive sedentarist, He rightly chose to send Cain into the desert. This means, however, first, that *sedentary life was sentenced again* and, second, that *within the nomadic way of life a division of labor was announced between those who cater to animals and those who have to do more or less sedentary 'services' occupying a lower status.*

At this point, Cain as a blacksmith becomes historically possible. A realistic example of this constellation can be found in the division of labor between the Tuareg of the Central Sahara and 'their' *sedentary* Inadan/ikalan who supply the work of the blacksmith etc.[27] (Here we see the difference from what Rost, the editor of the *Handwörterbuch*, told us about an alleged hierarchy *within* the Bedouin: the lowest level should be occupied by 'the pariah-tribes of blacksmiths and musicians'[28]). In fact, this reading of the case works out as a variant of my first interpretation. Both deviate from the existing stories which never look at Bible documents as historical sources written very long after Adam, Eve and their two sons lived. First, they were looked after as tools to legitimate political-religious positions not only in about 1000 BC but right up to 2000 AD and every period inbetween.

Theologically inspired Bible exegetes mostly defended a strong sedentarist solution but have a serious problem with explaining '*the sin of the second stage*'. Which solutions are given? Weber (and his sources) gave the simplest one by making Cain a proto-Bedouin as a consequence of God's punishment. His Cain-like aversion against nomads made him forget 'God's Own Bible'. Originally or better: from the standpoint of Genesis, it is not only impossible but also too strange to view Yahweh or 'Israel' as an eternal enemy of nomads. Apart from what was said before, one can ask: What to do, for instance, with the god-chosen 'patriarch' Abraham, undoubtedly a pastoral nomad on a large scale, or with Moses the Lawgiver who lived with his tribe in the desert. Here, in fact, the whole covenant scenario was constructed which gave these Bedouin their world-historical role in the formation of Christendom, Judaism and Islam? Who was responsible for '*the sin of the second stage*'?

26. *Genesis* 4:17. See J. Flight, The Nomadic Idea and the Ideal in the Old Testament, in: *Journal of Biblical Literature*, XLII, 1923 p. 213. Flight wrote in the important tradition of the alternative German theologian K. Budde, Das nomadische Ideal im Alten Testament, in: *Preußische Jahrbücher*, 85, 1896 p. 57-79 (earlier published in *The New World*, Boston 1895).

27. H.Derks, *De Koe van Troje*, p. 17-21.

28. BHH, I, p. 197.

Quite wild answers come from Mendenhall and Gottwald. For them, the Cain and Abel story presupposes, as a matter of course, 'that the shepherd and the farmer were brothers, just as most references ... presuppose that the shepherd is a member of a city or village community ...' The Bedouin of the Bronze Age as well as the modern Bedouin 'can be safely regarded as statistically and historically negligible'![29] Here, 'brothers' cannot refer to biological brothers. Such a close relationship is imcompatible with a division of labor between farmers and nomads. The pastoral nomadism with sheep, goats or cattle to which Mendenhall could point has at least three forms which are never considered. During summertime in the mountains and in the winter along the coast or in the valleys (with two important variations: long or short distance nomadism); the steppe-nomadism; and, third, the nomadism which uses the desert oases in wintertime and coastal regions in summer. Camel-nomadism is often mixed with the last two forms (see below). Therefore, 'brothers' can be found first and foremost *between* the several kinds of nomads. Mendenhall's exclamation sounds similar to Weber's failure to detect any 'traces of Bedouin within Israeli customs'. Gottwald specifies Weber's most popular Cain trick. From the whole story he isolates Cain as 'a fugitive and a wanderer' and, therefore, a nomad ('a tent-dwelling cattle breeder').[30]

As shown elsewhere, the monk Roland de Vaux occupies a slightly different position. First, he accepts that Cain was a farmer.[31] The desert behavior of Cain, however, is for him the ultimate proof of 'the condemnation of outright noma-dism'. Even the desert self shares in the burden because she becomes synonymous for Hell. This seems true for the reasoning as well. De Vaux: 'Before his crime, Cain was a farmer (Gn 4:2). So, in this story, the real desert is presented as the refuge of disgraced settlers and outlaws ...' What can be criticized here, in my opinion, is the lack of imagination for giving 'So' no meaning at all. The next example was related to no less a historian than Arnold Toynbee. It is told that he did not study his history very well because he gave Abel the peasant and Cain the nomad role in the story.[32] This message is communicated to Iraqi peasants and uncritical scholars who immediately discovered 'the terrible truth' about their own

---

29. G. Mendenhall, The Hebrew Conquest of Palestine, in: *The Biblical Archaeologist*, XXV, 1962, p. 69. Apart from this, it is worthwhile mentioning the meaning of *fields* in the O.T 'which make up much of the hill-country, and can never have been cultivated even for vines' says G.A. Smith, *The Historical Geography of the Holy Land* (New York: Harper Torchbooks, 1966), p. 72. As a general statement, Mendenhall is right to point to some interrelation between farmers and nomads, but in this region, this can never have had much impact.
30. N. Gottwald, p. 578.
31. R. de Vaux, p. 14.
32. This 'solution' is still defended in feminist Bible exegesis. See E. Fagel, *Adam, Eve and the serpent*. New York, 1988 (Dutch transl., 1989), p. 209. And what can be said about somebody who cannot see a nomad-peasant contradiction *at all* as happens with R. Hess in his article 'Abel' (note 126)?

Bedouin. The struggle between *these* Iraqi Cains and Abels is fixed as 'permanent' and used as a pretext to support the strongest possible State.[33]

AMALEK, THE ETERNAL ENEMY

Till now, I could show serious problems with Weber's use of 'blood vengeance', 'fratricide', the 'Cain-murderer-of-God' option and with the specific negation of 'Cain-the-peasant'. Weber did not stop creating problems in his conclusive text, quoted above. He also said that there was an 'eternal struggle between Yahweh and Amalek'. Who or what is 'Amalek', and what does Cain have to do with this 'Amalek'? Apparently a simple question but who re-reads the last sentence of the introduction of my book, is confronted with nothing less than the Shoah evil.

Amalek[34] seems to be the name of a 'nomadic tribe classified as part of the Esau tribe' (*Gen.* 36:12). Esau ('savage, hairy'), a son of Isaac and Rebecca, and older brother of Jacob, is supposed to be a representative of a hunters' culture, while Jacob represents the pastoral culture. Who can imagine a nomadic tribe and a pastoral one within a hunters' tribe? In *Genesis*, the Esau-Jacob story seems to be told as a metaphor for the interrelations between hunters and shepherds and for the slow development into a domination of shepherds over hunters. Weber again has his own interpretation of the professions of Esau and Jacob:

'As Abel is opposed to the peasant Cain, so is the soft Jacob as pious shepherd living in tents opposed to the raw peasant Esau. On the other hand, in the way that Cain becomes a Bedouin, Esau changes into a greedy hunter.'[35]

In the Old Testament, descendants of Esau, the Edomites, are seen as undifferentiated and rash people. For some reason, they are also considered especially wise people, which contradicts the first characteristics. In the New Testament, however, the people of Edom are considered symbolic of (materialist) Jewry.

---

33. Arnold Toynbee, *A Study of History* (Somervell Abridgement). New York, 1946 Vol. 1, p. 58-74. This *false* story is used by quite a famous Iraqi sociologist, Ali Al-Wardi, *Soziologie des Nomadentums. Studie über die iraqische Gesellschaft* (Neuwied: Luchterhand, 1972), p. 45-49. A worthwhile study about real interrelations between nomads and peasants is still J. Weulersse, *Paysans de Syrie et due Proche-Orient* (Paris: Gallimard, 1946); for the situation in Iraq see p. 302-314.

34. For this part see in BHH in particular the lemma's *Amalek, Bedoeienen, Esau, Hebreeën, Herder, Nomaden, Kain, Kenieten* and *Woestijn(reis)*; E. Meyer, B. Luther, p. 389-400; I. Finkelstein, *The archaeology of the Israelite settlement* (Jerusalem: Israel Exploration Society, 1988), p. 27, 38, 45; R. De Vaux, p. 215 ff., 256-261; D. Redford, p. 296, 349; J. Bright, *A History of Israel* (London: SCM Press, 1979), p. 122 ff.; M. Noth, *Geschichte Israels* (Göttingen: Vandenhoeck & Ruprecht, 1966), p. 57 ff. Around Weber's use of the 'Kenites', it is perfectly possible to come up with the same kind of analysis as with 'Amalek'. Somebody else should look into such a bunch of irrationalities if this would be interesting enough.

35. GAR, III, p. 58 note 3 and 4. Weber does not see any contradiction here.

Gottwald et al. identified Amalekites (and Amorites, Shosu, Midianites, etc.) as 'transhumant nomadic peoples who were predecessors or contemporaries of Israel'.[36] Other information shows that Amalek and the Amalekites lived only in the Negev desert. Sometimes they raided southern Palestinian areas. Already during the Long March through the Desert, a large defeat against them could be avoided because of Moses' endurance with keeping his hands in the air (*Exodus* 17:8-16). This battle seems to be the very reason why, one day, Weber could talk about the eternal struggle between Jahweh and Amalek.

Also later (1 *Samuel*, 15:6), Saul and David had to fight victorious battles against these desert nomads. The first went to war against the Amalekites who cooperated with Ammonites, Midianites and Qainites as well (Qain/Cain). Saul, however, asked the Qainites to leave the Amalekites before his attack because Qain had done him a favor in the past. And, indeed, Qain disappeared from the battle-field. Elsewhere (*Judges* 1:16), one can read 'Qain dwells with Amalek' or 'Qain, the father-in-law of Moses'. In 1 *Samuel* 15:5-8 there is also some information about a town and a 'king' of the Amalekites. Without any hesitation, archaeologists concluded from this 'fact' (created by the translation) that sedentarisation had developed.[37] Furthermore, the *Handwörterbuch* announces that this 'definitely broke their power'. With this, the aim of all (sedentary) governments is defined in their policies against nomads. Theoretically, in this way a serious problem disappears from the table.

What can be understood from this strange and contradictory information from the 'giants' in the profession? Before entangling ourselves in more details, it is necessary to get closer to the heart of the matter. One of Weber's main sources, Eduard Meyer, can probably help with this.[38] He is certain that the small tribe of the Qainites were part of the Amalekites,[39] and he believes that this was confirmed by the Qain-Abel story: 'Because here is Qain the wild tribe of the desert, which did not have a fixed dwelling place ...' This circular argumentation does not bring us very far. What else does he offer?

---

36. N. Gottwald, p. 231.

37. Take the example of Tel Masos in the south near Bersheba (oldest part ca. 1225 BC). This site was excavated in 1972-1979 and was considered the showpiece of the Israelite Settlement. The earliest phase of this settlement, therefore, 'marked the first phase of sedentarization by a group of semi-nomads' (op cit. I. Finkelstein, p. 41 ff.). Finkelstein makes it perfectly clear that on many grounds Tel Masos cannot be an Israelite Settlement site. His teacher Moshe Kochavi already identified the place as the '*city of Amalek*' (1982).

38. In particular E. Meyer, B. Luther, p. 394-396. Meyer's sources are Julius Wellhausen and Stade's analysis of the so-called 'Cain's sign'. Meyer mostly writes about 'Qain' (Qainiter) but he also uses 'Kain'.

39. This should correspond to M. Noth, p. 162 who looks at the Amalekites as a 'Nomadenstämmever-band in der südlichen Wüste' who lived 'more or less in a permanent enmity' with Israel. Earlier (p. 149 note 2) Noth remembered that the Amalekites, Midianites etc. in *Judges* 6:3-33 and 7:12 appeared with '*the Sons of the East*', i.e. the most general expression for the inhabitants of the eastern deserts.

First he states: 'Abel, in fact, like Wellhausen already knew, is identical with Jabal[40] the ancestor of all animal breeders, and he is the representative of the sheep breeders from the Negev desert.' A few lines further he also confesses 'that the idea, Qainites originally were peasants and then changed into Bedouin, is most unbelievable ...' Next, Meyer says: 'In Gen. 4 Qain plays exactly the same role as Amalek in the later stories ...' and '... the Rechabites are the only ones left from the Qainites...'[41] Weber, in the end, made Cain 'the ancestor of the Kenites tribe' and these Kenites (or Qenites) were mostly identified with Midianites (except by De Vaux).[42]

If both Abel and Cain are seen as ancestors of nomads who, in some way or other, are all related to 'Amalek', an expression such as 'eternal struggle between Yahweh and Amalek' is utter nonsense. The exaggerated language is also dangerous, while fundamentally discriminating against some party within religious tracts. This is the case despite the logical possibility of talking about an 'eternal struggle between Yahweh and the father-in-law of Moses'. Other conclusions are more important.

All of the authorities cited did not have many problems with nomads in a positive or negative ideological sense, but with Cain's peasantship in particular and with the act of sedentarization. For all these *sedentarized* ideologists/theologians, a peasant can never be the bad guy in a story, let alone 'an eternal enemy of Yahweh/God himself'. Such a basis for a religion should have deprived them of their most persistent followers. Furthermore, the peasant-agrarian component of an oikoidal economy is of pivotal importance because an animal-based economy is *by definition* market-oriented. From the start, i.e. the Cain-Abel story, the very purpose of Bible history is sedentarization, evolving into a solid agrarian economy and society. The Israelite Settlement (in capitals) is as such an ideological and not a historical model. *Within this model*, in my opinion, only the following variants can be constructed with Biblical data:

---

40. As usual, finding an absolutely contradictory opinion is rather easy. In BHH, II, p. 433 one can read about Jabal: '1. The son of Lamech and Ada in the pedigree of Cain according to J. He was the father of all shepherds (Gen. 4:20)?' Etymologically this name could be connected to the Arab *abbalun* 'camel-driver.'! Jabal's brother, Jubal, was the father of all musicians; Jabal's step-brother was according to *Gen.* 4:22 a blacksmith.

41. E. Meyer, B. Luther, p. 399.

42. J. Bright, p. 125 note 46. BHH, III, p. 28 states that they belonged to the Amalekites till the beginning of the monarchy. At that time they divorced the Amalekites and 'joined the Juda-tribe and transformed into peasants'. To blur the story again, BHH states that some Kenites (or Qenites) stayed nomads and, in any case, the nomadic Rechabites looked upon Kenites as their ancestors (see R. de Vaux, p. 15). M. Noth (p. 56-58) tells the same story and also points to other southern tribes (although he knows of Kenites in the northern Galilee as well!). First of all Judah, but also the Kalibbites (or Calebites, the inhabitants of Hebron) who are related to Kenizzites and Edomites. Furthermore, there lived Othnielites, Kenites, Jerachmelites and the Simeon tribe. See also G. A. Smith's story of the Kenites invasion of Palestine (p. 187 ff.).

A.   'In the end', agriculture must be established and a monarchy, etc. (the *Oikos model*). This supposes that somewhere 'in the middle' a transformation of nomads into peasants has to take place; the sedentarization must come from 'transhumant semi-nomads (shepherds)' and not from camel nomads from the desert; therefore, a good and bad (camel) nomad can be substituted 'in the start' of the development. The end result is: Cain and Abel were both nomads.

B.   'In the end', agriculture must be established and a monarchy, etc. (the *Oikos model*). This supposes that somewhere 'in the middle' a transformation of nomads into peasants has to take place; the sedentarization must come from 'transhumant semi-nomads (shepherds)' but also from 'nomadic agriculture' (see Weber[43]); therefore, a good nomad and a still bad peasant (who only has to become a real peasant in a later stage) can be substituted 'in the start' of the development. The end result is: Abel was the only nomad and Cain, the peasant.

Both models are 'not from this world'. Ideologically motivated students will not be bothered by this judgment. Christians have always known that there was a fundamental antagonism between the *civitas Dei* and *terrena civitas*. The two other interests in the Holy Land, Jewish religion and Islam, are both strongly divided by the fundamentalists. The pivotal Cain-Abel story will certainly divide them, too. I am not familiar with their theological debates, but I would guess that the Jews choose the second alternative and the Islamic theologians, the first.[44] The nomad Abraham is, in fact, the father of both religions; Jerusalem and Hebron are Holy Cities for Jews and Moslems. Mohammed himself experienced strong Jewish influences in the first years of his ascendancy and so on.[45] It must be clear that both models have everything to do with the (mis)understanding of a sedentarization phenomenon.

Back to '*Antike Judentum*'. Some general questions on this phenomenon can be posed already at this junction. If a from-nomad-to-peasant sedentarization is 'most unbelievable' (Meyer), what could be the alternatives in the history of this part of the Near East? First, of course, no sedentarization at all. This, however, can only be an academic question because every nomadic lifestyle has its peculiar elements of sedentarization. Far more realistic for this area is the next alternative: nomadic sedentarization as *market urbanization*. Recent anthropological or sociological studies can be combined with the latest archaeological results

43. Even nowadays this nonsensical concept is used in *Anchor Bible Dictionary* (note 126), vol. 1, p. 634.

44. At a 'basic technical' level see G.H. Cohen Stuart, *The Struggle in Man between Good and Evil. An inquiry into the origin of the Rabbinic concept of Yeser Hara* (Kampen: Kok, 1984) is interesting and K. van der Toorn, *Sin and Sanction in Israel and Mesopotamia. A comparative study* (Assen: Van Gorcum, 1985). Directly related to Weber's involvement is one of the many readers of Wolfgang Schluchter (Ed.), *Max Webers Sicht des Islams* (Frankfurt a/M.: Suhrkamp, 1987). The essays from Rudolph Peters (p. 217 ff.), Patricia Crone (p. 294 ff.) and Michael Cook (p. 334 ff.) are relevant here.

45. A. Hourani, *A History of the Arab People* (London: Faber & Faber, 1991).

(Finkelstein, Redford, Zarin, etc.). These have to be related to each other and also expanded in a somewhat more complex framework. That is not my task here, but elsewhere I will provide an alternative along these *market lines*.

I do not intend to show in further detail what was good or bad in Weber's 'practical' analysis. The question I posed at the end of section II (how he handled the *'attack'* from reality on his theoretical model) can be easily answered now: Weber fled from nearly all Palestinian realities and did not reply to any attack. Instead, it seems as if he was constructing a 'Wunderwaffe' to win a theoretical battle which was practically lost. He acted as an Icarus searching for the definite explanation of 'Judaism in World History', not content with only becoming a better Wellhausen, the most up-to-date (Lutheran) Bible scholar. Therefore, the second question posed (Why did Max Weber attack reality with his strong ideological point of view) could be more revealing in discovering the real content of his (or any other) *Nomadic Challenge*.

THE PARIAH COMPLEX

Again the Cain-Abel story can serve perfectly well to provide insight into a seemingly very different discourse. Why? Because the Bible, in fact, did *not* say that the peasant Cain became a *bedu* but only that he became a vagabond and, in any case, a *wanderer always in danger of being slain*!

> 'And the Lord said, 'What have you done? The voice of your brother's blood is crying to me from the ground. And now you are cursed from the ground, which has opened its mouth to receive your brother's blood from your hand. When you till the ground, it shall no longer yield to you its strength; you shall be a fugitive and a wanderer on the earth.' Cain said to the Lord, 'My punishment is greater than I can bear. Behold, thou hast driven me this day away from the ground; and from thy face I shall be hidden; and I shall be a fugitive and a wanderer on the earth, and whoever finds me will slay me.' Then the Lord said to him, 'Not so! If any one slays Cain, vengeance shall be taken on him sevenfold.' And the Lord put a mark on Cain, lest any who came upon him should kill him. Then Cain went away ... and dwelt in the land of Nod, east of Eden.' (*Genesis* 4: 10-17).

This text can be easily rationalized as a metaphor for the highly common migration of *peasants* following the loss of yields due to droughts, earthquakes, war, repression, etc. These facts could be symbolized in Yahweh's refusal of Cain's offer! That they sometimes have to flee through the desert in an area with deserts around every corner is not so strange. But with this, one can change the subject of the discussion from the *nomad versus peasant* part of the story to the more abstract *mobile versus sedentary* way of life. The last dichotomy has other elements than the former. The following example will show what I mean.

One of the interesting and valuable books by the historian Bronislaw Geremek has the title *La Stirpe di Caino*, Cain's sign, about which Weber wrote as 'a tribal tatoo' for a 'murderer on the move forever'.[46] The English writer Thomas Nash (1567-1601) already saw Cain as 'the first vagabond in world history'.[47] His Scottish contemporary, John Cleveland, however, introduced other dimensions in his *The Rebel Scot*: 'Had Cain been Scot, God would have changed his doom,/ Nor forced him wander, but confined him home'. The Scots were strongly discriminated against by the English in every sense and consequently had to flee the country or to migrate. For Cleveland there seems to be only one difficulty with Cain: he was not Scottish enough, although Cain was already a rebellious wanderer with a good cause! Nash's remark states:

> 'On one hand the concept [Cain] marks the nomadic existence the poor had to live while ... at the same time, a criminal connotation is added: this wandering is not of one's own free will but a matter of fugitivity caused by a crime.'

In the Middle Ages, this double meaning was well known in the stories about 'werewolves with Cain's sign' for vagabonds living in the woods as symbols for hypocrisy and fraud. But beggars who tried to get their alms by fraud were also seen as descendants of Adam's eldest son.

When going back in time, from the late Roman Empire beggars or vagabonds played a large role in plays from Lucianus of Samosata, Petronius or Apuleius. Here, marginal figures, in fact, were only perceived as criminal demi-gods busy with frauding and cheating to get money for alcohol and prostitutes. With Roman Christianity, indeed, there was a break with this perception: *poverty was praised as a virtue*, although nothing else gave rise to more hypocrisy. The reason why poverty became a virtue is simple. According to the Fathers, it is only a matter of God's grace whether you will become rich or poor and receive a high or low social position. So, you have to accept your destiny in all humbleness. What He has given to you is a virtue. Amen.

Furthermore, Christianity later developed an institutionalization of *eternal poverty* to organize real poverty and related phenomena by means of rural and urban cloisters, beggar communities or public *charitas* institutions. This became a most lucrative means of transmitting money and riches to the Churches. With care for the sick and education, this 'trinity' formed very effective instruments to creep into all corners of society. When the urban heir of beggars expanded too quickly and the rich started fearing for their position, hard repression by law, church and army was exercised. In particular, from the beginning of the 16th century on, this repression became systematized, large scale and often very cruel.

---

46. B. Geremek (note 105). In Kipling's *Jungle book* Shirkan the tiger, the Ultimate Evil, was provided with 'Cain's stripes'.
47. Idem, p. 9.

Then the stories about the 'richness' of the poor, their laziness to work, the cleverness to simulate illness and, in the end, their descendancy from Cain also started to be told. Last but not least, the place where all those sinful wanderers and beggars concentrated, the city, could be rather easily incorporated by something that became the absolutist (patrimonial) state, the *Super-Oikos*. It is surely no accident that Cain also became responsible for building The City As Place of Sin (see *Genesis* 4:17)[48].

There is a poor legitimation for poverty-as-a-virtue in the Old Testament. In a nomadic tribal society, there are certainly differences in individual prosperity but only 'collective' poverty due to droughts, pests, etc. Contrary to sedentary Christianity, here richness is a virtue. It is expressed first and foremost in the number of animals one has.[49] Everybody accepts that the rich are the most pious, clever, etc. and the poor (' the ones with fewer animals) only people with bad luck, not very clever and, therefore, a kind of sinner. But sharp distinctions cannot be made because all participants in this society know very well how relative richness is, how everybody has to rely somehow on each other, and what is the minimum number of animals for a 'good poor life'. Also, a poor man remains independent and free.

Real (unfree) poverty arises *in oikoidally organized urban and rural societies*. For a substantial part, the very hierarchy of that society rests on the existence of a relatively large real poverty and, therefore, on the (legitimation of) institutional dependency of 'the top'. Some prophets learned about this society for the first time in exile (*Isaiah* 14:32; 25:4; 49:13) and started to give poor people a profile as 'the poor from Yahweh'. In the New Testament and in apocryphal writings (*Tobias* for instance), there is already more talk about poverty in the Christian sense. Jesus, far from being a social reformer, used the poor as the first receivers of the richness of faith. Still, it is typical enough that Gottwald, who must have a strong interest in making his revolution theory acceptable, could not mention any *substantial* fact about poverty.[50]

---

48. Indispensable for the period concerned is R. Muchembled, *L'invention de l'homme moderne: sensibilités, moeurs et comportements collectifs sous l'Ancien Régime* (Paris: Fayard, 1988).

49. One example from Near Eastern nomads demonstrates present realities in the area. In a study of the famous Yörük of Southeastern Turkey, of the 168 nomadic families studied only six 'owned shares in fields or urban property from which they derived a predictable income. Variation in herd size therefore is an accurate measure of a family's economic standing'. D. Bates, *Nomads and Farmers: A Study of the Yörük of Southeastern Turkey* (Ann Arbor: Un. of Michigan Press, 1973), p. 161. Among this Yörük, with an average herd of about 250 sheep per family, there is 'a strong ideology which calls for supportive behavior among agnates, particularly in dealings across close descent lines.' The richness of people is generally demonstrated by acquiring second wives at high bride prices, by devoting much wealth to hospitality and charity and by interacting with kinsmen in a preferential way (Idem, p. 168). In my view, this means a high levelling rate of income distribution and, subsequently, a rather comfortable position for poor members.

50. It is also typical that M. Noth or J. Bright and even R. de Vaux do not mention the phenomenon at all. The latter provides some facts about oikoidal towns and cities (Id., p. 72-74). If poor people (*ebjonim*) can be found, Weber points to two possibilities (GAR, III, p. 55). In post-exilic times, the

This is clearly related to the obvious difficulties of coming up with a reliable picture of agriculture ('Cain's work').

All this has provided *sedentary* people within 'Western Culture' with one of the strongest prejudicial notions: *wandering peoples are criminals, uncontrollable scum.* The authorities and the ideologues did everything to foster these prejudices because they belong to the hard core of sedentary legitimation.[51] How is this non-conformist ('Cain') behavior treated in Weber's writings? And what about 'criminal wandering' behavior?

How Weber perceived the Bedouin is clearly stated at the end of section II. The two serious mistakes he (also) made can now be concluded from the discussion so far. First, he makes the overly strong suggestion that the so-called Cain's sign/mark indicates that the bearer is a criminal. From the *Genesis* text quoted, I can only conclude that this sign *protects the bearer from being slain*. The example of the *Yellow Star* is obvious here: this clearly had the first function. Second, here (again) it is proven that Cain is not damned *'to be on the move forever'*. Although *Genesis* in this case is not specific enough, the safest conclusion is that the peasant Cain had to wander till he settled again in the land of Nod, where he built a 'city' for his son Enoch. Therefore, *Cain is a sedentarian temporarily on the move because he committed a crime.*

Now, a quite different type of people come to the fore. They are no doubt wanderers but also 'in between' people: the *'Kleinviehzüchter'* and the patriarchs. In the entire passage, Weber gave the impression that the breeding of 'small' animals equals a socially and politically impotent constellation. Clans or tribes, however, can have enormous herds of sheep and goats. Only the power of numbers gave them substantial political power. I cannot imagine that patriarchs were people with only a few sheep. Sometimes these *'Kleinviehzüchter'* were for Weber synonymous with *'Halbnomade'* and another time with *'Hirten'*. A *'Halbnomade'* is comparable with 'a woman who is only a little bit pregnant'; a shepherd is only a short-distance manager of a flock. Weber's poor conceptualization in this respect is a fact with which I cannot deal further.

What about the criminal record of *'Kleinviehzüchter'* and patriarchs? In fact, Weber looked into the *perception* of these peoples in the common opinion of the so-called 'monarchy' ('the Patriarch legend'). In connection with this legend,

---

poor could be found only within the city-demos of petty traders, craftsmen etc; in pre-exilic times, however, Weber finds them only within the small peasantry exploited by town patricians. But a few pages later, he notes from a source 'aber es sollte eigentlich keine israelitischen Bettler geben' (Idem, p. 73).

51. The whole literature about the way gypsies are treated in police and other bureaucratic reports through the ages (to this day), or people who live in caravans, is illuminating. See, for instance, L. Lucassen et al, *Gypsies and other itinerant groups. A socio-historical approach* (London: Macmillan, 1998). For an interesting comparison between Jews and Gypsies see W. Wippermann, *"Wie die Zigeuner". Antisemitismus und Antiziganismus im Vergleich* (Berlin: Elefanten Press, 1997).

Weber reached the nucleus of the Pariah question, announced above as the hard-core of his ideological position. According to Weber, the legend provided a profile of patriarchs.[52] They were isolated house-fathers of large families who did not cooperate politically. They were pastoral-nomads, metics on sufferance [*geduldete Metöken*] and true believers in a peaceful God. They received land for animal breeding from the sedentary population in a peaceful way and subdivided this peacefully among their family members. They also did not have the charisma of heroes.

Still, one has the impression that Weber is reproducing coolly, as stated, the *perception* of the patriarchs. However, in telling the last element of this Patriarch legend, this honorable Wilhelminian scholar inexplicably produces an emotional exclamation lasting a full page. In Weber's work one will never read another passage containing so much sarcasm, distaste, wrath and indignation. After displaying that incriminatory 'last element', I will quote the first and last sentences of the passage and in between the emotional keywords. Here, again, one regrets providing a translation because it is necessary to read the German original to understand all the connotations.

First then the 'last element' of the profile: the patriarch is willing to provide his patron [*Schutzherr*] with the most beautiful women, even his own wife. He then asks God to liberate her by means of plagues, although it had not crossed his mind to defend her honour [*Frauenehre*]. Weber continues with:

> 'To them it seems quite laudable to get rid of their own daughters instead of their guests so as not to injure the holiness of the law of hospitality. One has to distrust the ethic guiding their manners [*Verkehrsethik ist fragwürdig*]. For years an amusing play full of blackmail was performed between Jacob and his grandfather. In it they haggled [*Feilschen*] about desired women or the cattle gained from his grandson's work as a lad. In the end, the Ancestor Israel sneaks off from his grandfather's Lord while stealing the Lord's house-idol to assure himself a quiet retreat.'

Weber continues with a catalogue of abuses from which I only quote keywords:

'Jacob's Fraud' (is) absolutely in order ... a pious pastoral nomad out-haggled [*abfeilscht*] his brother[53] pictured as a thoughtless peasant[54] and hunter ... (Jacob) cheats the father with mother's help ... prays a very miserable prayer for fear ... to kill a brother or sell him as a slave ... this Joseph shows fiscal qualities in exploiting

---

52. GAR, III, p. 58 ff.

53. Weber's note: 'In the same way that Abel is confronted with Cain, so is the soft Jacob confronted with the wild peasant Esau as if he is 'the pious nomad who lives in a tent'. On the other hand, as Cain becomes a Bedouin, so Esau is seen as a fanatic hunter' (Idem, p. 58, 59 note 4).

54. Weber's note: 'Because in this way one has to translate 'isch sadeh' ('Man of the field', Gen. 25,27) and not as is done at present: 'Man who wanders over the steppe' which is not the meaning of 'sadeh'.' (Idem, p. 58 note 3).

Pharaoh's subjects ...' Weber compares the patriarchal behaviour with 'the ethic of a pirate and merchant ... or (with) Odysseus' excessive complaints [*maßloses Jammern*] ... (this remains) for us beyond the virtues of a hero [*Heldenwürde*] ... These are the characteristics of the ethic of a pariah-people [*Pariavolksethik*]. Its impact on the external moral [*Außenmoral*] of the Jews in the period of their dispersion as an international guest-people cannot be underestimated. With the very articulated pious obedience, they form the whole of the inner stature of this kind of people ... without any doubt, this stratum is, like powerless *metoiken*, the same as pastoral nomads [*Kleinviehzüchtern*] living among free citizens [*wehrhaften Bürgern*].'

The vision like that given by Weber on *Exodus*, when not mixed up with the pariah option, could reveal a healthy relativism or sarcasm about those patriarch stories. It could be the same mood in which Donald Redford wrote about the ironies of the Exodus events and the curious use of them in modern religion

'as a symbolic tale of freedom from tyranny ... namely that of Pharaoh, (which) was mild indeed in comparison to the tyranny of Yahweh to which they were about to submit themselves. As a story of freedom the *Exodus* is distasteful in the extreme ... and in an age when thinking men are prepared to shape their prejudice on the basis of a 3000-year-old precedent, it is highly dangerous.'[55]

Of course, Redford's modern (democratic) English contrasts sharply with Weber's class-bound German elite language from around 1900. The main difference, however, is that scholars like Redford try to work on a 1:1 relationship with reality. Weber, however, seems to take blood vengeance because reality cannot be manipulated in the direction of his own 'Geist'. Here Weber used Wilhelminian bourgeois-aristocratic values as (positive) criteria. Who else worries in this way about '*Frauenehre*'? What to think about a '*(Kriegs)Held*' with its '*Heldenwürde*' for whom/which it is utterly impossible to make a difference between '*Außen- und Innen-Moral*' or to accept a '*würdelose Erniedrigung*'? And who else shall judge everything except 100% fidelity to the Master as fraudulent behaviour?

The (in his eyes) negative values Weber expresses to characterise 'Pariahs' are indicated here with the verb '*feilschen*' (to chaffer, barter or haggle) as the ultimate market behavior and with '*maßloses Jammern*' (excessive complaining) which is something like 'to barter with emotions'. Therefore, he could conclude that their '*Verkehrsethik*' is '*fragwürdig*'; a conclusion which could follow the classical (and false) complaint about the Jews asking foreigners for interest on loans but not fellow Jews.

---

55. D. Redford, p. 422. For his profile of Yahweh see p. 275 ff.

In this passage Weber, therefore, displays the moral and sexual indignation of the Wilhelminian elite and the strong (religious) disappointment about the fact that the '*Stammvater Israels*' (which must be, in his eyes, his own ancestors) is only a fraudulent, sexually perverted, dishonorable and criminal pastoral-nomad. At least, he reproduces the '1914-1918 German elite thought' about *Helden versus Händler* (heroes versus merchants) in his Judaism analysis of the same period. At the time, this was the usual talk in his own circle to be demonstrated by his friend and co-editor Werner Sombart.[56]

In his '*Die Juden*' Sombart gave a profile of the Jews as '*Händler*'. Only a few years later he wrote one of the most poisoned, nationalistic pamphlets in favor of the German war efforts under the title '*Händler und Helden. Patriotische Besinnungen*'.[57] Here he abused not only the English and England as '*der Feind des deutschen Wesens*' ('the enemy of the German spirit'), but he also tried to eliminate on paper the race of '*Händler*' as such. This race he had adored in '*Die Juden*'. Now he ridiculed '*der englische Seeräuber*' with their '*ewigen Handeln und Feilschen*' ('eternal hawking and haggling'), which could be only fought in a religious war. This had to be a war between two ideologies: '*händlerische und heldische Weltanschauung und dementsprechende Kultur*'. This dichotomy, '*Händler und Held* forms the largest contradiction ... the two poles of all human behavior in the world.'

Later in his 'Nazi book',[58] Sombart reproduced these texts. There, he openly adored Mussolini as a typical Hero, found it quite reasonable to refuse – '*ohne jede Begründung*' – Jews from commanding and responsible positions (no army officers, lawyers, university professors, etc.) and he gave the highest priority to getting rid of the 'Jewish Spirit'. In 1914, most Germans, in particular those in academic circles, saw the English as '*Krämer*' (pedlars, hawkers). They constantly used words like '*Krämerkultur*', '*Krämerideale*', etc. Weber connected these words with sexual connotations to violence as he wrote about the English with their '*rapes and immoral hatred of (their) 'krämerhaften' economic war.*'[59] This was the mood in which he at the same time wrote about Judaism.

It seems furthermore striking that the key concept 'guest people' is already used in Weber's above-mentioned text. Weber knew that he was dealing with a legend. Indeed, at the moment[60] it is still clear that no single item of the relevant Bible passages fits into a *historically* verifiable chronology of some Israelite, Hebrew, let alone Jewish history. Strangely enough, Weber provided the legend as the *first historical setting* in which all negative (also positive?) elements of Jews

---

56. Compare W. Sombart, *Die Juden und das Wirtschaftsleben* (Leipzig: Duncker & Humblot, 1911), p. 332-334.

57. (München/ Leipzig: Duncker & Humblot, 1915). The citations come from p. VI, 16, 21, 4, 64 in that order.

58. W. Sombart, *Deutscher Sozialismus* (Berlin: Buchholz & Weisswange, 1934), p. 76 ff., 192 ff.

59. GPS, p. 117.

60. D. Redford, p. 258-263, 422-429.

popped up. In other words, in a legendary birthplace of a concept, Weber comprehensively located the reasons why *later* people/Jews had to become a guest people. In this way it became the '*Tatort*', the place where Cain committed his crime and where an '*eternal enmity*' could be created.

It seems, therefore, appropriate to give a detailed reconstruction of 'the crime'. A further aim is to show the mutual connection of a bunch of Weberian concepts. It does not matter which concept one chooses as an example. Still, there is a particular reason to take the following step. Thanks to Weber, the discussion is politicized to the utmost. To counterbalance this situation, I shall take the least ideologically loaded concept Weber used in this context.

THE CRIME AND ITS 'TATORT'

The shortest description of '*Pariavolk*' Weber used here is '*geduldete Metöken zwischen wehrhaften Bürgern*'. As usual with Weber, this definition is also highly ambiguous if seen as a historically 'correct' comparison. In the Greek classical period, metics (*metoikoi*) were privileged foreigners without civil rights in the settlement where they lived. *Met-oikoi* means literally 'the dwelling together' (*metoikion* is the name of the fee they had to pay). They were often Greeks but came mostly from other parts of the Mediterranean. Some became very influential due to their money capital (ca. 400 BC the Athenian metics Pasion and Phormion belonged to the richest people 'in the world') or to specific talents such as the orator Lysias.[61] Some stayed poor, and most of them occupied small and marginal jobs in commercial, service or handicraft activities.

Contrary to Weber's suggestion, they could serve in the army in separate divisions and could become normal oarsmen in the Athenian fleet. They could get several dispensations and receive the same protection from the courts as citizens, but could not contract legal marriages with citizens or own real-estate property. They even had their own god of a high status, *Metoikios Zeus*. In short: apart from some political and legal restraints, they had practically the same social position as a citizen.

Therefore, they were not '*geduldet*' (on sufferance) but had a definite status distinguishing them from all other foreigners (*xenoi*); they were '*wehrhaft*'[62] as Weber knew perfectly well from Thucydides [II, 31]. To call them '*machtlose Metöken*' is, to say the least, a contradiction in terms also within his own ideology.

---

61. H. Derks, *De Koe van Troje*, p. 257-259.
62. 'Wehrhaft' refers to the possibility of bearing and using arms. As usual, Weber has something different in mind when he uses this word. For example: 'Die volle Wehrhaftigkeit und also: politische Macht lag aber in vorexilischer Zeit in erster Linie bei den stadtsässigen Sippen.' (GAR, III, p. 32). For Weber, political power is *by definition* the property and use of arms, nothing more or less. This is probably the hard core of his ideology but also of his mentality. In the meantime, the citation demonstrates once again his heavy reductionism.

A historical parallel with the patriarchs, furthermore, is not possible because these were nomads and not sedentarized foreigners from the moment they arrived in Israel, according to the stories. This was the case, despite the fact that there was no such thing as Greek citizen-rights in the area until Hellenistic times. The question remains of why Weber made the comparison between pariahs and metics.

Weber's text discussed here was a *conclusion* for him. He prepared his opinion on the issue carefully. In the introduction to the second section, I provided the whole framework of his model, which stood at the start of his argumentation: the largest contradictions exist between city (patricians) and the Bedouin; 'pastoral-nomads' (defined as '*Kleinviehzüchter*') cooperate with peasants against both the city and the *bedu*. There he already talks about the '*Wehrverband*', and he made the early settlements in the region similar to the Greek *poleis*. Due to this comparison, he already operates on an extra-reality level suggesting that most settlements were real cities.

In enhancing this model by detailing the '*Kleinviehzüchter*', he again referred to the Cain constellation.[63] Weber, of course, saw the way from the Bedouin to semi-nomads, peasants and 'city' as the phases to pass through successively in an inevitable sedentarization. The effect here is that the main differences between pastoral-nomads and shepherds (mostly caring for the animals of some proprietor in the neighborhood) are blurred. With this, the 'semi-nomads' automatically get an (ideal-typical) intermediate position: '... they were *gerim* ... could easily receive full citizenship in the cities for their economically best achieving clans by means of contracts or after violent conflicts.'[64]

Who or what were *gerim*? In answering this question, Weber used all the keywords already discussed in intermediate passages.[65] They were related to 'crafts-men', 'merchants', 'ritually unclean', 'ritual alienation from the tribe' ['*rituellen Stammfremdheit*'], 'guest craftsmen', 'pariah caste', 'Dan tribe', and 'Cain'. In addition, he referred to Kammalar craftsmen in the south of India. Surprisingly, after the return from exile, *gerim* are also identified with a 'typical urban 'demos''. In the same sentence Weber also identified *gerim* with a 'plebean stratum', as if *demos* and *plebs* could be compared here anyway. To make this opportunistic name-dropping fully indigestible, only one page later he confessed that there were differences between 'a real '*Demos*' in a technical sense' and 'a '*popolo*' ... as used in medieval times.'[66] He denies that the *ger* or *toschab* from the sources, translated

---

63. GAR, III, p. 44 – 51. If one reads p. 16 ff., p. 44 ff. and p. 58 ff. ('the conclusion) one right after the other, one has a good example of how a Weberian ideal-type is constructed. It is not a discussion of several alternatives and situations ending in a well argued conclusion (' the model), but an *a priori* statement from which the details (i.e. the pivotal concepts within the model) are repeated to a large extent in slightly different configurations.
64. Idem, p. 46.
65. Idem, p. 34, 35.
66. Idem, p. 36.

with *Metöken* by Meyer, were free men who did not belong to the 'highly valued clans' [*vollwertigen Sippen*].[67]

To illustrate his case, Weber gave as an ideal-typical example the Danites – a quite promising choice. According to him, the members of the Dan tribe were '*Wanderhirten*' (pastoral nomads, I guess) who could not obtain fixed places within Israel/Judea till they could conquer the city Lajisch in the north. He must have known from Meyer[68] that this is half of the Biblical truth (let alone the real truth).

First, they were settled in the hills west of Jerusalem in the 'cities' Sora, Estaol, etc. but had to leave these places because of the pressure of 'Amorites'. The Dan people were known because they produced well-known artists. They had great commercial talents and had services to perform in the harbours. Their adherence to sectarian religious beliefs, however, made the authorities afraid and suspicious. This must be the reason that much later it was predicted that the Antichrist would come from the tribe of Dan. (There is, however, no reason to be afraid according to Donald Redford.[69] As is the case with Amalek, there is no extra-Biblical evidence for a Dan settlement in the north, and it seems wise to reserve judgment also for the rest.) Of course, Weber knew the relevant Meyer passages about the Dan tribe as he himself reproduced many particulars, and it is, therefore, unbelievable that he was unaware of their very negative image.

But what did the Biblical sources really say about the *gerim*? Roland de Vaux provides the clue:

> 'Nomad life also gives rise, invariably, to a law of asylum. In this type of society it is impossible and inconceivable that an individual could live isolated, unattached to any tribe. Hence, if a man is expelled from his tribe after a murder or some serious offence, or if, for any reason whatever, he leaves it of his own free will, he has to seek the protection of another tribe. There he becomes what modern Arabs call a *dahilc*, 'he who has come in', and what their forefathers called a *jâr*. The tribe undertakes to protect him, to defend him against his enemies and to avenge his blood, if necessary. These customs are reflected in two Old Testament institutions, that of the *ger* (which is the same word as the Arabic *jâr*) and that of cities of refuge.'[70]

The old texts consider, therefore, a *gerim* as one who stays for some time in another tribe, clan or place. Patriarch Abraham became a *gerim* in Hebron to bury his wife Sarah on land with a cave given to him by the Hittites (*Genesis* 23:4).

---

67. Idem, p. 32 and note 1.
68. E. Meyer, B. Luther, p. 524 ff.; see for the following also BHH, I, p. 351 ff. See also GAR, III, p. 34 where Weber used the Dan tribe in relation to Cain and the *gerim* for the first time.
69. D. Redford, p. 296.
70. R. de Vaux, p. 10.

Moses fled to Midian, helped the seven daughters of Reü'el and could stay and had a son with Zipporah: '... he called his name Ger'shom; for he said, 'I have been a sojourner [ger] in a foreign land' (*Exodus* 2:22). *Ger(im)* could be used as part of the characterization of the Rechabites.[71] The family of patriarch Jacob comprises three generations. Included were the servants, 'the resident aliens or *gerim* and the "stateless persons", widows and orphans, who lived under the protection of the head of the family'.[72]

All these meanings reproduce a peaceful attitude against foreigners and a far-reaching hospitality. I cannot see any reason for Weber's denigrating opinion about nomadic hospitality and the marrying of daughters. Furthermore, no patriarch can be put into the constellation Weber sketched as typical for *gerim*/pariah in any context.

The use of *gerim* underwent changes.[73] After settling in Canaan, the Israelites considered themselves 'owners' of the country and the former inhabitants as *gerim* unless they were assimilated by marriage or reduced to slavery. In the beginning, the *gerim* as free people had to hire out their services like the Levites with their own profession. '*Resident alien*' became an inferior position compared by the Israelites themselves to their own *gerim* situation in Egypt. De Vaux discovers, therefore, a similarity with the Spartan *perioikoi*, the suppressed original population of the Peloponnese. The only comparison to be made is that also *metoikoi* is a Greek word.

Apparently shortly before the Exile, however, a series of new provisions were made for the *gerim* to reduce their differences to the Israelites, to enhance the assimilation of their own (Israelite) *gerim*, and to pave the way for the assimilation of foreign *gerim*. They came to share in the social and religious advantages and obligations. They were entitled to justice and liable to the same penalties, while in everyday life they experienced no difficulties whatsoever. They had to observe the sabbath, fasting on the day of Atonement or celebrate Passover with the Israelites, provided that they were circumcised. They were subject to the same laws of cleanliness and so on. If one likes comparing, this *gerim* could be seen as *metoikoi* in the same way as I sketched the *real* Greek position.[74]

---

71. Idem, p. 15: '...you are to dwell in tents all your life, so that your days may be long in the land where you live as aliens (*gerim*).' Is this the beginning of the Ahasverus legend with which the next chapter starts?

72. Idem, p. 20.

73. See for the following Idem, p. 74-76.

74. Weber criticized Meyer (GAR III, p. 32 note 1) for making a difference between *ger* and *tôshab* (for Meyer resp. 'Metöken' and 'Klient') while he himself did not see any difference. De Vaux, p. 75,76, concludes that a *tôshab* seems less assimilated (socially and religiously), less firmly rooted in the land and also less independent than a *ger*.

PRELIMINARY CONCLUSIONS

At the end of this chapter, some conclusions can be directly scrutinized thanks to a publication about the pariah problem by Hyam Maccoby, emeritus fellow of the Leo Baeck College in London.[75] One citation is enough to reveal the problems he raises. Maccoby writes:

> 'Max Weber never put forward an explicit theory of antisemitism, but his concept of the Jews as a pariah people has obvious implications for the study of antisemitism ... Since in this book, which is chiefly about antisemitism, I also put forward a theory of the Jews as a pariah people, it is important to state at once how my theory differs from that of Weber. The basic difference is that Weber argues that the Jews made themselves into a pariah people by their adoption of a separatist religion; while I argue ... that the Jews became pariahs only because they were cast in that role by Christians ...'

In this last section, I will comment on this theory, first, indirectly by starting with some simple logical conclusions regarding the repeated use of *Metöken/-guests/pariahs* by Weber. Afterwards I shall return to Adorno and, now, Maccoby as well.

It is perfectly clear from the last part of my analysis that the three possible *gerim* meanings from Bible texts do not correspond with Weber's pariah model for several reasons, and the real *metic* position is not appropriate either. Furthermore, it could be shown how the nomadic elements (hospitality, etc.) are denied in a fundamental and even hostile way. Now it is easy to verify Weber's firm universalistic statements in WG/EC and to see the very weak basis of his argumentation.[76]

Next, it seems obvious that Weber's use of the pariah concept does not refer to any historical reality nor to the perception of historical patriarchs but to the *negative perception of Jews and their 20th century position*. This perception is transformed into an *ideal type* and an universal truth suitable for all times and all corners of the world. Apparently, this is made possible through the immanent and original *anti-nomadic moment* (Cain-Abel syndrome) and, therefore, the general sedentarians aversion against non-conformism. Therefore, one can better speak of a *pariah complex*.

For all fundamentalist sedentarians, this complex serves as the historical legitimation to *stigmatize and discredit* nomads, all wanderers as such, and ir-regular, uncontrollable market peoples or the ones who are regarded as such, like

---

75. H. Maccoby, *A Pariah People. The Anthropology of Antisemitism* (London: Constable, 1996). The negative opinion I have of this book is only the result of reading of 'Weber' passages. In passing I read many interesting things on which I cannot elaborate here. In particular, I fully agree with his thesis (last chapter) that the Holocaust is no mystery, although I probably have a different argumentation for this. The citation is from p. 20.
76. See WG, p. 748 and EC, p. 1247.

the Jews. Furthermore, there is envisaged a negatively loaded *guest* position in order to keep the 'guests' only temporarily within your reach and *to avoid any form of assimilation*. In the next chapter I shall elaborate on this point. At last one can conclude: in Weber's time, as the many given examples have shown, the *Nomadic Question* and the *Jewish Question* are strongly intertwined in the sense that the *former is the general and the latter the specific 'question'*.

These results confirm Adorno's opinion that there is a mutual relationship, first, between nomadism and Jewishness and, second, that this relationship must be connected in a profound way to the nomadism-sedentarism antagonism. This opens a new avenue of fundamental research. From the above analysis it also follows that Adorno's *Urgeschichte des Antisemitismus* can be reconstructed through a study of the *Urgeschichte* of the Patriarchs. Paradoxically enough, this leads to confrontation not with a real history of so-called 'patriarchs' in old Palestine, but with 19th and 20th century anti-Judaism (Meyer, Sombart, Wellhausen, Weber, etc.).

From this follows, next, that it is highly preferable to make the distinction between *antisemitism* (racially oriented -ism from the 19th and 20th centuries in many European countries, the USA, etc.), *anti-Judaism* (religiously oriented -ism originating in the West-European Middle Ages and still active today), and *anti-Jewish measures* (secular measures from a social, cultural and economic nature taken against some Jews sometimes in antiquity but mainly from the Middle Ages onwards).[77] So, only in the 19th and 20th centuries could all three phenomena be active together, but they have their own history and are in need of their own explanation. In my view, many misunderstandings (see the Goldhagen hype) about the un-mysterious so-called 'Holocaust' could be avoided by adopting the given distinction.

In this way of defining problems it is easier to see why, for example, Weber is a diehard anti-Judaist in his Bible studies. Because he universalized and secularized his *pariah* concept while making it also a 'secular' concept, Weber contributed to antisemitism and to anti-Jewish measures (not very different from anti-foreigner measures). He, furthermore, 'confessed that, personally and subjectively, I am inclined to value highly the meaning of the biological heritage [*Erbgut*]'[78] because of 'highly rewarding' racial studies which probably shall be significant in the future. Apparently for this reason, Weber thinks a 'racial' determination ["*rassenmäßige*" *Mitbedingtheit*] of Jews as '*Fremdvolk*' must be 'certainly available'

---

77. Of course, there are also anti-Israel measures or critique which are erroneously considered by some as 'typical antisemitism'. They belong to the species anti-americanism, anti-arabism and all down the alphabet of the day-to-day political discourses.
78. GAR, I, p. 15.

[*sicher vorhanden*] although one cannot prove it yet.[79] Apart from this, Weber adopted the erroneous and highly ambiguous general thesis: 'wherever the Jews appeared, they were the agents of the money economy'.[80] With all this he is practically an antisemite as well.

Maccoby documents another and quite serious problem, namely, the acceptance of the stigmatization and criminalization by the victims. He is rather critical of Weber's *Antike Judentum* and sometimes comes to the same conclusions as I do. However, as a responsible and critical Jew, he accepts that all Jews are pariahs because they are named so by Weber and others. This is not just Maccoby's problem.

In 1944, Hannah Arendt wrote an article about *The Jew as Pariah*, which is, strangely enough, unknown to Maccoby.[81] Arendt created the same problem: uncritically accepting Weber's concept as representative for her own position. In chapter nine of this book, when enough material has been gathered to make more definitive conclusions, I will come back to this problem. Furthermore, Maccoby did study Weber and his circle through the writings of, in particular, Arnaldo Momigliano who displays curious attitudes (see chapter 1).

The latter stressed that 'the Patriarchs lived before the Hebrews received their God-given law and God-given land' and, therefore, there is no need to define the Jewish status; exit pariah-problem. In other words: once sedentarized ('The Settlement') one is liberated from the primitive, inimical nomad who may be a pariah, too. Thanks to this ostrich policy, we come across a most fundamental aspect of the pariah complex, the denial of the own ancestral history. Furthermore, here one can find the source of the discrimination of the 'Diaspora' in favour of 'Jerusalem' and – in secular terms – the source of the Zionist creed.

Whatever the difficulties with Max Weber's *Antike Judentum* or his sociology of religion in general, a world historical panorama could be unrolled in his defence of theological and ideological positions against historical or social realities. The dimensions of the most profound antagonism between the nomadic and the sedentary modes of life or production have been shown in this part of the study. Weber's biased analysis of the Chinese and Central Asian realities revealed in particular the weak empirical basis of his work, and now his weak ideological basis can be demonstrated. However, without Weber's extensive and wide-ranging studies, it would have been more difficult to discover the world historical dimensions of the nomadic – sedentarian antagonisms *and* interdependencies. Furthermore, it must be clear that the *Nomadic Question* and the *Jewish Question* are inseparable.

---

79. WG, p. 720 and EC, 1202 with a remarkable translation. Instead of Weber's certainty appears 'probably exist in one sense or another'. Weber's use of a word like 'Blutsfremd' in this context is not very innocent either.
80. WG, p. 721 and EC, 1203.
81. Reprinted in JP, p. 67-91.

This interrelation must now be discussed in an even more dramatic context, the European one. Again, Weber gave us the hint on how to do this. His *gerim* analysis resulted in a profile of an intermediary position: no longer pariah and nearly pariah again. Within a European context it is this highly ambiguous, social, cultural or intellectual status of 'the Jews' which is coupled with the most dramatic events in European history, not in Asian or African, let alone American history. The theory and practice of the *guest principle* in Europe will give the pariah position a much less abstract profile.

The Courts of the Inquisition. Documentary representation, Bernard Picart (1722). Source: M. Hroch, A. Skýbová, *Ecclesia Militans* (Leipzig: Edition Leipzig, 1988), p. 127.

AN EUROPEAN HISTORICAL CONTEXT

'The first World War exploded the European comity of nations beyond repair, something which no other war had ever done. Inflation destroyed the whole class of property owners ...something which no monetary crisis had ever done so radically before. Unemployment ... reached fabulous proportions ... Civil wars ... were not only bloodier and more cruel then all their predecessors; they were followed by migrations of groups who, unlike their happier predecessors in the religious wars, were welcomed nowhere and could be assimilated nowhere. Once they had left their homeland, they remained homeless, once they had left their state they became stateless; once they had been deprived of their human rights they were rightless, the scum of the earth. ... Every event had the finality of a last judgement, a judgement that was passed neither by God nor by the devil, but looked rather like the expression of some unredeemably stupid fatality. Before totalitarian politics consciously attacked and partially destroyed the very structure of European civilization, the explosion of 1914 and its severe consequences of instability had sufficiently shattered the facade of Europe's political system to lay bare its hidden frame. ... The very phrase "human rights" became for all concerned – victims, persecutors, and onlookers alike – the evidence of hopeless idealism or fumbling feeble-minded hypocrisy.'

Hannah Arendt, *The Origins of Totalitarianism* (1951, 1979)

4. GUESTS IN GHETTOS

'Ich will stehen und ruhen, du aber sollst gehen!'
Jesus against Ahasverus, the 'eternal Jew'.

Traditionally, the Netherlands are known for their hospitality. Since the end of the sixteenth century, Jews have formed a small and rather influential part of its population. They dwelt mainly in the city of Amsterdam, although small pockets were spread over the rest of the country as well.

This remained so up to April of 1943 when the deportation of 75-80% of all 160,000 Jews in the Netherlands was completed. Certainly in light of this deportation, the idea of typical Dutch hospitality has to be revised and be given realistic dimensions. The other country where Jews lived for centuries and were destroyed, Poland, has displayed from time immemorial a harsh antisemitism which did not substantially decrease after 1945. Whether we have to blame Dutch hypocrisy or Polish discrimination as additional reasons for the German destruction of Jews, in both cases we are confronted with a minority tolerated for centuries as what Weber and many others should call 'guests'. How dangerous these objects of hospitality could live becomes apparent in a concept like 'ghetto'. A rather strange conceptual relationship between both can be discovered.

Everywhere in Christian Europe, Protestant or Roman Catholic, reference was made to the Ahasverus legend when talking about Jews (and sometimes Gypsies). Not, however, to the contradiction in the answer Ahasverus got from Jesus who, according to a German legend from 1602, wanted to rest a while during his dramatic walk to Golgotha. Of course, this story is treated as if Jesus was not a Jew but a typical blue-eyed, blond and Christian West European. A misunderstanding which seems typical for the way the hospitality principle is treated in our regions.

There is, however, a more important contradiction between the one who eternally has to roam around and the one who is seated and, therefore, quite sedentary: *Nomadic Man* is confronted here with *Sedentary Man* as a consequence of a curse which made the former a criminal and the latter a copy of a god, a near saint and, certainly, an innocent and good man, as sympathetic as the guest principle. However, a typical childish question while pointing to an emperor is: why were these cursed wandering Jews so often viewed as ghetto dwellers by nature and, therefore, sedentary in a strict sense as well? Let's try to unveil this mystery by looking first at the nomadic side of the guest problem.

THE NOMADIC JEW AS 'GUEST'

In publications from Dutch pre-war Protestant writers, one can find the following characterization about

> '... the Jewish people, a pastoral people from Arabic blood. All the characteristics of a nomadic people can be discovered in the Jewish blood. Freedom, experienced by the nomads of the desert as a delicate thing, is of a very different type to that of the Germans [the ancient Germanic tribe] ... The space in which nomadic tribes live is without many limits, but the means of existence are very few .... The Germans [the ancient Germanic tribe] were fixed to specific spaces. They did not wander ... Agriculture was their age-old business and from this they developed all kinds of means of existence. The unity of the soil brought a solidly based property-law ... These characteristics... show till today the main difference between Jew and what is called Aryan.'[1]

The author, Dr. Diemer, a sociologist and newspaper reporter in Rotterdam, was an influential member of the Calvinist party (and trade union) from which the Dutch pre-war prime minister, Dr. H. Colijn, originated. The latter wrote a preface for one of Diemer's books. In any case, these two, the Protestant politician (The Hague) and the journalist (Rotterdam), were in a good position to indoctrinate parents of the yelling children in The Hague (see introduction).

In pre-war Holland Colijn was well-known as 'Deutschfreundlich', and recently he became seen as a war criminal thanks to his 'duties' in the former Dutch East Indies. In his book on National Socialism, Diemer in his turn accepted so much of the Nazi propaganda that he, in fact, acted as a full-fledged antisemite in the usual hypocritical Dutch way (after 'Calvinism is utterly incompatible with National Socialism', this Calvinist stressed time and again only the Roman Catholic support for Nazism). There is, of course, nothing against using sources like the publications of Hitler, Goebbels, Rosenberg, Fritsch or Günther, and of NS-German Protestant opinion leaders or well-known Old Testament scholars like G. Kittel with his antisemitic *Die Judenfrage* (1933). They all were used, however, without any criticism. But above all, Diemer reproduced Werner Sombart's opinions in adoration.

In a typically racist way, Sombart once fanatically condemned the *Assimilations-Juden* as those who committed '*Artvernichtung*' (extermination of the Jewish

---

1. H. Diemer, *Het Duitse Nationaal-Socialisme. De west-europese democratie op de proef gesteld* (Kampen: Kok, 1934), p. 90.

race)![2] These Jews are immoral; they are *'Duckmäuser und Leisetreter'* (roughly to be translated as people who secretly lie and copy); they destroy one's personality and create *'Jammerlappen von denen uns Gott bewahre'* (peoples who constantly lament, Heaven forbid). Sombart even told them that 'they left their own people and went over to the enemy.' He threatened them:

> '...this kind of Jew shall never be able to deny their Jewishness ... even not when they change their names because their physiognomy will always betray them, and every hour they shall tremble for fear of being discovered.' Sombart only wanted to support the 'aufrechter Nationalljude ein ... Kerl den man hassen mag, aber vor dem man Respekt haben muss' ('honest nationalist Jew, a fellow which one may hate but must also respect').

This is a fellow who, notwithstanding his social and physical sufferings, sticks heroically to his own creed. In fact, Sombart used here the same kind of Wilhelminian elite value pattern as Weber in his patriarch analysis. In even stronger words the same argument is used today by no-one less than the Sefardic Chief Rabbi of Israel, Baksi-Doron: the Jewish People was threatened less by the Holocaust than by the assimilation of Jews into modern society![3]

Why the famous Sombart interfered in this hot issue will be shown below, but the effects of this can be discovered through the influential Protestant opinion leader Diemer. Sombart inspired him to give the following 'politically correct' demonstration of his guest principle:

> '... the Jews have to accept the new thinking in Germany ... surrender their privileges [hoogheidsrechten] ... (They) cannot try to infiltrate within original German circles by means of assimilation ..(or).. propagate their own opinions which, in any case, are not based on a Christian foundation ... the great problem is whether there is a possibility to build a real Jewish community which can

---

2. W. Sombart a.o., *Judentaufen* (München: Georg Müller Verlag, 1912), p. 16-19. See also his small essay *Die Zukunft der Juden* (Leipzig: Duncker & Humblot, 1912), p. 54-61. After the publication of his international bestseller *Die Juden und das Wirtschaftsleben* (1911), Sombart stayed involved in debates about the 'future of German Jews', etc. The still unknown *Judentaufen* is a booklet with one long lecture from Sombart and reactions from famous people like Alfred Weber (brother of Max), Friedrich Naumann, Frank Wedekind, Heinrich Mann, Matthias Erzberger, etc. To study the antisemitic character of his writings, both booklets are indispensable. The official antisemitic circles started a campaign in support of *Die Juden und das Wirtschaftsleben*, while additional booklets were published like J. Henningsen, *Professor Sombarts Forschungsergebnisse zur Judenfrage. Eine zeitgemäße Betrachtung* (Hamburg: Deutscher Verlag, 1912). H. was the 'Generalsekretär' of a rather important antisemitic association. The antisemitic bible Th. Fritsch, *Handbuch der Judenfrage. Die wichtigsten Tatsachen zur Beurteilung des jüdischen Volkes* (Reprint, Bremen: Faksimile Verlag, 1991) relied heavily on Sombart.

3. *NRC-Handelsblad* 28-1-1999. See also the comparable sloganizing from the theologian Emil Fackenheim quoted in A. Dershowitz, *The Vanishing American Jew. In search of Jewish Identity for the Next Century* (New York: Simon & Schuster, 1997), p. 63.

remain as a guest among the German people under alien-laws but not as members of the German nation.'[4]

Assimilation must be avoided in order to prevent racial, religious and cultural mixture; they may be guests from some foreign country apparently without protection under German law as if Jews had not received religious freedom and equality under the law since 1871. But let's look into Sombart's influential 'nomadic theory' in more detail and compare it with other more or less theoretical or ideological approaches in his time before we return to Diemer's other hero.

Sombart's (Jewish) Nomad

One of the reasons Weber started his analysis of a *Wirtschaftsethik* of Judaism was the publication a few years earlier of Sombart's *Die Juden und das Wirtschaftsleben.*[5] At that time, the author was already an internationally acknowledged economic historian, while Weber was still unknown outside certain German circles. The book is certainly a new demonstration of Sombart's erudition, but it is also often packed in quasi-objective and often very arrogant scientific language.

In his introduction Sombart symptomatically confessed that he does not want to contribute to a '*rassenmäßige*' (racially directed) historiography. This seems to reflect a bad conscience, as P. Mendes-Flohr rightly suggests.[6] Here Sombart also pointed out how he 'by accident' came to write a book, which can easily be reduced to two 'accidental' thoughts. The first is: that fabulous capitalism is very bad; and those fabulous Jews are responsible for capitalism, therefore .... On this always supported opinion ('Is not the largest money speculator in the world, Mr. Soros, a Jew?' etc.), I do not want to elaborate. The other, and the interconnection between the two, must be introduced as follows.

From Weber, indeed, Sombart received the first inspiration for this book. With Weber and Jaffé, Sombart issued the *Archiv für Sozialwissenschaft und*

---

4. H. Diemer, p. 95, 96; italics from Diemer. Not only Protestants were influenced by Sombart but leading Catholics as well. See J. Ramaekers, The Attitude of Dutch Roman Catholics towards the Jews 1900-1940, in: *Dutch Jewish History* (1989), pp. 371-387. It is always possible to point to more serious examples as, for instance, W. Mühlmann, *Rassen, Ethnien, Kulturen. Moderne Ethnologie* (Neuwied: Luchterhand, 1964) who restored after 'Auschwitz' fully uncritical the whole pre-war racial humbug from Von Eckstedt et al., including Max Weber's guest-principle (p. 194, 198).

5. Sombart's *Die Juden* is translated (not very accurately) into American by M. Epstein with the title *The Jews and Modern Capitalism* (New York: Franklin, 1913). It went through six reprints; in Germany it was sold until 1928 (ca. 15,000 copies); translations followed in French, Polish, Hebrew (only 4th chapter!), Italian, etc.

6. P. Mendes-Flohr, Werner Sombart's *The Jews and Modern Capitalism:* An analysis of its ideological premises, in: *Leo Baeck Yearbook* 21 (1976), p. 87-107; Idem, Martin Buber and the Metaphysicians of Contempt, in: J.Reinharz (Ed.), *Living with Antisemitism. Modern Jewish Responses* (Hanover: University Press of New England, 1987), p. 145 ff.; p. Vidal-Naquet, *The Jews*, p. 118.

Sozialpolitik, and here he read Weber's first essay in *Wirtschaftsethik* (1904/05). In Weber's (false) thesis positing a profound relationship between Protestant puritanism and some 'Capitalist Spirit', he pointed several times to Jewish characteristics.[7] Of course, Weber and Sombart were quite different personalities. Mostly, they covered their quarrels by being silent about each other's work but, in the end, this was an untenable position for both.[8] Why they were sharp antipodes cannot be discovered through ambiguous Freudian speculations but by studying, for instance, their different opinions about Jews and nomads. Against which theories, then, could Weber come up with his alternative sketched in the former chapter?

Sombart discovered that

'a very special People – a desert People and a nomadic People, a hot People – is dispersed under fundamental alien Peoples – wet – cold, irresolute [*schwerblütig*], and soil-bound Peoples; they lived and worked here under, again, very special living conditions.'[9]

If Jews had not sedentarized among an antagonistic 'race', according to Sombart's thesis, there could never have exploded that *'Knalleffekt der menschlichen Kultur: (der) moderne Kapitalismus ...'* ('that explosion of human culture: modern capitalism'). In this case, the maximum they could have achieved was comparable to the role Armenians play 'nowadays' in the Caucasus (Sombart wrote at the time of the genocide of the Armenians by the Turks), the Kabyl in Algeria and the Chinese or Persians in the Indies. In the meantime, he also says that at present the large influence of Jews in economic life is decreasing. One of the main reasons for this is that, starting with the big companies and banks, bureaucratism is spreading rapidly at the cost of commercialism.

His thesis is told as well in this way: capitalist society is the result of a union of Jews with an extraordinary capacity for commerce and of 'Nordic peoples' (in

---

7. For example GAR, I, p. 5, 17, 33ff., 38 ff., 181 in particular the long note 2 were Weber already talked about the Jewish 'Paria-Kapitalismus'. See also Weber's attack on Sombart's theory in WG, p. 367 ff., 720 ff. and EC, p. 611 ff., 1202 ff. For a comparison of the two see A. Mitzman, *The Iron Cage. An Historical Interpretation of Max Weber* (New Brunswick: Transaction, 1985), p. 256 ff. or Idem, *Sociology and Estrangement. Three sociologists of Imperial Germany* (New Brunswick: Transaction, 1987), p. 186 ff. and Idem, Personal Conflict and Ideological Options in Sombart and Weber, in: W. Mommsen; J. Osterhammel (Ed.), *Max Weber and his Contemporaries* (London: Unwin Hyman, 1989), p. 99-106 and many other passages in this interesting reader.
8. From Sombart's point of view see, for instance, his books like *Der Bourgeois* (München: Duncker & Humblot, 1913), p. 7, 305 ff.; Idem, *Der Moderne Kapitalismus* (München/ Leipzig: Duncker & Humblot, 1919), Vol. I, p. 881 ff. Idem, *Idem* (München/ Leipzig: Duncker & Humblot, 1927), Vol. III, p. 428 ff.
9. Sombart, *Die Juden*, p. VII, VIII. For Sombart's position see also H. Derks, *De Koe van Troje*, p. 8, 11, 41-48. Also Hannah Arendt was not impressed by Sombart's thesis as can be seen in OT, p. 13 ff. note 4.

particular the German tribes) with their equally remarkable abilities for science and technology.[10] Jews are one of those Oriental races 'bred and burnt' in the dry-hot air of the deserts. Agriculture is only possible in an oasis culture in which farmers constantly fear for drought, scorching winds, locust swarms and, in particular,

> 'Bedouin tribes which can appear any moment out of the desert robbing, killing, pillaging people and country, sometimes even taking possession of his holding if the fancy seizes them. ... Such a tribe of restless wandering Bedouin were the Hebrews, when about the year 1200 BC they fell upon Canaan, plundering and killing as they went and, finally, decided to stay here resting from their eternal wanderings.'[11]

Thus, Sombart constructs the reverse of the Ahasverus legend: the eternal wandering Bedouin, Hebrew, had to rest and settle to become Jew. In his opinion, after The Settlement these ex-Bedouin established a so-called *Fronhofwirtschaft*, the typical Sombartian expression for an Oikos. In this case, the powerful lived in cities and the repressed peasants (the original population) outside in the country. Probably, also impoverished Bedouin were able to populate the country.

Strangely enough, Sombart supposes that the oikoidal upper layers of the twelve ex-Bedouin tribes also remained nomads or semi-nomads, cattle farmers (he cites: *'Judah's teeth are white with milk'*). Sombart's Oikos, however, is a self-contained or autarkic economy of some lord. To be clear, the *Fronhofwirtschaft* is originally a manor[12] of a Frankish lord strictly based on a grain-growing agriculture within some feudal relationship. It is utterly incompatible with (large scale) market-directed animal husbandry.

The above opinion we have to call 'Sombart I' because, referring to Wellhausen and Budde, he demonstrates a remarkable intellectual flexibility by supporting the opposite position as well: Jahweh is a desert and nomadic divinity; old nomadic traditions were maintained by Ezra and Nehemiah without taking heed of the intervening period of agriculture. The Priestly Code, he allowed Wellhausen to say, 'takes care not to mention the settled life in Canaan ... it strictly limits itself

---

10. Sombart, *Die Juden*, p. 403. For the next passage see in particular the last chapter, p. 403-434.
11. Idem, p. 405. See also W. Keller's text in note 14 previous chapter.
12. In the German '*Fron*' both the 'being a Lord/Herr' and 'doing a service' is combined. '*Hof*' means in this case the same as the Latin '*curia*' used in relevant documents as a medium-large, alleged 'autarkic manor' of a free landowner during the 8th -12th centuries in Western Europe. Within this so-called 'Fronhofs- or Villikationssystem', unfree laborers and dependant tenant farmers are used for production, etc. The Lord's whole *oikos*-household was guided in his name by a *meier (villicus)*. Often this landowner was the administrative head of the surrounding region, sometimes also a judge, sometimes a not too high person in the religious hierarchy, etc. Often he combined these functions but always as part of a larger (administrative) whole: a large 'Grundherrschaft', a diocese, etc. Sombart must have a rather specific perception of old Israel.

to the wanderings in the desert, and in all seriousness wants to be regarded as a desert Code'.[13]

Now, Sombart does not doubt that as late as the fifth century BC there must have been strong nomadic influences, and not only in the ruling classes. Since the Babylonian Exile, the vicissitudes of the Jewish people could not but arouse any slumbering desert and nomad feelings. This, even if we were inclined to assume a 'partly sedentary life' for about five hundred years:

'... Nomadism and Saharism ... was kept alive through adaptation or selection ... throughout the centuries, therefore, Israel has remained a desert and nomadic people.' Only one page further he arrives at the far-reaching conclusion, that 'the Jews (are) an eternal desert and nomadic people either by the process of selection or of adaptation.'[14] ('Sombart II').

Thanks to both Sombarts, the argumentation becomes wholly based on analogies, combinations from half- and whole truths, interlarded with many suggestive comparisons. These suggestions will certainly arouse more suspicion against Jews than civilities. Subtly, in Sombart II he recalls the legend of Ahasverus, the Wandering Jew, or he qualifies big cities, the preferred dwelling places of Jews, 'the direct continuations of the desert'; he even tells the reader that the Jews found here in the Nordic Germanic countries 'at last their Canaan'.[15] This implies in Sombart's social Darwinistic thinking and suggestive writing that Jews arrived or settled to conquer and repress the 'original population'!

The heart of his reasoning, therefore, can almost be seen as a powerful work of fiction which is able to inspire scientific work as well. Sombart assumes that the notorious 'Jewish drive to accumulate money' can be found in the following constellation[16]:

'From the endless wastes of sand, from the pastoral economy, springs the opposite of that old 'bound-to-earth' way of life: capitalism ... only in the shepherd's calling, never in the farmer's, could the idea of gain [Erwerb] have

---

13. Idem, *Juden* p. 407.
14. Idem, p. 409.
15. Idem, p. 415.
16. Idem, p. 425-427. Ismar Elbogen in a noteworthy article on *Judaism* in the *Encyclopaedia of the Social Sciences* (New York: Macmillan, 1949), Vol. VIII, p. 430-442 wrote about Sombart's 'most impressive' book: 'In the light of careful study of the sources this view is completely one-sided and exaggerated. Only this can be proved: the traditional mode of life of the Jews enabled them to participate in capitalistic activities and their religion did not hinder them from exploiting these opportunities, notwithstanding the fact that the spirit of both the Old and New Testament is diametrically opposed to the spirit of capitalism. It is not Judaism, but the individual Jew who has contributed to the development of the modern economic system...' (p.437, 438).

taken root, and the conception of unlimited production have become a reality.[17] Only in the shepherd's calling could the view have become dominant that in economic activities the abstract quantity of commodities matters, not whether they are fit or sufficient for use. Only in the shepherd's calling was counting a prime necessity. Moreover, the rationalism which ... is inseparable from nomadic life, here entered into play... Nomadism is the progenitor of capitalism.... Now desert and wandering ... are not the only forces which moulded the Jewish spirit. There were others, not as effective as the first, but supplementary to them.... Money was the burden Jews in particular had to bear... For in money ... are united both elements which consume the Jewish spirit: desert and wandering, Saharism and Nomadism. Money is as little concrete as the land from which the Jews sprang; money is only a mass, a lump, like the herd; it is mobile as the wandering life; nowhere it is rooted in fertile soil like the plants or the trees. Their constant concern with money distracted the attention of the Jews from a qualitative, natural view of life to quantitative, abstract conceptions and ways of valuation. The Jews fathomed all the secrets that lay hidden in money... They became lords of money and, through it, lords of the world...'[18]

For preaches like this, Sombart obtained substantial support in particular from antisemitic groups or writers like Theodor Fritsch (1852-1933), the main anti-semitic propagandist at the time. However, several (too few) scholars criticized his words; one example will suffice here. Countering such 'askewed and invidious' thoughts, the metaphysician Martin Buber came up with counter-arguments without considering the differences between Sombart I and II. They concern the untenable thesis that Jews in their formative period (whoever that could be at the time) were diggers of the soil and nothing else:

'All of the Palestinian period attests to so great a love of the soil and the exal-tation of its cultivation as is found but in a few other nations ... Seldom has there been another people so self-contained and so glorying in its rootedness ... The whole spiritual and religious life of ancient Judaism was closely bound up with the life of the soil, the life of the familiar earth.' (1915)[19]

---

17. Idem, *Der moderne Kapitalismus*, Vol. III, p. 426 ff. Sombart strongly ridicules Weber's ideas about a capitalistic impact of the Puritan belief. Twenty years after his *Juden* he writes here: 'It belongs to the most stupid opinions ... to perceive the *Erwerbstrieb* as a primitive drive of Man. On the contrary. Natural man does not bother about earning as much as possible money.' Etc.
18. For a detailed comparison and the real relations between nomadism (and animal husbandry in general), a money-economy and the peasant/ farmers way of life see the first chapter of my *De Koe van Troje*. Sombart only wildly associates things which are unrelated. The most remarkable for a learned historian and economist like he is his laymans equation of a money-economy with capitalism: the latter is, of course, a money economy, but not every money-economy has something to do with capitalism.
19. P. Mendes-Flohr, Martin Buber, p. 147. See also W. Mosse, Judaism, Jews and Capitalism. Weber, Sombart and Beyond, in: *Leo Baeck Yearbook* 24 (1979), p. 3-15.

Buber came up with the antagonistic position for the after-Exile situation: it was only with their Exile that 'the Jews indeed became a nomadic people... robbed of its natural context'. In this critique of Sombart's study (first peasants, later nomads), he demonstrated the main rift through Jewish discourse between *diaspora* and *homeland* (Zion). Both positions are attacked and defended in a way comparable with Sombart's and Buber's mutually incompatible ideological stands. The Zionist view, for instance, was and is 'that antisemitism was a permanent condition of the Jewish dispersion, and homelessness was thus its specific cause'.[20] Indeed, we are dealing here with a typical sedentarian ideology. Its negative valuation of, for instance, diaspora or homelessness will be discussed in the chapters six to nine.

The Police and the Medical Doctor

In an optimistic mood one could label Sombart's and Buber's approaches as social scientific and theoretical. The following example demonstrates how a classical problem is solved from a practical way of coping with nomadism. At the end of the 19th century also in Germany as elsewhere rules and laws were framed regulating the life of Gypsies.[21] The Munich police in Bavaria took the lead and established an office for coordinating actions against Gypsies (*Zigeunerzentrale*) which soon was extended to vagabonds or Gypsy-like itinerants. All possible data, photos, horses or fingerprints of Gypsies were registered and in 1925 there existed a databank of about 14,000 names of these people all over Germany. Twenty years earlier the head of the *Zigeunerzentrale*, Dillmann, published a *Zigeunerbuch* the first handbook for police officers with all kinds of information which became a bestseller among authorities. In other German states authorities copied these activities, conserted actions became possible, laws and regulations streamlined.

The pattern of control and regulation was so pervasive that it was difficult for Gypsies not to collide with the law. However, there existed far from a uniform legislation and every state or part of it sought to get rid of 'its own Gypsies' by pushing them across borders. Again it was the Bavarian authority who took the initiative to organize a conference in Munich (1911) in order to uniformize laws and regulations in all jurisdictions. That was not very easy. Fundamental differences of opinion appeared already with the first question *how to define a Gypsy*.

> 'The conference working paper [from the Munich police. D] had stressed that there existed few pure Gypsies and that it was therefore the Gypsies' way of life, their occupation and nomadic lifestyle, and not membership in a tribe or race,

---

20. B. Halpern, Reactions to Antisemitism in Modern Jewish History, in: J. Reinharz (Ed.), p. 14.
21. For the following see G. Lewy, *The Nazi Persecution of the Gypsies* ((Oxford: Oxford Univ. Press, 2000), p. 5-9.

that should be the decisive criterion. ... Eventually agreement was reached on a compromise formula: "Gypsies, in the eyes of the police, are those who are Gyosies according to the teachings of ethnology as well those who roam about in the manner of Gypsies." .... On July 16, 1926 .. the Bavarian legislature approved the Law for the Combating of Gypsies, Travelers and the Work-Shy ... travelers (*Landfahrer*), or Gypsy-like itinerants, had been included in the law because they had become even more of a nuisance than those belonging to the Gypsy race ... The implementing regulations for the new law .. provided additional details and definitions. "The concept 'Gypsy' .. is generally known and does not require further explanation .."[22]

At least one thing was clear that the primary purpose of the authorities was to penalize the nomadic lifestyle, to sedentarize and controle every 'movement abroad', and that an attack on a racially fixed group was of a minor or no importance for the practical repression but, eventually, only for its legitimation.

The last approach I want to mention here is another sedentarian ideology *par excellence*, the Social Darwinistic one, which was widespread in Western Europe since about 1890. Its (mis)application to human societies of ideas of biological evolution are quite antithetical to those of Darwin.[23] Social Darwinism originates in the end from the English and North American bourgeois fears for internal and external non-conformistic behaviour undermining their political and economic superiority at home and in the world. There programme 'will intensify race consciousness. It will furnish us the means of a rich culture without internal exploitation .. It will insure to the world the continued domination of the whites.'[24] Its influence covered the entire political spectrum in England (including, for instance, the British Fabian socialism) and North America (including, for instance, the strongest supporters of *laissez-faire* capitalism). On the European continent the (radical) conservatist element of Social Darwinism prevailed, although so-called liberals like Sombart and Weber or German Socialists[25] had joined this bandwagon as well. All believed in the abilities of biology to come up with new proofs in racial matters.

An international authority like Charles Davenport (1866-1944), director of the 'Department of Experimental Evolution' in the highly influential Carnegie Institution of Washington, was the right man to satisfy their needs. Davenport, Laughlin and other 'racists' were very active to restrict immigration on the shaky grounds that immigrants had a disproportionate percentage in insane asylums,

---

22. G. Lewy, p. 7 and 8.
23. See P. van den Berghe, Social Darwinism, in: A. and J. Kuper (Ed.), *The Social Science Encyclopedia* (London: Routledge, 1999), p. 783 ff. What Hannah Arendt tells about Darwinism is, in fact, only applicable to Social Darwinism. See her OT, p. 178 ff.
24. Quoted by Th. Gossett, *Race. The history of an idea in America* (New York: Schocken, 1963), p. 401.
25. See my article: Social Sciences in Germany 1933-1945, in: *German History* 17 (1999), p. 181-187 about the racism of the important socialist ideologue Th. Geiger.

jails and poorhouses because they had 'inborn socially inadequate qualities'. Like Sombart Davenport was a most positive advocate of the theory that race inter-mixture must be avoided; the biologist argued that this led to biological abnormal-ities: 'hybridized people are a badly put together people and a dissatisfied, restless, ineffective people.'[26] He was not only one of the leading spirits in the international eugenic movement but threw a bright light upon the nomadic problem as well.

In fact, Davenport considered nomadism as a desease which eventually could be cured.[27] It's quite easy to laugh now about the accumulation of stupidities or primitive reasonings, but one has to remember the serious consequences of the spreading of these thoughts at the time, their contribution to totalitarian regimes or to the 'New Genetic Movement' of nearly a century later.[28] In the first page, as his 'laboratory work' not yet started, Davenport states that

'human locomotor responses from sessility and extreme domesticity to "ambulatory automatism" [and he is in need of] a term .. to apply to these cases in all of their variety .. "Wandertrieb" is satisfactory .. Vagabondage and vagrancy connote too much to pauperism .. Fugue is usually applied to the extreme cases .. On the whole, I am inclined to use the word "nomadism" just because it has a racial connotation. From a modern point of view all hereditary characters are racial. Moreover, the term "nomadic" is in good use for the restless, wandering type.'[29]

When he and his collaborators finished their work, one can quote from the last pages that it strikes in the family histories how frequent is the

---

26. Both quotes are from Th. Gossett, resp. p. 401 and p. 379. See also H. Kaupen-Haas, C. Saller (Ed.), *Wissenschaftlicher Rassismus. Analyse einer Kontinuität in den Human- und Naturwissenschaften* (Frankfurt/ New York:Campus Verlag, 1999), p. 99, 114.

27. C.B. Davenport, *The feebly inhibited. Nomadism, or the wandering impulse, with special reference to heredity ...* (Washington: Carnegie Institution, 1915), p. 3-70. It concerns paper no. 24 of the 'Station for Experimental Evolution at Cold Spring Harbor, New York'. This paper is published here together with another one about 'Inheritance of Temperament with Special Reference to Twins and Suicides' (p. 71-123). After a classification of nomadism a chapter follows about the wandering instinct in anthropoid apes, among primitive peoples, in children and in adolescents. Next comes a summary in tables of '100 family histories of nomads', a hypothesis and test of the inheritance of 'the nomadic tendency'. Before the summary, literature cited and the abstracts of 100 family histories we learn something about 'nomadic occupations' and the 'association of the nomadic impulse with psychoses.'

28. For the direct links between the USA – eugenicists and the Nazi regime see S. Kühl, *The Nazi Connection. Eugenics, American racism and German National Socialism* (Oxford: Oxford Un. Press, 1994). Kühl compares as well the present eugenic ideas of Americans like R. Pearson, A. Jensen, W. Shockley, etc. with the pre-war eugenic movement. The most shocking were articles like the one of T.E.Ellinger in the *Journal of Heredity* (1942) in which he argued about Jews who were urged to be sterilized that 'it would have been a great deal more merciful to kill the unfortunate outright.' This was not an exceptional opinion!

29. C. Davenport, p. 7.

'association .. of nomadism and various well-known aberrant nervous and mental states .. periodic psychoses, with depression and frequently suicide .. fits of temper, including various explosive tempers .. migraine and periodic headaches .. epilepsy .. hysterical attacks .. sprees .. sexual outbreaks or general weakness of sex control ..'[30]

One gets the impression that one only finds what is posed *apriori*. The following supports this view.

Davenport writes how in older studies students of epilepsy, for example, concluded that nomadism is a symptom of epilepsy, or is sometimes 'caused by' epilepsy; the student of hysteria is struck by cases of nomadism – occurring as 'ambulatory automatism' – and ascribes them to hysteria.

'The new light brought by our studies is this: The nomadic impulse is, in all the cases, one and the same unit character. Nomads, of all kinds, have a special racial trait – are, in a proper sense, members of the *nomadic race*. This trait is the absence of the germinal determiner that makes sedentariness, stability, domesticity. Under the influence of the *mores* – or social pressure – the nomadic impulse is often repressed, but periodically – due to the same sort of internal tension that in .. especially other members of their families leads to epileptic, hysteric, depressive, and sexual outbreaks – they are unable to inhibit the impulse and it breaks out. ... One other class of nomads .. belongs to strains showing feeble-mindedness and dementia .. To this class belongs many typical rolling-stones or ne'er-do-wells, some tramps, the gypsies, and the other nomadic tribes .. The relation between this class and the other is much the same as between the steady drinker and the dipsomaniac.'[31]

It takes a while before one discovers that Davenport does not talk about individual patients with serious illnesses in a medical practice, but of *all people* who are periodically or permanently on the move for whatever reasons. In fact, from the second page of his paper he makes this perfectly clear when he presents elaborate and simple classifications of nomads.

There are, indeed, 'legitimate nomads': 'labourers without work, exiles, representatives of traveling professions (traveling men, peddlers, explorers, missionaries)'. Apparently all the rest is illegitimate. This *seems* obvious with 'delinquent nomads' like 'fugitives from justice, recidivists of prisons and asylums, and certain dangerous degenerates'; it's an inapt classification for 'nomads of morbid origin' with physical and/ or psychic insufficiency (neurotic, psychopathic, etc.,

---

30. Idem, p. 24. The other quotes are from page 25 and 26.
31. Davenport refers here to the *mores* i.e. the concept coined by the main American ideologue of Social Darwinism, William Graham Sumner. Sumner states (1906): 'Bad mores are those which are not well fitted to the conditions and needs of the society at the time ... morality .. in higher civilizations restrains passion and appetite, and curbs the will.' Quoted in P. van den Berghe, p. 784.

etc.) and for 'nomads of ethnic origin' from which Davenport mentions 'Goths, Saxons, Huns, Normans; Crusaders; Gypsies, Arabs, Sioux, etc.'!

From the 100 interviewed people, always called 'patients', Davenport and his collaborators wanted to know everything about their family history and, in particular, the occupation and behaviour of parents and grand-parents. What aroused their suspicion and could be a new proof of the thesis in this highly biased investigation was italicized. This gives keywords like: 'one is wild and gambles, one sister has headaches'; 'part Indian, incarcerated for theft'; 'never content to remain in one place'; about father's fathers: 'Western desperado' or 'bear-hunter', 'in vaudeville stage', 'deserted from the army', 'escaped from slavery and ran away to Kansas'; about mother's mothers: 'had migraine', 'erotic', 'painful menstrual periods', 'loves country walks'. And so on.

Main characteristics of Davenport's approach, at last, are demonstrated in sentences like: 'Thus all the evidence supports the hypothesis that the nomadic impulse depends upon the absence of a simple sex-linked gene that "determines" domesticity.'[32] The classical and still actual confrontation between professional social scientists and biologists as laymen in social problems (see the recent Edward O. Wilson row) is already given in Davenport's time. He opposes the obvious remark of the opposition that nomadism has everything to do with the nature of specific work, occupations and many other ecological, economic, etc. circumstances: 'Inquiry will frequently reveal the fact that the nomadic occupation has been selected because it accords with the innate tastes and impulses of the restless man.'[33]

Some conclusions can be drawn from this short overview of approaches and theories. The formulation of Davenport's racial nomadic problem, how nonsensical it may be, leads first and foremost to medical-biological solutions. To eradicate nomadism and to domesticate nomads one has to rely on collective treatments of the population (vaccination), individual medication, a cure in a special medical institution, specific mechanical treatments like (compulsory) sterilization, etc. What could be and is subsumed under 'etc' is well-known. The chance that this road is chosen is greater the larger the bureaucratic institutions which have to execute the 'solution work'. These are able to concentrate large amounts of 'non-conformists' but to create as well unmanageable problems leading to fantastic solutions.

A serious difficulty from the point of view of eugenicists, racist and their all too clever advisers is that they are more or less outspoken supporters of the avoidance of assimilation or racial intermixture. Whatever treatment is available, a true racist must say: once a Jew, Gypsy or nomad, always one. It's probably possible to domesticate all itinerant people (for a while or permanent) but they

---

32. C. Davenport, p. 23.
33. Idem, p. 24.

stay Gypsy, etc. This 'natural' dilemma easily leads to the desperate solution: A good Gypsy is a dead Gypsy.

Another difficulty concerns the question whether the greatest thread and nuissance was the uncontrollable mobile, nomadic life or a racial inferiority. Directly related was the question of the *name and location* of the thread: what is its *definition* and is it an *internal* or an *external* matter i.e. a sedentarian (agricultural) or nomadic. The existence of Sombart I and II side by side seems a good demonstration at issue of the possible confusions. A comparison of the Davenport case with the police-actions in Bavaria could lead to the conclusion that if there is an *external* 'danger' one does not rely, in the first instance, on a medical but on a juridical, police and eventually military response and repression. Is it, however, an *internal* 'danger' one seems to rely first and foremost on a race-concept and not on occupation or work.

Beginning with the next paragraph a proof of this can be given. In any respects, in the Shoah-, let alone the Holocaust-research, these relationships are fully neglected. It's also clear that here could be found a clue to the relationships discussed in the first chapter those between insiders – outsiders and incasts – outcasts.

A New Hero and his nomads

After this basic treatment of some theoretical backgrounds, I can return to Diemer and his other hero whose relevant statements can now be better understood. Diemer proudly reproduced in his book Hitler's party-member's ticket, which is directly followed by his own (visually similar) admission ticket to Hitler's famous *Reichstag* meeting of May 17, 1933.[34] However, he should have used his time to read his *Führer* a bit better. Adolf Hitler had his own theory about nomads-Jews as he criticized Sombart without mentioning his name:

> 'Since the Jew never possessed a state with definite territorial limits and therefore nevercalled a culture his own, the conception arose that this was a people which should be reckoned among the ranks of the nomads. This is a fallacy as great as it is dangerous. The nomad does possess a definitely limited living space, only he does not cultivate it like a sedentary peasant ... Probably the Aryan was also first a nomad settling in the course of time, but for that very reason he was never a Jew! No, the Jew is no nomad: for the nomad had also a definite attitude toward

34. On this day Hitler delivered in the *Reichstag* a major declaration on foreign policy: he is a man of peace and during the next five years he is prepared to agree to substantial arms-reductions if other countries will do the same. All MP's agreed, including the remaining SPD members. At that time, the intention was to produce a '*Wiederwehrhaftmachung*' as Goebbel's diary shows. J. Goebbels, *Tagebücher* (München: Piper, 1992), Vol. 2, p. 788-803. On May 17, Goebbels not only dined with Leni Riefenstahl discussing a new 'Hitler-film' but wrote in his diary as a reaction to Hitler's peace-offensive: '*Wehrminister ist von mir wieder aufgerichtet worden.*' For Diemer's direct interest had to be Goebbel's quarrel about '*Gesandter im Haag*' (p.803)!

the concept of work ... in his whole being he may seem strange to the Aryan peoples, but not unattractive. In the Jew, however, this attitude is not at all present; for that reason he was never a nomad, but only and always a parasite in the body of other peoples ... This, however, has nothing to do with nomadism, for the reason that a Jew never thinks of leaving a territory that he has occupied but remains where he is, and he sits so fast that even by force it is very hard to drive him out.'[35]

Here we are confronted with the other guest-principle. A guest is not somebody *coming from somewhere* but the already sedentary ('never thinks of leaving') *being inside* considered as an alien and damaging element. Hitler demonstrates, therefore, the typical sedentary way of arguing about 'parasites' as all categories of people which do not want to conform to the (dominant) sedentary political or social rules, which only trouble society or which are seen as dangerous to what was called 'the health, hygiene, racial purity, etc. of the social organism'. In this reasoning (big) city life, for instance, is always seen as 'evil'. Therefore, this variant of the guest principle has nothing to do with hospitality but has the significance of a verdict, is a life-threatening concept.

Also in this respect, Adolf Hitler was not very original. Not only is there a striking similarity with Weber's opinions at issue; antisemites at the end of the 19th century eagerly quoted Father Johan Gottfried Herder (1744-1803):

'Like the Egyptians, the Jews detested the sea and since then, they dwelled ... among other nations; this was a quality of character against which Moses already struggled ... (they did not have a national political culture and therefore) did not receive either that feeling for honour and freedom ... The People of God is a parasitic plant on the trunk of other nations.'[36]

---

35. A. Hitler, *Mein Kampf.* American translation R. Manheim; introduction K. Heiden (Boston: Houghton Mifflin Co., 1971) p. 303-305. Although he quotes half of this passage, Goldhagen declares that Hitler told his readers '*that although the Jews are a nomadic group they are unlike nomads ...*' but Hitler denied precisely this nomadic option! D. Goldhagen, *Hitler's willing executioners. Ordinary Germans and the Holocaust* (London: Little, Brown, 1996), p. 285. Even more serious is that Goldhagen misses the chance to understand the real meaning of the prevailing cultural cognitive model of Jews and their 'work-ethic'. While he refers here to Max Weber several times (p. 557 note 4; p. 558 note 15), you can, furthermore, conclude that he does not understand Weber's position in this question. The *relationship* between nomads – guests – parasites with their derivations like 'guest country'(*Wirtsland*) and related prejudices within a particular context is of paramount importance to understand sentences like: '*der Parasit folgt seinem Wirtsvolk auf dem Wege in die Großstadt*' (Quoted from a bookreview of K. Ahlheim, *Geschöntes Leben. Eine deutsche Wissenschaftskarriere.* Hannover: Offizin, 2000) in: *taz* 26-7-2000).
36. Cited in a famous antisemitic tract *Die Sittenlehre des Talmud und der zerstörende Einfluß des Judenthums im Deutschen Reich* (Berlin: A. Niendorf Verlag, 1875) p. 66,67.

Herder, certainly, is one of the sources for Weber's honour concept which was implemented in his patriarch analysis (chapter 3).

Which guest perception one supports depends on the same attitudes exhibited in preferences for *das Primat der Aussenpolitik* above *das Primat der Innenpolitik* (and the reverse) and many other inside-outside dichotomies. It would be wise, however, to remember how the sedentary way of arguing also depends in many respects on thoughts attached to the 'Soil [*Boden*]', 'the Peasant [*Bauer*]' and his pure 'Blood [*Blut*]' and on the policies derived from them like the aggressive economic autarky-policy, typical population and settlement policies, etc.[37] The more radical the policy, the more clearly these items come into the picture. An example from Hitler, who was not the most radical Nazi:

> 'The acquisition of new soil for the settlement of the excess population possesses an infinite number of advantages ... For one thing, the possibility of preserving a healthy peasant class as a foundation for a whole nation can never be valued highly enough. Many of our present- day sufferings are only the consequence of the unhealthy relationship between rural and city populations ... For Germany, consequently, the only possibility for carrying out a healthy territorial policy lay in the acquisition of new land in Europe itself.'[38]

Furthermore, it would be unwise to forget how both perceptions can be combined. Between the 'being inside' and the 'coming from outside' lies the *settlement* problematic. The 'in-placement' could have the purpose to transform a nomad into a parasite or a pariah-guest. Assimilation seems to be the logical end of the 'in-placement' process. The 'out-placement' aims to eliminate the pariahs/-parasites by expelling them from 'the trunk', 'the Guest-land' [*Wirtsland*] into a new wandering life or worse. In other words, for antisemites it seems perfectly plausible to support both a Weberian and a Sombartian reasoning and subsequent policies; Weber's and Sombart's positions are or can be mutually connected.

In Germany and many other countries like the USA, the dominant sedentary ideology results in a double perception of foreigners: the 'inside' and 'outside' foreigners, which differs, for example, between the (sedentary) Jews and the (nomadic) Gypsies. In Germany, both were considered as guests, which gave this word its very nasty meaning so far from the normal hospitality rules in real nomadic societies. While formulating their definition of '*das Wesen des Judentums*' (the essence of Jewishness), Fritsch et al. repeated most of Sombart's opinions but stressed only a nomadic heritage of Jews which made them parasites:

---

37. On these elements see my archival study *Deutsche Westforschung. Ideologie und Praxis im 20.Jahrhundert*; (Leipzig: Akademische Verlagsanstalt/ 2001) and the following extensive debate about this book in, for instance, the 1100 pages of B. Dietz et al. (Ed.), *Griff nach dem Westen. Die "Westforschung" der völkisch-nationalen Wissenschaften ...* (Münster: Waxmann, 2003).
38. A. Hitler, p.138, 139.

'To the essence of Jewishness belong the close connections between its religion, e.g. its priests-church and nomadism, mammonism and rationalism. To live upon and from alien peoples is the divine destiny of these nomads. The temple in Jerusalem became the central bank for the dispersed believers and folk-members.' Later more clearly: ' It was other peoples which worked ... in agriculture and animal husbandry. Jews have been only hawkers, usurers and exploiters ... the dispersion of the exploiting Jews among the value-producing peoples is a precondition for their pure parasitic life'.[39]

In these exclamations, Fritsch et al. approached the clear statement of Hitler, but he was still technically confusing in his analysis of sedentary versus mobile elements in society. This limitation does not stop Fritsch from demanding time and again the 'destruction' of the Jews. Later this advice could be followed up by Hitler within the general aim of destroying 'all parasites', knowing about the widespread consent in most scholarly circles in Germany as well as in other European countries or America.[40]

Notwithstanding this, nomadism remained a hot and deadly topic. In 1938 a German book was published with the following title: '*Der nichtseßhafte Mensch*' (Non-Sedentary Man) with the subtitle '*Beitrag zur Neugestaltung der Raum- and Menschenordnung im Großdeutschen Reich*' (Contribution to the Renewal of the Spatial and Human Order in the Reich).[41] It could be a demonstration of Davenport's work.

In this publication important psychiatrists, medical doctors, lawyers, etc. demand 'to kill [unschädlich machen] the anti-social people ... who abuse public social services or offend the law' (Prof. Polligkeit); for the lawyer Prof. Exner, tramps are 'wandering herds of microbes causing a moral focus of infection from which our people must be saved'; the medical doctor Prof. Villinger calls it scientifically proved that people who avoid work suffer from a genetic defect; his colleague Stumpfl delivers the 'proof' that tramps are, in fact, psychopathic and feeble-minded; the female Führer of the so-called 'Nichtseßhaften' bureaucracy, Frau Eiserhardt, concludes that 'every labourer shall have to be used according to

---

39. Th. Fritsch, p. 54.
40. This worldwide consent in the biological, in particular, eugenetic studies and opinions at the time should be complemented by studies from other disciplines. Besides this, it seems obvious that studying only one aspect is never enough: you have to study *relationships*. For instance, knowledge about the sedentarian concept *par excellence*, HOME, HEIMAT, etc., should be completed by, at least, HOMELESSNESS, HEIMATLOSIGKEIT, etc. but also by NOMADISM, WANDERUNGEN, etc. Therefore, one could consult in another discipline I-M. Greverus, *Der territoriale Mensch. Ein literaturanthropologischer Versuch zum Heimatphänonomen* (Frankfurt a/M.: Athenäum, 1972) together with U. Gerhard, *Nomadische Bewegungen und die Symbolik der Krise. Flucht und Wanderung in der Weimarer Republik*. Historische Diskursanalyse der Literatur (Opladen, Wiesbaden: Westdeutscher Verlag, 1998).
41. See Ernst Klee, '*Euthanasie' im NS-Staat. Die 'Vernichtung lebensunwerten Lebens'* (Frankfurt a/M.: Fischer, 1985), p.65 ff.

the needs of the state and the economy'; a mayor demands that wandering peoples should be transferred to the '*Arbeitseinsatz*'; etc.

In the same time that all these scholars and bureaucrats collaborate to legitimate and execute a broad spectrum of killings of wandering and sedentary 'parasites', SS-Führer Himmler begins in January 1938 the 'Aktion Arbeitsscheuen Reich' (Operation Striker in the Reich) from which the first victims (tramps, Gypsies, beggars, people without work, etc.) were brought to KZ Buchenwald. The euthanasia program started up in this year with the nationwide reshuffling of young and adult 'parasites' from institutions of the disabled, etc., facilitating their destruction. In June 1938 a nationwide Gestapo search for 'Nichtseßhaften' (Non-Sedentaries) started; already half a year later the SS reported that 'much more than 100,000 of these anti-socials attend re-education courses in special concentration camps which are highly effective for this purpose'. That occurred not only in Buchenwald but more specifically in KZ Flossenburg (erected in 1938) which had the same deadly 'facilities' as Mauthausen a bit later (from a granite-mine to continuously torturing guards). This large-scale forced sedentarization and elimination of wandering peoples was the beginning of the most unprecedented destruction of 'guests' in world history.

Now, after we looked into the dramatic nomadic side of the guest problem we are also obliged to study the sedentarian side of this problem. The contradictory relationship between both indicated in the Ahasverus legend can be discovered by studying the traditional sedentarization policy to make 'guests' dwell in ghettos.

The sedentarized 'ghetto Jews' as guests

One of those always repeated slogans in antisemitism concerns what was stressed by Weber time and again that Jews themselves wanted to be *pariahs* and ghetto dwellers. If clever people like Weber are using this argument, one has to study it carefully. A pivotal Weber text in this respect is the following:[42]

'In particular for external use, the Jews [*das Judentum*] accepted increasingly the type of the ritually isolated guest-people (pariah-people). This happened voluntarily and not as a consequence of some pressure from outside. The general dispersion of 'antisemitism' in antiquity is a fact. But it happened as well that this

---

42. GAR, III, p. 434, 435. See also GAR, II, p. 39, 40 where Weber came with the theory about the 'voluntary ghetto' compared even to the origin of the 'Christian freedom'. Because of the building of the "Sharon Wall" in Israel this issue became topical as well. On the 18th of the October 2004 the journalist Alain Menargues, a Director of the state-run Radio France International (RFI) had to resign because he called Israel a racist state by building such a ghetto-making wall. He, however, also told the people: 'Where was the first ghetto? It was in Venice. And who built it? It was the Jews them-selves in order to be separated from the rest. After that, Europe put them in ghettos' (www.free-public.com from an article in the Jerusalem Post; www.oualala.net). Only with the last statement he became an antisemite (see below), but he was dismissed thanks to the first oversimplified remark!

increasingly growing aversion against Jews was paralleled by a growing Jewish aversion against communication with non-Jews. The opposition against Jews in antiquity was far from a 'racially' determined antagonism .... In the first instance, the negative attitudes of the Jews themselves were without doubt responsible for the mutual relations.... If one wants to go to the heart of the matter, the 'misanthropy' of the Jews again and again was in the end the definite reproach: the fundamental denial of marrying and living together [*Connubium, Kommensalität*] and every kind of brotherhood or closer relationship, even in commercial matters ... The social isolation of the Jews, this immanent 'ghetto', was primarily chosen by themselves and wanted by themselves and this in an increasing degree ... Hand in hand with this radical isolation ... energetic propagandistic and proselytic work to the outside...'

This theological declaration is a most astonishing Weber text, although it did not appear unexpectedly. Weber substantiated its content by quoting from the New Testament about the competitor in the struggle for souls (*Math.* 23:15). When a Christian complains in a scholarly text about the proselytic and propagandistic work of another belief, this is worst than hypocritical; apart from the fact that the Jewish belief is generally not known for proselytic activities (and, if so, who could care about the proliferation of an anachronistic belief from a very tiny sect within an overwhelming Christian environment in the Middle Ages and an overwhelming 'pagan' world in antiquity ?).

It makes no sense either to discuss the shadowy empirical basis of this declaration. For example, it is certainly untrue that there is something like a 'general dispersion of antisemitism in antiquity' (even if it is not racially determined). This is a good example of the usual exaggerating out of proportion of things related to Jews. First we are dealing here with a span of time of at least two thousand years. Within this very long period there are *sometimes*, in Hellenistic and Roman times, specific anti-Jewish measures as, for instance, in Alexandria. Recently, Feldman[43] proved how tolerant the Persian, Greek and Roman governments generally were. The same was true for the 'pagan' intellectuals who often were in favour of the personality of Moses and of Jewish characteristics like their courage, temperament, justice and piety. Only the 'masses'- whatever that may be - sometimes showed anti-Jewish sentiments if they were directed by influential people against rich citizens who called themselves Jews.

Furthermore, Weber does not indicate clearly that these anti-Jewish measures have nothing to do with the typical Christian anti-Judaism, let alone with the

---

43. See L. Feldman, *Jew and Gentile in the Ancient World. Attitudes and Interactions from Alexander to Justinian* (Princeton: Princeton University Press, 1993). Weber's unfounded exclamation fits perfectly well in the background of war-publications like E. Fischer, G. Kittel, *Das Antike Weltjudentum* (1943). See L. Siegele-Wenschkewitz, *Neutestamentliche Wissenschaft vor der Judenfrage. Gerhard Kittels theologische Arbeit im Wandel deutscher Geschichte* in: *Theologische Existenz Heute*, Nr. 208, 1980.

modern racial antisemitism. In fact, Weber's verdict concerning the so-called Jewish misanthropy originated from the Hellenistic anti- Judaism as found in Alexandrian writers like Apion and Roman authors such as Tacitus. Here I only want to reflect on the important ideological question of the alleged ghetto mentality which presupposes 'ghettos for Jews' and on the Jews' own initiative to become pariah/ghetto-dwellers.

The text appears at the end of *Das Antike Judentum* as Weber's final conclusion and verdict. In the former chapter we have seen how he already concocted a pariah model in his patriarch analysis with a maximum of Wilhelminian values and a minimum of scholarly rigour. By using the Matthew quotation as an attack on Jews, Weber proved that he saw himself primarily as a propagator of the Christian faith. Here he also introduced the definition of the Sin and Punishment of Amalek/Cain/Jews, the *eternal enemies of Yahweh*: their Sin is the misanthropy, their *eternal enmity of Mankind*, and the Punishment becomes *the eternal isolation within a ghetto*.

This highly ideological thesis about, of course, the personal guilt of the Jews for their persecution was a fixed part of every antisemitic tract in Weber's time and later. As such, it was a modern redefinition of the old thesis about the Sin of the perpetrators of the New Testament Jesus Christ.[44] Sometimes rather serious scholars accepted it in the form of false theories about '*the voluntary ghetto*' and of the existence of ghetto's in specific historical periods.[45] These 'facts' had to prove

---

44. See the highly relevant H. Maccoby, *Judas Iscariot and the Myth of Jewish Evil* (New York: Free Press, 1992), p. 27. For the stigmatization policy of the Christian churches, see also W. Klassen, *Judas. Betrayer or friend of Jesus?* (London: SCM, 1996).

45. Also many Jewish scholars accepted this opinion. See L. Wirth, *The Ghetto* (Chicago: University of Chicago Press, 1928), reprinted 1956 p. 18 ff. See also the good overview of J. Lestschinsky, Ghetto, in: *Encyclopaedia of the Social Sciences* (New York: Macmillan, 1949), VI, p. 646-651. In the same encyclopedia wrote Benjamin Ginzburg the article about antisemitism in which he mentioned 'the hermetical social isolation of the Jews in the ghetto' in medieval times. Idem, Vol. II, p. 120. Most influential was also B. Bettelheim, Freedom from Ghetto Thinking, in: Idem, *Freud's Vienna and Other Essays* (New York: Vintage, 1991; orig. 1956), p. 243-273. Even the recent and interesting study of Ariel Toaff, *Love, work and death. Jewish life in medieval Umbria* (London: Littman Library, 1996) comes up with the, in itself contradictory, opinion: 'Although there do not appear to have been any explicit ecclesiastical rulings limiting the Jewish presence to designated areas, or confining them to particular parts of town, a profusion of local ordinances was issued from the middle of the thirteenth century in France, Spain, and Italy obliging Jews to live exclusively in the localities they themselves has already chosen, often known as *giudecche* or *juderie*.' (p. 187). As argued in my text, there is no way that people could occupy space freely in medieval towns (except the original builders-proprietors), and if so, strangers had the least chance to do so. This apart from the fact that it is not clever to issue laws which give 'malicious people' the opportunity to stay where they are. Already a page later, Toaff tells us: 'In point of fact, in Italy, attempts to confine Jews to a particular area were sporadic and short-lived until the middle of the fifteenth century.' (p. 188). And thirteen sentences later he states more correct: 'It was only in the second half of the fifteenth century, and more particularly towards its end, that efforts to impose specific areas of residence on Jews began to proliferatie ...'. It took another three sentences to come up with nearly the whole truth 'that such confined areas were the direct precursors of the ghettos, officially set up only from the sixteenth

the presence of a ghetto mentality within the Jewish DNA or something of that order. At the same time, these 'facts' excuse, in particular, State and Church for their violent repression (now liberals and socialists could say, 'they had no other choice' and conservatives, 'they did the right job'). This matter was further complicated because some Jews also accepted the ghetto in one way or another. I want to deal with this last phenomenon in chapter 6, but one recent example can be mentioned here.

According to a newspaper, Dr. Avi Beker of the Jewish World Congress informed us while displaying new demographic figures of Jews in the world that ultra-orthodox Jews (*harediem*) prefer to live in ghettos fully isolated from other Jews in cities like New York, Los Angeles, Miami, Antwerp and London.[46] So, was the ghetto the typical form of Jewish settlement? First, I have to take a quick look at the beginning of ghetto history. The end we know all too well,[47] although this cannot refer to Avi Beker's information which, of course, does not concern ghettos at all as will be shown below.

The ghetto argument runs as follows. A ghetto is a concentrated isolation; already in the Middle Ages Jews lived in isolation; Jews, therefore, have chosen voluntarily for a ghetto. A better theological justification like Weber's for this 'argument' is difficult to find. However, the medieval reality is forgotten which shows how Jews, *like everybody else*, could only travel 'voluntarily' *between* places. Inside the town and city walls, *like everybody else*, they had to stick to the rather harsh rules relative to all settlements (mostly these places were too overcrowded and had too many difficulties concerning water, pollution, food deliveries, etc.). It was common practice for craftsmen and other professions to concentrate in specific streets or places. From early in the Middle Ages, it was also the usual practice to give *all* merchants (with a minority of Jewish merchants) a *claustrum negociatorum* inside or directly outside the town or city. So, segregation was a normal effect of spatial and social divisions.

As today, also in the Middle Ages there were several kinds of Jews. If they were merchants, they mostly travelled in groups, and the popular Jewish *mercatores* in, e.g., the Champagne or Rhine valley received security, a synagogue and so on as the usual service for merchants from all 'nations'. The first attempt toward the

century.' (p. 188, 189): this truth concerns, of course, only the ghettos, but there is no direct link with the alleged 'precursors'! A recent reader R.Po-Chia Hsia, H. Lehmann (Ed.), *In and Out of the Ghetto. Jewish-Gentile Relations in Late Medieval and Early Modern Germany* (Cambridge: Cambridge University Press, 1995) demonstrates the ritualism perfectly well. Many interesting and relevant data are discussed in the 22 contributions, but starting with the title the generally accepted image of the ghetto-Jew is not attacked (enough). If ghetto 'should be understood only metaphorically rather than literally', as one reviewer wrote (*German History* 16,3 (1998), p. 428), than this research has only a metaphorical basis.

46. *NRC-Handelsblad* 23-2-1999.

47. H. Derks, De joodse opstand in het getto van Warschau, in: Idem (Ed.), *Kroniek van 3 eeuwen revoluties* (Groningen: Wolters-Noordhoff, 1989), p. 248-256.

establishment of a *Judenviertel* appeared in a grant of the bishop of the Rhine valley town Speyer near Mannheim (1084). Bishop Rudiger wanted to attract Jewish merchants to his city to 'add to its honour', and he promised protection so that 'they might not be readily disturbed by the insolence of the populace'. The bishop did not erect a ghetto. Elsewhere, Jews could dwell in a *bourg public*. All this happened in the period of the first crusades, in which sometimes Jews were massacred by crusaders and their followers.

Sedentary Jews, craftsmen or bankers, had a much more difficult life in this respect than ambulant merchants. After the council of Lateran IV (1215) codified an anti-Jewish ideology, Jews increasingly came under a rather systematic ideological attack. Still, the *juiveries* in Paris and comparable constellations elsewhere were not ghettos but a *jewry* (England), *Judenviertel, -stadt, -dorf* and so on (Germany), *judena* (Spain), *mellah* (North Africa), *ulica zydowska* (Poland) and so forth.

During the time of the plagues in the 14th century, a new wave of massacres occurred, and the papal inquisition started its terrible work, which continued to the Napoleonic era. In a few cases in the next century, Jewish communities formed loose 'ghettos': 'the peoples who were looking for a security guarantee sometimes asked for it ... most of the time, however, (a ghetto) was ordered by the authorities or the (non-Jewish) public.'[48] From the 15th century onwards, real anti-Jewish ghettos became possible. They must be defined as: the enforced internment in an urban setting of a specific part of the population.

THE ORIGINAL GHETTO

It was, however, not earlier than the beginning of the sixteenth century that these compulsory institutions appeared in Italy and that the legitimation for the general segregation of the Jews in a locked ghetto was given by Pope Paul IV in 1555 in the bull *Cum nimis absurdum*. From here they spread only to central and eastern Europe, which means that the largest part of Europe did not have ghettos at all. Apart from this, the majority of all Jews came to live in Moslem countries, in which neither ghettos nor pogroms existed.

A quick look into the birth history of what is called the 'most liberal ghetto', the one in the capital of the mighty commercial Venetian republic, substantiates my argument.[49] Furthermore, it provides the opportunity to reconstruct the intriguing power-play which led to the drastic decision of making a ghetto. Here, in the 15th century the Jews were no longer allowed to be merchants; they had to

48. G. Duby (Ed.), *Histoire de la France urbaine* (Paris: Seuil, 1980), II, p. 53, 61, 99, 538 ff.

49. Data and following quotations about the Venetian ghetto come from R. Calimani, *The Ghetto of Venice. A History* (New York: Evans, 1987), p. 28-41. See for general background R. Bonney, *The European Dynastic States 1494-1660* (Oxford: Oxford Univ. Press, 1991), p. 458-463.

confine their activities to banking. The Italian rulers, Jews and the Church adapted to the rather subtle interweaving of religious (against usury or lending on interest), economic (commerce and credit facilities) and political (need for money for waging war) factors. Toward the middle of this century, however, this slowly changing balance deteriorated rather suddenly because one of the parties, the Church, did not stick to its position.

The rebellious Franciscan Friars Minor started a vigorous campaign against usury. They took the most radical stand: lending money for even the smallest profit was usury; those who practised it (Jews) were 'enemies of the people'. The fundamentalist Minorites castigated not only Jews but were radically intolerant against the luxury of the ruling class or the moral laxity of their colleagues, the Dominican and Augustine friars. This led to harsh theological disputes between these friars and, sometimes, to strong reactions from city governments against these provocative preachers.

A practical consequence of their preachings was the establishment of the so-called *monti di pietà* to combat the Jewish pawnshops. A true fight of *oikos against market* started to rage. In the very beginning, most *monti* gathered capital from donations, etc., and they asked no interest for their small loans to poorer townsfolk. Soon they had to rely fully on the generosity of an increasingly smaller group of richer people. Next, the Minorites themselves started to ask (a small) interest to pay their operating costs, i.e., 'a class of hired employees who became increasingly parasitic'. The rulers preferred the Jews as good taxpayers (the friars had tax exemption); they were less troublesome and were valued as a rather reliable credit institution in a commercially expanding environment.

In the city of Venice, the Jewish pawnshops enjoyed a strong position: 'Jews asked no questions, they did not require official declarations of poverty, they appraised pledges generously ... and in rural areas they accepted the future harvest as security. Moreover, the Venetian government could levy extra taxes on the Jews in times of crises.' In short, the radicality of the friars established a new inroad of the oikoidal powers into the world of the markets, but they stopped short at the moment they began to compete with the secular banking institutions, including the Jewish ones (a minority in the Venetian banking world). The inevitable bureaucratization led to the usual corruption, lack of freedom of the clients and autonomization of the institutions: one has arrived at charity as business. It made the friars' radicality rather ambiguous, and within the Catholic Church antagonisms, they became formidable competitors.

In Trent the Minorites succeeded in provoking false accusations of ritual murder of a little boy, Simone. This happened at Easter when Jews ('murderers of Christ!') are supposed to stay at home. During the trial (1475) a converted Jew, Giovanni da Feltre, provided the 'proofs' of the accusations, and torturing of many Jews did the rest. Although a papal commissioner sent from Rome declared the Jews innocent, in other places new accusations of ritual child murder were launched under the direct influence of the Minorites' fiery sermons. (Later the boy, Simone of Trent, was beatified by the Pope in 1562, and it took four hundred years, after Vaticanum II before the Catholic Church officially rectified the anti-Judaism at issue and abandoned the Simone cult).

The Minorites activities in charity-banking increased as quickly as their anti-Jewish campaigns, and in 1492, the year of the great Spanish expulsion, a wave of riots and persecutions swept through the cities and towns of the Venetian Republic after the sermons of Minorites under their leader, Bernardino da Feltre. Now the Spanish Catholic kings had spoken, the Italian friars-mobs could gain secular support even from the Venetian government. The Jews had to leave Venice, and they fled to Mestre, a town on the mainland directly across from Venice.

The Jews continued to go back and forth to Venice to do their business, but times had definitely changed. The yellow hat was introduced (1496), periods of residence restricted, control over the pawnshops tightened, etc. The culmination of Venetian power, culture and luxury marked the years around 1500. A year earlier, however, the failure of three banks announced the economic crisis in which the Venetian Republic was in constant need of large sums in order to continue business and to wage war. A cat and mouse game followed between the Jewish moneylenders and the Venetian government.

Already in 1503 they could come back to the city, rent houses for families and personnel of the pawnhouses, they were allowed to bear arms and to go without the yellow hat under dangerous circumstances. Thanks to the war, most Jews fled to the city. After 1509 a new campaign of the priests started to preach against the presence of the 500 Jews within a population of 102,000 inhabitants: they were 'the root of all evil'. In particular, the few Jewish doctors were accused of fraternizing with Christian invalids, while they were successfully competing with the Christian healers.

At the time the charter with the Jewish bankers had to be renewed for the next 10 years or large amounts of money had to be borrowed, the Venetian political powers were willing to use their force (imprison important Jews, confiscate goods, etc.) to 'negotiate' better terms. The Jews, in their turn, could always threaten to leave the city and disappear with their money. In 1515, after such a period of suspense, an agreement was reached. The Jews had negotiated nine new business enterprises, and they could expect a rather bright future.

Now, they lived dispersed all over the city. One of their families, the Meshullams, belonged to the wealthiest and most important banking families of Venice. But they became controversial. The highly respected Asher was the hero of the negotiations with the political powers. His brother Chaim imprudently occupied a palace and displayed a luxury which was, within the explosive Venetian atmosphere, a psychological blunder, to say the least. The same was true concerning the imprudent public appearance of Jews at Easter (see above). Asher's son, Jacob the jeweller, bribed judges after he was accused of having purchased stolen goods; Chaim and Jacob got into bitter public fights. So, the richest Jews started to demonstrate the usual conduct of the established elite to which they wanted to belong (Jacob later converted to Catholicism with the blessings of the Pope and the Doge). All this coming so soon after the succesful negotiations was a mistake.

'At that precise moment there was a counter-reaction that seems almost surprising.' Now the continuously screaming friars received unexpected support from certain nobles within the power system. In March of that year, the Senate received a proposal requesting that all Jews be confined to the Giudecca, probably a Jewish quarter in earlier times. In March 1516 a new violent attack with many political implications was launched by the nobles. Now the request was that the Jews be confined to an ancient site resembling a fortress which was, in fact, an old foundry, named *Ghetto Novo*. The proposal was accepted in the Senate with an overwhelming majority of 130 to 44 and 8 abstentions.

The decree of March 29, 1516, ran as follows:

'The Jews must all live together in the Corte de Case, which are in the Ghetto near San Girolamo; and to prevent their roaming about at night: Let there be built two Gates ... which Gates shall be opened in the morning ... and shall be closed at midnight by four Christian guards appointed and paid by the Jews at the rate deemed suitable by Our Cabinet.'

New high walls had to be erected, all the exits were to be locked, and the doors and windows walled up. The Jews had to pay two patrol-boats to watch the ghetto from the canals as well. Even Asher Meshullam and his family '*were forced to move into the ghetto*'.

It is hotly debated why the ghettoization occurred in Venice and why so quickly. In my view, this sudden change of mind and policy was mainly of a *political-economic* nature and only for a small part based on (religious) anti-Judaism. An occasional coalition of otherwise competing factions within the oikoidal power-play of the republic took the ghetto decision. The first faction wanted to enhance the development of the *monti di pietà* (certain nobles and friars) at the cost of the Jewish pawnshops. Another faction wanted to take over these pawnshops for themselves '*no longer at the controlled rate of 20 percent but at 50 percent or more*' (other nobles). The strict anti-Judaistic friars' position was directed at a total expulsion of the Jews. The Doge and the Council of Ten, however, wanted to counteract all these factions because their intention was the disappearance of the Jews, who were such excellent power-instruments in the hands of the Council and badly needed for the economy.

The Council could have had another important reason: the combination of nobles and friars was such an explosive mixture that, for the first time, it had to fear its own powerbase. Therefore, the one saw the ghetto as an acceptable alternative punishment, the other as a means to provoke the Jews to leave the city, while still another hoped the locking up of the Jews (without removing their ways of earning an income) should save them for the city. At very least, the ghetto could result in taking the wind out of the opposition's sails. In my view, this constellation worked out less unfavourably for the Jews than elsewhere, while the ultimate power-holders in the republic were pragmatic allies of the Jews (hence, 'the liberal ghetto').

A REFLEXION ON THE 'EASTSIDE OF THE GHETTO PROBLEM'

When we return to Weber's verdict, it is easy to see why his and other's idea of a 'voluntary ghetto' is dangerous nonsense comparable to that of the so-called 'Jewish Selbsthass'. The latter is invented by Jewish authorities to stigmatize criticism from 'the own ranks', whatever that may be; the former is invented to stigmatize all Jews including their authorities. To my knowledge, no Jewish group ever build a ghetto for itself in some town or city; even if they should have helped to build a construction like that, they were forced to do this by, at least, the insecure circumstances.

The only way to 'save' the *voluntary ghetto thesis* is to call every homogeneously populated urban quarter a ghetto in which a certain proportion of Jews or other special groups like, for example, white upper middle class, are concentrated (see Avi Beker above). In this case one demonstrates nothing but a bad conscience or simply poor social understanding: 'ghetto' symbolizes all that is negative in city life (high crime rates, pollution, noise, bad sanitation, and so on); 'ghetto' is emotive and racist in its connotations.[50] However, for people who are brainwashed in some ideological sense, historical arguments like the one discussed above do not work.

The immanent excuse built into the thesis has been needed up to the present day as a consequence of a most serious historical paradox. Jews (and comparable minorities) had to expect help and security from State and Church which they often served wholeheartedly. These *super-oikoidal powers*, however, were and are responsible for both the repression and execution of minorities on a large scale. The strong military or bureaucratic hierarchy of a Super-Oikos only survives through the (forced) sedentarization of different groups and functions to a proper place.

A most important oikoidal rule is: What is divided and separated from each other in order to rule can only be ruled if bound to the (societal) soil. Therefore, any oikoidal power is bound to, first and foremost, an *agricultural* power base and

---

50. See the article 'ghetto' in E. Cashmore (Ed.), *Dictionary of Race and Ethnic Relations* (London: Routledge, 1994), p.127 ff. which again suggests that Jews 'voluntarily' establish ghettos.

people as fixed to locations (sedentary) as possible. The main origin of this policy is to be found in the early rural power base of the aristocracy and Roman Catholic Church. Whatever some Jewish and other historians may think about an early medieval origin of an *urban* 'ghettoization' policy, it's cristal clear that this received its original shape as a contrareformatorial measure (Pope Paul Vl, 1555). In that period the so-called nation-states as absolutist and imperialistic states came also into existence with their immanent anti-aristocratic policies.

However, in both the feodal as the absolutist oikoidalism the following had to be done. First, the most mobile and uncontrollable groups and phenomena (from Jews, Lombards or vagabonds to market interests) and, second, the most dangerous groups in an ideological sense (from heretics to witches and again Jews) had to be eliminated in some way or other. This was meant not only to control or to get rid of these non-conformistic minorities but primarily *to discipline the majority in a double sense:* to make it instrumental to the aims and purposes of the leading elite and to make it conscious of its exploiting capacity against minorities. The last measure is the protection of an undisturbed flow of capital and capital goods in order to sustain or expand state and/or church power.

Small wonder that within the oikoidal grid highly antagonistic interests arose and that often the one hand did not know what the other hand was doing. Therefore, the pinnacle of the State and Church often protected Jews but made it clear to everybody that it had the 'potential duty' to exile, repress or kill this minority. Sociologically speaking, the pinnacle was as isolated as possible because its members had to fight everybody in order to press them within its self-invented oikoidal grid (see the position of Doge and Council of Ten in Venice; the Jewish policy of Charles V, etc.). And if there were no or not enough enemies to establish this grid, enemies could easily be invented under any kind of pretext. The oikoidal *fear-producers* like the Friars, their successors or imitators were and are always in great demand.[51]

What else can be learned from these historical examples for our general subject, the treatment of nomadic and sedentary 'guests'? In about two centuries up to ca. 1650, the mutual learning process of State and Church vis-à-vis many kinds of guests/ minorities was more or less executed (see also next chapter for the dramatic expulsion of Jews from Spain). Some of these Jews were most profitable and kept sedentarized as guests in ghettos or otherwise, to have them on hand for all kinds of dubious affairs of monarchs, church dignitaries or important aristocrats in southern and eastern Europe.

In the latter, the tight control of Russian, Polish or Austrian governments and churches was the main reason for the creation of that special brand, the *Ostjuden,*

---

51. J. Delumeau, *Sin and Fear. The Emergence of a Western Guilt Culture 13ᵗʰ – 18ᵗʰ Centuries* (New York: St. Martin's Press, 1990), part 3 and 4, afterwards one can read the first two parts with much more profit.

which were seen as 'rude, dirty and superstitious' also by 'Jews in the West'.[52] From about the early 17th to the early 20th century, however, they mostly did not live in ghettos but in *shtetl(mestechti* in Russia), hamlets or market-towns more or less regionally concentrated in Eastern Poland and Western Russia. The *divide et impera* policy demonstrated in the Venetian case was ruthlessly executed here as well by giving these Jews (a few) more opportunities than the local population which was terribly repressed and, in the same time, incited against Jews.

That is, in my view, the basic reason why *Ostjuden* in Russia, Poland, Rumania, etc. epidemically suffered from bloody pogroms in which a primitive subjective cruelty was displayed by mobs and at the same time 'enjoyed more protection by kings and nobles, more civil autonomy and religious freedom than anywhere else in Europe'.[53] Indeed, Lindemann forgot to consider the relativity of this remark: in the Dutch Republic at the time they did not need this costly protection and had still those freedoms![54] A more serious omission is that he did not recognise the *divide et impera* trap of the Christian elite and its effects on Jewish communities.

Instead of urban ghettos there was the so called *Pale of Settlement* which 'enclosed' those large territories (together nearly twice as large as France!) in which substantial clusters of rural and urban Jews could live in a rather oikoidal and autarkic way.[55] Within the 'walls' of this 'ghetto-land', Jews were mostly free to do what they liked. They, however, clung together, preserved their customs and were isolated from their non-Jewish environment for several internal and external reasons. Later this type of life encouraged rather romantic stories (Isaac Babel, Bashevish Singer, etc.) or paintings (Chagall) about *shtetl* life or handsome *kletzmer* music.

Babel's immanent cruelty reproduces, in my view, the other side of this isolation which left the eastern Jews too long under primitive circumstances, too long in oikoidal dependence because of their service work for the antisemitic royalty and nobility. This and the internal Jewish contradictions (see below) gave the

52. A.S. Lindemann, *Esau's Tears. Modern Anti-Semitism and the Rise of the Jews* (Cambridge: Cambridge Univ. Press, 1997), p. 51.

53. Idem, p. 59.

54. I. Israel, *The Dutch Republic. Its Rise, Greatness, and Fall 1477-1806* (Oxford: Oxford University Press, 1995) from the first page on; S. Schama, *The Embarassment of Riches* ; Dutch translation (Amsterdam: Contact, 1989), p. 585 ff.

55. This Pale of Settlement (Cherta Osedlosti; 'pale' is also 'fence' and 'boundary') was an administrative construction from the Czarist regime in 1835; it remained until 1917. Around 1900 it had about 5 million Jewish inhabitants, 11% of the populations in the territories of the most western part of Russia from the Baltic Sea to the Krim. Jewish inhabitants were not allowed to move outside this huge area without a special individual permit. Notwithstanding this about 2 million Jews left this *Pale* between 1880 and 1914 in the direction of, in particular, the USA, Britain and other European countries. It's the period in which the West-European and American antisemitic movement received its first and broad popularity.

younger generation a too narrow career perspective which made them leave the region *en masse,* weakening in a fundamental way those what and who was/ were left behind. Last but not least, this remarkable concentration in the East made *Ostjuden* to a large extent an easy prey for bloodthirsty pogrom leaders, e.g. the end assault during the Shoah. All this was impossible or less possible in 'the West', the Utopia for most of them.

Did all this result in a ghetto mentality as well? What does this mentality look like? Probably the answer can be discovered in the following episode of the Shoah. In October 1997, a German female journalist, Ulrike Meyer, visited Czernowitz (Cernauti, Chernovtsy) in the Ukrainian heartland of Jewish life and destruction, the Bukowina.[56] Happily, she had a good feeling for the 'dialectical changes' in the history of this rather unimportant spot on the European map, while she found a spokesman who represented this history perfectly, the 68-year-old Mathias Zwilling, the youngest of the few German-speaking Jews in town.

Czernowitz is now a poverty-stricken, middle-sized city, but in 1775 the village was chosen to become the showpiece of the Austrian Habsburgian government where Jews were given the task to teach the Ukrainians and Rumanians the benefits of German-Austrian civilization. A theatre and a university were established along with many Habsburgian government and military buildings. The Germanspeaking Jews belonged to the bourgeoisie and lived in the centre while Yiddish-speaking Jews lived their *shtetl* life as craftsmen in the outskirts.

Whatever happened in World War II, they are still not on speaking terms; their place in the oikoidal hierarchy is even reproduced in the cemetery. 'We have nothing to do with these people!' says Mathias Zwilling, the Jew who is undoubtedly still proud of his German name, while an important representative of the Yiddish-speaking part, the poet Josef Burg, states: 'During my life, four nationalities have been imposed on me ... This does not matter to me at all ... I am nothing but a Jew.' The German-Austrian language represented here the higher echelons of the oikoidal hierarchy and Yiddish, the German dialect for the lower classes.[57]

Burg was right: in 1918 Rumanians replaced the Austrians; in 1945 the Bukowina became part of the USSR, and now it forms the south-western part of the Ukraine. During the Soviet regime, Jewish life slowly returned to Czernowitz thanks to immigration from elsewhere in the USSR. In 1990 about 18,000 Jews were living again in the town, but today most of the young people have emigrated to the USA, Germany or Israel, and only 5000 Jews, the old ones, stay behind.

In this town the poet Paul Celan was born as Paul Antschel (1920). He studied at its university; he who coined the phrase, *Der Tod ist ein Meister aus Deutschland.*

---

56. *Die Zeit* oct. 1997. For background information see W.O.McCagg Jr., *A History of Habsburg Jews, 1670-1918* (Bloomington: Indiana University Press, 1989) under 'Bukowina' and 'Cernauti Jews'.
57. See the highly interesting S. Landmann, *Jiddisch. Das Abenteuer einer Sprache* (Berlin: Ullstein, 1986).

Indeed, according to Meyer, Czernowitz was visited in the middle of 1941 by one of the worst *Meister*, Dr. Otto Ohlendorf and his *Einsatzgruppe D*. They promptly killed 6000 Jews and deported the remaining 46,000 Jews from the total of 120,000 inhabitants. However, these figures and the circumstances cannot be correct according to Raul Hilberg's rather detailed description of this history.[58]Hilberg reports about Ohlendorf's murder of 682 prominent Jews, while the main thrust of the destruction of the Czernowitz Jews came on the weak shoulders of the highly unreliable Rumanian army and police. Ohlendorf urged the Rumanians 'to start the organization of the ghettoization of the Jewish communities'. That, we learned, was the classical method to get Jews 'at hand'. The Rumanians, however, had other plans: while the Germans killed the Jewish intellectuals, they did the same with the Ukrainian ones who gave them so much trouble during their earlier Ukrainian policy. The Germans were not amused because the Ukrainian nationalists were strong and useful supporters of the Germans who now had to negotiate a major deal with the Rumanians of Antonescu: you shall get your Jews and Communists; we want our Ukrainian nationalists. This is what happened, but a few weeks later both parties collaborated to kill many thousands of Jews. Ohlendorf's group alone was responsible for ca. 100,000 murders in their region of operation.

From Hilberg's data one can deduce that the Czernowitz Jews had to walk very long death marches without food; their Rumanian guides killed them at will in groups or alone; they were decimated quickly, but a substantial part could bribe the Rumanians to leave them fully exhausted in some village. At last they were free to go back to their '*Heimat*'. What freedom, though? To be shot by Ukrainian soldiers, some German *Einsatzgruppe* or other Rumanians roaming around like wild animals, or to be put on trains to a KZ for a definite treatment. Nearly no one returned to Czernowitz. Paul Celan ended up in a KZ, lost his parents but survived; before he could move to Paris (1948), he worked for three years in the Rumanian capital, of all places.

Hilberg tells how there was a remarkable difference in reaction between Jews from different towns. In June 1941, at the moment the Soviets started deportations in the region, the Germans opened their large offensive on the Soviet Union, and the Soviets had to flee. At the moment the Soviets started their evacuation, 'they also urged the university students to leave the town ... but only a few Jewish students followed the retreating Red Army in the end. Most of them [including Paul Celan. D.] stayed, along with the largest majority of the Jewish population. In Kischinew, however, the Germans found only 4000 Jews when they captured the city ...'[59]

---

58. VEJ, in particular p. 822-832.
59. VEJ, p. 822.

Hilberg explicitly reminds the reader that the Czernowitz population was German-speaking and traditionally highly influenced by the German-Austrian culture, which was apparently not the case in the more southern Kischinew, the present capital of Moldavia. It was even more correct to say that only the elite was wholly German-oriented, and its members had apparently so much influence that the 'Yiddish rest' followed the 'inner voice of the *Meister*' as well.[60]

One representative of that elite was mother Zwilling, a medical doctor, who could stay with her 11-year-old son in Czernowitz, but had to move from her comfortable house in the centre into the 'ghetto', a street in the north of the city. Here the journalist found the poor Mathias Zwilling, a retired textile-engineer who still lived 'in this rat lair'. In high spirits Mathias spoke about how he saved the German language with two old Jews byreading together German papers like *Der Spiegel*. Still pleased, he remembered his father as a captain in the Austrian army but not as a Zionist: 'Happily he died in 1936, otherwise we would not have survived the German occupation nor Stalinism'. The journalist further notes: 'My grandfather was appointed an imperial adviser by the Emperor Franz Joseph,' stressed the engineer proudly and, after a pause, continued with 'in 1943 he was killed in Theresienstadt; from his seven children only one survived.' Apparently, Zwilling did not see any contradiction here, but at the cemetery he could not suppress some regret. He was surprised that the Soviets allowed Shoah victims to be buried only as 'innocent Soviet citizens', not as Jews. His deepest regret came from a recent experience concerning the graves of soldiers from the First World War.

The Austrian Black Cross, specialized in repairing these graves, left without caring for the Jewish soldiers' graves after finishing its work for the Christian soldiers. Zwilling's whole family tradition was jeopardized, and he asked for an explanation. Meyer then writes: 'The short answer from Vienna was shocking and highly disturbing for him: "They wrote me that the Black Cross had nothing to do

---

60. Probably the last scholarly investigation before the war in the area – in this case the present most western part of the Ukraine around cities like Uzhorod, Mukacevo, Chust, etc. – is the still highly important J. Mousset, *Les Villes de la Russie Subcarpatique (1919–1938). L'effort Tchécoslovaque* (Paris: Librairie Droz, 1938). He stresses among others (p. 24 ff.) the sharp differences between rich and poor Jews. The first lived in the cities, had alcohol and grain monopolies while they were also managers (see "meier" in note 12) of the domains of the aristocracy which they sub-rented to the peasants. In this way these were exploited in a threefold way. The poor Jews lived only in rural areas. They were as poor as the other, Ruthenian, peasants but could not make common protests: they had a too sectarian belief which isolated them strongly of the rest. A very critical report about this situation was already published around 1900 by an Hungarian government official who was killed afterwards. Mousset concludes that in 1938 this situation was not altered. He defends these poor people who are in need of much external help. Their lethargy could be the very reason why a few years later a SS officer is astonished about the total absence of any protest among Jews of a.o. the Mukacevo region: they could easily flee to the mountains because there was nearly no supervision. Yet, they embarked quiet on the trains to their last destination. See , Hilberg, VEJ, p.906.

with these graves," tells the convinced Old Austrian with a weak voice, "because, in the end, these soldiers were Jews!'"

That's how Jews were and still are made '*vaterlandslos*', 'without a Fatherland', i.e. nomads. The question of what is wrong with this is not unimportant because even today too many people think it worthwhile to die for something like a 'Fatherland'. German Jews in particular thought of it as a definite proof of their assimilation. Those who died as German soldiers (World War I) are used to make an impression in debates.

In this whole dramatic story I am concerned most with traces of a 'ghetto-mentality' which I cannot discover. This is, first, due to the absence of a definition in Weber's or even Wirth's work.[61] Lindeman, in any case, reproduced some 'ghetto traits such as servility, deviousness, clannishness, and fearfulness', which circulated in even the moderate antisemitic circles of German Socialism in the Interbellum.[62] Next, it is due to the absence of ghettos in large parts of Europe and to the existence of the 'ghetto-like' region, the Pale, in Eastern Europe. If we confine ourselves for the time being to a definition like 'social narrow-mindedness', then this qualification must be connected in the story to the persistent adoration for the century-old oikoidal Austrian superpower combined with the persistent denigration for lower classes of such an attitude like toadyism vis-à-vis the oikoidal mighty and kicking at lower-class groups or peoples.

Life in the Pale was, however, also characterized by circumstances in which, normally, the mighty had nothing but disdain for those servile people who did all kinds of good or dirty jobs for them like tax-farming, which made them 'intermediaries between the nobles and the peasantry on the one hand, and the keen competitors of the burghers on the others'.[63] This means not only that they were closely confined to the sedentary agrarian oikoidal life with its immanent tensions but also to a harsh kind of town-country contradictions. As intermediaries, they could gain influence and income from two sides, but they earned without doubt also the suspicion of both sides!

Last but not least, this constellation is also characterised by the reproduction of the Pale classes in the different languages used in the many compartments of life from Latin and French for the mighty to Polish (etc.) for the repressed subjects or higher and lower German for Jews as supporters of the mighty; a dialect for the low factions, a language for the high ones. It is clear enough that the Yiddish-speaking craftsmen and peasants and their Polish (etc.) dialect-speaking colleagues in the lower middle classes had to bear the main burden of the whole system whatever their mutual enmity.

---

61. Compare, for instance, L.Wirth, *Ghetto*, p. 75-97.
62. A.S.Lindemann, p. 174.
63. Idem, p. 59.

Of course, religion had practically no other function than bringing some cohesion to a specific, underdeveloped social compartment. For simple-minded subjects it could bring some consolation, but there is a much greater chance that it was only another instrument of repression, which explains why the clever subjects were eager to get rid of its burden as soon as they could escape the region. Judaism was as primitive as Roman Catholicism or Greek Orthodoxy; Hebrew lent only its alphabet to Yiddish, which was ultimately a German dialect; religion was nothing more than a kind of folkloristic practice adhering to the oikoidal structure, comparable to different kinds of clothes or haircuts. Why? The *Ostjuden*, until the middle of 1941 the largest single concentration of Jews in the world, were here fully assimilated into the sedentary oikoidal life.

From the perspective of the so-called 'ghetto-mentality' and from the historical examples given, therefore, one can only conclude that the adoration-denigration complex was part and parcel of *all* oikoidal rules, governed as these are by deep hatred against each group (and a lesser deep hatred between parts of these groups) in order to sustain the whole oikoidal edifice. More specifically, it is a quality of the centuries-old monarchical or aristocratic social *body* which has to bind its different members closely to its own survival ('Blut') and its own agricultural-based sedentarianism ('Boden').

To support this answer, I could illustrate how after about 1650, in western, central and northern absolutist Europe, that brand of 'Jews at hand' was best reproduced in the *Hofjuden* (court Jews), which in the 19th century transformed easily into what can be called the *Staatsjuden* and into the Jewish minority of the European *Hochfinanz*.[64] Most of them became Christianized, and a substantial part became members of the aristocracy; the largest part earned their substantial capital in state/Oikos-related transactions.

Notwithstanding this apparently total absorption into the traditional oikoidal or governing elite, Jews remained guests, now 'honourable guests' indeed, rendering their oikoidal state-services. Arnaldo Momigliano's description (chapter 1) of their loyalty and deceptions seems proof of this and of Arendt's assimilation thesis mentioned in the beginning. The position of the Jews, from the 'Hofjuden' to the 'Ostjuden', in Venetian as well as Polish or Ukrainian history, seems to be marked by their 'hospitality' within an oikoidal hierarchy, resembling the hierarchy in a so-called *Ständestaat*. This is opposed to a class-society, which developed in the 19th century, with its typical place for a liberal bourgeoisie and town-country contradictions between – say – Polish peasants and urban industrial workers.[65]

---

64. TOT, 11-28; B. Barth, Weder Bürgertum noch Adel, in: *Geschichte und Gesellschaft*, 25 (1999), p.94-123. M. Reitmayer, *Bankiers im Kaiserreich. Sozialprofil und Habitus der deutschen Hochfinanz* (Göttingen: Vandenhoeck & Ruprecht, 1999), p. 163-195.
65. For this subject see my analysis in *Stad en Land, Markt en Oikos*, chapter 8.

Everything points also to the answer that this *oikoidal* kind of assimilation, in the end, could not overcome a deep-rooted defect *within the oikoidal elite* itself. Because the religious branches of it were (and still are!) the most persistent elements and these had to provide the ideological cement of the oikoidal edifice, we can discover the nature of this defect there. In the next chapter it is this constellation which will be scrutinized in its original setting. Thereafter, further conclusions about the relationship between the Jewish and the Nomadic Question can be made.

5. A SPANISH EXPULSION

'What do you say, Jew? What do you propose?
What do you impute? What do you oppose? What do you object?
Behold, our Virgin is of your race, of your descent, of your people,
your nation, your origin. Truly, however, she is of our faith, our belief,
our glorification, our reverence ...'

from Ildefonso de Toledo, *De Perpetua Virginitate Sanctae Mariae* (ca. 657)[1]

In previous chapters the 'Spanish Expulsion of 1492' is referred to as a major mark in the European history of Jews. In its historiography some even perceive it as *The First Holocaust*. Whatever this unbelievable (and irresponsible) exaggeration,[2] for many Jews it concerns the single most important European event before the 20th century Shoah because of its specific political, economic, cultural context. A chain of major European events occurred in a relatively short period known under entries like 'The Unification of the Spanish Catholic Monarchies', 'The Discovery of the Americas', 'Reformation', 'Contrareformation', 'Inquisition', 'The End of the *Reconquista*', 'The Fall of Grenada', 'The Establishment of the Absolutist State', and so on.

However, within this fundamental reshuffle of power, its new Christian legitimation and the modernization of the power organizations, the expulsion of Jews and the related fall of Grenada, i.e. the expulsion of Islam[3], could be seen as historically necessary but superficial happenings. Indeed, in this framework of events, one wonders whether this was 'really necessary' and, why – from a 'Jewish

---

1. Quoted in N. Roth, *Jews, Visigoths and Muslims in Medieval Spain. Cooperation and Conflict* (Leiden: Brill, 1994), p. 19.

2. It is always possible to go further. In *NRC-Handelsblad*, 20-4-2002, some New Yorker journalist, Ron Rosenbaum, who could not stand the extensive European criticism on the Israeli occupation policy, warned the Dutch readers for the last time that they would be supporting '*The Second Holocaust*' if they should continue with their bad habits. We were to believe that Rosenbaum was an authority, because he had already 'explained' Hitler by studying films! Between the given 'first' and this 'second' Holocaust existed the real one from which these demagogues only know the name.

3. The expulsion of 1492 (Jews and/ or *conversos*) is followed by one involving the Moors in 1502-1525 and again eventually in 1609-14.

point of view' (whatever that may be) – the rather unknown 'Spanish pogroms around 1391' could not be of much greater importance.

The interrelations between the Christian, Jewish and Muslim elites in the previous nearly thousand (!) years of Spanish history were mostly close. How close? The Visigothic bishop Ildefonso's exclamation quoted above demonstrates the specific quality of these interrelations: familiar to each other and inimical at the same time. What is the impact of this *competition*? One symptomatic answer: fourteen hundred years later scholars like Max Weber still wrote like Ildefonso and contemporary writers about Cain who, by slaying Abel, was a 'prefiguration' of the Jews who crucified Christ.[4] The mutual false accusations and paranoid exaggerations of elite groups of a most barbarian society apparently survived millennia! Did the profile of the non-conformists, the pariahs, the outcasts remain unchanged as well?

The history of this expulsion of Jews from Spain and Portugal, subject of a whole library, is only discussed here in a few pages because an *archaeology of the pariah complex* can be sketched in a typically European context. I hope to demonstrate why and how the Jewish-Nomadic Question became an *exclusively European problem*.

THE RISE OF THE (JEWISH) PARIAH

What can be called 'Jews' lived in Spain always as a (very) small minority. They are purported to have settled in the Iberian peninsula by the third century; they, anyway, lived here longer than anywhere else including Palestine. Under the Christian Visigoths (6th – 8th century), they were subject to increasing hostility, but the Muslim invasion (711) liberated them from the Christians for many centuries.[5]

---

4. N. Roth, p. 20. Ildefonso and Isidore of Seville were the first ones in Spain to make this comparison, but patriarch Ambrose (ca. 337-397) was the first in Italy to do this. See for the use of Cain in the European and American literature, R. J. Quinones, *The Changes of Cain. Violence and the lost brother in Cain and Abel literature* (Princeton: Princeton Univ. Press, 1991), p. 34 for Ambrose. Quinones's use of Max Weber, by the way, is fully beside the mark (p.64, 240 ff.).

5. For the Catholic interpretation of Visigothic history, see H.I. Marrou and M. Knowles' parts of L. Rogier et al., *Geschiedenis van de Kerk* (Hilversum/ Antwerpen: Paul Brand, 1964), Vol. II, p.232 – 237; Vol. III-1, p. 16-19, 65-71. It is not impressive, but it is worthwhile to quote Knowles who says: 'The short but brilliant period of Visigothic Spain started with the conversion of King Reccared I in 589 ...' (Vol. III-1, p. 200). If Islam had not conquered this land, it would have become 'a very important factor in Europe's development .. (it) .. threatened the Jews to convert or expelled them ..(it) .. had a mighty influence on literature and science of Ireland ..' (id.)! For other interpretations of this history the Internet often provides splendid help. See, for instance, the *Internet History Sourcebooks Project* with a full text of the famous *Visigothic Law* (http://libro.uca.edu/vcode), a special Jewish History Sourcebook with some dramatic documents from 654 and 681, professions of faith from Jews in the Catholic faith, etc. See also S. Alfassa Marks', The Jews in Islamic Spain: Al Andalus, in: www. sephardicstudies.org or the text of the World Jewish Congress on 'Spain' in: www.wjc.org.il. It is, however, much better to start with reading Ramsay Macmullen's *Christianity & Paganism in the*

Before I go in some detail about this short history, two general remarks are in order.

First, the fundamental question of the definition of 'Jew'. Roth thinks that in Visigothic society and in the Roman perception at least, 'Jew' was not so much related to a specific religion as to a certain *ethnos*, a people.[6] Roth does not define 'Jew' and he has forgotten that *ethnos* was a much more general concept than what ethnographers study nowadays. It was related to a group, class and people as well as to a crowd or herd. As a hebrarism, however, it was even similar to 'pagans' and directly related to *ethnos toon Judaioon* (often hopefully translated as Jews as 'the chosen people'). In short, both are *religious* connotations. In addition, in a recent review of the ethnos discussion, medieval Jews are even subsumed under 'pariah castes'.[7]

Most important, however, is the rapid change in the historical repressive practices from the fourth century onwards. The Christian leadership, Byzantine emperors and their governors and generals executed *pagans* on a mass scale in the East and the West, whatever their ethnical background, in order to convert them. Therefore, time and again and still today the Roman Church and its successors and supporters boast that Christ and His Church never look at the colour of a person's skin: they practice a terrible tolerance using the believer – unbeliever dichotomy. It was 'conventional wisdom among the leadership of the church that fear constituted a most essential element' in their several approaches to "the other".[8] The differences between the latter were valued as more or less devilish depending on their subordination under Rome and/or Constantinople. In this respect, Jews as one of these "inimical others" do not form an exception; they had to wait nearly two millennia for their *Sonderbehandlung*.

For this period of the formation of the *Imperium Christianum* in East and West, i.e. the strongest possible unity of church and state, the mutual communication with the large *majority* of people was controlled by the rule that no truce with religious error was allowed:

'Christians might point with envy to the *concordia* that prevailed among non-Christians, just as non-Christians pointed with amazement at the murderous intolerance within the now dominant religion; but there could be no compromise with the Devil.'[9]

Fourth to Eighth Centuries (New Haven/ London: Yale Univ. Press, 1997).

6. N. Roth, p. 35 ff. See also S.K. Jayyusi (Ed.), *The Legacy of Muslim Spain* (Leiden: Brill, 1994), Vol. 1, p.5 and, in particular, p.188-200 (the success story about the Jews in Muslim Spain).

7. A.D. Smith, The Politics of Culture: Ethnicity and Nationalism, in: *Companion Encyclopedia of Anthropology*, Ed. T. Ingold (London, New York: Routledge, 1997), p. 715.

8. R. Macmullen, p, 11.

9. R. Macmullen, p. 14. The first chapter 'Persecution' gives so many shocking examples of these murderous practices that the usual optimistic and innocent 'Praise the Lord's Victory' historiography is definitely replaced by a realistic one. This start could be as disastrous for the legitimation of

The second general remark concerns Roth's continuous use of the term *antisemitism* in his study of the Visigothic – Jewish relationship. He is not the only one.[10] The Visigothic lawgivers could not be antisemites but were anti-Judaists first and foremost because they only dealt with a Jewish *religion*.[11]

Antisemitism started after about 1850 as a consequence of the combination of Social Darwinism with biological, anthropological and cultural theories. This resulted in racial theories which strongly supported practical social, economic, etc. segregation measures not only relative to some 'Jewish and many other races' but also to divisions between so-called 'biologically worthwhile and worthless' people(s). Antisemites and antisemitism paid little attention to religious matters, not least because so many Christians supported antisemitism.

It is, therefore, historically and intellectually false to project antisemitism to the Visigothic era.[12] It seems that even fine historians as Roth are "converted" to conceptual ambiguities only for apologetic reasons. Later I shall return to this issue.

The Visigothic law-fanatics also designed the harshest and most ridiculously detailed anti-Judaistic laws in the Middle Ages, which remains, indeed, a puzzling phenomenon.[13] In my view, the explanation starts with transfering the following remarks from Roth's[14] Visigothic context into a logical one. He agrees that the

---

Christianity as the Holocaust and Shoah. Notwithstanding the enormous number of publications on these latter subjects, there has not yet been a breakthrough into realistic historiography: apart from some archival studies, most of it still belongs to intolerant apologetics. Let's hope that it will not take another 1,600 years as in Macmullen's case (see his p. 12).

10. B. Saitta, *L'Antisemitismo nella Spagna Visigotica* (Rome: L'Erma di Bretschneider, 1995). See also http://ccat.sas.upenn.edu for a long critical review of A.Fear. Saitta is doing the same as Roth (p. 26-35), providing the anti-Jewish laws diachronically, but then over 158 pages. Roth is also to be preferred because he does not force an open door like Saitta who uses his introduction to morally condemn antisemitism. This has been unnecessary, however, for half a century. In addition, he makes a greater blunder than Roth (see text).

11. H. Berman, *Law and Revolution. The Formation of the Western Legal Tradition* (Cambridge, Mass.: Harvard Univ. Press, 1983), p. 52 ff., 511 about the practical meaning of law in this tribal society. For the workings of the tribal law in Visigothic Spain, see also R. Bartlett, *The Making of Europe* (London: Allen Lane, 1993), p. 207. It appeared that Visigothic kings also persecuted Catholics and made use of Jews to collect taxes for them. See Michel Rouche's contribution to R. Fossier (Ed.), *The Middle Ages 350-950* (Cambridge: Cambridge Univ. Press, 1990), p. 67, 89 ff.

12. A. Fear does not criticize Saitta in this way but opposes that 'we must not assume that they were not motivated by a sincere belief that what they [the lawgivers Isidore, Braulio, Sisebut] were doing was right.' Better than this strange motive against the background of Ramsey Macmullen's studies is the question of why Saitta fails to address the problem 'why anti-semitism should have been such a potent tool to employ in such struggles' (p. 2).

13. I fear that a large part of the solution will come from scrutinizing the ideology of the scholars involved and not so much the historical practice which is known already today. From the literature I have consulted, one gets the strong impression that it is still mostly apologetic 'church history'.

14. Roth's apologetic stand is so fundamentalistic and therefore exclusive that he even states: 'No single author has hitherto given more than the most superficial, and hence faulty and incomplete, treatment of the anti-Jewish polemical writings ... My chapter...' etc., etc. (p. 40).

Visigoths did not consider Jews as a 'separate race' and that Jews did not suffer any inferior judicial status.[15] This supports both of my general remarks above. Roth further reveals the fact that there is 'no way of ascertaining even remotely the number of Jews .. and it is nearly as difficult to determine *where* the Jews lived.'[16] He also mentions that there is no evidence as to what a Jew looked like, nor what their language was at this time, and that there is also no evidence of any popular animosity (except when Jews were acting as a tax collector).[17]

From these remarks, one can only conclude that the many harsh anti-Jewish laws issued within a period of a hundred years by Catholic Kings and Councils were just paper without any much effect on the life and goods of the inhabitants called 'Jews'. Roth fails, of course, to come up with victims (still writes about the laws as 'Written in Blood'!), except when he perceives conversion as a negative act.

Anyway, there must have been Jews! A mysterious remark leading to this conclusion is: 'Garcia Iglesias .. notes that the anti-Jewish legislation of Sisebut (612) was directed specifically to the bishops of Tucci (Martos and Jaén), Cordoba, and Montesa (La Guardia), which indicates a preponderance of Jews in those communities.'[18] Supposing that these bishops were not of Jewish descent, the logical conclusion to draw from the above data remains: those are the only locations with (some) Jews, concentrated in a rather small southern area, since there were hundreds of bishoprics in Visigothic Spain.

The given supposition, however, is not so strange because Roth also mentions one convert, bishop San Julián de Toledo (ca. 642-690). Julián wrote a treatise on the soul after death 'that for centuries remained the classic work' on this subject.[19] Roth, however, makes of it 'one of the most important and influential of medieval

---

15. N. Roth, p. 35. Wolfram Drews's interesting analysis of Visigothic terminologies supports the view of the denigrating character of anti-judaistic laws. W. Drews, Jews as pagans? Polemical definitions of identity in Visigothic Spain, in: *Early Medieval Europe* (2000), p. 189-207. However, he also mentions the tendency to put Jews, pagans and Christian heretics (Aryans) into the same category, which deviates from the official religion of the Empire. Even then ' .. Judaism still retained its time-honoured status as a *religio licita*, whereas pagans and heretics were outlawed.' (p. 193; *licita* is something like 'permitted, lawful'). In Visigothic Spain Jews had the right 'to adhere to the religion of their ancestors' until the third council of Toledo in 589. Even then 'the Jews preserved their rank as Roman citizens which they had held ever since the *Constitutio Antoniniana* was passed in 212 ... it was only finally abolished in the middle of the seventh century' (p. 194). Even after Sisebut ordered a wholesale baptism of Jews, 'they do not seem to have been socially isolated ... royal laws blamed catholic clergy for illegally offering support to the Jews.' (id.) Drews ends this part of his article with: 'All this leads to the conclusion that – contrary to official ideology – Jews were not regarded as outcasts; on the contrary, they could rely on the help of Christian neighbours, who seem to have sympathized with them' (p. 195). The words "outcasts" and "neighbours" receive a special meaning in my study. See for the latter, for instance, Prinz's quotation in the beginning of the Introduction.
16. N. Roth, p. 11.
17. Idem, p. 35.
18. Idem, p. 236 note 20.
19. M. Knowles, Vol. III-1, p. 200.

theological treatises ...' while it is difficult nowadays to find Julián's name.[20] The importance here is, however, that Julián as *conversos* was one of the strongest Visigothic anti-Judaists.

An explanation is needed because it seems one of the earliest examples of typical pariah behaviour, to be the harshest critic of one's own tradition. Also, the position of this *conversos* seems to be typical as well: later in the medieval period this man, who earned a sainthood for his anti-Judaism, was accused of heterodoxy by Mozarabic Christians. In other words, he became a kind of "in between" figure, which may be why he disappeared from history.

Other features here of the *pariah complex* are the way *conversos* were and are judged by contemporaries or present partisan historians from *both* sides. A dangerous hypocrisy develops here: when he is doing well, one of the traditions claims it is "because he is now converted" and the other "because he still sticks (secretly) to the old belief". There is seldom understanding for the all too reasonable decision to leave the "old stubborn village" and look for a new existence elsewhere; to risk assimilation into another culture; seldom is there the willingness to comprehend the many difficulties of newcomers in a strange environment.

In closing these Visigothic remarks, a rather hidden conclusion drawn by Roth can receive its logical place:[21] the harsh anti-Jewish paragraphs in the laws of these rather fanatic law-makers were not so much for internal Visigothic as for external use. At that time, the Byzantine religious influence was important in Spain, while the Byzantines had to fight a cruel war against Persians and Jews in the East. A new danger, the Muslims, arrived on the scene as well. All parties tried to massacre as many of its enemies as possible. In addition, the Eastern Jews were perceived as incorrigible conspirators with Persians, Muslims or other enemies of Christians.

In short: these laws were to please more powerful outsiders (in this case, for example, the Roman Church) and to warn less powerful outsiders not to attack or immigrate and insiders not to conspire. Additional measures to overcome Visigothic fears were *compulsory* conversions aimed at transforming potential internal enemies into controlled supporters.[22] Everybody, except powerless

---

20. N. Roth, p. 25. Many Julians played a role in church history, but the man from Toledo cannot be found in, for instance, *The Oxford Dictionary of the Christian Church*, Ed. F. Cross (London: Oxford Univ. Press, 1958) or its concise edition, ed. E. Livingstone (Oxford: Oxford Univ. Press, 1990) nor in *The Cambridge History of Later Greek and Early Medieval Philosophy*, Ed. A. Armstrong (Cambridge: Cambridge Univ. Press, 1980) or C. Andresen, G. Denzler, *Wörterbuch der Kirchengeschichte* (München: DTV, 1984).
21. N. Roth, p. 9 plus 37.
22. See R. Collins, Visigothic Spain 409-711, in: R. Carr (Ed.), *Spain. A History* (Oxford: Oxford Univ. Press, 2000), p.60 states that there is no evidence 'as to how, if at all, those regulations and prohibitions were translated into practice ..' The state measures could have been a fiscal measure but also ' a reflection of the worries that were then being felt concerning the rapid expansion of the Arabs through the former Byzantine provinces of North Africa.' A. Fear (p. 2) supposes that the legislation 'might simply have been a gesture towards an ideology which was not to be taken seriously or possibly

minorities, used this measure, and it remained for many centuries a beloved means to achieve a *strong unity of church and state interests*.

Is it, therefore, understandable that Elie Kedourie and his collaborators did not even mention Jews in Visigothic Spain?[23] And later Jews? Even Roth is flabbergasted that the 'later medieval Spanish Jewish tradition almost revered' the harsh anti-Jewish polemic of Isidore of Seville, the main ideologue in Visigothic Spain; he cannot explain this 'astonishing veneration of .. a bitter enemy of the Jews.'[24] Perhaps, they were proud that several of "their" *conversos* even could become famous bishops? Was this not their best stepping stone to a brilliant carreer in the new Christian society?

This directly leads to the bridge between the beginning of the Christian – Jewish relationship in Spain and its alleged end in 1492. Roth built it in the following way. Concerning the ideological influence of Visigoths on the later Christians from (Northern) Spain, who started the Reconquista, he remarks first, that 'the cruelty and tyranny of the Visigothic kings towards the Jews went for centuries unremarked and unrebuked.'[25] That is right! Thanks to Roth, it is even very difficult to discover today. Furthermore, he stresses several times: 'Visigothic Spain was very far from the democratic and tolerant atmosphere of medieval Christian Spain' or 'the almost *total lack* of any continued impact of these Visigothic attitudes and laws in later Christian Spain' and the 'Christians of the Reconquest were a different breed altogether, and they learned .. the lesson .. of cooperation, of *convivencia*.'[26]

First, it is a chutzpah to talk about 'democratic and tolerant' in these times and particularly from a Jewish point of view. Perhaps in some cities this minority could constitute up to 10 per cent in quiet and prosperous times, but throughout the whole of Spain during the period of about 700 to 1492 it was about 0.5 per cent.[27] Every minority had to accommodate to the wishes and orders of the majority (for a long time Islamitic rulers in the South, Christian ones in the North). It is called 'a myth of the modern liberal imagination' that medieval Islamic Spain was a tolerant society; the same could be said of the fortunes of the

---

of theoretical theology ..' (complaints by Pope Honorius for Visigothic apathy towards anti-Jewish measures).

23. E. Kedourie (Ed.), *Spain and the Jews. The Sephardi Experience 1492 and After* (London: Thames and Hudson, 1994), the best survey to date of the historical facts, opinions, etc. In this matter, by the way, H. Ben-Sasson (Ed.), is silent as well, which is rather puzzling.

24. N. Roth, p. 16 ff.

25. Idem, p. 18.

26. Idem, resp. p. 18, p. 37 and p. 38 (his italics.D.). For the denial see Collins, p. 61 with, for instance, the statement: 'Simply put, the Goths could have come to be seen as the ancestors of the modern Spaniards in the way that the Franks are so regarded by the French and the Anglo-Saxons by the English.'

27. See J. Casey, *Early Modern Spain. A Social History* (London: Routledge, 1999), chapter 1 (An inhospitable land) and 2 (The fewness of people) for the demographic and 'physical' context.

Mudejars (name for Islamic minority in Christian society) and Jews under Christian rule. Religious minorities were subject to all sorts of discrimination; in art and literature one displayed a dismissive arrogance towards Muslims and Jews. In addition, Muslims and Christians 'were simply not interested in one another'.[28]

The only possibility of using the word 'democracy' in Spanish history is given after the death of Franco. Furthermore, it is not true to talk about 'a *total lack*' of continuation regarding the Visigothic laws. The famous *Lex Visigothorum* 'regulated everyday life in the Asturian-Leonese kingdom' and 'would apply over much of Spain until at least the thirteenth century'.[29] In this 13th century the main laws from Alfonso X the Learned of Castile, *Las Siete Partidas* (The Seven Divisions, 1251-1265), were directly inspired by among others the *Lex Visigothorum*, while this 'compendium of legal and customary information remains the foundation of modern Spanish law.'[30] How Alfonso's law is a major step in the "codification of the pariah" is shown in the *Seventh Partida*, the last of the *Seven Divisions*, which fully concerns the dark underside of society in the following sequence of titles: accusations; treason, infamy, corruption; homicide and violence; robbery, theft, larceny, fraud; sex crimes; sorcery and magic; jews; mudejars; heretics, assassins, blasphemers; prisons, punishment, torture, pardons. That is the proper context in which Jews and Muslims (Mudejars, Moors) belong: between accusations and pardons with all sorts of cruel uncertainty in between.

Why exactly this place for Jews (Muslims and heretics) within this sampling of nonconformistic behaviour? The answer should be simple: because for the dominant power in the realm, the Christians, they demonstrated as dangerous a non-conformism as the other 'sources'. The Catholic historian and theologian Robert Burns, however, answers this question in a more complicated way discussed at length in the previous chapter:

> 'Alfonso would probably have responded that Jews and Muslims were guests within Christendom and therefore required a few basic ground rules for their external relations with the host community. ... Jews and Muslims appear under the rubric of crime because the crown feared two kinds of serious crime extrinsic

---

28. R. Fletscher, The Early Middle Ages, in: R. Carr (Ed.), p. 84 ff.

29. Resp. R. Fletscher, p. 68 and R. Collins, p. 58.

30. Cover text on *Las Siete Partidas*, R. Burns Ed.,(Philadelphia: Univ. Philadelphia Press, 2001), Five volumes, in total 1492 pages. Only title XXIV concerns the Jews (p. 1433-1437) and the Moors (p. 1438-1443). 'In Spanish America and the Philippines, the *Partidas* were and are the common basic law.' In California, Louisiana or Texas this law was used until 1924! See http://faculty.washington.edu. For the Visigothic inspiration see, for instance, Vol. 5, p. X ff. If Roth is looking for something democratic, it can be found in the strategicaly important testament laws where the Germanic laws against the Roman law 'enjoined equal shares for all children male or female, rejected the "Universal Heir" so absolutely central to a Roman law will...'(p. xi). Notwithstanding a prohibition of the Visigothic civil law in 1251, this older system survived. For the negligible influence of Judaism and Islam on the development of the European law systems, see H. Berman, p. 588-590.

to the situation of these minorities but omnipresent – apostasy by Christians and conversely mistreatment or coerced conversion of the guest communities to the detriment of public order and Christian belief .. Muslims, Jews, and heretics .. are the ultimate Outsiders, each in their very different way... [That Muslims and Jews appear] with sorcery/magic has nothing to do with the common superstition that Jews were often magicians. Alfonso rather follows a rhetoric in which diviners seek to penetrate God's secrets .. whereas conversely Jews refuse to accept God's workings.'[31]

From the complex background of this law and the situations it covers, I only mention the following in order to provide a possible explanation for the 'rise of the pariah' in this social or cultural context.[32]

Around 1300 Spain was the centre of Jewish and Muslim life in Europe. Like the Christians, both had long traditions, fixed customs, etc. The elites of the three groups 'obsessively feared assimilation', and they established parallel, semiautonomous societies with independent legal, administrative, festive systems. Besides the fact that Burns's *guest* concept is typical 20th century language, with the given characteristics of the mutual communication, the "other" can be only perceived as an enemy with which you can make a deal to arrive at an armistice for the time being. Probably it is this constellation which tempted Roth to use the word 'democracy', but in my view, this contains the ultimate weakness of the whole constellation and the main reason why in 1391 everything exploded in a most terrifying way.

All three parties fostered orthodox religiosity to a large extent and constructed regulations which made the mutual cultural communication officially or formally difficult or even impossible. The smallest of the three, the Jewish minority, officially or formally had to pay the highest price if only because it could only serve the other two. Servants can be dismissed at will. From these regulations those of the largest majority, the Christian one, are well-known. Let's look a bit closer at this variable, i.e. *Las Siete Partidas* and its impact.[33]

First, there is the matter of the *definition* of 'Jew' and 'Moor'. Title XXIV law I states: 'A party who believes in and adheres to the law of Moses is called a Jew, according to the strict signification of the term, as well as one who is circumcised, and observes the other precepts commanded by his religion.' With the definition of 'Moor' in this law, we are confronted in a peculiar way with the Abraham story in chapter 1. The preamble and law I of Title XXV says: 'The Moors are a people who believe that Mohammed was the Prophet and Messenger of God, and for the reason that the works which he performed do not indicate the extraordinary

31. Idem, Vol. 5, p. xxvi. For the following quotations see Idem, p. xxvi-xxxii.
32. See further E. Kedourie (Ed.), p. 42 ff.
33. For Islamic regulations see, for instance, *Las Siete Partidas*, Vol. 5, p. xxxv and the excellent chapters on Mozarabs, Mudejars, Moriscos, etc. in S.K. Jayyusi (Ed.), p. 149-273.

sanctity which belongs to such a sacred calling, his religion is, as it were, an insult to God.' And further: 'Sarracenus, in Latin, means Moor, in Castilian, and this name is derived from Sarah, the free wife of Abraham, although the lineage of the Moors is not traced to her, but to Hagar, who was Abraham's servant.'

What belongs, in fact, to the definition of Jew is the *historical reason* why Jews have been fallen deeply in Spain (XXIV law III). They

> 'were formerly highly honored, and enjoyed privileges .. for they alone were called the People of God .. they disowned Him who had honored them .. humiliated Him, by shamefully putting Him to death on the cross .. and therefore from the day when they crucified Our Lord .. they never had either king or priests among themselves, as they formerly did. The emperors, who in former times were lords of all the worlds, considered it fitting and right that .. they should lose all said honors and privileges, so that no Jew could ever afterwards hold an honorable position, or a public office by means of which he might .. oppress a Christian.'

The differences are obvious: Jews are called 'a party' and Moors 'a people'; the title concerning the latter gives the strong impression that the lawgiver is much more prudent than in the Jewish case and his knowledge about this people and their religion is negligable (for instance, that Moors are usually circumcised as well, is not yet known). In some way or other, Jews are historically accepted as failing ancestors of Christians. The Moors, on the other hand, are relatively new and still dangerous "external strangers"; the Jews are "internal strangers" you cannot trust anymore, because the (Christian) Bible and (Christian) emperor ordered their punishment. Even if Moors are called a 'people', they are still judged only in *religious* terms. More differences appear in the following laws.

Title XXIV states that 'no force or compulsion shall be employed in any way against a Jew to induce him to become a Christian' (law VI); the same was said about Moors. It could be a formula borrowed from the 8th century pact between the Muslims and the Christians after the former conquered Spain.[34] However, what cannot be found in Muslim regulations is: 'Where a Christian is so unfortunate as to become a Jew, we order that he shall be put to death just as if he had become a heretic..' (law VII). Law VIII forbid 'any Christian man or women to invite a Jew or a Jewess, or to accept an invitation from them, to eat or drink together ..', etc. Law IX states that Jews who have sexual intercourse with Christian women 'shall be put to death' (the same applies to Moors), and also copied from the Visigothic Code is the order 'that all Jews, male and female, .. shall bear some distinguishing mark upon their heads ..' (does *not* concern Moors), otherwise they apparently could not be identified.

---

34. M. de Epalza, Mozarabs: an emblematic Christian minority in Islamic Al-Andalus, in: S.K. Jayyusi (Ed.), p. 152 ff.

Concerning the Moors (Title XXV) there are several marked differences apart from the more prudent and circumstantial language. Its law IV concerns the punishment reserved to Christians who become Moors. After giving several reasons why people can 'become insane' to accept this faith (not given in the Jewish case), comes: '.. they are guilty of very great wickedness and treason .. [again explanation. D] .. Wherefore we order that all those .. shall lose all their possessions, and have no right to any portion of them, but that all shall belong to their children (if they have any) who remain steadfast in our Faith .. and in addition to this, we order that if any person who has committed such an offense shall be found in any part of our dominions he shall be put to death.' Here is a substantial difference with the comparable Jewish law which is very short and deadly.

This Title XXV also has other characteristics. Although it concerns Moors, law III gives *general* directions to be very kind to all converts who anyway 'acknowledge the superiority of our religion', because they have already suffered so much trouble in leaving their old habits, family, belief, etc. Also, law VI concerns Christian married women who want to become 'Jewess, a Moor, or a heretic'. Her only punishment is that her property shall belong to her Christian husband. Then follows: ' .. we decree that her husband if he becomes a Jew, a Moor, or a heretic, shall undergo the same penalty which we stated should be inflicted upon his wife.' This nullifies, in my view, law VII of the former Title in which a death penalty was prescribed for a Christian who became a Jew.

Next, there is law VIII of the Moor Title in which a Christian 'who becomes a Jew or a Moor' and who afterwards repents shall 'be pardoned, and released from the penalty of death which we stated in the fourth law preceding this one' if he will 'render some great service to the Christians resulting in the substantial benefit of the country..' This gives a chance to make a deal with the authorities, a possibility which is only open to rich people.

I shall now come to a general conclusion about the 'rise of the pariah' in this Spanish history so far. Maybe Burns's answer, Jews are considered as guests, is quite right from the Catholic religious point of view. Although it seems contradictory, he may also be right to reassure us that, in fact, *Las Siete Partidas* was promulgated with a view to pleasing 'the clergy and the rabble, always clamoring for the persecution of heretics and infidels.'[35] There was, however, not only a "technical" discrepancy between the letter of the law and its practical application, there were large social and cultural discrepancies as well. In addition, *Las Siete Partidas* did not take deep root in society, and the pressure of the localities to keep their own customs still blocked the unification efforts of the kings.[36]

Around 1300 the three groups (Christians, Jews and Muslims), which were mutually strongly divided, each had *internally* sharp antagonisms between elite and

---

35. Idem, Vol. 5, p. 1437 note.
36. H. Berman, p. 513.

'base'. Members of the elite (in itself already divided between 'priests/rabbis/imams and laymen') could make many sorts of deals with their colleagues in the other groups, but notwithstanding this they remained strangers to each other. At the 'base-level' there was only an elementary communication between the three groups, which explains why a rather profound enmity prevailed. All this resulted in a hypocritical atmosphere on all levels of society. The last quotation from Burns continues with:

> '.. for it was notorious that they [these laws. D.] were constantly violated. Ecclesiastics sold Christian slaves to Jews, without any attempt at concealment. Individuals of each [group] kept concubines belonging to the other openly in their houses, and even kings did not hesitate to entertain beautiful Jewesses as their mistresses before the eyes of the court.'

In chapter one Momigliano's family history revealed a comparable situation. The existence of this assertive and morally lax 'upperworld' also created a favourable climate for all possible *conversos* relations between the elites. However, after 1350 an increasingly orthodox tendency in the 'basic world' seriously undermined this upperworld culture, including the *conversos* position. At the moment this ambiguous constellation was confronted with a general worsening of the situation in Spain, and all nasty elements of the *conversos* movement as pariah movement rose to the surface.

An European model of the pariah complex developed which I want to discuss in the next section looking back from that notorious year 1492 in which so many institutions and persons squared their accounts with each other.

THE "PIGS" OF 1492

In the years 1492-1496 Jews were expelled by the 'Catholic Kings' Ferdinand and Isabella of Spain and, later, by Don Manuel, king of Portugal. One hundred years earlier, anti-Jewish pogroms had swept through Christian Spain, the likes of which had *never* been seen before. What was going on in this long Spanish 15th century? Only Fernand Braudel, traditionally, looked at the expulsions as a result of overpopulation and an attempt to redistribute the scarce resources.[37] For early

---

37. F. Braudel, *The Mediterranean and the mediterranean world in the age of Philip II* (London: Fontana, 1975), Vol. 1, p. 415. If Braudel had only studied the very small percentages of Jewish population (0.5 per cent in Castile, elsewhere probably more) he would never have made these statements. At this moment in the whole of Spain the numbers of inhabitants must have been about 4 million people (J. Casey, p. 21). If Jews attained something about – say – 3 and 0.5 per cent, there were between 120,000 and 20,000 Jews, but the latter figure must be too low (see below). Since Malthus, the alibis for expelling undesirable folk have increased with the powerful and magic 'overpopulation' slogan. At the moment, in one of the richest countries of the world with plenty of space, the Netherlands, right-wing and fascist politicians incite followers with the idea to expel

modern Europe, others say, this expulsion had the impact of the Holocaust in our century. Certainly, it was a major but not unprecedented event which did not have strong effects in other parts of Europe like the Mediterranean.[38] Is it, indeed, to be compared with the 20th century Holocaust or Shoah?

The shortest answer is: no. First, not with the Shoah because the expulsion concerns *not so much Jews as baptized Christians*.[39] There are, secondly, many motives behind this expulsion, but the main one according to Kamen was to convert all Jewish inhabitants and leave them in Spain. This should concern also the subsequent decree of 1502 directed against the Muslims of Castile. More about motives later; there are other things to consider as well.

An act of expulsion is so often used in Spanish history up to 1492 against Muslims in 'reconquered' regions and probably against Jews during a Visigothic or Almohad regime; after 1492 it is used again in Spain several times. That does not sound very original. To compare this with a wholesale extermination in a system of concentration camps and killing machines 450 years later is impossible. It is an irresponsible downgrading of the 20th century phenomena of the Holocaust and Shoah with its many millions of victims in a highly civilized society.

Not only is the number of Jews involved in each case in no way comparable, the expulsion has nothing to do with physical killings as in the 1391 pogrom.[40] This '1492' is, furthermore, often used by Zionists and their predecessors as a horror

---

foreigners with the slogan: 'Holland is full!' (while the established parties – including left wing ones – easily jump onto this bandwagon). And, indeed, in 2004 this Christian country and their parties decided against all international agreements, mores and modest opposition to expel 20,000 foreigners.

38. J.H. Elliott, *Imperial Spain 1469-1716* (Harmondsworth: Pelican, 1978), p.99 – 110. See, in particular, H. Ben-Sasson (Ed.), p. 713-723, 754 ff.

39. Even a fine historian as Henry Kamen in E. Kedourie (Ed.), p. 76, dares to talk about 'a veritable holocaust by the normal civilized standards of western Europe, unprecedented in the history of Spain or any other country...'. Then follows his italicized warning quoted in my text. The question of why these scholars exaggerate in such an irresponsible way is in need of a special study.

40. Most of the time, one reads about 300,000 Jews who were expelled, but S. Katz, *The Holocaust*, p. 370, note 241, mentions 215,000, and a figure of 100,000 seems to him 'too cautious'. E. Kedourie (Ed.), p. 114, states that '200,000 Jews left, of whom 120,000 crossed the border into Portugal .. The rest went by sea to North Africa and eastwards ..' It is a mistake that J. Casey, p. 223, still writes 'up to 200,000 may have left', although he could have known better. In a review of Kedourie's book (*TLS*, 17-2-1992), David Wasserstein informs us that the newest research must lead to the conclusion 'that the total number of exiles cannot have been very much higher than some 50,000.' Henri Kamen reaches lower: 'Possibly not more than 40,000 to 50,000 ..' in: E. Kedourie (Ed.), p. 90. Interesting are the figures in Ottoman statistics in Idem, p. 165. In his newest study, *Empire. How Spain became a world power 1492-1763* (New York: Harper, 2003) Kamen even states that 'no more than fourty thousand' Jews left (p. 22; 'few Jews', p. 342), among them the richest families (so the poor stayed and converted, while the rich left?). The practice was very different from inquistitional theory or laws: Jews 'lived freely in most territories of the empire long afterwards.' (p. 343, 378). Anyway, in this so-called "First Holocaust" one cannot use the abstract "victims" but the concrete "exiles" only because there is the false suggestion that – say – all 50,000 "victims" were 'killed Jews'.

scenario of what modern or old assimilants could do against supporters of colonizing Palestine.[41] Some present Israeli historians, still writing history based on religious principles, are upset about the widespread anti-Judaism of the *conversos* or *marranos* (Spanish for *pigs*), although many *marranos* had to flee or were killed as well.[42]

There are several other relevant features in the events which should be treated here because they concern patterns of behaviour in competing parties which are seen here for the first time and reproduced time and again in Western European history.

In 1492, the fall of Granada symbolized the very reason why Jews had to disappear. Granada was the last stronghold of the pagans, of the foreigners, of a superb *secular* culture, of 'The East' which had always highlighted by its very existence the general backwardness of the *religious* oikoidal war-machine. Now the centralization process of the king's bureaucratic power base could be completed with a victory over the regional overlords including those of the Church. The time had come to show who dictated the (secular) norms throughout Spain. Certainly, '1492' proved the military and ideological superiority of the new Spanish ruling elite centred around the royal court. Later, this elite would crown itself with a new capital, Madrid (ready ca. 1562), at the summit of this development.

Here, for the first time in a new world, the Spanish secular and Roman religious *universality claim* was announced (1493): possessing the divine right of justifying and sanctifying the conquering of everybody's land, the suppression of everybody's mind by God's fire and sword. The spirit of pope Gregory's and emperor Justinian's Christian world domination not only started to haunt the Mediterranean again but Western and Northern Europe as well.

---

41. Before the war, a study about 'ethnic identities' of peoples from many regions in the Netherlands also included a chapter about the dispersed living Jews. Many Jews in this country were *marranes* coming from Spain and Portugal in the 16th century. A Jewish historian (Izak Prins, 1927) is quoted who writes about the *marranes* as people 'for whom religion is a means and a lie', 'who betrayed Judaism ...', 'who knew that they only deserted Judaism for the money ...', '... they hated their former co-religionists the most whom they considered stupid and narrow-minded.' The author states that the *marranes* asked the king to repress the Jews. However, these *marranes* became Jews again after living for some years in Amsterdam! J. Leydesdorff, De Nederlandse Joden, in: P.J. Meertens, A. de Vries (Ed.), *De Nederlandse Volkskarakters* (Kampen: Kok, 1938), p. 486, 487. The author, social psychologist and, in many respects, a self-complacent Zionist, considers the Dutch Jew still as 'privileged compared to his brothers elsewhere' (p. 499) because he is more assimilated. In the next sentence, however, he paints an apocalyptic scene in which the Dutch Jews come close to annihilation. This is not due to Nazi Austrians or Germans but to their assimilation: 'his family-ties, his sexual chastity, his modesty, they are in the process to disappear; vices which were unknown to him appear, like dipsomania, fornication and licentiousness'. The medicine for these diseases is found in emigration to Palestine, the promised country, the 'empty land without people' suitable for 'a people without land'.
42. See H. Ben-Sasson (Ed.), 758 ff.

The *Expulsion of 1492* has to be placed within this basic framework. Mostly, it is seen as the endresult of the *Reconquista*, but that is more a matter of chronology. In my view at least, this reconquest ended in the middle of the thirteenth century (in military terms: fall of Cordoba), after which the Spanish immediately started with the usual dynastic policies (marriages, military and diplomatic interventions to influence successions, etc.) on a Mediterranean (Italy, North Africa) and later European scale. The most famous marriage, that between the rulers of Aragon and Castile (1469), belongs to the prelude of the expulsion history. 'Cordoba' signalled the end of 600 years of "military cooperation" with the Muslims, paralelled by a substantial social, economic and cultural 'cooperation'.

Compared to the Islamic legacy in Spain, the Jewish legacy was of minor importance. Nevertheless, a highly arabised and converted elite of Jewish descent flowered as courtiers, scholars, etc. Its members were simply retained when the Christians took over power. They were experienced in government administration and diplomacy,

> 'but, as before, they were not contenders for ultimate power and were thus more trustworthy than Christians ... [They] were outside the feudal system; they were completely dependent on the ruler to guarantee their rights and to protect them against the masses and the Church ... the Jewish courtiers were desirable as the bearers and mediators of the culture of prestige among the far less sophisticated knights and clerics of the Christian kingdoms.'[43]

One effect was that the 'Jewish' communities gained considerable autonomy, and 'as before', the courtiers were seen as heads of these communities. A process of assimilation into the Christian world started. By the end of the 13th century, however, in the large reconquered areas, the Jewish culture had almost completely lost its Arabic cast and, therefore, Jews had lost a substantial part of their attractiveness as courtiers, etc.

Meanwhile, its elite started to copy the behaviour and lifestyle of the Christian aristocracy. It could do this thanks to their oikoidal work *par excellence*, in particular as tax-farmers; they invested substantial capital in land, started a marriage-policy into the aristocracy, converted and so on. In short: this elite *sedentarized* in the most classical way and, like all "new money" and parvenus, tried to be the largest, the biggest, the richest, not realizing how much jealousy and envy they aroused among "old money". Once they were called *marranos*, it was rather difficult to get rid of this invective.

Jews were not only active in the oikoidal part of society but also in the market. What can be said about their commercial gains and losses in, for instance, the

---

43. See for this and the next quotation, S.K. Jayyusi (Ed.), Vol. 1, p.196, 197.

highly mobile and uncontrolled world of "international" seatrade and merchants?[44] In the Visigothic period there were already Jewish traders, they were mentioned in legal statutes as ship-owners, slave traders and marine merchants. Not before the late 10th century are Jewish traders mentioned anew. The cities of al-Andalus like Almería, Seville or Málaga were main trading centres in the Mediterranean during most of the 8th till the end of the *reconquista* (13th century).

In the beginning Muslim traders dominated fully (economically, politically and socially), and Jewish traders played a minor role. Later, Jews from Christian Spain joined the merchants in the Mediterranean, and from the east of this sea came another Jewish contingent. In the 11th century, therefore, Jews gained substantial profits with trade in many products. As the reconquest continued Christian traders also joined this sea trade. Jewish traders then apparently disappeared in the middle of the twelfth century from Muslim Spain. Why this happened is rather unclear, but it is likely that the arrival of the Almohad regime had something to do with it. The information is contradictory, because under this regime Jewish trade continued. It is possible that they decided to play the Christian card.

It is striking how the merchants separated themselves by their choice of associates into religious and, less importantly, geographically based groups (Andalusis with Andalusis, etc.). This religious division was apparent even regarding the trading routes and the sort of cargo (Christian merchants did not buy and sell Christian slaves; Jews never traded timber, etc.). Jews and Christians traded freely with all regions, whereas Muslim merchants generally restricted their activities to the Islamic realm and the southern coasts of the Mediterranean.

In particular, Muslim traders were well-known for the merchant-scholar phenomenon.[45] Many of them were also ship-owners, doctors, soldiers, government officials and scholars. A study among 14,000 entries describing Andalusi Muslim scholars in biographical dictionaries revealed that 4,200 had some trade in textile products, foods, jewels, books, perfumes, leather-work, etc.

Later, Ibn Khaldûn (1377), who commented extensively on the various aspects of making a living and acknowledged that 'honest traders are few', perceived two distinct types of merchants.[46] First, there is the crafty, tenacious businessman concerned

---

44. For the following see O. R. Constable, *Trade & Traders in Muslim Spain. The commercial realignment of the Iberian peninsula, 900-1500* (Cambridge: Cambridge Univ. Press, 1995) and her article, Muslim merchants in Andalusi international trade, in: S.K. Jayyusi (Ed.), Vol. 2, p. 759-773.
45. See Idem, *Trade*, p. 54 ff. and S.K. Jayyusi (Ed.), idem, p. 769, 770.
46. See Idem, *Trade*, p. 56. The quotations come from Ibn Khaldûn, *The Muqaddimah. An Introduction to History.* Franz Rosenthal edition (Princeton: Princeton Univ. Press, 1967), Vol. 2, p. 342-343. Italics from Rosenthal.

'with buying and selling, earning money and making a profit. This requires cunning, willingness to enter into disputes, cleverness, constant quarreling, and great persistence ...qualities detrimental to and destructive of virtuousness and manliness .. Those who are of a very low type and associated closely with bad traders who cheat and defraud and perjure themselves .. [d]eceitfulness becomes their main characteristic. ... *If a merchant always practices cunning, it becomes his dominant character quality. The quality of cunning is remote from that of manliness which is the characteristic quality of rulers and noblemen.* .. There exists a second kind of merchant .., namely, those who have the protection of rank and are thus spared (the onus) of having anything to do personally with such (business manipulations). They are most uncommon ... have come into the possession of a good deal of money .. or have inherited money from a member of their family .. they have obtained the wealth that helps them to associate with the people of the dynasty and to gain prominence and renown .. they are too proud to have anything personally to do with such (business manipulations) .. It is easy for them to have the magistrates confirm their rights, because (the magistrates) are familiar with their beneficence and gifts .. Their manliness, therefore, will be .. very remote from these destructive qualities.'

In this way Ibn Khaldûn sketched the sharp distinctions between market and oikoidal interests and behaviour; it's clear where his sympathy as famous adviser of kings lies. Whatever his criticism of the market behaviour, he is honest enough to provide us also with a clear insight into the dark sides of the Oikos: the typical immanent corruption of (aristocratic) oikoidal life; its dependence 'on the dynasty' which must be buttered up constantly; its protection-against-gifts policy; its hollow macho-ism, etc.

Whoever switches for whatever reason from the market into the aristocratic and monarchical Oikos has to change his conduct in a fundamental way. The author of the *Muqaddimah* prepared a concept and proverb for this switch: *to sedentarize, sedentarization.* For him, they express the connotation of a civilization which settles itself in a city to grow in power, splendour, wisdom and luxury. It's the reverse of the harsh and pure life of the *nomadic* Bedouin. As indicated, a highly mobile, rich segment of the Jewish population in Christian Spain took the former road and created the first prototype of what later would be called the (Christian) *Hofjuden*. Bonds between Oikos and Market were also coined in other sectors.

In the 13th century Christian Spanish and Italian traders dominated because they now had the advantage of support from the new Christian rulers, and Barcelona and Valencia became booming tradeports. This political, commercial and naval Christian hegemony was, as usual, much more discriminating than the Muslim one. In, at least, the north-western Mediterranean

'... non-Christian traders were forced to do business according to Christian rules. Muslim and Jewish travelers were likewise obliged to seek passage on Christian ships, even though Muslim authorities might object to this mode of transport. The latter trend was already clear by the late twelfth century ..'[47]

These inimical acts were aimed at saving the Christian world from foreign influences. As shown above, it is the same lack of communication as demonstrated earlier within Spain between Christians, Muslims and Jews.

Slowly, the Mediterranean became a largely Christian lake in this way. Several developments point in the same direction. Aside from some data about Granadan Muslim traders, there is little information of their business in the 15th century. Jewish merchants 'were no longer useful as commercial go-betweens and they concentrated their activities within either the Christian or Muslim commercial spheres.'[48] They also did not venture into the Atlantic trade. However, the Muslim minority in Christian Spain, the *mudejars*, apparently took over the go-between role. In Valencia, from the beginning of the *Reconquista* tolerant against un-believers, these Muslim natives of the city developed a flourishing trade with Granada, Venice, etc. and Muslim countries in the 15th century.

Not only in commerce but also in production, nearly everything was turned upside down in Spain. Notwithstanding the Christian (Spanish, Italian and even Dutch) dominance in seatrade, the Peninsula had lost the commercial importance of the Muslim period. Dutch/ Flamish cloth was sold which effected Spanish textile production; a dramatic decline in production of some staple exports (silk) and a rise in the wool exports had serious regional consequences and determined the fate of its rulers. Spain was no longer a major international entrepot.

This wool sector demonstrates as no other what happened in the long term with Spain and which great conflict existed permanently in (early) modern Spain. The economist Caxa de Leruela phrased it in 1631 as the conflict *'between Cain and Abel, between pasture and arable.'* With this we are back in the problematic of chapter 2 and 3 so that I can confine this to a very few remarks.

From early on throughout Spain, a nomadic-pastoral economy was the main feature of the mountainous and hilly country, while people also practised a 'nomadic' shifting cultivation, adapted to the poor soil and shortage of rain.[49] They both formed a true frontier society 'something akin to the range war of the American West – the battle between the rancher and the dirt-farmer.' This form of extensive farming was only possible due to the lack of 'private property', while for the nomads the word 'property' was anathema at all.

---

47. Idem, *Trade*, p. 252.
48. Idem, p. 254.
49. For the following including its quotations see J. Casey, p. 47ff.

Against this "moveable block", the cities, the feudal rulers, the church, the monarchy, the 'normal arable and propertied interests', etc. fought a constant battle because they could not control the huge movements of animals from high in the North to deep in the South and back (the largest and best organized *Mesta* since 1273), from high to low areas and back, from mountains to coasts, etc. They not only could not control the movements of millions of beasts, but they were also dependent on the nomadic work: (merinos) wool was for centuries the main Spanish export product; leather products, meat or milk were in high demand in the cities and elsewhere.

Only at the places of export or other points of delivery could church and state satisfy their permanent tax-hunger. A constant negotiation about transhumance routes, the use of grasslands, the prices of wool, meat, manure, etc. was the result of their refusal to pay taxes to the tax-farmers (often Jews or *conversos*). The Crown had to allow the *Mesta,* but it also did everything to undermine its power, for instance, by allowing the establishment of enclosures for arable land.

In 1492, however, the *Mesta* and all other nomadic activities were still in full swing: a new law forbade owners of land once rented to the *Mesta* to offer the lease to anyone else at a higher rent. A few years later a law allowed the *Mesta* to stop the 'conversion of any of its pasture to arable.' Two fundamental blows to the dealers with land and property. Who was Cain and who Abel?

Against this political economic background, we have to place the decline and fall of the Jewish presence in Spain, which certainly started in 1391 and officially ended in 1492.

First, the Northern 'Jewish' elite increasingly had to face the Christian ideological attacks and, therefore, the creation mechanisms of the 'eternal enemy'. They, however, reacted *accordingly* (instead of looking for alternatives in the Maghrib, for example, as many Arabic-Jews had done[50]) by taking over *religious* and Northern European features of these mechanisms. The growing antagonism was certainly aggravated by the internal adoption of a deliberately isolationistic policy as expressed in the use of Hebrew, Talmud or Kabbala. Last but not least, the sedentarization of Jews as described earlier made them underprivileged and mostly of modest means.[51] Therefore, their possibilities to chose alternatives were limited.

The other side of the coin was the unavoidable distancing from all this in a conversion to Catholicism. After this act, *Jew* has to be placed between brackets for a large part of the former Jewish elite. In many cases this alternative was chosen

---

50. R. Fossier (Ed.), *The Middle Ages 1250-1520* (Cambridge: Cambridge University Press, 1986), p. 360-373. For the next passage, see J. Genot-Bismuth, Le Mythe de l'Orient dans l'eschatalogie des Juifs d'Espagne ...., in: *Annales ESC* (1990), p. 819-838.

51. H. Kamen's article in E. Kedourie (Ed.), p. 79.

more or less voluntarily, but in times of social and political crisis it was often forced upon Jews and other sects.[52] The introduction of these converts caused traditional factors to predominate within Islam itself. In the later Spanish Muslim culture, a conversion to Islam was comparable to assimilation in a modern USA society, while the new wave of forced conversions to Spanish Catholicism seemed to create only zealots.

In other words, at least sociologically, the small minority of religious Jews which was established in Christian Spain had to struggle with a dominant alien belief system, with *conversos* who loudly ceased to be Jews and with its own drive to Jewish sectarian orthodoxy.[53] Therefore, by the end of the 14th century, this Jewish part of the *entire* religious climate had developed fundamentalistic traits in its upper and lower ranks with all its consequences.

Next, a gradual emancipation of nobles and clerics from dependency on Arabic-'Jewish' and Jewish court influences resulted in an increasing competition between the old Jewish/new Christian and old Christian oikoidal powers in the four parts of Christian Spain. The scenario painted in the story about the Venetian ghetto can be discovered at the end of the 14th century in Spain as well. Now, for the first time in European history, it is played out in all its harshness. As such it is historically much more important than the expulsion of 1492.

So, around 1390 the (lower) nobility connived with the monks – this time Dominicans – using the mob to spark anti-Jewish and anti-*conversos/marranos* riots, killings, a mass of forced conversions, etc. in order to put pressure on the secular and religious leadership with their courts and 'highest circles'. It's obvious that, first and foremost, the poor or non-elite Jews were the main victims of this power-play.

The next lesson which was learned for the first time was how the ruler, the government or the state had to operate within growing political, economic and religious tensions.[54] Backed by the best theologian of the Roman and Catholic Church, Thomas Aquinas and his natural law (still official doctrine today; thus, homosexuals, lepers and Jews are 'unnatural'), and by the usual demonization and

---

52. S.K. Jayyusi (Ed.), Vol. 2, p. 850 ff. See also Idem, p. 899 ff. about the heretics in Al-Andalus and their treatment around the 11th century. In particular, here the so-called *zindiq* are interesting,'an apostate who has secretly fallen away from Islam under the cloak of outward conformity, and he must be beheaded ... in fact his hypocrisy and concealment of his true belief' was the basic accusation. In the 14th and 15th century converted Jews were similarly accused by Catholics.

53. See, for instance, the drive of the Alconstantinis family to greater wealth and influence in E. Kedourie (Ed.), p. 37 ff. and its impact. The most remarkable fact is that Jews tried to enlist the help of the Fransciscans and Dominicans to destroy their Jewish competitors. It was these monks, among others, who acted later as the murderers of Jews. See also the *Jewish* attacks on 'the wealthy, corrupt, and irreligious Jewish aristocracy [which] were made .. in the *Zohar* and by an anonymous .. kabbalist ..' (p. 39).

54. For the following, see A. Mackay's and E. Gutwirth articles in E. Kedourie (Ed.), p. 33-74.

for Catholics very 'natural' rumours (ritual murder of a boy, host desecrations, blood libel, etc.), kings started to act accordingly.

One ruler of Castile tortured and killed his most devoted chief treasurer, tax farmer, confiscator of the lands of rebelling nobles, the Jew Samuel Halevi (1361). True, the latter played a rather dangerous double game by using his job for amassing a fortune for himself. His king apparently became too suspicious. Probably, Halevi was a typical parvenu who also build in Toledo 'the most beautiful synagogue' with a Christian name (*Tránsito*) to honour himself and his king. Was all this at that time a legitimation for murder? This seems to be an 'after Auschwitz question': *Las Siete Partidas* gave numerous cases, methods and reasons for torture as lawful means.

A few years later a civil war with foreign interventions plunged Castile into anarchy, and the unscrupulous Henry of Trastámara *invented a tradition* in order to win his crusade against another tyrant with its infidel helpers. One of the main factors of his victory 'was undoubtedley his skilful use of antisemitic propaganda.'[55] Therefore, the first feature of the invented tradition is: the creation of a foreign, inimical, *partly* invisible (*some truth* must be known) and terrifying power as a means to win a power game over a competitor at home.

It is unimportant here that Henry's activity had nothing to do with anti-semitism, but with anti-Jewish and anti-Morish measures. These were serious enough: Jewish communities were forced to pay very large sums to Henry, and they did (Burgos, Toledo, 1366). Next year, he came back with its soldiers and asked for similar sums. In the case of Toledo, for instance, Henry ordered the official of the city

> 'to sell by public auction ... all the Jews and Jewesses of the Jewish community of Toledo and all their landed and moveable possessions until the sum he had demanded had been raised. To facilitate matters, his treasurer was empowered to torture any Jews who offered resistance.'

One may suppose that this Henry did not believe the fantastic stories he propagated about Jews and Moors, but – and that was new – they served as legitimation for strong repression of a minority to gain the support of the majority.

After his victory, Henry reverted to the traditional royal policy as Henry II (1369-79): a Jew or *conversos*, Joseph Picho (see next paragraph), was nominated as his next treasurer; a Jewish medical doctor had to look after the king's health; Samuel Abravanel had to farm his taxes, etc. With this, his invented tradition gained another new feature with a remarkable future: Jews as leading administrators and/or executors of the ruler's decisions were 'not contenders for ultimate

---

55. Idem, p. 48 also for the next quotation.

power' (see above) and, therefore, trustworthy and replaceable at will as if they were a pair of shoes.

Henry understood the other side of this coin also very well: "they" had apparently the ambition to function as a "pair of shoes" for the mighty and powerful, knowing that without these tools, the mighty cannot walk at all. Why did this ambition exist? Jews and other people in the same position in Visigothic, Muslim and Christian times belonged to small minorities without any competing power and always at the mercy of *alien* rulers. They cannot resist being killed; to serve as best as one can is probably perceived as a stay of execution. Why was Joseph Picho prepared to serve the murderer of his companions in distress as treasurer, knowing how much blood his predecessor had on his hands? Why did Samuel Abravanel farm Henry's taxes, never the most pleasant work?

Another feature of king Henry's *invented tradition* is the creation of the one who must receive the advantage of the tradition. He is, namely, also known as the first ruler who tried to replace charismatic war leaders by heads of a more permanent hierarchy of command, while he exercised 'more ongoing authority' on the frontier with Granada 'than did any of his predecessors'.[56] Also, this primitive beginning of a power centralization by decentralization of power in a hierarchy – in fact, the Catholic church model of the Counterreformation – had an important future in the secular world.

The last feature of his *invented tradition* was an inevitable *consequence* of it: his example was highly infectious. It was not surprising that the first who understood its value was a churchleader, the most dangerous competitor for so pious a king as Henry II. Someone like an archbischop, Ferrant Martines, gave Henry a strong dose of his own medicine. He was an even harsher and uncompromising propagandist and rebel seeking open confrontation with his king as well. From 1370 onwards he started rabble-rousing sermons and continued doing so despite whatever warning Henry issued. By 1389 Martines

'was indulging in the most cynical antisemitic propaganda possible, publicly preaching, for example, that the king and queen secretly wanted Christians to kill Jews and that, if they did so they would be forgiven in both legal and religious terms.'[57]

Thus, here Henry's propaganda definition was improved by an important item: if you follow my advice to kill, you are morally doing a good job for king, god and country. Martines jumped into a power vacuum and stimulated the beginning of an unprecedented pogrom on 6 Juni 1391 in Seville with Jews being massacred and synagogues being converted into churches. In Cordoba, Toledo, Valencia,

---

56. J. Casey, p. 89,90.
57. E. Kedourie (Ed.), p. 49.

Orihuela, Jativa, Barcelona, Logroño up to Lerida, the same bloodshed was executed. It is impossible to quantify the number of deaths or the destruction: it was the beginning of the end of Jewish communal life in Spain. With this pogrom the *invented tradition* of the end of the 14th century was completed; in future, its characteristics could be refined but not invented anymore.[58]

So from 1450 onwards, for instance, monarchs and popes tried everything to avoid the strengthening of feudal and local powers and to establish a bureaucratic centralization accompanied by secular and religious universality claims. In Spain, at this time, one sees the birth not so much of the modern nation-state as of the modern empire-state, the state with universalistic, world-domination aspirations: the 'nation' was subsumed under this 'empire', and in turn this 'empire' connived with the only possible ally, the top of the transforming Roman Church.

This church brought in its traditional universalistic outlook but lacked the effective secular bureaucratic centralization. The first reforms in that direction immediately resulted in numerous 'heretic' actions, and at the end of the day, the Roman pope had to accept that the Roman Church had been divided into several large and powerful competitors. They all organized their resources and power-networks and abandoned as many of the feudal traditions as possible, comparable to the main tasks of the Spanish monarchs. It is not a coincidence that only a year after the expulsion of the Jews, Pope Alexander VI issued the Bull of Donation which gave the Castilian crown a principal claim to *dominium* in America (1493).[59]

To promote the *internal* organisation and hierarchisation of the new 'empire-state', the notorious inquisition revivalist, the Dominican monk, Tomás de Torquemada, started his awful work. It was mostly directed against heretics and not Jews. The latter were no threat to the highest power-positions as is shown above with Samuel Halevi or Joseph Picho. They were still a functional and theological threat to the nobility and modernising church power-lawyers. In particular, the unity of state and religion in this empire had to be secured at the top. The internal consequences of the strong alliance between the Spanish rulers and the Pope made the 'Catholic Kings' abandon their relative tolerance against *all non-conformists* including Jews.

This had something to do with a new tool in the ideological instrumentarium, the *limpieza de sangre* laws. These 'purity of blood' laws had been introduced during the anti-Jewish agitation of about 1450. Of course, one is eager to consider

---

58. This does not mean, of course, that from here on there is a direct line to the Holocaust or Shoah; It is even doubtful if there should or could be a 'line' like that!

59. A. Pagden, Dispossessing the barbarian: the language of Spanish Thomism and the debate over the property rights of the American Indians, in: Idem (Ed.), *The Language of Political Theory in Early-Modern Europe* (Cambridge: Cambridge University Press, 1987), p. 79-99. For the history of the Papal claims, see part 1 of Harold Berman's *Law and Revolution* and for the early modern doctrines of princely power K. Pennington, *The Prince and the Law, 1200-1600. Sovereignty and rights in the Western legal tradition* (Berkeley: California University Press, 1993).

this policy a prelude to the 19th century Social-Darwinistic and biological racism (including antisemitism),[60] but that would be a serious mistake. In my view at least, this stressing of prerogatives of *descent* is to be seen as an expression of a genuine medieval and renaissance aristocratic exclusivity. This had to be stressed now that society was being increasingly modelled in a hierarchical way. In short: it concerns here a reactionary Don Quichotery which becomes instrumental for the introduction of a new rank order.[61]

---

60. A staunch defender of this position is the arch-Zionist and father of Benjamin, Benzion Netanyahu, *The Origins of the Inquisition in Fifteenth Century Spain* (New York: Random House, 1995), in particular pp. 975-1005, 1052 ff., 1141-1147. This is a highly apologetic work which is difficult to control: his theses are seldom supported by the many interesting facts he reveals. See, for example, bishop Cartagena's defense of Christian unity, 1450 (p. 516-578), which does not produce a single criticism of what could be compared to a 19th century racial theory as N. claims. He is one of those who perceives the history of Jews from the start to today as one long period of suffering with the Shoah as only the largest in a long chain of pogroms. Based on the few incidents in the whole period called 'Antiquity', he states for instance: 'Our own view, in contrast, is that the Jewish question in antiquity was produced by essentially the same factors that fashioned it in later times' (p.15). Hellenist Greeks, in his view, definitely spoiled everything for Jews in world history (p. 26, 27). Furthermore, every act of violence against or criticism of Jews is for N. antisemitism and racism whatever the circumstances, time or conceptual clarity. Therefore, it is rather impossible to argue with this believer, certainly when he also starts to construct proofs for antisemitic racism like the Spanish *limpieza de sangre*. See what S.Katz, *Holocaust,* passim quotes about it (Villanueva's warning, for example, against attempts to identify old Spanish concepts with new 19th century ones) and what A. Lindemann, *Esau's Tears,* p.74 ff., says about the 'blood imagery' in history. Netanyahu thinks (p. 513) that the Spanish *generación* means 'race' (in his mind, of course, in the Shoah meaning), whereas the real words for 'race' (*raza, casta, estirpe*) are hardly provided in original Spanish quotations. In addition, all of them have many meanings. *Casta,* for example, 'genus, tribe, caste, clan, blood, race, character, nature, etc.' Torquemada himself is quoted (p.1250 note 60) as saying: *de limpio y noble linaje* which is for N. a typically racist connotation and for T. nothing but a quality of descent. What could be discovered here, but not by N., are historical roots for the 20th century differences between the Southern European Fascism and the Germanic Nazism. Here, one can also find the historical roots for the ridiculous racist idea that the biological and not the cultural ('the real') father should be the right, juridically correct father (in *racist* terms it is still better to say that the biological mother is the correct mother). The same is true for N.'s appendix B (p.1103-1105) in which he acknowledges that already in 1414 and 1418, 'purity of blood' did *not convey* a racial meaning (!) and that '*limpio sangre* signified noble descent, or rather noble blood that remained unaffected by plebeian or other deleterious admixtures' (p.1105). Now his problem is transported to the 16th century. For the expulsion of the Jews, the 'first Holocaust', apparently Netanyahu's book is written in vain. See now the excellent article by J.P. Zuñiga, La Voix du Sang. Du métis à l'idée de métissage en Amérique espagnole, in: *Annales ESC* (1999), p. 425-452.

61. J. Casey, p. 140 ff. for more relevant details. 'Purity of Blood (*limpieza de sangre*) was an added, complicating factor in the whole story of hierarchy in Spain.'(p. 141) etc. See also idem, p. 231 from which can be concluded that this 'purity of blood' claim has no effect whatsoever on the expulsion of 1492. Between the Cordoba (1449) to the friars action (1495), the Seville chapter's exclusion (1515) and Philips II (1556) approval in this dossier lies more than a century! That the Inquisition was first and foremost a tool in establishing centralisation and absolutism was already known in the first constitutional history of Spain, H. Gmelin, *Studien zur Spanischen Verfassungsgeschichte des neunzehnten Jahrhunderts* (Stuttgart: Enke, 1905), p.5.

The Roman Church could not support these ideas in principle or on ideological grounds, as the powerful criticism of the Bishop of Burgos, Alonso de Cartagena, clearly demonstrated. An opportunistic support, however, could always be expected from any side, as was abundantly proved during the expulsion process.

It is not necessary to provide details of the nationwide Spanish expulsion of Jews (preceded by one in England in 1290, and several regional ones) to understand how many parties and motives were involved. Katz gives an incomplete but relevant summing-up of motives for the expulsion of Spanish Jews:

> '... the state's desire to protect *conversos* from other Jews who remained true to the faith of the fathers ... an abiding "bad conscience" on the part of those Jews who had converted; and ... there were influential *conversos* who saw the expulsion of the Jews as necessary to protect their own position ... the inauthentic conversion of some Jews caused difficulties for other *conversos* who ... were under suspicion because of the marranoism of their fellow apostates.'[62]

At the end of this section the following should be added. Katz's conclusion means that the state, backed by anti-Judaist representatives of the clergy, took sides with the religiously assimilated ex-Jews against the orthodox; this often happened after creating *conversos* as the first state victims. These *conversos/ marranos* (*pigs*[63]) were often 'dangerous victims' and much more 'trigger-happy' than the Spanish perpetrators; sometimes, they were transformed into fundamentalist Christians demonstrating the usual anti-Jewish hatred in an exaggerated form. Mostly, they stood under the constant suspicion of having converted only *pour besoin de la cause*. The fundamentalist Jews considered them as their worst enemies.

The given reasons, motives and circumstances are all more or less related to the religious side of the expulsion problem. The result is that, in particular, the *marranos* must be considered as 'nowhere people', 'in between people', luxury pariah's 'wandering between an abandoned Christianity and a scarcely understood Judaism.'[64] Therefore, messianic expectations were far stronger in *conversos* circles before and after the expulsion of 1492 than among Jews, whether they could stay in the country or left Spain.[65] However, much more about the political economic

---

62. S. Katz, *Holocaust*, p. 576 and note 214.

63. A new history of the 'Jew as pig' by Claudine Fabre-Vassas, *The singular beast. Jews, Christians, and the pig* (New York: Columbia University Press, 1997) I could not use. From Adam Bresnick's review in *TLS* 14 Nov. 1997, p. 14, I quote: 'For it was always necessary to reaffirm the connection between the Jew – the entire Jew – and the animal he judges unclean, and, at the same time, to make the pig, with its shady origin, again become the meat that proclaims the difference of the Christians, the Christian meat par excellence.' This dialectic in the perception of Jews has its own theological basis in the church doctrines: 'In short, the blood of the pig becomes "that metaphysical bodily fluid that the alimentary rituals of Easter have already revealed", an avatar of the blood of Christ's resurrected body.'

64. D. Wasserstein in his review of E. Kedourie (Ed.) in: *TLS*, 17-7-1992.

65. See the highly interesting contribution of M. Idel in E. Kedourie (Ed.), p. 123-139.

or sociological sides of the phenomenon, should be studied as is done in the relevant literature.

As indicated above, Jews and *conversos* were mostly traders during the first centuries of our story (but some even became bishop or scholar). Roughly after the 13th century, they *sedentarized* (definition Ibn Khaldûn) and got quite specific jobs as treasurer, tax farmer or financial adviser to their kings. One receives the strong impression that they tried to be nobler than the old aristocracy, more unscrupulous in amassing wealth than 'old money' and more eager to execute the monarchical 'dirty work' as the established courtiers. In this perception, they did everything to make themselves not the most beloved of people. Anyway, '1492' was a fundamental break as many Jews and *conversos as marranos* had to change their sedentarized into a nomadic existence once again.

In any event, this is all quite a different story than one of antisemitism relative to a Shoah[66] while, at this juncture, the anti-Judaist circles were not effective enough and the monarchs/state still had to rely on Jewish and *conversos'* capital and goods; there were no genocidal actions. This changed once the Inquisition could extend its uncompromising dark power, but even then, it is not possible to accuse this body of committing 'genocide'.[67] It was introduced (it seems as a *conversos* initiative) to stamp out religious non-conformism, which was always seen as dangerous for the state as well.

Last but not least, the intellectual and religious battle around the *conversos* – pariahs made another question urgent: who was or remained a Jew? It seems worthwhile to receive an impression of an answer by studying this expulsion complex from some individual perspectives.

THE EXPULSION REACTIONS

A key Jewish figure in the events of 1492 was Don Isaac Abravanel (1437-1508). He had a typical job for (ex-)Jews in the elite: financial adviser to the king of Portugal and, afterwards, in Spain. He was a colleague from the prototype of the wealthy Jew, Abraham Seneor, the royal tax collector of the rulers Isabella and Ferdinand.[68]

---

66. If necessary, one should better talk about 'Holocaust' because among the massive executions of the Inquisition and its regional branches there were far more victims than Jews. Also in this respect, they are a small minority. S. Katz, *Holocaust*, p. 373, note 245. From 1480-1700 in Spain about 50,000 Judaizers (most of them *conversos,* and that are no Jews) were tried and 1,850 killed (mostly *conversos*). In a regional branch like the Aragonese Inquisition, only 16 Judaizers were killed between 1540 and 1640 along with 181 Muslims, 122 Protestants and 167 homosexuals. See also E. Kedourie (Ed.), p. 108-119.

67. E. Cashmore (Ed.), *Dictionary of Race and Ethnic Relations*, p. 123-125.

68. See E. Kedourie (Ed.), p. 10 ff., 68 ff. for Seneor and for the theological side of Abravanel, Idem, p. 134 ff. For the latter, see also J. Genot-Bismuth (note 299). For the importance of the 'Jewish tax farmers' and *contador mayor* (treasurer) activities, see B. Netanyahu, p. 959 ff. Interesting in this respect is Mackay's *nearly* correct warning 'not to allow ourselves into being deluded that the Jews

The latter two persuaded him successfully to convert in 1492; on the same occasion Isaac Abravanel refused and left Spain.

Isaac was a member of the very wealthy Abravanel family to which also the famous Samuel belonged.[69] Isaac was not only a money-maker for his royal bosses like Samuel and Seneor. he also had intellectual ambitions expressed in many (political) theological treatises. Therefore, he is also called a rabbi, although it is uncertain whether this was the case in his own time. Anyway, in this framework it is probably not strange that he identified himself with the Old Testament patriarch Joseph, himself an adviser to Pharaoh.

Thus, in spite of his high and rewarding position, he left the country. Later, he would write in a highly exaggerated manner:

'So, in one day 300,000 men, old and young ... men and women including myself had to take their walking-sticks ... only a few could reach the destiny of their desire ... I arrived in the famous city of Naples, which was ruled by a tolerant and pious government ... there I could live in peace ...'[70]

In his new environment, Abravanel soon became an influential and apparently wandering courtier again who became well-known from Venice to Naples.

---

controlled the major share of fiscal and financial transactions (in fact the opposite was the case), ..' E. Kedourie (Ed.), p. 35. Netanyahu, however, supports the other extreme by strongly suggesting that the Jews occupied nearly all these positions notwithstanding harsh opposition (murder of Picho[n], 1379, etc.). He continues even with: '..no Christian, it seems, was to fill that position [of *contador mayor*. D.] .. It would seem that the powerful Jewish tax farmers objected to having a Christian in that office, and as a result, the *contaduria mayor* continued to be run .. by Jews.' (p. 960). N., therefore, follows the policy: the more splendid and powerful the Jewish position, the more pity one can earn at its destruction and the higher the satisfaction can be. *Both* opinions are wrong in the sense that they talk about *The* Jews, instead of clever, reckless or – for my part – self-destructive individuals.
69. See B. Netanyahu, The Conversion of Don Samuel Abravanel, in: Idem, *Toward the Inquisition. Essays on Jewish and converso history in Late Medieval Spain* (Ithaca/ London: Cornell Univ. Press, 1997), p. 99-126. He was also a 'Jewish leader' and not only in Spain but in France as well, as sources in his time reveal. Notwithstandig his position as top courtier, he was converted to Christianity. This did not happen during the riots of 1391 (p. 100) and not as other sources suggest, at the time he 'was impoverished and forced into wanderings that .. brought them to Portugal.' (p. 101) N. makes it clear that Samuel 'followed a course of economic expansion and social elevation': he and his large family converted to amass his fortune (gained as *contador mayor* of the King, tax-farmer, treasurer of the Queen, etc.) and to assimilate/ intermarry with the Spanish nobility (p. 107). His further story could be a clear reproduction of the given Venetian 'ghetto story' with all its Jewish and other murderous intrigues, the nobilities' exploitation of anti-Judaism, the very sharp antagonisms between the very rich upper class and the very poor people, 'fodder' in the pogroms around 1400, etc. It makes no sense here to criticize Netanyahu's interpretation (p. 124) which is, in its kind, a reasonable explanation of Samuel Abravanel's conversion.
70. P.Navè, Kirche und Synagoge, in: F.Bautz (Ed.), *Geschichte der Juden* (München: Beck, 1992), p.80. For Abravanel, see also R. Calimani, p. 41-44 ; G. Weiler, *Jewish Theocracy* (Leiden: Brill, 1988), p. 69-86; N. Roth, p. 165, 229; A. Cohen, P., Mendes-Flohr (Ed.), passim. It is highly remarkable that H. Ben-Sasson (Ed.) not even mentions his name.

As a thinker he was quite radical. He tried, in fact, to attack the Christian theft of the Jewish tradition and the Christian overlordship which was founded on the sword, 'an artificial instrument, made in order to destroy natural things'.[71] He saw the 1492 expulsion as the sign of the Messiah's apparition, and this drama was his ultimate inspiration for his radical criticism: the various forms of human government ('city, state, kingdom') are all described as alien to man's nature; they are artificial structures directed to false goals (*honor and power*) and founded upon confrontations (*war and rivalry*), and the same is true for the existing religions:

> 'For most wars among the Gentiles are occasioned by their religious differences, as in the wars between Edom [for A. the Christian nations] and Ishmael [the Muslim world]...'

The beginning of this sad part of human history Abravanel found in the Book of *Genesis*: man's expulsion from the Garden of Eden, the first bloodshed committed by Cain, and the advent of Tubal-Cain 'who sharpened instruments of brass and iron, sword and spear, for the sake of bloodshed'. Thanks to our Cain/Abel analysis (chapter 3), it is not difficult to discover the real background of his thoughts.

In other words, Abravanel had a quite modern outlook: an anti-church religious and anti-state political stand complemented by a criticism of their weapon technology. Therefore, his criticism is purely anti-oikoidal, formulated by an expert in oikoidal matters; it is purely anti-sedentarian as well, while he implicitly and explicitly points to the nomad Abel, patriarch Joseph, the 'natural' way of life, etc. For him, the disappearance of all national and political boundaries ('the freedom to move wherever one wants') is as synonymous with redemption as the abrogation of political and religious structures or the adherence to a strict monotheistic faith.

Abravanel belonged to the many Spanish-Jewish theologians who were responsible for a plethora of competing systems of dogmatics created to define what a Jew is and what Judaism is vis-à-vis the *marranos*. The remarkable thing is that they all differ in their definitions, but this did not lead to the establishment of schismatic sects as was usual in Christianity.

Furthermore, these theologians except two, Abravanel and Bibago, were not dogmatic in the sense that non-conformism with a rule could lead to heresy. Most of them stuck to the traditional rabbinic concept that, for example, ignorance of the law is an exculpatory factor. Only Abravanel raised *every* teaching of Judaism to the level of dogma 'requiring absolute doctrinal orthodoxy from every Jew on every issue'. Kellner did not understand this as the end of all dogmatics, which would be the right conclusion. Anyway, Abravanel contributed to an original

---

71. A. Cohen, P. Mendes-Flohr (Ed.), p.697 (Ravitzky on peace); see also p. 144 ff. (Kellner on dogma) and 220 ff. (Eisen on Exile).

solution for the 'eternal' problem of the Jewish identity, although Zionism as a strictly sedentarian ideology cannot rely on him as a 15th century predecessor, as has been suggested.

It is not only the theological and high-brow reactions to '1492' that are still vivid. The other effects of the non-genocidal actions are still felt nowadays. In about 1930 in a remote corner of Portugal, a *marranos* ('*pigs*') village was discovered. Here lived descendants of coercively baptised Jews from the period before 1492. The *present* inhabitants feared every foreigner because he could be a spy of the Spanish Inquisition come to burn them alive.

Today in Mallorca one can find *chuetas* (also means '*pig*') with the same history. Only recently was it disclosed who belonged to these *chuetas*, namely the majority of commercial people and the intelligentsia of the island. Before the publishing of this history, it was one of the common secrets of Mallorca.[72]

The existence of a true *marranos* village in 1930 points to basic contradictions. I do not know the specific history of this place, but someone who intends to do historical research on such a *marranos* village could consider at least the following possibilities. On the side of the villagers, a serious 'time lag' must exist between fact and fantasy, which points to a mentally blocked life resulting from an isolated autarkic world so well-known from histories of sects or from Dracula-versus-villagers stories. The strongest friend-enemy dichotomies are part and parcel of its highly oikoidal village life, which not only have their effects on the present situation but on the village history as well.

Who could have fulfilled the enemy 'function' in the past? In principle, it was unnecessary for these converted Jews or neo-Christians to fear an Inquisition. But what about the hate of the original perpetrator, the Inquisition, if its burning suspicion against these 'pigs' could be affirmed, when these *marranos* were indeed tarned as pious believers in some (Jewish *or Christian*) faith? And what about possible antagonisms between the rich and powerful *conversos* and these poor villagers?

Furthermore, it indicates how the (fundamentalist) Jews were normally the worst enemies of the *marranos*, while non-sedentary people cannot sympathize with autarkic and stubborn village life. The latter, however, cannot be seen as enemies thanks to their possible arrogance or misconception of sedentaries. Often the position of inhabitants of neighbouring and competing villages is different as they could use the *marranos* status as a pretext to isolate competitors on the agrarian market. The same status could invite the local or regional aristocracy to repress the *marranos* by threatening them with the Inquisition in order to create cheap labour.

---

72. P. Navè, p. 77 ff. In antiquity Jewish rites were insulted by Roman writers as mere pig worship; see R. Lane Fox, *Pagans and Christians* (Harmondsworth: Viking, 1986), p. 428.

Last but not least, 'normal' Catholics are not the friendliest people towards fundamentalist Catholics, which *marranos* often were. Thus, the very existence of such a *marranos* village leads to a highly complicated reflection on all of the intricacies in which Jews or people with some (anti)Jewish background were entangled in the past.

The non-sedentary side of this coin is eloquently told in Calimani's history of the ghetto of Venice. From among the many Inquisition cases, he selected the 'very typical Marrano story' of the nearly 60 year old Licentiato Costa (1555). This Costa lived in Venice dressed as a Christian with a black instead of a yellow hat, etc. His father was a converted Jew from Portugal, and his mother remained a Jewess: 'My father and brothers have told me I was snatched from my mother's bed and baptized'. Had he then lived as a Christian? 'At the time they told me, I was living outwardly as they told me to ... went to mass with other Christians ... Inwardly I lived as a Jew, and then I left for Lisbon. I stayed eight months, and never gave any sign of being a Christian ... I went to Flanders and Antwerp, and then I came here.' Licentiato Costa lived in Salamanca, Salonika, Ferrara and Viana as well. In this last place he married 'one of our own nation', and he had all of his five children baptized 'for fear of the Inquisition'.

The Inquisition continued to demand an adequate answer about whether he was a Jew or a Christian. Costa, in his turn, refused to provide clear and non-contradictory answers: he had never behaved as a Christian or prayed as a Jew; if he wanted meat, he went to the ghetto to buy it. Was he circumcised? *'I have no recollection of it, unless it was when I was a baby.'*[73] Licentiato Costa, the 'archetypical Marrano', was immediately released and could continue wearing his black hat. Let's suppose that even members of the Inquisition could laugh at a good joke.

CHOICES BETWEEN LIFE AND DEATH

It seems as if in the discussion of the Jewish – Nomadic Question so far, we have already arrived at its 'heart of darkness'. This, however, is reserved for the next chapter as the 20th century "Holocaust of the Common Man" comes to the fore and as clear victims' perspectives will be chosen. Still, it is quite appropriate to circumscribe here this Jewish – Nomadic Question anew, whatever its preliminary character.

Many sources of prejudices about wandering people, pariahs, Jews, Muslims, other internal or external minorities are evident now. The perpetrating role science and religion played in their collaboration with political regimes could be demonstrated in a world historical as well as an European (historical) context. Sharp differences between antisemitism, anti-Judaism and anti-Jewish measures

---

73. R. Calimani, p. 72-74.

were given, and unexpected and rather unknown relations between (the perceptions of) several 'groups on the move' discovered.

There is a 'natural relation' between perpetrators and victims. After the 20th century Shoah, many questions arose about the role of the religious and secular (absentee) Jewish leadership vis-à-vis the German perpetrators. The same occurred with the non-Jewish leadership in the Holocaust. They could all too easily hide themselves behind some accusation of 'blaming the victims'. For Jews, however, who are sometimes perceived by others and themselves as 'eternal' victims, it is certainly unavoidable and necessary to scrutinize their historical role as victims. Also in this respect many prejudices could be discovered, some of which are discussed above but most of them in the next chapter.

From the basic perspective of this book, the '1492' and 'ghetto' stories and reactions display the familiar contradictions between the sedentary life with all its rigidities and the wandering life with all its flexibilities. According to Costa, the latter was the real Jewish life.

Many rich members of the Jewish elite, however, sedentarized, often feodalized and assimilated into a dangerous world after their highly mobile trading and commercial interests and activities declined. I also feel that among all minorities the Jewish elite was always the most active in *risking the perpetrators' deal* by making themselves very visible in the oikoidal searchlights.[74]

Here we also come across the famous contradictions between sedentary ('Jerusalem') and *diaspora* Jews or rich German Jews versus poor Eastern Jews or the serious conflicts between the Spanish *conversos* and orthodox Jews.

It is easy to find recent examples. Concerning Jews in Palestine, Bruno Bettelheim once constructed the reasoning: 'I cannot help feeling that this anger against the British was a projection of the anger of American Jews against themselves for not doing their duty towards the Jews in Europe.'[75] Also relevant in this context is Raul Hilberg's quote of the Jewish barber in a labour camp who remarked to the camp commander on the day of the camp's liquidation: 'But I have always shaved you well.' For Hilberg this remark was so typical of the victim's behaviour that he made it the device of the 'Victims' part of his book.[76]

The most recent example concerns Henry Kissinger as portrayed in Christopher Hitchens's biography published *after* "the 11th of September".[77] According to

---

74. A relevant comparison between the fate of the early Christians and the old Jews in this respect is provided by R. Lane Fox, *Idem*, p. 428-434.

75. Quoted by R. Dinnage, The Survivor, in: *New York Review of Books*, June 20 (1996), p.14.

76. R. Hilberg, *Perpetrators*, p. 103.

77. C. Hitchens, *The Trial of Henry Kissinger* (London/ New York: Verso, 2002). For reactions related to this book, see www.enteract.com/~peterk/henry.html. The quotations come from the interview with C.H. by R. Suudi, translated in *Vrij Nederland* 3/10 August, 2002. Hitchens is right to call Kissinger a mediocre scholar which is supported by the dissertaion of E. J. Kautsky, *Die Vergangenheit als Muster. Kissingers Analyse der Geschichte und seine Tätigkeit als Staatsmann* (Leiden: Univ., 1982),

most reviewers, Hitchens convincingly proofs how Kissinger as top-adviser for 'national security' to Nixon and Ford and as minister of Foreign Affairs was responsible for war-crimes in Vietnam, Laos, Cambodia, Chile and Eastern Timor. Hitchens:

> 'People like Kissinger permanently try to prove how harsh and ruthless they can be. Just give them the chance and they shall demonstrate a terrible misconduct. Nixon was a mixed-up petty-bourgeois and a paranoid antisemite. That was not his choice, but his nature. Kissinger, however, wanted to rise from a mediocre scholar unto a political potentate. For him it was a conscious change in order to get power.'

It is tempting to compare this with the behaviour of people like Halevi, Seneor, Abravanel, Picho and their many colleagues in the tax-farmers guild of the Spanish 14th and 15th centuries who – as it is called above – 'risked the perpetrators' deal'. Anyway, Hitchens's conclusion refers directly to our next chapters: 'This man is, what Hannah Arendt called, the radical evil'. Apart from the fact that Arendt could not have said this, Hitchens's dictum seems to reflect genuine antisemitism as this always presupposes this kind of *pars pro toto* comparison.

It is a pity as well that in explaining the Kissinger phenomenon, even a critical man like Hitchens falls into the prefabricated trap by referring to the 'Jewish self-hate'. The last thing you can prove of all the peoples mentioned above is that they hated themselves, let alone, that this kind of hate should be a typical characteristic of all Jews, which seems to me an antisemitic generalization, too. Did Kissinger demonstrate *typical Jewish* behaviour? No, not at all. The only thing I can imagine what all these persons belonging to a Jewish *elite* had in common was an extreme need for recognition, sociologically based in their tiny minority positions, which expressed itself in a exaggerated non-conformism.

One thing is certainly clear: the examples given have to be explained in relation to the perpetrators involved. In Abravanel's Spanish case, for instance, one cannot avoid thinking that the responsible Spanish kings expelled or killed the wrong people, i.e. those who served the royal Oikos like that of all their predecessors, whatever their religion and aims, with all their skills and devotion. Thus, there are many potential perpetrators (new) and motives (old) to discover in these cases, which also make the victims' problem within elites highly complicated.

The other thing which seems clear enough is that the Christian religious traits of this perpetrator-victim relationship are of fundamental importance. Not the sectarian Jewish belief system; throughout history, it attracted only a few people, and it could increase its share only by seeking some understanding with the two

---

p. 63 ff. One could also refer to highly influential people like Paul Wolfowitz or Richard Perle in the present Bush administration or neo-conservative coterie.

great monotheistic religions, Islam and Christianity. With the former it had a generally peaceful relationship but could not receive a secular power position of any significance; with the latter it had an inimical relationship from the moment the Jew and apostle Paul stole its tradition, which – periodically – exploded in deadly cruelties.

In generalizing, one could say that in this perpetrator-victim relationship, both needed the other: the one to reassure himself that he was an invincible power and the other that he could always flee if he was about to be crushed. However, it is impossible to generalize that what is said concerns the Jewish elite only; for the 'ordinary Jews', quite a different story should be told the reverse of Goldhagen's '*willing executioners*'.

In a strict oikoidal monarchical, aristocratic and church setting, it seems a typical feature of the Jewish elite that its representatives often functioned as the *naucrates ductor* vis-à-vis the leading sharks. From the middle of the 19th century in bourgeois society, many things changed so drastically that the rather simple and predictable perpetrator-victim relationship was abandoned, and much more dangerous animals took over the initiative. One thing is clear from the above texts: pilot-fishes remain, but new alternatives come to the fore. The next chapter starts to discuss this completely new situation.

Which of the given motives were active and turned the *marranos* and Jewish worlds historically upside-down is not clarified further. The way the *conversos* assimilated within the Iberian cultures (from Visigothic to Islamic or Spanish) also determined the '*pigs dirt*' non-converted peoples had to swallow and the alibis used by the perpetrators. The cognitive complexity of the whole problem, however, is provided by the Holocaust and Shoah and will not disappear when we try to transform its content into consumable proportions for simple-minded spirits.

The analysis of Arnaldo Momigliano's behaviour and thinking as a kind of Italian *marrano* (chapter 1) receives here its ultimate basis. Many examples of this sort could be given here as, for instance, of a Dutch *conversos*, the famous pre-war Dutch author of regional novels, Herman de Man (1898-1946). He was born as Salomon ('Sallie') Herman Hamburger and raised like his humble father as an itinerant merchant in everything. In a short time he became famous as a novelist, and rich and converted to Catholicism together with his Jewish wife (1927). Naturally, he was accused of betrayal of the Jewish belief; in the Catholic church he only met (proto-) fascist priests or 'an undefined distance'. Nothing new. However, as one of the very few he published a booklet in 1933, *On Jews and their perpetrators,* in which he defends both his conversion and his Jewishness (racial definition!) while attacking antisemitism and Nazism.[78] A few years later he lost his

---

78. H. de Man, *Over de Joden en hunne vervolgers* (Baarn: Hollandia Drukkerij, 1933). It has 67 pages; on the cover a cross is designed with in its heart a smaller Jewish star; directly after the cover page appears the *NIHIL OBSTAT and EVULGETUR* of the Catholic religious censor. The quotation is on

wife and five of his seven children in the Shoah; he did not want to write anymore and returned to being a merchant in everything. He lost his life in an air crash (1946).

The only thing I want to quote from Herman de Man is the way he circumscribed his perception of the essence of Jewishness:

> 'The Jew .. whatever the vehement denials among some of them, remains a passer-by in the street where he temporarily exists, for a century or a day. But whether it is a century or a day, he immediately spins himself an intimate home. That is, in fact, the greatest tragedy of the Jewish people: the one who is marked as a wanderer and remains a wanderer because of the enforcement to do so, is by nature a patriarch who basks in the tenderness of an own, enclosed yard. This [last] characteristic leads inevitable to preservation and – in a political sense – to conservatism. The majority of Jews belongs ... to the conservative groups.'

According to most people before the war, De Man also thought about Jews in racial terms. He, furthermore, reproduces the myth of the Cain's mark (chapter 3) and of Ahasverus (chapter 4). Most interesting is how he demonstrates in the clearest way, in his life and writing, the *contradictions between oikos and market*.

Through all these examples, an explosive problem is brought to the fore, which I want to address in the following reflections and chapters. What does it look like?

For example, is it possible to discover similar antagonisms where the Zionist sedentarization drive and big power cynicism resulted in establishing a Jewish mini 'minority State and Church', Israel, as a most typical Oikos? With some exaggeration one could perceive this Oikos as a new *marranos* village and, consequently, as a (dwarf-) oikoidal power, *by necessity*, one could create, and repress, its internal (dwarf) minorities.[79]

Also, this problem is directly related to choices between life and death: If these choices are at stake, most but not all people will choose 'life', while they do not believe in a case which brings death to its followers, knowing that still others are willing to be martyrs for a case which promises only life in some Valhalla. These choices between life and death become an existential necessity, because 'the state' and/or 'the church' with its main supporters accuse groups or people of something

p. 22.

79. These propositions could be substantiated by Tom Segev's brilliant analysis, *The seventh million. The Israelis and the Holocaust* (New York: Hill&Wang, 1993) as, for instance, in the first chapter titled *HITLER: The Yekkes Are Coming*. Hermann Hesse's antipathy against the German Jewish bourgeoisie seems to be reproduced in Israel's lack of sympathy for German victims of the Holocaust. See H. Hesse, *Ausgewählte Briefe* (Frankfurt a/M.: Suhrkamp, 1974), p. 108. Israel's discrimination of these so-called *yekkes* resulted, in my view, in Hannah Arendt's lack of sympathy for several Zionist ideological assumptions (Segev, p. 358). This is one demonstration of her *'German fixation'*. See further chapter 9.

and are urged for some reason to perpetrate these groups. Their interrelations are at stake; any attempt to moralize this discussion and to create the 'good' and 'bad' dichotomy will bring the reader only into an 'ugly' position.

Which interrelational problem, then, is to be studied from what angle? In my view, the given examples prove the intensity of the behavioural change (including mutual conflicts) on the side of victims of the Church/State persecution activities. They also display the spectrum of reactions: from accommodation with the perpetrators to the hiding away in a personal, closed, worldly or celestial utopia based on fear and expectations concerning some supernatural destiny and the real outside world with an 'unreal past'. Is not it in this spectrum that we have to look to find the sociological characteristics of the pariahs (in the elite)?

Next, they demonstrate the alternatives available to those who choose to be sedentary and flock together. Only *these* sedentaries had to answer *yes* to a particular question: are we clever enough to expect help and security from our potential murderers? They are the ones who had much to lose by making such a deal, hoping for a stay of execution and, therefore, doing their utmost to please the potential perpetrators. Also, religious and/or conservative spirits had to affirm the question while, almost *by definition*, they always expected all good things from (state) authorities and still believe that Allah, God, Yahweh or Mao will save their lives.

Another kind of people, probably religious and/or progressive, deny the question but still want to flock together and sedentarize: inevitably, they have to look for an alternative settlement to organize their own particular little world which will be, almost *by definition*, a copy of the oikoidal world the *marranos* established.

Finally, there is the Abravanel case: he served the most powerful perpetrators in the Mediterranean, and at the end of his life, he chose to go into exile with his last employer, the King of Naples, an 'exile' which corresponded the most to his ideal way of life and thinking. If possible, this Spanish Don should have supported – say – Herman de Man's wandering definition of Jewishness and, therefore, the awareness of Jews as Nomads, as '*secret gypsies*'.

This psychology, geography and sociology of the problem already bring to light the main elements of a problem definition which is to be tackled through a reflection on the *pariah concept* in the hope of discovering a modern answer to the Jewish identity question. The historical investigation of the Spanish Expulsion did not result in a convincing story about the seriousness of this event in an European context, although it was an important stage in the creation of a pariah-complex on an European scale. At the moment, however, many millions of people suffer from the same expulsion problems, which gives this question so many universal characteristics that it will be difficult to discover something typically Jewish.

After this problem definition, my thesis for the following reflections is obvious: by acceptance of the *pariah* concept, as a most important part of the Jewish identity, not only is the sedentary victim's role of Jews stressed and the perception of the alternative, i.e. 'the democratic market-nomad', blocked, but at the same time a definition of 'the Jew' is implied which makes the Holocaust (not the Shoah) predominantly a non-Jewish affair. The following thorough discussion of the victims' positions in modern times, in the real Shoah and Holocaust, should bring us to the very "heart of darkness" of this problem; in my view, it is not only a prerequisite to clarify our problem, i.e. Hannah Arendt's choice, in the best scholarly way possible, but also to come to terms in a subjective way with a most crucial European historical complex. More than the other parts of this study, indeed, the next chapter in particular should be seen as a series of reflections directed to a new way of thinking about the Holocaust phenomenon and, therefore, the contradictions between *Truth and Politics*.[80]

---

80. It is the title of Hannah Arendt's seventh exercise in political thought in her *Between Past and Future* (Harmondsworth: Penguin, 1977), p. 227 ff. It was incited by the so-called Eichmann-in-Jerusalem controversy. She is concerned with the question whether 'it is always legitimate to tell the truth' and with a counterattack against 'the amazing amount of lies' in the controversy but particularly with 'the gap between past and future'. I have the impression that this gap looms larger than ever before because the moral and political crisis of "Jerusalem" today makes "Eichmann's shadow" visible anew .

Source: J. Struk, *Photographing the Holocaust.* (New York: Tauris, 2004), p. 65.

6. VICTIMS AND THEIR PERPETRATORS IN EAST AND WEST

'The chief difference between the despotic and the totalitarian secret police lies in the difference between the "suspect" and the "objective enemy". The latter is defined by the policy of the government and not by his own desire to overthrow it. He is never an individual whose dangerous thoughts must be provoked or whose past justifies suspicion, but a "carrier of tendencies" like the carrier of a disease. Practically speaking, the totalitarian ruler proceeds like a man who persistently insults another man until everybody knows that the latter is his enemy, so that he can, with some plausibility, go and kill him in self-defense. This certainly is a little crude, but it works – as everybody will know who ever watched how certain successful careerists eliminate competitors.'

Hannah Arendt[1]

In the recent debates about my *Deutsche Westforschung*, in particular, in the mega-publication *Griff nach dem Westen,* one subject is not discussed at all, and I am inclined to see this as symptomatic. It concerns the position of the Jewish and other victims in the (occupied) Western countries during World War II. When studying the *Ostforschung,* it is impossible to overlook this subject, not only because Aly, Burleigh, Gerlach, Heim, Hilberg, etc. wrote such penetrating studies about the Eastern European situation, but because the *Vernichtungslager* were situated there, the highest concentration of other distressing places to eliminate Nazi victims, and the largest military operations occurred there.

Only recently has the study of *Westforschung* started (in itself remarkable enough), and we are still in the beginning of the power games about who will decide how its history should be written. Anyway, now the necessary and interesting possibility of comparison with *Ostforschung* is given. This chapter about the situation of the Nazi victims in East and West will reach into the very core of these comparative studies; hopefully, it is able to give the victims a face which they are still missing in the *Ostforschung.* Most authors of *Griff nach dem Westen* suffered a symptomatic loss of memory when they forgot to consider even a most *mini-*

---

1. H. Arendt, *The Origins of Totalitarianism.* (New York: Harcourt, 1979), p.423, 424.

mally defined Holocaust victim in the West ("dead Jew") and, therefore, (the homelands of) about 260,000 victims caught in the West and killed in the East.

Therefore, I have to start with a *step by step strategy* in explaining the problems at issue before I come to discuss, in particular, the Dutch situation of the Jewish victims which will be followed up in chapter 8. Hannah Arendt's text quoted above provides the method for this strategy.

The (invented) traditions which made the Holocaust and Shoah possible reveal the roots of an *eternal enemy*. It mached an *eternal victim*: generally speaking, no European Jew could ever have defended himself and his kin against any physical attack except by fleeing. It is said these circumstances produced specific Jewish character elements; indubitably, however, this tradition is directly responsible for the Shoah but only partially for the Holocaust and is, anyway, to be seen as a 'white collar part of the crime'.[2]

This *eternal victim* also became a 'suspect' and an 'objective enemy' of secular despotic and totalitarian states existing in Europe from – say – 1850 onwards, in particular Austria, Germany and Russia. They followed the procedure Hannah Arendt sketched above.

In this chapter I will only reflect on the criminal relationship between perpetrators and Shoah victims with its own history of police and military forces or state bureaucracy, its own criteria, rules or attitudes. Arendt rightly concludes that the most important aspect involves these rulers and their secret police who *define* the suspect, objective enemy and, therefore, the victims. This relationship is not very well understood by most Shoah historians and the general public, let alone its consequences. Time and again we are confronted with Jewish writers who without any difficulty accept the definition of Jew from their perpetrators while compre-

---

2. One of the reasons of distinguishing between the Holocaust as the general and the Shoah as a specific concept is this case which will not be substantiated further: for the Christian Church the role of the Jew in history is part of the dogmatic doctrine which is not the case for all the other victims in the Holocaust. Gypsies (Sinti, Roma,etc.) apparently belong to old tribes, but they did not got the general spiritual dedications from the Christian elite but only from common people. Interesting is the comparison W. Wippermann made between Jews and Gypsies in *Wie die Zigeuner. Antisemitismus und Antiziganismus im Vergleich* (Berlin: Elefanten Press, 1997). Homosexuals were given a serious chance, but sodomy never received the same status as general evil; the same is even true with the victims of the euthanasia programm for which several churches developed different theories, practices and reactions. The historical study of these subjects is, for that matter, still in an infant phase because the first studies appeared in the 1980s like V.L. Bullough, J. Brundage (Ed.), *Sexual practices & the medieval church* (New York: Prometheus, 1982); the highly relevant J. Brundage, *Law, Sex, and Christian Society in Medieval Europe* (Chicago: University of Chicago Press, 1987). For the 20th century position of homosexuals see, for example, R. Lautmann, *Seminar: Gesellschaft und Homosexualität* (Frankfurt a/M.: Suhrkamp, 1977). In the meantime this literature has become rather abundantly. For the euthanasia problematic a typical 19th century history with some Enlightenment influences still must be written although the Holocaust aspects are well covered by the many studies of Ernst Klee a.o. For gypsies see below.

hending the life-threatening impact of these definitions. In other words: we have to face the fact that the antisemitic and/or anti-judaistic definition of Jew is accepted by Jews and Jewish victims.

Here the relationship perpetrator – victim is not the only question. Take, for instance, the problem of the status of crimes committed. In her strongly debated *Eichmann in Jerusalem* Hannah Arendt rightly argued that the local Israeli law was/is not fit to judge crimes against humanity. I do not want to elaborate on this item here; a few remarks must suffice. When she reacted to Karl Jaspers's ambiguous booklet, *Die Schuldfrage* (18 August 1946), Arendt also made a principal statement about the perpetrator-victim relationship: 'The Nazi crimes, it seems to me, explode the limits of the law; and that is precisely what constitutes their monstrousness. For these crimes, no punishment is severe enough ... That is, this guilt, in contrast to all criminal guilt, oversteps and shatters any and all legal systems. ... And just as inhuman as their guilt is the innocence of the victims. Human beings simply can't be as innocent as they all were in the face of the gas chambers ... a guilt that is beyond crime and an innocence that is beyond goodness or virtue.'[3]

Although I sympathize with the emotional gist of this statement, it is difficult to defend in juridical terms. There is, first, the practical possibility to remove the limits of the laws if they form an obstacle to tackle these crimes. With universal declarations, tribunals and international courts, *local* limits can be removed; probably not yet far enough, but that is another problem. If one were to remove international limits, one would arrive in an intellectual 'outer space' far beyond human history or, practically, in an international jungle in which a mighty state (at the moment only the USA is doing this in their present practice of a preemptive war) creates a situation in which it can repress or blackmail all others. In both cases it becomes, theoretically speaking, impossible to understand, to research and to talk about all these human acts as genocide, a Holocaust or Shoah.

Still, a lawless situation is defined by laws. While it concerns acts of inimical human beings and reactions of 'other' human beings, it is always impossible to negate past and present, otherwise you are forced to mortgage a future life in an unmanageable way. There is, next, the consideration that these perpetrators could escape their punishment very easily if their guilt was inhuman: nobody will be able to sue them (that is why the USA strongly attacks international courts). At last, within a perpetrator – victim relationship, the position of the (innocent) victims also becomes highly unmanageable (no claims are possible, etc.) and their history, morality, etc. *as victims* become "footloose". Of course, there is more to say about this problem, but I do not want to address this case of international law or ethics.

There is, furthermore, the painful problem of the Holocaust rhetoric and the policies behind it. Too often, one is confronted with attempts to forget or seriously distort a Holocaust past as the explicit aim of many governments and specific

---

3. AJC, p. 54.

interests. For all kinds of very human purposes, the Holocaust is often made a mystery by those who utilise metaphysical or ideological manipulation daily. Then the well-known local political leader with a crime record can be transformed into a Hitler, and the cruel acts of the strongest army in the Middle East against childish casters of stones or during the destruction of nearly unarmed and poverty- stricken Palestinean fugitives can be legitimated by 'the Holocaust'. For instance, critics from Germany labelled these Israeli acts as 'hemmungslosen Vernichtungskrieg' as if the *Wehrmacht* raged again its *Unternehmen Barbarossa*. Compared to all this rhetoricism, the restricted activities of the very few so-called Holocaust deniers are fully negligible and only food for publicity seekers: people like Irving, Faurisson, etc. are not worth either a word or a penny.

In my view, it is necessary to keep both feet on the ground in the course of our intellectual walk through history. Let's start, therefore, with some preliminary considerations about victims and their (rhetoric) enemies.

An aggressive relationship

Only one who is 'another' can be a victim of an offender, a perpetrator, whatever its/his/her impersonal appearance, for example, a bureaucracy or an army.[4] In popular language one can be a victim of a natural disaster, but at least juridically and politically speaking, that is not possible because an avalanche cannot be the object of a *sentence* if not induced by *humans*,[5] and whatever *power* we apply, it remains impossible to arrest an avalanche. Morally it is impossible as well, because it is rather difficult to make an avalanche the object of a *good-evil argument* if you do not support an animistic belief system. In a sociological sense, it is also difficult to speak of victims in these cases, because we always have to deal with a *relationship* between the victim and the offender/perpetrator.

Objections against my avalanche example will certainly come from religious fundamentalists: it can be the will of some god(s) to punish humans by means of an avalanche; the only thing one can do is to accept this fate and wait, praying that death will be quick and painless while regretting all the time that one fell victim to one's own sins i.c. not to listen (enough) to a god or to have read his words long or loud enough. Many rabbis told and still tell Jewish believers this kind of story,[6] and recently I heard the same words from Amsterdam vegetarian sectarians who were socially threatened by several fatal accidents: their Leader told them that these

---

4. I am not convinced of the possibility that this relationship exists in a suïcide case, but I cannot substantiate this here.
5. However, not only in fables are lawsuits held but in medieval times, animal trials were celebrated. We keep it simple!
6. See Yehuda Bauer in HH, p. 18 ff. who, strangely enough, connects these attitudes with Jewish self-hate/-accusations and even with antisemitism (!) as if these are not very common reactions among isolated and desparate sectarians of whatever kind.

occurred *because* they were too lax in following the dietarian rules while, in fact, it was these rules which undermined reason and body and caused the accidents.

Whatever one can say about this behaviour, it must be clear how here the victim-offender relationship is blurred: the offender/perpetrator (including his rules) receives not sub- but superhuman qualifications, thus losing his offensive character; the victim becomes disoriented (an avalanche transforms in a godly present), loses his identity as victim and can only become the obedient follower of something which has lost or hides its own identity. Result: *the danger not only remains but becomes the true salvation*. The pessimistic variant of this constellation is that the god becomes the cruel offender, the avalanche the means to express its will, and the human being only the 'willing victim'. There are still people who can discover in the latter the Old Testament god and in the former the New Testament one.

Historians are earth-bound. They cannot believe in mysteries and note, therefore, that clever religious and secular offenders/perpetrators, knowing how to play this divine game with their victims, can gain substantial victories. Experienced politicians and all other professional pretenders must have a basic knowledge of these mechanisms. In larger social settings than a sect, however, this game is bound to fail because there are too many 'circumstantial variables'. In my view, therefore, the Nazis were able to produce so much pressure on their own and other societies that comparable sectarian policies could be applied. On the largest possible scale they rather systematically played their divine cat-and-mouse games with their victims before killing them off (Jews, Gypsies, Russian POWs, etc.) or transforming other victims even in 'willing executioners'. With the former, the 'pessimistic' and with the latter, the 'optimistic variant' could be executed. Below I'll take the opportunity to discuss this perspective further.

My analysis of the relationship will start this time from the victims' side because in former chapters the perpetrators' view came to the fore. It is, subjectively, a much more difficult task than commenting on the perpetrators' role for which there is the easy implementation of old-fashioned moral views. 'After Auschwitz', the victim problem has become nearly a taboo question as Raul Hilberg experienced while gathering his data and writing his notes.[7] He, together with Bruno Bettelheim and others, were sharply attacked for their scepticism about Jewish

---

7. R. Hilberg, *Unerbetene Erinnerung. Der Weg eines Holocaust-Forschers* (Frankfurt a/M.: Fischer Verlag, 1994), p. 105-137. See the review drained in acid from M.A. Bernstein in *Times Literary Supplement* 7-3-1997, p. 3-4. This review seems to be symptomatic for the American Jewish reactions on Hilberg's writings, whereupon he reacted with the declaration that he 'became an European author' (Idem, p.150). For the perpetrators side of the problem see the works of the Dutch jurist Rüter c.s. or the detailed casuistry of H. Jäger, *Verbrechen unter totalitärer Herrschaft. Studien zur nationalsozialistischen Gewaltkriminalität* (Frankfurt a/M.: Suhrkamp, 1982).

resistance in 1933-1945: Jews apparently behaved like 'sheep to the slaughter' which gives us, indeed, a serious problem (see below).[8]

A recent debate can teach us other things about the perpetrator-victim relationship. The victims were apparently used for political aims as, for instance, a warning against the newly united Germans which should be *by nature* 'willing executioners'. In hindsight this Goldhagen row was quite unpalatable:[9] the Holocaust or Shoah victims' terrible fate had to prove something of a collective guilt of the Germans from the beginning of history. Therefore, he retold, among others, the famous Browning study about police battalion 101, already an eye-opener in 1992,[10] in more cruel detail. The revealing of these details was consequently transformed into the ultimate proof of the faulty German character and into a quasi-scientific theory (instead of a journalistic act) to give it a status of value. Most experts reacted as if they were stung by a wasp, but the media event around the book was a success in Germany and the USA where a 'moral row around a Holocaust subject' is never difficult to arrange.

'Humanly speaking' it is nearly impossible to replace Raul Hilberg's *Destruction* (new German edition), and it was, indeed, premature for a beginning non-professional historian like Goldhagen to announce he intends 'to explain why the Holocaust occurred ... how it could occur'. The media event enlarged this arrogance out of proportion, and a new Holocaust row was born. The author also set a subjective tone in his descriptions which was new compared to the cool

---

8. Recently, the 'sheep to the slaughter' indignation in A. and H. Edelheit, *History of the Holocaust. A Handbook and Dictionary* (Boulder: Westview Press, 1994), p.91-109. For Raul Hilberg see last paragraph of this chapter. For Bruno Bettelheim see, for instance, his *Freud's Vienna & other Essays*, p. 189-273; HH, p. 585-647 and for Bettelheim p. 772 ff. Generally, one can conclude that the psychoanalytical approach is not very helpful for understanding the victim-perpetrator relationship in Holocaust matters.

9. This qualification is not only a conclusion of *what follows* but is also based on the way the row has been concocted and developed. In the shortest possible time supporters and critics of Goldhagen stood facing each other as if orchestrated to assure a good selling climate to the book; both sides made rather stupid and unproven accusations; the public reactions in Germany were alarming: from a kind of teenager adoration of the author to a highly unfounded prize distribution (G.'s 'contribution to democracy'!) by none other than good old Jürgen Habermas, who apparently is available to defend everything that some *Kanzler* or ambiguous state action (Berlin Holocaust statue) deserves; the *fine fleur* of the Holocaust experts came to the fore from which a large majority (including Hilberg, Vidal-Naquet and Wehler) provided a devastating criticism but, strangely enough, a Yad Vashem expert as Gutman apparently came to G.'s rescue; G.'s extreme oversimplification, demagogic descriptions of frightful atrocities and his ridiculous claim he could uncover the truth about the Holocaust, can only lead to the question: why all this? Whatever its shortcomings, this book was important as a catalyst for discussions about the Holocaust problem, but the shift between American-Israeli and European + non-Israeli-American research seems greater than ever. See N.Finkelstein, R.Birn, *A Nation on Trial. The Goldhagen Thesis and Historical Truth* (New York: Holt, 1998) and G.'s reaction in the journal *German Politics and Society* (1998), 88. For specific criticism see below.

10. Chr. Browning, *Ordinary Men: Reserve Police Battalion 101 and the Final Solution in Poland* (New York: HarperCollins, 1992).

analytical Hilberg and his direct opponent, the highly skilful Browning. I have no difficulty with this if the necessary argumentative basis is supported. A very 'willing reader' should recognize something of the second generation's impatience, but this did not come to the fore enough to be taken seriously. Apparently, Goldhagen was too busy as a skilful shyster in his own case.

Problematic was, furthermore, that he did not see or consider the historical relativity of the dirty work the German military and police executed. Not even later in the row did he discover that while he was writing his book, a racist genocide of unprecedented proportions took place in Rwanda: in 100 days in 1995, about 900,000 Tutsis and some Hutus were slaughtered by Hutu murderers; in one terrible move extreme representatives of the large majority of sedentary agricultur-alists wiped out the minority, the largely sedentary pastoralists, about 13% of the population.[11] One can be certain that if there had been 6 million Tutsis in Rwanda, they all would have been killed down to the last child; the murderers' physical exhaustion seemed the only limitation. It is clear that Goldhagen himself repro-duced only a one-sided perpetrators' view without even the remotest idea about the need to reflect on a victim-perpetrator relationship.[12]

---

11. Now the history of this apocalyptic event is written by Philip Gourevitch: *We wish to inform you that tomorrow we will be killed with our families* (London: Picador, 1999). The extreme Hutu racialists later terrorized their own people from which about a million had to flee to neighbouring countries where a majority died from cholera, starvation and mass killings. Although the Germans were the first colonizers of Rwanda, then together with Burundi (1897-1919), the Belgians and the Catholic missionaries were most of the time responsible also for the racist divide and rule between the Tutsis and Hutus (and Rwanda and Burundi). In 1959 they left overnight while Rwanda was in a bloody civil war. Now it was a French puppet-regime which executed the killings; trained and armed by the French (including the son of socialist prime minister Mitterand, acting as a leading arms dealer in the region) and backed by the French till the bitter end. The USA with their large mineral interests in the whole region did the rest by blocking every possible solution and every military intervention. They made it possible that in this 'biblical time'(Moses Isegawa) neighbours killed their own neighbours, doctors their own patients, priests and nuns their own flock with machetes and machine guns. And so on and so forth. In 1971 at the time, the Tutsis were in full power thanks to their 'property' of the army; they killed all the educated Hutus they could catch after a failed Hutu coup. That was about 350,000 peoples or 7% of the 1971 population! See A. Mazrui (Ed.), *General History of Africa. Africa since 1935* (Paris, Oxford: UNESCO/ Heinemann, 1993), pp. 209, 212-214 for the preceding period.

12. See Goldhagen's answer to Browning's study about 'Ordinary men' for which he wanted to substitute 'Ordinary Germans' in HH, p. 301-307. For Browning this was not a matter of principle as it was for G., who told the same story. The latter wrote for instance: 'Had a battalion of ordinary Danes or ordinary Italians ... *with the same opportunity to have exempted themselves,* would they have slaughtered, deported, and hunted down, with the same efficacy and brutality, Jewish men, women, and children, as these ordinary Germans did?' (italics from G., p.305). Later on he 'simply did not believe' that the people of this police battalion 'would be willing to kill as these men did, simply for the asking' (p. 306). While writing his book, G. could read nearly daily how thousands of Christian housefathers in Serbia as weekend leisure went into Bosnia to kill many tens of thousands of men and children in a cruel way, raped the women in collective actions, burned houses, villages, mosques, etc. and went back to Belgrade, etc. to work in their offices, restaurants, bakeries, etc. until the next weekend. It was not the professionals of the 'Sonderkommando' Arkan or general Mladic who

One commentator explained the remarkable success of *Hitler's willing executioners* from the transition to a new *culture of victimization* which popped up in the American 1990s in the wake of cases like O.J. Simpson, the anti-smoking actions or sexual abuse affairs.[13] The inherent warning was that a rewritten Holocaust history, used as a political-ideological instrument, could transform a powerless past into a powerful present. The precondition is an uncritical historiography which is aimed at describing history as one long episode of suffering.

Furthermore, it is envisaged that an identity crisis within the American Jewish community could be 'solved' by means of books like Goldhagen's. One is also confronted with opinions that this book or the claims for restitution of Jewish war money fit perfectly into a strong American and Jewish anti-Europeanism: Currently, Europe is definitely trying to unite in a highly competitive political and economical sense and has definitely abandoned her pro-Israel policy (using streetfighters like Netanyahu or Sharon as the ideal pretext), and thus every means is suitable to fight 'perpetrator Europe' politically, culturally, etc. Goldhagen's book is not that important, and the instrumentalization of the Holocaust victims will rebound as the following examples suggest.

A new competition between continuously growing numbers of victims is a circular game based on dubious comparisons between Hitler's, Stalin's and Mao's atrocities (Nolte, Conquest, Black books, etc.): now China remains the only serious threat. Mao's body count increased to a 100 million victims while, in fact, nobody (not even 'willing Chinese') can provide any reliable figure of 'real victims' or of the starvation cases which make the bulk of the body-counters' exercises. The only thing one knows is that, for example, Mao made 'very many' victims. The other side of this coin is, that in such perspectives a Holocaust remains nothing but a regrettable accident or that Hitler's responsibility diminishes to a negligible level;

---

slaughtered most of the Bosnians, but ordinary Serbs. Much more 'ordinary' than G's police battalion! During World War II 'ordinary Croatians' probably acted as cruelly as possible in their Ustasha movement with their many priests-helpers and, in particular, the special long Ustasha knifes: it was the sport to slit open a body from belly to head in one stroke. The SS who often had to accompany these people who killed their Serbian neighbours in masses, with whom they had lived for 25 years or so; these SS became confused about so much cruelty. Several hundreds of thousands of Serbs and Jews were killed . G. had to know that they did the dirty work also as helpers of the Italians! And what did the Rumanian police battalions do during the war, as told by Raul Hilberg? About Danes I do not know anything, but probably the Dutch are good enough: recently one found the most cruel and detailed descriptions from the pre-war Prime Minister, Colijn, about his adventures in the Dutch colonies where he was an officer and time and again his soldiers bayoneted women and children after killing their fathers and men and burning their villages. Directly after World War II 'ordinary Dutchmen' made for year-long murder trips with the Westerling 'Sonderkommando' in Indonesia. In short, G. is in this respect an uninformed demagogue. Other people accuse him of racism because his unsubstantiated opinion leads to the acceptance of special German genes for cruelty.

13. Gulie Ne'eman Arad, Ein amerikanischer Alptraum, in: J. Schoeps (Ed.), *Ein Volk von Mördern? Die Dokumentation zur Goldhagen-Kontroverse* .. (Hamburg: Hoffmann und Campe,1996), p.176-186.

even worse is the twist that the latter is to be *praised* because he attacked Stalin, which was the biggest threat to 'us'.

For political, ideological or business reasons, Jewish, Polish, Israeli, American, Dutch, and many other authorities and interest groups recently confronted others with their own victim histories. For instance, this history of the Russians with by far the greatest number of World War II victims still remains largely unknown (how reliable is the generally accepted figure of 20 million?); despite the fact that these victims also suffer from a 'Land of Evil' image! To this category of state propaganda also belongs the use of the Holocaust in the sense that Israel could be promoted as a kind of privileged nation in its struggle with the Palestinians: perpetrator and self-styled victim.

Nowadays, a country like Austria has gained its identity from a similar conjunction. Thanks to the Cold War it has managed to become a sentimental victim land instead of a country with nearly the worst perpetrators, which it, in fact, has been since – say – 1900. In 1997, officially, a quarter of the total Austrian population (Haider's so-called 'liberals') was explicitly antisemitic and neo-nazistic, although there are only a few Jews left in the country, except for Simon Wiesenthal; another third, the Catholics, are still in the infant stadium of anti-Judaism; another third, the so-called 'socialists' (after 1967 led by the second remaining Austrian Jew, Bruno Kreisky), failed in a fundamental way to avoid the rise of the neo-Nazis. At present, Austria is the worst example in Europe of blurring the antagonisms between victims and perpetrators. Here, it seems to be the rule that the judges acquit important neo-Nazis of reprehensible antisemitic deeds and convict people who protest against these acts.[14] I shall return to this Austrian constellation because here the victim-offender relationship reveals clear traits. Today, 'small events' like the following belong to that relationship as well.

Directly related to the Holocaust were the confrontations following appalling actions like those of Polish Catholic churchleaders and nuns who began exploiting 'Auschwitz' with antisemitic overtones; or after a Polish entrepreneur tried to open a supermarket right in front of the gate of the Auschwitz concentration camp.[15] The official commemoration of '50 Years Auschwitz' was celebrated with all the pomp of gatherings of world political leaders, heirs of those who were co-responsible for the genocide. At the time the first *intifada* broke out, Israel 'pulled out its secret weapon, the Holocaust' (Margalit); a substantial part of the Auschwitz tourist trade is apparently aimed at indoctrinating Israeli youths for a dubious war against their neighbours, while at the same time on Israeli television a Holocaust quiz was to be seen 'shot on location in Poland ... participating in it were Jewish

---

14. Karin Jušek in *NRC Handelsblad,* 10-5-1997.
15. C. Rittner, J. Roth (Ed.), *Memory Offended. The Auschwitz Convent Controversy* (New York: Praeger, 1991).

boys and girls who were ... awarded two points for each correct answer.'[16] The Amsterdam-based Anne Frank multinational definitely opted for a place in mass tourism after its last, highly criticized, multi-million investment program. It looks like, furthermore, as if Mr. Spielberg is gathering 50,000 video performances of Holocaust victims to conduct business under the pretext of correctly sustaining the Holocaust memory. This again is an element of the prediction about the year 2010 that the americanization of the Holocaust has resulted in the opinion: 'every American' thinks the Holocaust took place somewhere in the United States;[17] and so on and so forth.

The largest and most astonishing omissions in *all* Holocaust and Shoah discussions are, first, the neglect of the *living victims* from the years 1933 to 1945: until recently in all Holocaust statistics you are only a victim when you are dead; the physically or traumatically injured does not count, nor the one's who lost everything but their lifes or who had to perform compulsory labour. After more than fifty years some of the latter received a tip and others got a restitution for the lost family shares, etc.[18] For a very long time, furthermore, *dead victims* were only Jews: it took again half a century before it was well-known that Gypsies, disabled, Poles, Russians POW's, homosexuals, Jehova's Witnesses, etc. belonged to the dead victims as well, and that the latter together easily outweigh the 5 to 6 million victims called Jews. These omissions had and still have serious consequences not only for the historical record but also for the acknowledgement of claims as is recently proved.

For many reasons, therefore, the situation is as diffuse as possible thanks to a substantial knowledge gap, a widespread instrumentalization of the Holocaust for alien purposes, blank cynicism and pure propaganda. One must regret that 'the real Holocaust victims' are increasingly being driven into the background and not just because they are slowly becoming extinct. I suppose that there is a clear link between the neglect of the Holocaust victimization and the deplorable public or political perception of, for example, the recent Bosnia and Rwanda genocides or the near disappearance of support for an "Israeli versus Palestinians case".

Still, it is not necessary to become totally pessimistic when confronted with all these events and tendencies. First, it is possible to question the seriousness of the many allegations hidden in the above 'facts'. Apart from this, in the last decade

16. A. Margalit, The Kitsch of Israel, in: *The New York Review of Books*, Nov. 24 (1988), note 13, p. 24.
17. Dutch and German publications tell about ambiguities of the Spielberg Survivors project and the Americanization or Hollywoodisation of the Holocaust: B.Blokker in *NRC Handelsblad*, 19-9-1998 and A. Kilb in *Die Zeit*, 3-12-1998. Not even 500 survivor-stories should be ready for circulation at the time!
18. The most thorough studies at stake come from Gerard Aalders, *Roof. De ontvreemding van joods bezit tijdens de Tweede Wereldoorlog* (The Hague: SDU, 1999; German translation: *Geraubt...* Cologne: Dittrich Verlag, 2000) and *Berooid: de beroofde Joden en het Nederlandse resititutiebeleid* sinds 1945 (Amsterdam: Boom, 2001).

historians, sociologists or journalists developed substantial falsification capacities, and many fiction writers or artists broke down the unnecessarily high barriers between the scientific and the real worlds. They are few in number and sometimes influenced by or even subordinated to the daily political rivalries. The so-called German *Historikerstreit* with its international effects demonstrated this clearly. The considerable and nearly universal criticism of Goldhagen's *scientific* performance and the massive *journalistic* support show the substantial limits.

A more serious problem would arise if under influence of 'the street' the public opinion institutions or universities were not eager and diversified enough to sustain and expand a sound democratic discussion and culture which is being undermined by the substantial new support for right-wing policies, hidden agendas of opportunist 'Third Road' politicians and anti-democratic market policies. Here a lot of work is still to be done. Concurrently, I have to conclude that the victims' panorama displayed above is far too broad to treat here. What is to be done now?

THE PERPETRATOR'S CREATION

I intend to discuss several ambiguous attitudes of victims. However, this seems impossible without a differentiated idea of who, in fact, were and are the Holocaust and Shoah victims. The tensions described so far presage a minefield of highly explosive opinions and feelings. The advantage could be that one can avoid common mistakes in these discussions.

In daily conversations one was (and, too often, is) confronted with a meaningful 'but': '... but aren't Gypsies thiefs?'; ' ... but Jews are all bolshevics, aren't they?'; '... but Jews are behaving like parasites, aren't they?' and so on. I myself had a similar experience in 1964 as well.

A few minutes before he was shown the door, a rather famous Jesuit professor, who had played a role in the Dutch resistance, objected in the same way: 'One cannot approve what happened, but the Jews possessed the whole middle class in Poland.' After 'but', several variants of *the own guilt thesis* are displayed, which always convince far too many people. The question, therefore, of which species victims belong to, needs a specific clarification.

We learned from the above that perpetrators and their representatives determined for some reason or other who would be victims; they defined the sins in order to gain from the fears they sowed; it is their value system which was the original impulse for the punishments and exterminations. It is a common policy of (potential) perpetrators to *create victims by means of making 'wholes'* ('Ganzheiten') which do not allow for exceptions or tolerance, let alone for reasonable argumentation; they define ambiguous concepts as laws, as happened with *Jew*, *heretic* and so on. The European bourgeois-aristocratic form of this aggressive 'wholistic' thinking with its concepts like *race, nation, honour, hero, enemy* and so on is a heritage of the 19th century, which in the 20th allowed too much room for committing mass murder, including the later rationalizations. It is not only oikoidal thinking in the extreme, but received a widespread legitimation beyond the usual state environment of government, police, military and other bureaucrats.

Furthermore, a general problem with victims from a car accident, a rape, a fraudulent practice, etc. is that 'the other' or 'society', being a constitution, judge or neighbour, does not have a more or less standardized set of moral or juridical rules from which to estimate the victim's position. Among the many reasons for the Austrian juridical failures, Jušek stresses the extreme oikoidal character of the juridical organization and university education. One accepts, for example, the opinion that the punishment of neo-Nazis belongs to *discrimination* cases.

Also elsewhere, a typical class judgement is the rule: the more important, richer, etc. the victim, the more he/she can claim as recompense for the offence. In addition: the more important the offender, the less certain his/her sentencing. In a highly civilized country like the Netherlands, it is a rule that famous singers or soccer players, who are to blame for killing people in traffic, get off with no or a light punishment instead of the usual years in detention; time and again highly fraudulent or dangerously incompetent bureaucrats have a chance to get away with a *golden handshake*. At the moment, the worst criminals, once they become ruler of a country, still receive an effective immunity. Consequently, also being a victim is not always a bad position, in which case the creation act becomes interesting.

The ultimate way to repay the sufferings of victims was – and often still is – (blood)revenge. At the time this was forbidden thanks to Christian ethics, victims were only referred to heaven in which they were promised a sufficiently comfortable place. Why? The so-called Christian pacification (by means of the 'iron fist' killing real or alleged opponents so that a mortal peace could be introduced) gave the new authorities the obligation to protect the new subjects. In other words, the oikoidal (state) authorities took over the revenge task, whereas 'the market' only provided defective insurance opportunities. Even today, the authorities have largely failed to perform protection tasks in nearly all countries but, at the same time, they do not allow others to perform the 'revenge work'. Secret services, death squads and other institutions close the gap between safety claim and reality.

Thus, the state became a major problem, which in the 20th century was mostly unbearable because the state not only failed to protect, but actually started to attack citizens on an unprecedented scale and with all available means. Weber became one of its main ideologues simply by ascribing to it a 'monopoly in legitimate coercive violence' – *Monopol legitimen physischen Zwanges* – only in the hands of its 'administrative staff' – *Verwaltungsstab* ! Here we reach the core of those 20th century dilemmas and dramas in the so-called First World but also in the Second or Third World countries. 'The state' became the single most important perpetrator in our time after having been pushed into the background in the 19th century: the 20th century victims are mainly its creation. Let's look closer at the fate of its classical victim in our time.

THE CLASSICAL VICTIM

After the survivors returned from the *Lager*, in Germany as elsewhere in civilized countries, they had to fight a long battle to become acknowledged as victims and to get their belongings back. Some of them organized themselves to take physical revenge on specific Germans. For the great majority this was not possible; for them, the bureaucratic struggle was all that remained. This battle about acknowledgement as a victim had to be won as otherwise no subventions, allowances, restitutions, etc. could be awarded. Still, thanks to their better help organizations, Jews had a relatively easier job than homosexuals, gypsies, forced labourers and so on. The last category, the deserters, received their 'victim stamp' in Germany in May 1997. Symbolically, it was the same time in which the *Wehrmacht* was definitively transformed from victim of a lunatic Hitler and a barbarian SS into an institution as criminal as the other German perpetrators thanks to a controversial German exhibition of its warcrimes in Soviet Russia during Operation Barbarossa.

For the real victims it did not matter. Once the point was reached that a relevant discussion could start about some material compensation for incarceration in a concentration camp and other sufferings, many survivors were exhausted by the bureaucracy, new discriminations and antisemitism, or had simply died.[19] However, in these long-lasting battles the second-generation victims were created.[20]

A striking example of the bureaucratic war which had to be fought is the following verdict of the *Bundesgerichtshof* in Koblenz (1956) after lengthy lawsuits:

---

19. There is a substantial literature on the problems met by those who returned from the camps in 1945-1946. Now, fifty years later, the restitution of capital, paintings, etc. has become a hot item nearly all over the world. Here only the stories about the Netherlands, antisemitic as never before, and the BRD as usual: D. Hondius, *Terugkeer. Antisemitisme in Nederland rond de bevrijding* (The Hague: SDU, 1990); M. Bossenbroek, *De Meelstreep. Terugkeer en Opvang na de Tweede Wereldoorlog* (Amsterdam: Bakker, 2001) and H.H. Fischer-Hübner (Ed.): *Die Kehrseite der 'Wiedergutmachung'. Das Leiden von NS-Verfolgten in den Entschädigungsverfahren.*(Gerlingen: Bleicher Verlag, 1990); L.Herbst, C.Goschler (Ed.), *Wiedergutmachung in der Bundesrepublik Deutschland* (München: Oldenbourg, 1989). Interestingly H. Ben-Sasson, pp.1306-1321 does not say anything about this problem.
20. See last paragraph. A specific kind of psychoanalytical literature was created as well like A. Eckstaedt, *Nationalsozialismus in der 'zweiten Generation'. Psychoanalyse von Hörigkeitsverhältnissen.* (Frankfurt a/M.: Suhrkamp, 1992) or J. Eland et al, *Tweede generatie Joodse Nederlanders* (Deventer: Van Loghum Slaterus, 1990), but also an interesting political literature like E. Gans, *Gojse nijd & joods narcisme* (Amsterdam ; Platina, 1994). They document together the main reactions: a strong attention for the personal troubles of children with '(camp)victim-parents' or '(camp)perpetrator parents' and a strong political interest in Zionism (to leave perpetrator Europe) or opposition activities (to change existing society so that 'it' never could happen again). Alas, the latter belong to a very small minority.

the '*Umsiedlung von Zigeunern*' to the Generalgouvernement was '*keine national-sozialistische Gewaltmaßnahme ... im Sinne des & 1 BEG.*' Why was it not a Nazi crime? Everybody knew that the word '*Umsiedlung*' in SS jargon nearly always was the euphemism for 'killing'; even if '*Umsiedlung*' was taken literally as 'transportation to', the destination 'Generalgouvernement', the region containing the most important death-camps and ghettos, meant 'killing' as well. By 1956 everybody also knew that, at least, a half million gypsies were killed in Treblinka, Sobibor and elsewhere.

This verdict directly robbed most gypsy survivors and their next of kin of any material allowance. The judges told the public: because it was already very common in 1936 for the police to take measures against a '*Zigeunerplage* ... *Asozialen* ... *Zigeunerunwesen* ...*' ('gypsy plague ... anti-socials ... hostile behaviour of gypsies'), the wartime SS measures against the gypsies can be considered as a normal part of German life! Only after Himmler declared his so-called *Auschwitz-Erlaß* (March 1943), and the gypsies could prove that they were (still) victims, could they receive the so-called *Wiedergutmachungs* (compensation) payments.[21] At this time, most of them had already been killed. Thirteen years later the guards of the oikoidal norms and values still could not deviate from 'normal' treatment of the most nomadic elements in European society.

The other side of this coin concerns what can be called the 'vacuum position' of victims: their isolation often transformed them into something like saints or martyrs for their environment because their sufferings and the reasons for their sufferings were made incomprehensible for many people, non-victims and former victims alike. Nearly all political and cultural leaders and institutions were afraid that the victims should talk too loudly and asked too much. This vacuum position gave the opportunity to transform the Holocaust into a mystery and, therefore, to keep a solemn silence. This artificial edifice broke into pieces during the 'Roaring Sixties' as for the first time the 'fathers' were taken to task in these Holocaust matters as well.

Everybody tumbled down to earth including the victims. They were discovered as humans and neighbours with all their shortcomings; camp victims could be (Jewish) Nazis or criminals and only a very few could (re)act like Primo Levi; the rest were, for example, highly obstinate to their environment including most second-generation victims. In short, all these victims together reproduce

---

21. H. Derks, De joodse opstand in het getto van Warschau, in: Idem (Ed.), *Kroniek van drie eeuwen revolutie*, p. 249 ff. A recent example is the following about Jews in the former 'Eastern Block' (*Die Zeit*, 16-5-1997): '*Aber wer ist schon ein NS-Opfer?*' The Ministry of Finance in Bonn nor anybody else gave criteria for answering that crucial question. Of all the people in the Ukraine who receive a war subvention there are only 2% Jews; Lithuania and Estonia both received 2 million marks but nobody knows who put it in his pocket; in Latvia SS veterans who served in the camps got 'Kriegsopferrente' while the Jewish neighbour, a former camp victim, received nothing.

human society under the strongest forms of pressure from some higher oikoidal power, probably a fierce Christian or Old Testament god.

Most important, is it not very difficult or even impossible for the large majority of Nazi victims to express a *cause* for which they could be martyrs or saints; a cause defined in the end by 'a fierce Christian or Old Testament god'? Did Primo Levi, for example, state why and how he suffered for a cause? Another consideration is that, apart from minorities like Jehovah's Witnesses or political prisoners, no one was victimized for his/her religion. The Christian religion was the basic creed of the perpetrators and, in our culture, this is the only (oikoidal) background for saints and martyrs.[22] On May 10, 1997, a most astonishing event occurred to elucidate the meaning of this statement.

The Polish Pope, himself a descendant from a fascist background, beatified a Spanish gypsy for the first time in history. The newsreel showed a gathering of gypsies with candles, pious faces and so on in the company of praying Catholic priests. The public relations department must have studied the case carefully before launching such a symbolic event: the converted gypsy in question was beatified because he had saved the life of a Catholic priest during Franco's ascent to power in the 1930s. Whoever constructed this event must have been a 'spiritual pervert': the Catholic church never protested against and was a willing supporter of the harshest treatments of gypsies (now, in Rumania, they are being hunted again, and there has been no Catholic protest); this church fanatically defended the fascist Franco regime (*Opus Dei*) including the many atrocities against humanity it has committed; the gypsy could only be beatified after being baptised and after he saved the life of a church executioner. Thus, you can only become a saint/martyr if you are first accepted within the ideological and institutional framework of this (or any other) church.

Christianity has definitely lost her position in Western and Southern but not in Eastern Europe, where Catholics started an agressive competition with the Greek-Orthodox churches at the time genocidal battles are raging in ex-Yugoslavia between the Croats/Catholics and the Serbs/Greek-Orthodox as well as against their common enemy, the Bosnians+Albanians/Islam. For the time being in Western Europe, Christianity has to follow the well-known minority strategy of supporting old left-wing themes like poverty, etc. By choosing the above gypsy case in Franco Spain, at least, three such themes were handled in one stroke: the suggestion could be made that this Catholic Church was neither the harsh co-repressor of anti-Franco groups, nor the supporter of the negation of nomadic peoples such as gypsies, and is, in fact, a highly progressive institution.

Here again, as in the case of the Austrians, an incredible travesty of the victim-perpetrator roles/functions is achieved. It also demonstrates the European

22. Against E. Fackenheim's religious perception of the Holocaust in A. Cohen, P. Mendes-Flohr (Ed.), *Contemporary Jewish religious thought* (New York: Free Press, 1988), p. 406.

perpetrators' strategy of changing colours at the moment they castigate their subjects too heavily. At such a moment they will assume the victims' position in trying to dictate who may be a victim and who not. In this policy one will meet again 'the old friends' and 'the classical victims'. These victims can be easily connected to another characteristic.

It may be difficult to understand the ultimate depths of being a victim or a murderer in Nazi camps, during death marches and so on. It is, however, astonishing how religious interests did their utmost after 1945 to exploit 'Auschwitz' by transforming it into a mystery. In this way, one could avoid to investigate uncomfortable problems, and it is the vehicle to download Auschwitz onto the original 'Christian harddisk'. It may also be difficult not to blur the large differences between (the behaviour of) a group or institution and an individual person for which, generally, very different standards must be accepted. The reality, however, is that also 'after Auschwitz', too many intolerant elites kept looking at homosexuals, gypsies, Jews or communists as 'wholes' (Adorno would say 'specimen') and as *Untermenschen*. If you study the source of this intolerance, you will find mostly: the 'secular religious' institutions.

Enough about the fate of the classical victim in the post-war world and its general characteristics. Is it possible to 'emancipate' victims from this victims model, to get rid of this model as such, or to reflect in a different way on victim problems 'after Auschwitz'?

OIKOIDAL AND NOMADIC VICTIMS

Of course, the famous question of how to define a 'victim after Auschwitz' has first to be answered by '*the drowned and the saved*' (Primo Levi): drowned by and saved from German perpetrators and their allies. In this way camp victims became part of a much larger victimization related to the 1933-1945 period and its aftermath. It is not my intention to describe a differentiated casuistic of victims including the second and even third generation but only to discuss some rather unusual perspectives in order to develop a new perception of the victim. This can be, first, discovered by making the differentiation between victims (dead or alive) from within or from outside the *Lager* system.

Recently, Gudrun Schwarz announced that 50 years after the war there is still a 'large gap' in our knowledge about this system, as well as the number of *Lager* in and outside Germany. She discovered that there were at least 17 different kinds of *Lager* and (only!) a few more than 10,000 *Lager* known, which is perceived as 'a fraction' (*Bruchteil*) of some total! From these 10,000 about 60 per cent were located in Poland and 40 per cent outside this country.[23] This means that the extension and density of this whole extermination system was much greater than previously thought and that many more categories of victims were involved. It also means that the pace at which this system could be extended was considerable, because the impulses to augment the victims (categories) and their dwellings came from several directions which did not necessarily work together.

It is equally difficult to come to terms with the situation *outside* this extreme oikoidal and highly extensive Nazi underworld (for the internal organization, see below). Here a very fluctuating and flexible situation existed. Thanks to Hilberg, Browning, Goldhagen, Pohl and many others, the about ca. 100 death marches or the actions of the notorious 40 police battalions and 8 *Einsatzgruppen* became known. For several years they all roamed around '*in the East*', busy with multifarious cruel and lethal actions which resulted in several million dead victims and very few survivors. Furthermore, the extent of the numerous, loose *Erschiessungsaktionen* in the Soviet Union executed by the German army during the Barbarossa campaign is unknown. Here, for example, about 2 million Russian war prisoners were killed in a few months (August 1941 to February 1942) by means of shooting, intentional starvation and freezing in open fields.[24] Against the oikoidal and

23. G. Schwarz (Introduction, note 3). Strangely enough, her quantifying research is not considered in HH, although it differentiates the existing perception in a rather *fundamental* way. In ENS, p.550 B. Distel writes referring to the first edition of Schwarz's book: 'Till the beginning of the war seven concentration camps were erected; till 1945 there were within the area of NS-power 22 main camps with 1202 additional camps [*Aussenlager*] and outposts.' In A.&H. Edelheit, p. 271-295 there are mentioned already 2275 camps and 43 categories. Now Schwarz concludes: 'The empirical research resulted in 17 categories and far more than 10,000 national socialist camps in which people of different ages, different sex, different nationalities, different ethnical or religious origins were kept.' (p. 261) Then follows a list not only with the Distel figures but also, for example: 'sechs 'Euthanasie-Anstalten', 29 Psychiatrische Anstalten und 30 Kinderfachabteilungen, in denen Patienten durch Medikamenten-Vergiftungen ermordet wurden ... 11 Sammelstellen für unheilbar geisteskranke Ostarbeiter ... 399 Ghettolager in Polen ... 941 Zwangsarbeitslager für männliche und weibliche Juden ... acht Jugendschutzlager ... 645 Lager für ausländische Zivilarbeiterinnen und Zivilarbeiter in Berlin ... 136 'Germanisierungslager'..' And so on. Schwarz stresses how much is still unknown about this whole system from which 5877 *Lager* were erected in Poland; just in Berlin there existed 645 hard-labour *Lager;* etc. The newest data can be found in K. Orth, *Das System der nationalsozialistischen Konzentrationslager. Eine politische Organisationsanalyse* (Hamburg: Hamburger Edition, 2002).

24. H. Boog et al., *Der Angriff auf die Sowjetunion* (Frankfurt a/M.: Fischer, 1991), p. 1195-1202; ENS, p.553-555 tells that the Russian POWs got the worst treatment of all prisoners of war: from the total of ca. 5.3 million Russian POWs between 2.5 and 3 million died during the war 'because of racial and communist hatred'. See also O. Bartov, *Hitlers Wehrmacht. Soldaten, Fanatismus und die Brutalisierung des Krieges* (Reinbek b/H.: Rowohlt, 1995); H. Prantl (Ed.), *Wehrmachtsverbrechen. Eine deutsche Kontroverse* (Hamburg: Hoffmann & Campe, 1997) and C. Hartmann, Massensterben oder Massenvernichtung? Sowjetische Kriegsgefangene im 'Unternehmen Barbarossa', in: *Vierteljahrshefte f. Zeitgeschichte,* 49 (2001), pp. 97-158. The best publication to date is the exhibition catalogue of the Hamburger Inst. Für Sozialforschung (Ed.), *Verbrechen der Wehrmacht ... 1941-1944* (Hamburg: Hamb. Edition, 2002) which should be read together with H. Heer, *Vom Verschwinden der Täter. Der*

sedentary camp victims, therefore, one has the 'nomadic' victims as a result of all kinds of mobile activities.

There are other aspects of the same inside-outside problematic. The contradiction between the sedentary and mobile constellation had (and has) an important legal basis. World War I was characterized by the extreme oikoidal way of making war, the absolutely immobile trench warfare. Although World War II generally showed a much more mobile character (even a '*Blitzkrieg*' is possible for a moment), thanks to the massive implementation of all sorts of traction, a new way of warfare, *the mobile guerilla*, was introduced on a large scale. This happened, in particular, in Eastern Europe from the Finnish North to the Greek South. During this war international law did not apply to the deeds of these nomadic-warriors: if caught by the perpetrators, they who were the victims in their own country were immediately tortured, hanged, shot, etc., and international law gave the perpetrators the full right to do this.

Consequently, nowadays, the best of German military historians assess the deeds of their army in foreign countries as legally correct.[25] They dare to construct an excuse for the atrocities by pointing to an allegedly 'inhumane' way in which the Soviet army was commanded. Even if this should be true, it is totally irrelevant in this context. Paradoxically, to support this construction, they also point to the alleged similarity of the notorious mobile *Einsatzgruppen* and special forces of the NKVD (Soviet secret police) which had to do the most immobile, oikoidal job imaginable, i.e. guard a camp system and, if necessary, execute prisoners. All this is part of a dreadful Soviet history which cannot be mixed up with the German invasion activities and so on. For our discussion, however, there are more important elements considered by these (and most other) military historians.

They stick to the rule: an (immobile, oikoidal) standing army has to be fought by a standing army; every other possibility is *illegal*. This is not only a question of (lack of) professionalism but also of subordination to the, in the end, mysterious rules of the battle order and absolute, monarchical leadership of generals/warlords. Nomadic warfare is seen as *dishonest* because these partisans fight 'from behind the

---

Vernichtungskrieg fand statt, aber keiner war dabei (Berlin: Aufbau Verlag, 2004).
25. The 'official' historiography of the *Militärgeschichtlichen Forschungsamt,* H. Boog et al., p. 920, says, for instance, that the hanging of those young guerillas may be a pity but '*so darf man doch nicht übersehen, daß es nach den unerbittlichen Kriegsgesetzen vielleicht unabwendbar gewesen ist*'. It is a reason for the authors to make the German atrocities excusable by means of comparing them to those committed by the Russians, which is certainly going too far: the Germans started to invade a foreign country, and the Russians defended themselves by all means. In an oikoidal view of history, it must be cowardly and dishonest not to take responsibility and hide away behind the atrocities executed by the victims who are eager to retaliate. It is the same mechanism with which the Israeli always approve the occupation and repression of foreign territories. For a better treatment of this war, see O.Bartov, *The Eastern Front 1941-45: German Troops and the Barbarisation of Warfare* (Basingstoke: 1985), p. 119-141; K.H. Pohl (Ed.), *Wehrmacht und Vernichtungspolitik. Militär im nationalsozialistischen System* (Göttingen: Vandenhoeck & Ruprecht, 1999) in particular the article of Christian Gerlach (p. 89-115).

enemy's back' ('*Kampfauftrag im Rücken des Feindes*'). Partisans were not recruited from the privileged but from the amateuristic, uncivilized, wild outlaws of society who can hide themselves in the wilderness under difficult circumstances, being only supported by the poor. Of course, these clever men seek the weak spots of the enemy in order to succeed. The Germans should have been warned by their history books telling dreadful stories about the hit-and-run Cossacks during Napoleon's Russian campaign. Later, the Americans discovered them in and even below the Vietnamese jungle.

Heroic men, however, look for big tasks and the strongest spots, otherwise they cannot gain the medals and honour and cannot enter into the shadow of those mysterious oikoidal powers. Compared with the umbrella abstract oikoidal ideals, a hero's life is absolutely worthless. Nomadic warriors, in any case, are individualists with strong ties to endangered but concrete elements of their own environment like family, work, etc. They defend common men and common causes; therefore, they cannot match heros, and heros cannot fight them without making themselves look ridiculous. An ideal of oikoidal warriors is also *fairness*, which historically is derived from old aristocratic rules of fighting behaviour. Guerillas have to choose their means as opportunistically as possible.

The military historians of the Barbarossa operations apparently cannot understand common men nor common causes (see also below). Even in retrospect, they could not but defend the German *Oberkommando* case by stating ambiguously that '... in the first instance [it was] the NKVD troops and ... the partisan groups and organizations which violated international law and also the general laws of humanity.'[26] Historically, the defeat of the largest and highly successful standing army in history by means of (among others) very mobile

---

26. H. Boog et al, p. 923. In all respects, this part of the extensive and important study morally and intellectually falls short of what is required: here one can read how the present historians, still like defenders of the former German *Oberkommando*, accuse the Russians of making a bad (?) kind of war propaganda in 1941 (as if the usual German anti-Jewish writings which were issued for ten years at least, were examples of pure literature): the Russians suggested that this war was '*nicht ... einen Krieg im üblichen Sinne, sondern um einen kriminellen Akt handelte, die Soldaten der gegnerischen Armee somit nicht als reguläre Kombattanten, vielmehr als Verbrecher und Banditen anzusehen seien.*' (Idem.) What we now know about the aims, performance and plans of the German Wehrmacht, etc. in the Soviet Union these last qualifications seem to be quite polite. Of course, this does not mean that all (individual) German soldiers in Russia behaved like wild animals. The principles which clash here are discussed in G. Dill (Ed.), *Clausewitz in Perspektive. Materialien zu Carl von Clausewitz: Vom Kriege.* (Frankfurt a/M.: Ullstein, 1980) in particular in the contributions of H-U. Wehler (p. 474-511), S. Haffner (p. 652-664), but see also p. XVII ff. with notes. Historians like Boog et al. had time enough to read these articles with much profit. Recently (*Frankfurter Rundschau*, 18-6-1997) Bavarian lawyers tried to sue historians of the Hamburg Institute of Social Research for their exhibition about and interpretation of the suspect role of the army in Hitler's Eastern War. Again, these lawyers mentioned as one of the main arguments that the historians did not clarify the role of the Russian *Partisanen* and their 'bei der deutschen Wehrmacht verursachten Opfer an Menschen und Material.'! See also ENS, p.636, 637.

guerilla fighters had to be followed by a Vietnam war to learn a straight lesson about the definite end of these oikoidal armies. Francis Ford Coppola's *Apocalypse Now* (1979, 2001) evoked the dilemmas discussed in a most dramatic way.

ON ORANGISTIC STATE VICTIMS AND 'ORANGE-JEWS'

From the above one can conclude, for instance, that the oikoidal-nomadic differentiation is not as artificial as it seems. This is to demonstrate further with another and much more complicated war-case from which the previous history will be analyzed in a later paragraph.

In the past, many authors (Poliakov, Hilberg, Dawidowicz, Marrus/Paxton and even a few Dutch historians) wondered why, relatively, the largest number of Jewish victims was deported and killed in the Netherlands of all occupied countries (except Poland), i.e. about 70-75 per cent. In countries like Denmark or Bulgaria, this percentage was practically zero; in France 25 per cent, Belgium about 40 and in Germany itself about 23 per cent from the 1933 Jewish population. This high death toll should have sounded a warning that something is wrong with the "Dutch tolerance".[27] Why was this so although several times a courageous collective behaviour in general strikes was shown, and many Dutch men and women bravely resisted the German oppressor?

Recently, good comparative material about this question appeared, and thanks to the highly critical study of Nanda van der Zee and my *Deutsche Westforschung* the notorious role of the Dutch elite in the Holocaust could be highlighted. A comparison of the Dutch and Belgian situation during the war, indeed, will show the impact of the oikoidal-nomadic differentiation.[28] Let us recall that during the war the Netherlands had a (German) civilian government under a strong NSDAP/SS influence whose overall aim was to incorporate the country within the *Reich*. This was, among others, a consequence of the manner in which Queen

---

27. See above in the preface István Deák in: *New York Review of Books*, 31-5-2001. H. Ben-Sasson, p. 1271 tells how in the Netherlands 'large parts of the population' showed great sympathy for the Jews. Therefore, the remarks a few sentences later must be ambiguous: 'Only in the Netherlands the public behaviour was not able to save much Jews for their destiny.' But there are also sound reasons for sympathy as mentioned, for instance, by G. Kolko, *Century of War. Politics, Conflict, and Society Since 1914* (New York: New Press, 1994), p. 244 ff.

28. R.Zeller, P. Griffioen, Judenverfolgung in den Niederlanden und in Belgien während des Zweiten Weltkriegs, in: *1999. Zeitschrift f. Sozialgeschichte*, 3 (1996), p. 30-54 and 1 (1997), p. 29-48. Irrelevant in this respect is J. Blom, The persecution of the Jews in the Netherlands in a comparative international perspective, in: *Dutch Jewish History* (Jerusalem: 1989), p. 273-289. For the first time a kind of Dutch mini-*Historikerstreit* raged as an effect of N. van der Zee, *Om erger te voorkomen: de voorbereiding en uitvoering van de vernietiging van het Nederlandse jodendom tijdens de Tweede Wereldoorlog* (Amsterdam: Meulenhoff, 1997). Now my *Deutsche Westforschung*, based on new archival research, gives a more elaborate picture of the problems at stake. For the Belgian situation see chapter 3 and for the Dutch chapter 4.

Wilhelmina and the government had left the country, practically giving the new (German) rulers the status of correct legal successors.[29] Apart from this, the perpetrator regime could easily look for and find every kind of *active* cooperation within the Dutch bureaucracy to centralize the rounding-up and deportation of the Jews. At every level the Dutch bureaucrats correctly executed the German deportation orders, and too often, they felt obliged without being asked to act in a brutal way against their fellow citizens. Adolf Eichmann was astonished about such favourable cooperation.

However, the crucial factor in the notorious Dutch efforts is the following. The state bureaucracy under the leadership of the Dutch heads of the ministries and large bureaucratic institutions, who now could act according to the *Führerprinzip*, used the occupation to realize their centralization dreams from before the war. Without much ado this leadership was prepared to pay the price, 'a few Jewish guests', in order to plan and execute these aims. It was constantly 'argued' that this could avoid more serious problems. And, indeed, the Germans welcomed and *followed* the Dutch bureaucratic centralization in nearly all fields except, of course, in military matters. Therefore, in my *Deutsche Westforschung* the concept of the *Second Occupation* (the one of the Dutch state-bureaucrats) could be coined.[30]

For the execution of the deportation decision, in particular, the notorious Amsterdam bureaucracy was of strategic importance because most Jews lived and were collected in this city.[31] Certainly, as a protest against this deportation, there

---

29. After the war the SS-Leader in the Netherlands, Rauter, relied, among others, on these circumstances during his trial, whereas the present hagiograph of this Queen, N. Fasseur, a-historically and demagogically denies that one can believe a SS-man: a scientist is obliged to (double)-check; his/her belief can be shown in a church. See *Het Proces Rauter* (The Hague: Nijhoff, 1952), p. 272 ff. For Fasseur's dubious opinions see *NRC-Handelsblad* 21-5-1997 in which he reacts on J. Michman's strong defense of N. Van der Zee's book (in: *Idem*, 14-5-1997). M. is a high official in the Israeli Ministry of Culture.

30. In the newest research, which I could use only superficially, this perspective is supported. M. Croes, P. Tammes, *"Gif laten wij niet voortbestaan". Een onderzoek naar de overlevingskansen van joden in de Nederlandse gemeenten, 1940-1945* (Amsterdam: Aksant, 2004) looks into the regional and local organisation of the Jew-hunt in the Netherlands. Based on new archival sources a largely quantitative analysis of this hunt could be given. The regional German organizations (*Außenstellen*) with the field-tasks to catch the Jews and other 'enemies' operated relatively independent of their headquarter in the Hague or had their own communication with the SS-headquarter in Berlin (RSHA). Whether this was caused by the always active drive of the SS to intervene secretly in the business of other Nazi institutions (Wehrmacht, etc.) is not told. Anyway, these German organizations showed rather autonomous behaviour and a highly differentiated performance, although the endresult still astonished Eichmann. Dutch parallel organizations, however, from voluntary police forces to the regular police or the municipal bureaucracies and their mayors were strongly hierarchically organized and centralized. They all had to do the dirty work of the rounding up of the victims, although the degree of cooperation with the Germans was not everywhere the same. Only thanks to the effective Dutch work the "job" could be done so quickly and lethal.

31. G. Meershoek in HH, p. 284-300. See also his *Dienaren van het gezag. De Amsterdamse politie tijdens de bezetting* (Amsterdam: Van Gennep, 1999). More interesting is F. Roest, J. Scheren, *Oorlog in de stad. Amsterdam 1939-1941* (Amsterdam: Van Gennep, 1998).

was a brutally repressed widespread strike against the Germans (February 1942). This was, however, a mainly communist initiative and had to be played down by the elite whereas the protest remained an Amsterdam affair only: in the end, as usual, 'the Reds' were again the real bad guys, often a variant of the 'blaming the victim'.

Favourable to the quick deportation was that the Queen and the government in exile urged too late and in a rather irrelevant way the Dutch population to bother about their Jewish citizens. The Dutch resistance began late as well (after April 1943 when most Jews had already been deported), was small and only partially effective. The population was not very cooperative in hiding Jews (25,000) and of these, at least, 8,000 were betrayed. However, *after* most Jews were deported, it appeared that 200,000 to 300,000 people could have been hidden easily! Last but not least, for the Germans there were perfect and undisturbed infrastructural facilities available (large camps, smoothly running trains, etc.).

Also, the 160,000 Jews cooperated surprisingly well with the Dutch government and the Germans. In the first place this was through the centralized Jewish Council. This Council under the chairmanship of A. Asscher and D. Cohen, comprised of representatives of the Jewish elite, urged the Dutch Jews in the strongest words to collaborate with the German perpetrators. Then the following black humour joke circulated: Asscher and Cohen first deported all so-called 'orange-Jews' ('sinaasappeljoden'; 'orange' here the fruit; 'orange-Jews' a name for petty traders) and this was always necessary "to avoid more problems with the Germans". Then the elite had to follow. The time came when they were the only two left. Then Asscher told Cohen: 'You have to go now to Westerbork Camp to avoid serious difficulties!'

There was nearly no Jewish resistance or refusal to wear the Yellow Star. Most important was that nearly all Jews (86%) were Dutch citizens, and the degree of assimilation was 95 per cent. Although there were many Jewish organizations, it was too difficult for them to cooperate with each other. Their identity was formed through non-Jewish organizations like the established Dutch political parties, trade-unions, churches, etc. The last thing to be mentioned here is that the possibilities for flight were hardly used (only 500 fled to the UK). What about the Belgian situation?

In contrast to the Netherlands, here was a German *military* occupation with only a weak relationship with NSDAP or SS circles and a weak antisemitic motivation. This military government got only limited support from the Belgian bureaucrats. They often refused active collaboration at the central level, while German orders were not or only ambiguously supported at the local level. Although he was comparatively German-friendly, the Belgian king objected openly against anti-Jewish measures (it is said that the Danish king even wore the Yellow Star by way of protest). In particular, the Belgian police insufficiently collaborated with the Germans.

It is a remarkable fact as well that practically from the start of the occupation, there was an active resistance movement: the Belgians had had an earlier experience with a German occupation in 1914-1918, which gave them some advantages. For instance, there were not only many more hiding places for Jews, but these were available right from the beginning. The forces specialized in executing anti-Jewish measures had to compete with the German military. Thanks to this situation, a kind of Jewish Council could not be established earlier than eight months after the Dutch example. At the time the largest majority of Dutch Jews were deported (April 1943), only a third of the Belgian Jews had been caught. An important reason for this was the absence of an efficient and adequate infrastructure.

In Belgium at an early stage, the 66,000 Jews initiated their own resistance movement, and generally, they did not cooperate with or listen to their Jewish Council. For instance, half of them refused to wear the Yellow Star. An important reason for this behaviour was the fact that nearly all Belgian Jews were *foreigners* and not Belgian citizens. They mostly fled from the East and were *not* assimilated (92 per cent). This did not mean that they had no organizations. In contrast to the Dutch Jews, there were almost no disagreements between the eastern Yiddish and other (Portugese) Jewish organizations (see below). They strongly supported each other, and their identity was formed by their own political, etc. organizations. One of the effects of all this was that these mobile Jews used all possibilities for flight: not 500 but 20,000 fled.

Many conclusions could be drawn from this comparison, but I restrict myself here to the following. The brave Dutch people in the resistance movement mostly came from the lower echelons of society and not from the elite. Whatever the political creed of members of this elite, in some way or other, they all had accommodated before the war to the oikoidal ticket (strong state authority with an orange colour, highly hierarchical social order and so on) and differed only in the degree of this accommodation and the ideological legitimation.

At the end of the long 19th century, in 1914-1918, Dutch society had already received its principal shape: three of the four 'pillars' or compartments (in party political terms: the Protestant, Catholic, Liberal; Social-Democrats practically joined in the Thirties; in the 1960's the first two became one 'pillar' with what they called two 'blood groups') with different but all inward-looking world views; the same hierarchical form and (very) weak democratic spirit. All 'pillars' had to bear the orange roof of an anti-democratic state bureaucracy and authoritarian monarchy. However, nobody cared for the *space in between* these 'pillars' which, therefore, could be used for everything. [32]It was not before the roaring 1960s that

---

32. One of the most discussed themes in Dutch contemporary historiography and political science is the so called "verzuilde samenleving" (*pillard society*) by scholars like Hans Daalder, Siep Stuurman and the like. See recently R. Schuursma, *Jaren van Opgang. Nederland 1900-1930*. Amsterdam, 2000,

this *space in between* could function as recruting field for a new opposition. All compartments were threatened and badly needed fresh air could pour in. In the same period the relevance and legitimation of the 'orange roof' were injured for the first time. All sorts of non-conformists from the 'pillars' also jumped into the free space and this strong cocktail lead to the so-called 'cultural revolution of the Sixties'.[33] However, the endresult was that the 'pillar' structure could not effectively be undermined but was thrown back on its ultimate limits and modernized only its repression machine. The restoration in the 1980s strongly supported by the Social-Democrats and carried out by a grimly weaponed state provided some compensation for the inevitable internal erosion of the 'pillars'. The 1990s saw the decline of this presumptuous undertaking and the subordination of this state under multinational constructions. The erosion of the 'pillars' is still continuing slowly.

Certainly until the end of the 1960s Dutch tolerance has only been a negative attitude: it meant nothing but the highly opportunistic, if not cynical, acceptance of an enemy as a coalition partner. Remarkable social characteristics were a national hypocrisy of saying publicly the reverse of what was told internally; a formal decision-making network *between* the elites of the 'pillars', but a highly intolerant ideological and intellectual repression *inside* the compartments. Therefore, tolerance was the 'automatic' effect of the existence of an unavoidable *space in between compartments* and of the continuous negotiations between elites over the next compromise. If one wanted to assimilate into this type of society, one had to become a Dutch member of one of the existing 'pillars' ('Dutch tolerance' as 'Dutch comfort'): it was practically impossible to erect a new 'pillar' as the so-called 'humanists' experienced after the war or the Ashkenazi and Sephardi Jewry in the 19th and early 20th century.[34]

The full consequences of the 'space between the pillars' is demonstrated with the dramatic Second World War history of Dutch Jews. Already in the first days of July 1940 a high Dutch state bureaucrat, Verwey, introduced without a serious German hint the official outlawing of 'antisocials, for example, those who experienced already a serious detention; persons with a clear communist past, and

---

p. 188-195 and literature. Nobody, however, discovered how the in-between-trap worked as soon this pillar system was in full swing from 1925 onwards.

33. H. Derks, De Nederlandse culturele revolutie, in: Idem, *Kroniek van drie eeuwen revoluties*, p. 215-225.

34. For the following see H. Daalder, Dutch Jews in a segmented society, in: P. Birnbaum, I. Katznelson (Ed.), *Paths of Emancipation. Jews, States, and Citizenship* (Princeton: Princeton Un. Press, 1995), p. 37-59. In his earlier work Daalder did much to elucidate the element of the Dutch segmented ('verzuilde'; litt. 'pillared') society. Here, again he made some interesting and necessary remarks but failed in my view to come up with sound reasons why Jews were deported wholesale. This must be due to his specific view of the 'pillared' society itself.

Jews'.[35] It did not have much effect but at this very moment also the latter were pushed into the 'space between the pillars'. For the state supporting elite this space functioned, therefore, as a *drain* for non-conformists, better: for those who are defined as non-conformists by the state.

In other words: the orange-coloured state roof on top of the construction with nearly impenetrable compartments equalled a classic immobile *oikos* closed to foreigners except when they were willing to become members of a compartment and to be subordinated under 'the roof'. Foreigners, traditionally, could also profit from the undisturbed *space in between* if they did not try to become Dutchmen. The assimilation of Jews not only made them Dutchmen and Orangist but also made them part of an oikoidal construction which always eradicates its non-conformists. Before 1940 this Dutch 'roof', monarchy plus state bureaucracy, was strongly influenced by German ideas and it was friendly (to say the least) to the Nazis. In most compartments the same feelings or the usual 'friendly reservations' existed, but antisemitism could receive only marginal support, not even in right wing circles. The pillar-construction of society was an effective preservative for extremism.

In May 1940, it seemed as if the 'roof' exploded by the flight of Queen and government, but this was more than compensated by the strongly increased strength of the state bureaucracy and the new rulers: any kind of tolerance for non-conformists was immediately gone. Apart from this, the fugitive Queen and her London entourage, who perfectly knew what was going on in the Netherlands, did not protest against the anti-Jewish measures until it was too late.[36]

In my view this is the main constellation in which, without serious antise-mitism, the highly assimilated Jews were driven out of the compartments by the Dutch state bureaucrats and into *the space in between*. Here they were concentrated and outlawed. In this way normal state-citizens, who had to be protected by the so-called 'monopoly of the legitimate and coercive power' (Weber), could be made sociologically invisible for the rest of the Dutch population and abandoned to their own fate. They did not have time to accommodate to the chances of a now possible

35. J. Presser, *Ondergang*. Vol. 1, p. 18 ff. Verwey was the director of a governmental departement for labour-services etc. and his problem was, who should be forbidden to work in Germany 'due to their fysical and psychological condition'!

36. N. Van der Zee, p. 194 ff. Meershoek in HH, 296 still repeats in the end the official opinion of his 'Doktorvater' Blom and of Dutch orangistic historiography about the subordinate role of the bureaucrats, notwithstanding the possibility to come up with an alternative based on some passages. He also states, for example, that the actual course of the persecution in Amsterdam indicates 'that the German contribution to the achievement of this result can easily be overrated. Most German authorities were not in a position to deal with the Dutch administration effectively.' A few lines further one can read: 'The Dutch administration wanted to retain controle, apparently at any price. In their own circles this strategy was referred to as "keeping one step ahead of the occupying forces."'

nomadic life; 'dis-identified' they were only prey in a 'de-civilized' desert without protection from the willing German-Dutch hunters.[37]

Therefore, the Dutch Jews and those who had to bear the same stigma became part of the 'Western victims' and had to demonstrate that classes and status-groups played a decisive role even in the way of dying.

EASTERN AND WESTERN VICTIMS

If the *Shoah* only refers to Jewish victims, one could conclude that the other part of the dead and survivors of the German *Holocaust* (to be defined as: the systematic and wholesale victimization, including murder, of selected unarmed groups of people by the Germans in 1933-1945) were non-Jewish victims like Russians, Poles, gypsies, homosexuals, Jehovah's Witnesses, political prisoners and other categories. This means, in other words, that through the Holocaust the 'Jewish Question' inevitably became connected to the fate of, for instance, the gypsies. If one wants to emphasize the complexity of the question, one must point to the fate of Polish dead and survivors who were often perpetrators for Jews and gypsies. If the Germans had won their eastern war, according to *Generalplan Ost* and its consequences, another thirty to forty million 'Slaves' would have been killed through the *Lager system*.

It is clear that for some strange reason or other, a hierarchy exists *between victims-survivors*, one group/ individual is (a) better dead than another: nationality, religion, the name of the camp (a large majority of these camps is still unknown

---

37. This image of the primitive hunt is used by Wolfgang Sofsky in his impressive *Traktat über die Gewalt* (Frankfurt a./M.: Fischer, 1996), p. 155 ff. Croes, Tammes (note 30) were more or less able to quantify the problem to what extent the pillarization of Dutch society decreased the chance of survival of Jews (chapter 7). They concluded: 'The lower the degree of pillarization, the higher the percentage of Jews that survived the occupation.' (p. 603) based on the occurence of intermarriage between the pillars. This supports my theory about the effects of this pillarization. The authors had no explanation for what they also found: in Catholic municipalities the chance to survive for Jews was substantially larger than in Calvinist ones. There is nothing mysterious about this! One should know, first, that in the whole southern part of the Netherlands (nearly for 100% Catholic in 1940-1945) social and cultural life was (and still is) much more abundant, mutual contacts between neighbours etc. much more easier than in the Northern Calvinist regions, where suspicion and hatred too often reigns too often. Obedient to "the authorities" were all of them, but one has to know that the Catholics were first and foremost obedient to their own religious leadership, while the Calvinists too often accepted everything from the secular state-power which is perceived as installed by God himself. Both groups left to their authorities to make the principal decisions, but for Catholics this means that they themselves are freed from trouble, while the Calvinist remain predestined and (socially) isolated within their pessimistic belief-system. A small minority of the Calvinists, however, questioned the religious thesis of the government send by God and, therefore, in this group many people joined the resistance. The same mechanism worked also into the wrong direction: in the other group Calvinists too many people joined the SS, the Nazi party or its many cultural organizations. Besides this, in the Catholic South intellectuals and specific groups were much more oriented to the Italian fascism and not to Nazism.

for most of us and *'therefore'* the lowest in this hierarchy), the seriousness of the suffering, the presence of a camp number, the location inside or outside the *Lager*-system and many other elements play their morbid game. Primo Levi gave the particulars of another hierarchy among the victims within 'his' Auschwitz. From the very top of the 'Prominenten' – often privileged criminals, sometimes extraordinary political prisoners like Eugen Kogon – to the 'Muselmänner' (inmates on the verge of death) at the bottom there was a deadly influential victims hierarchy based on the chance of survival.

Wolfgang Sofsky's description of these 'Muselmänner' belongs to the most distressing part of his record of the concentration-camp terror.[38]

> 'The majority were Jews, Russians and Poles, the pariahs of the Lager ... Their lethargy was often interpreted as laziness ... Because of his chronic violation of the camp laws and orders on cleanness, he became the universal scapegoat ... He did his needs in soup plates, he begged and stole without caring about punishments ... His apathy provoked every kind of brutality against him ... The passivity of the Muselmann was in the end highly insulting for the powerful ..'[39]

From a Muselmann position everybody else belonged to this 'powerful'. Indeed, nobody, neither other victims nor perpetrators, cared about these walking skeletons, bestial humans/living deaths who had definitely lost the rat race within the most extreme oikoidal setting possible. These 'no-mans' could hide outside social camp life and roam around searching for food, because they were not allowed to have a fixed place: they acted as the nomads of the *Lager*, as the absolute outsiders. In fact, the *Muselmänner* and *-weiber* were set free to die: for the time remaining to them, their misery brought them the relative advantage of neglecting every authority; they did not belong to the oikoidal camp hierarchy anymore, but were 'promoted' to its absolute antagonists. All the others, however, guards and prisoners alike, looked for some salvation up to the centre of this oikoidal monstrum in which every higher level had the most absolute power over the lower ones and in which every recognizable group remained in a most lethal struggle with competitors on their own level.

The etymology of their name is said to be a mystery, but the 'Muselmänner' (*Muslims*) from Auschwitz equalled the 'Kamele' (*camels*) in Neuengamme or the 'mude Scheichs' (*tired sheikhs*) in Buchenwald, the 'Muselweiber' (*Muslim women*) in Ravensbrück. They are supposed to display the body language of Muslims

---

38. W. Sofsky, *Die Ordnung des Terrors: das Konzentrationslager* (Frankfurt a./M.: Fischer, 1997), p. 229-237.
39. Idem, p. 234.

prostrating themselves in prayer.[40] I do not know what is mysterious about these names, because they – in some way or other – all refer to the strongest external enemy of the oikoidal, sedentary powerful: the eternal enemies, the damned nomads. And are they not metaphors for the 'Eastern' peoples like the Askhenazim, Poles and Russians? They could *not* belong to any oikoidal hierarchy but had to disintegrate below and outside levels where 'real humans' could live (and die but in that case like heroes) whatever their slavish existence. Both the gate-text, '*Arbeit macht frei*', and the related phenomenon of the 'Muselmänner' in the *Lager* system confront us with dialectics of lethal truth under oikoidal preconditions. The underlying warning seems clear enough: only at the outer limit of our power domain can freedom be found, but we shall do our utmost to make it the threshold of death as well.

Still, my answer is not satisfactory. There are also other people from the East who played a vital role in the Nazi conscience and, traditionally, in the minds of the usual (conservative and progressive) opinion-makers. First, there are the 'Mongols' and related peoples named by the *Oberkommando* during the Russian campaign. In their messages to the soldiers and in accordance with the normal (SS) war propaganda, the generals and lower officers ordered:

'the eradication of the Asiatic influence on the European cultural sphere ... In the East the soldier is not only a fighter according to the rules of warfare, but also ... the avenger of all the bestialities which have been committed against the Germans.' 'Here in the East spiritually unbridgeable concepts are fighting each other: German sense of honour and race, and a soldierly tradition of many centuries, against an Asiatic mode of thinking and primitive instincts, whipped up by a small number of mostly Jewish intellectuals ... (against) the advancing Asiatic barbarism.'[41]

In 1942 the SS issued a book and translated it into all possible languages. The title was *Der Untermensch*, and this person was defined as the predecessor of the Soviet *Untermensch* who originated in the following past:

'The challenge of the Untermensch began with the bloody rides of [the Hun] Attila and [the Mongol] Genghis Khan ... On ugly little horses, almost grown

---

40. Idem, p. 363 note 5. See also Rüdiger Lautmann in HH, p. 351-353 who translates it as 'musselmen' (p. 352) which is absurd, although he does not treat the homosexuals (the pink triangles) in the same way. Besides this, his thesis that antihomosexuality 'in its ideological and administrative practice assures essential features of fascist society' and is intrinsically connected to Latin American and (southern)European countries, is challenging. Against his thesis are anyway several contributors of R. Kolpa et al (Ed.), *Fascisme en Homoseksualiteit* (Amsterdam: SUA, 1985).
41. Cited in R.Van Pelt, D.Dwork, *Auschwitz 1270 to the Present* (New York: Yale University Press, 1996), p. 261. For the relations between Nazis and Russians, etc. see J.Connelly, Nazis and Slavs: From Racial Theory to Racist Practice, in: *Central European History* 32 (1999), p. 1-33.

together with the skin of their animals, the Hun hordes dashed against Europe. Their chink eyes glowed with the lust to kill, and behind them they left only wasteland, murder, fire, and destruction.' The accompanying pictures showed a dramatic scene of cruel nomads but also Soviet prisoners of war with the inscription: 'Now they are here again, the Huns, caricatures of human faces, nightmares that have become reality, a punch in the face of all that is good.'[42]

The lowest and most detested

The second major group of people *'from the East'* are the gypsies. The first thoughts about their inferiority *because of their oriental origin* already date from the end of the 18th century. At that time, the Lutheran theologian Heinrich Grellmann published a highly influential book, *Die Zigeuner* (1783). It was translated into many languages, abolished many prejudices and created many new ones: the Sinti and Roma have an oriental way of thinking; are thoroughly bad and lazy by nature; are notorious thieves; spy for the Turks; make a living by stealing young children who sometimes will be eaten; gypsy women display a strong sexual activity and independence: they even wear men clothes, smoke and drink too much, and so on and so forth.[43] In the 20th century and long before 1933, there existed in most countries state institutions specialized in preventing the effects of wandering gypsies, caravan dwellers and the like. Without exception, their guiding thoughts were as primitive as possible. In Holland, for example, a state committee of 1907 stigmatized these peoples as 'the lowermost strata' of society, forming a 'genuine plague', 'a social nuisance' and 'a source of danger'; gypsies in particular were

---

42. Cited in R. Van Pelt, D. Dwork, p. 260. The German architect of German Auschwitz, Hans Stosberg, send a New Year's greeting card to friends (Dec. 1941) with the ideological statement: 'In the year 1241 Silesian knights, saviors of the Reich, warded of the Mongolian assault at Wahlstatt. In that same century Auschwitz was founded as a German town. Six hundred years later the Führer Adolf Hitler fends off the Bolshevik menace from Europe. This year, 1941, the construction of a new German city and the reconstruction of the old Silesian market was planned and initiated.' Id., p. 19; see also p. 77.

43. W. Wippermann, *Wie die Zigeuner*. p. 97 ff.; A. Fraser, *The Gypsies* (Oxford: Blackwell, 1994) (Dutch translation Amsterdam: Atlas, 1994), p. 196 ff. There are, at least, also 15th century sources for some of these anti-gypsy prejudices. Most important for understanding the 'gypsy-problem' are Leo Lucassen's publications like *En men noemde hen Zigeuners.. De geschiedenis van Kaldarasch, Ursari, Lowara en Sinti in Nederland 1750-1940* (Amsterdam: IISG, 1990) and his *Zigeuner. Die Geschichte eines polizeilichen Ordnungsbegriffes in Deutschland 1700-1945* (Köln: Böhlau, 1996). Lucassen clearly shows the large differences between the stigmatization of wandering people whatever the motives and reasons (called by the police 'gypsies') and an 'ethnification' of people (called by police and often by themselves 'gypsies'). To a large extent we are dealing, therefore, with bureaucratic creations. Certainly in the first case, we are dealing with police measures of 'expurgating' the lower classes from 'elements' who could cost the community too much money (poor relief, etc.). Also the large amount of (small) states in Germany before 1870 lead to the administrative combination of belonging to a 'Heimat' and to a 'State' which resulted not only in an expulsion from a town or village, but also from a state. Too often, people were made nomads thanks to the police (p. 216-230).

qualified as 'the terror of the population'.[44] In most countries rather extensive and highly repressive measures were taken to sedentarize the nomads or to extradite them. In Weimar Germany two 'Konzentrationslager' in Prussia were erected (Cottbus, Stargard) as early as 1921, called as such, and organized to catch *Ostjuden* and *Zigeuner*. The poor treatment by the army led to protests in which Jews complained of being treated 'like gypsies'.[45]

Also in this respect, the Nazis could harvest what was sown long before by representatives of all kinds of (democratic) governments. In occupied countries, all authorities were always eager to repress gypsies and gypsy-like nomads without a second thought, and they continued to do this after the war. In these countries the German gypsy-ideologue Robert Ritter had the last word on the subject (in many countries like Holland also after the war), and he aroused a lot of confusion in the heads of peoples like Himmler, Heidrich, etc. Ritter saw large differences between 'racially pure gypsies' and 'gypsies'. The former were remnants of a primitive Indian tribe or caste and could be seen as a kind of ancestral Aryan who deserved some respect. Most of the German Sinti and Roma, however, descended from the latter, who were comparable to 'the lowest and most detested caste of the pariahs'; they were gypsy-bastards and, therefore, born criminals, defective and so on. Ritter et al. claimed to be able to make the selection between pure and bastard gypsies by means of blood tests.

The *Zigeunerforscher* surrounding Ritter and his girlfriend, the radical Eva Justin, were the ones who not only did the scientific research but were also directly involved in the gypsy genocide. An insight into thinking about the subject at top levels and the division of labour between the Germans and Dutch authorities is provided by a letter from Rauter, the highest ranking SS officer in Holland (May 13, 1943) to the highest Dutch police authority:

> 'In the four northern provinces [of the Netherlands] there live many 'germanic gypsies' who roam around with their vans and horses. Herr Reichskommissar [Seyss-Inquart] ordered me to make an end to this 'germanic nomadism'. I beg you to give the horse-material of these 'germanic gypsies' to the Wehrmacht or

---

44. B.A. Sijes, *Vervolging van zigeuners in Nederland 1940-1945* (Den Haag: Nijhoff, 1979), p. 167. One year earlier in Prussia, a law was issued about the 'Bekämpfung der Zigeunerplage'. So, in this respect, the Dutch did not lag behind with the proverbial fifty years. For the pre-Nazi period see also Wippermann, p. 73-136 under the title 'Volk des Orients'. About the European scale of the anti-gypsy movement see A. Fraser, p. 245 ff. From 1912 (till 1972)in France shields at the entrance of the communes warned '*Interdit aux nomades*'. Here earlier as in Germany one started with the registration of 'vagabonds, and nomads' even by means of photos (1907), fingerprints (1912), a so called *carnet anthropométrique* (1912) which was for heads of families no less than a book of about one hundred pages with data about the journeys of family-members, etc. Certainly there were also defenders of the gypsies in several countries like the *Gypsy Lore Society* from 1892 onwards till this moment. See www.gypsyloresociety.org or www.pe.net/'kathys/gypsy.html.
45. W. Wippermann, p. 131.

to agriculture. I want to order through the Dutch police that they stop these 'germanic nomads' with their gypsy crafts, which means that they are given a fixed place to live by the police and that they start an orderly life.'[46]

Rauter's 'start of an orderly life' coincided with a highly orderly trip to Auschwitz. Here, at last, 'Muselmänner', 'Mongols' and 'germanic nomads' were definitely sedentarized. Each represents a specific part of the *Eastern complex* of Nazis, Germans and also other orderly living Europeans. Jews were also part of this complex; now we meet them as 'Ostjuden' who did not want to be treated 'like the gypsies'.

'West' is rich and 'East' poor

Here in the *Lager* system the victims-victims hierarchy is interconnected with the perpetrators-victims hierarchy which underlies the former. The latter is already expressed in the daily food rations in occupied Poland: in the middle of 1941, the average German in Warsaw received 2310 calories per day, ('Aryan') strangers 1790, Poles 634 and Jews 184.[47] Poles, therefore, were four times and Jews thirteen times less valued than their German enemy. The Polish Jews formed a lower rank and, therefore, belonged to the real *Untermenschen*.

There are other elements of this sub-human hierarchy imposed by the perpetrators. Van Pelt discovered that in Auschwitz 'the concentration camp inmates had almost six times the space allocated to the Soviet Untermensch. The standard concentration camp barrack provided eighteen times as much light ... The design of the wash barracks and the privies was, in fact, lethal'.[48] The German Jews, however, were much higher in this hierarchy, at least practically. Hilberg: ' ... in Germany (the bureaucracy) made deals with Jews who fought in World War I, worked for a long time in the service of the state, or who deserved well from Germany. In Poland these considerations did not work at all.'[49] And Hermann Hesse, one of the sharpest critics of antisemitism in Germany criticized the contradictions between German and Eastern Jews from another point of view: ' .. Die traurige Mentalität der deutschen Juden ist mir leider seit langem bekannt, ihr Verhalten gegen die Ostjuden war schon lang vor Hitler ein Verrat und eine Schande, beinah möchte man sagen: ''es geschieht ihnen recht'', wenn das nicht gegenüber ihrer jetzigen Lage unerlaubt roh wäre.'[50]

Furthermore, we cannot close our eyes to a wider strained East-West anta-gonism. Once many Jewish victims-refugees from Germany and elsewhere arrived

---

46. Quoted by B.A. Sijes, p. 85.
47. H. Derks, *Kroniek*, p.250.
48. R.J. van Pelt, D. Dwork, p.267, 268.
49. VEJ, p.198.
50. H. Hesse, *Ausgewählte Briefe* (Frankfurt a./M.: Suhrkamp, 1974), S. 108.

at the Dutch border (1938), they had the great choice of being refused, handed over to the German police by representatives of the "tolerant" Dutch government or brought already in the refugee camp Westerbork, which was not long afterwards transformed into the main Dutch transitcamp to Auschwitz, etc. Once in the Netherlands, a Jewish commentator wrote about the East European Jews in particular: 'They irritated the [Dutch] Jews, who understandably worked off their own problems on these innocent persecuted peoples of their own race. And they irritated ... also the non-Jews, who did not want to meet this kind of folk in Amsterdam-South [the rich quarter of the city. H.D.] as if they were niggers in America.'[51]

In their turn, the large majority of the Dutch Jews had their roots in the East European Ashkenazi-Jewish 'tribe' (litt.: unknown people; also another name for Germans); they were in all respects different from the most Western 'tribe', the Portugese Sephardim who formed about three per cent of the Dutch Jews. For obvious reasons, the eminent Dutch historian Presser sketched the position of the latter in a rather cynical way: they made a serious effort to prove their non-Jewishness and their understanding for the National Socialist case, 'das neue Deutschland', while keeping aloof from East European Jews.[52] According to them, these Ashkenazim could only be 'Schmarotzer' who came to the Netherlands 'aus raffgierigen Motiven' alone.

Already in 1933 these Sephardim inquired at the German Embassy in The Hague about the happenings in Nazi Germany. They learned from the ambassador's secretary: 'O yes, you have to understand, gentlemen, that whenever we had to deal in Germany with Portugese Jews, there could not be a Jewish Question at all!' During the war this ambiguous explication was used time and again as an 'argument' to save Portuguese Jewish lives. A German Jew hunter studied the question for some time in 1941 and concluded that 'around 1600 the percentage of Jewish blood in the Marranos could not be more than 1/32nd ... and that they later did not increase in Jewishness.' Till 1750, he discovered no particle 'ostjüdisches Blut' in their veins; even 'Spinozza', he wrote, was in a racial sense not a Jew. This historical research was also in vain: they all perished in the death camps. Still, it is true that in France the most easterly living Eastern Jews in Europe, the Caucasian Jews, successfully argued that they did not belong to the Jewish race, whereupon

---

51. Cited by D. Hondius, p. 29. Nearly all official Jewish organizations and the *Nieuw Israelitisch Weekblad* did not bother about the Jewish newcomers of the East: they warned, in German, about '*Überfremdung*' and for the danger of antisemitism! The same inter-Jewish contradiction is seen in Switzerland even *during* the war where the sedentary Jews were as eager to refuse the Jewish fugitives as the Swiss police and the bankers. This happened also with many rich fugitives who, in most cases, had first to leave their substantial capital in Switzerland before definitely starting their last journey. See J. Ziegler, *Die Schweiz, das Gold und die Toten* (München: Hanser,1997); T. Bower, *Bloodmoney – The Swiss, the Nazis and the Looted Billions* (London: 1997).

52. For the following quotations see J. Presser, *Ondergang*. Vol. II, p.72-83. For the background of this highly dramatic controversy see my *Deutsche Westforschung*, p. 190-195.

they were saved. But, again, is there a Jewish race or 'Volk', and who decided this to be the case?[53]

From some Jewish East, things could be described differently as Kafka's youthful experiences demonstrate. Within the German-speaking parts of Prague, Jews were strongly represented; the Czech or Bohemian allegiances were not attributed to Jews 'and in truth they looked elsewhere for their rights, to Franz Josef in Vienna ... (although he was personally anti-Semitic) and beyond him to Prussia's Bismarck, another anti-Semite ...'[54] The main problem for eastern German-speaking Jews was the assimilation question if the dominant language in the country was not German. In Poland assimilation was out of the question. In Prague, however, the assimilationist movement was quite strong and, therefore, a rather tough opposition to Zionism flourished. Father Kafka, who spoke most languages well and did his business everywhere, found himself and his family 'moving toward a kind of no man's land in terms of ethnic and religious identification.' There was a definite loss of Jewish rituals and indifference to Judaism in 'German Prague':

'While unacceptable in the Czech community, the Kafkas did not enter deeply into the Jewish community. They remained marginal to both, and Kafka always lamented the fact that he had been denied an anchor in any culture or ethnicity. His cry that he was an acculturated, assimilated Westernized Jew was a cry of deracination, or marginality, of a kind of isolation that began well before he was born and would control his direction.'[55]

A German policy for the 'East'

In any case, the German perception of the Eastern Jews was related to a more general distaste for Polish people. How could this perception receive its pejorative content in the 20th century apart from medieval German colonization sources? In 1914 about 3.5 million German subjects were Polish (about seven times more than Jews); at the time every tenth Prussian was Polish. After the unification in 1871, the

---

53. The question will be dealt with in the next part of this study. Here only three examples. In the text is quoted a SS-researcher arguing that 'Spinozza' (his writing) is not a Jew. Hannah Arendt cited her boss, the famous Jewish publisher Schocken, who refused to publish something from Spinoza because 'Spinoza wasn't a Jew'. See AJC, p. 199. Who and what are Jews is the subject of an informative and scholarly study: S. Feist, *Stammeskunde der Juden* (Leipzig/ Leiden: Hinrichs/ Ginsberg, 1925) with many interesting illustrations. Still, here you will meet more than in any antisemitic tract, the highly ridiculous 'theories' which lead to those strange differentiations of the so-called Jewish tribes. They were still the basis for somebody's decision in present-day Israel to transport Ethiopian falaschas to their 'real, holy fatherland' with its many holy racists. The last example concerns present-day Holland were the bureaucrats used without any sense of shame the old SS-definition of Jew in order to pay Holocaust victims their newest restitution allowance.
54. F.R. Karl, *Franz Kafka. Representative Man* (New York: Fromm, 1993), p.14.
55. Idem, p. 15.

concentration of the East Elbian agricultural enterprises increased tremendously which, inevitably, brought the abandonment of most small-peasant farms, a strong depopulation of Germans, an emigration to western provinces and large cities or abroad to the USA, and a massive influx of cheap Polish day laborers.

This became a national political issue and a main concern for many *Reichs* and Prussian decision-makers. In Bismarckian and Wilhelminian Germany, a specific *Polenpolitik* developed with *Reichsnationalist* and racist germanizing overtones, sudden mass expulsions of Polish 'guest workers', harsh criticism of the mighty East Elbian estate owners (including Polish aristocrats) and the *Junker* class. Together, they clearly foreshadowed anti-Polish measures from 1933 onwards.[56]

In 1894 Max Weber defended the nationalist and racist position within this *Polenpolitik* during one of the rather notorious *Evangelisch-sozialen Kongresse*. The Christian Social Party which had been organizing these nationwide manifestations since 1890 also expressed a strong antisemitism or anti-Judaism inspired by the court priest Adolf Stoecker, its leader from 1879 onwards. For the first time, in 1890, young theologians like Adolf Harnack, Friedrich Naumann, Paul Göhre and Otto Baumgarten joined Stoecker's initiative and invited people like Weber or the economist Adolf Wagner.[57] At that time, these people could not make an unbiased decision, because Stoecker was sentenced for his antisemitic behaviour.

Weber had just published his extensive report on the East Elbian rural laborers which led to sharp political attacks on the powerful East Prussian *Junkers* and Polish aristocrats. Within the nationwide anti-Polish commotion, he was singing before his Lutheran audiences the tunes of the street about the seasonal Polish *'nomads'* (comparing them indirectly with Argentine 'savages'), while he even

---

56. H.-U. Wehler, *Deutsche Gesellschaftsgeschichte* III, 961-965, 1068-71; M. Broszat, *Zweihundert Jahre deutsche Polenpolitik* (Frankfurt a/M.: DTV, 1972), p. 129-173. Furthermore, the articles of W. Mommsen, H. Berding and S. Volkov in M. Hettling, P. Nolte (Ed.), *Nation und Gesellschaft in Deutschland* (München: Beck, 1996). For the perception of the *Ostjuden* in Germany see T. Maurer, Ostjuden und deutsche Juden im Kaiserreich und in der Weimarer Republik, in: *Gesch. in Wiss. u. Unterricht* 9 (1988), p. 523-542.

57. In the Netherlands, for instance, the Protestant leader Abraham Kuyper was highly inspired by the German example and a notorious anti-Judaist if not antisemite as well. For the history of this rather small but very influential party see C.M. Kegge, *De Evangelisch-Sociale Beweging in Duitschland* (Rotterdam: Libertas, 1916). W. Mommsen, *Max Weber* p. 20 ff., 28-36. W. Gerlach, *Als die Zeugen schwiegen. Bekennende Kirche und die Juden* (Berlin: 1987), p. 23 ff., 142, 330. Frank Stern, Evangelische Kirche zwischen Antisemitismus und Philosemitismus, in: *Geschichte und Gesellschaft* 18 (1992), 22-50. H. Wehler, *Deutsche Gesellschaftsgeschichte*, III, p. 921-924. An example of the strength of the combination of secular anti-Jewishness, antisemitism and anti-Judaism is the *Denkschrift 'Vorschläge für eine Lösung der Judenfrage'* (1943/'44) produced by the Protestant resistance (!), the Bonhoeffer circle: these resistance-theologians proposed that *after the war* the State should be allowed to take measures *'um dem unheilvollen Einfluß einer Rasse auf die Volksgemeinschaft zu wehren'*. At that time all these people knew perfectly well what was going on in concentration camps. Doris L. Bergen in HH, p. 566 – 583.

sneered about 'Polish animals'.[58] A year later, his notorious *Antrittsrede* about the differences between 'Deutschtum' and 'Polentum' was founded on a strictly racist basis:

> 'One is quickly persuaded to believe in physical and psychological racial qualities if differences in adaptability of the two nations to different economic and social living conditions are at stake. And, indeed, this is the case...'[59]

Apart from the fact that we meet here again the pejorative use of nomads (or racist and other antagonisms between sedentaries and mobiles), Polish people are degraded in an extraordinary way by German opinion leaders. Notwithstandig this, *both* parties mixed antisemitism with their own nationalistic creeds. This *deadly triangle* between Germans, Jews and Poles is already characteristic for this region of Europe at the end of the 19th century; here, where about 40 years later the most unprecedented destruction of human beings was organized. Around 1900, Polish antisemitism was triggered by their fear of 'the competition of German or Jewish merchants and craftsmen'.[60] Furthermore, it is remarkable how a Polish trade union in Germany accepted the Polish Catholic ideology with its strongest possible form of anti-Judaism in their fight against the German Catholic party (*Zentrum*). This party, in spite of its strong agitation against the Wilhelminian *Polenpolitik*, did not receive any sympathy from its eastern co-religionists.

A good insight into the critical German-Polish relationship is given by the daily juridical practices in the Third Reich with their particular *Polenrecht* (laws concerning Poles). If one looks for examples of justice which is only directed against the lower classes and motivated by racial 'arguments', they can be found in abundance.[61] It is not well known that in these courts, for instance, sexual relations between German Jews and 'Aryans' were less severely punished as so-called *Blutschande* (a kind of social incest) than the sexual relations with Poles, Russians and the like. As *Angehöriger der Ostvölker* the latter were seen as inferior to the former.

---

58. See also K. Tribe, Prussian agriculture – German politics: Max Weber 1892-7, in: *Economy and Society*, 12 (1983), p. 181-226, in particular p. 211; W. Mommsen, p. 24 ff.

59. GPS, p. 4. Here, one can learn (p.7) how the political agitation of the street works as Weber writes about '*die polnischen Wanderarbeiter, Nomadenzüge, welche, durch Agenten in Rußland geworben, im Frühjahr zu Zehntausenden über die Grenze kommen...*' (p.7). Elsewhere (p. 6) he even assures that 'by nature' the '*slawischen Rasse*' is accustomed to the lowest means of existence and culture and that this is the reason why this race could conquer the Germans. If one should replace 'Polentum' etc. by 'Judentum' one got exactly the kind of text which was always written about the Eastern Jews

60. M. Broszat, p. 154.

61. H.H. Wüllenweber, *Sondergerichte im Dritten Reich. Vergessene Verbrechen der Justiz* (Frankfurt a/M.: Luchterhand, 1990). For the practice of the *Polenrecht* see '*Das Verbrechen, Pole zu sein*', p. 121-185; for the extent of the class justice see p.52-59. The given example about sexual relations is on p. 181, 193.

However, from the Polish perspective things were and are quite different. One of the most embarrassing examples comes from an important pamphlet issued in the beginning of August 1942 by a secret Catholic organisation, the Front for the Resurrection of Poland, FOP (5000 copies). At that time, the destruction of the Warshaw ghetto had already started, and the pamphlet was one of the very few Polish reactions to the happenings which remained nearly unknown until recently.[62] This appeal to protest starts with a detailed description of the atrocities within the ghetto and during the transportation to Treblinka ('on the other side of the wall hundreds of thousands of condemned persons are waiting for their death. There is no hope of being rescued; from nowhere does any help arrive ...'). After this description the FOP concludes that already millions of Jews must have been killed in all Polish cities and towns: 'The World looks at this crime from which the atrocity exceeds everything known in history and it remains silent. ... Neither England nor the United States protest; even the influential international Jewry (*Judentum*) remains silent ... The Poles keep silent as well ... This silence cannot be tolerated any longer ... Therefore, we as Catholics and Poles raise our voices.' So far, it seems an honest and even a brave protest. The pamphlet continues, however, with:

> 'Our feelings against the Jews have not changed. We do not stop to consider them as political, economical and spiritual enemies of Poland. Even more, we are conscious of the fact that they hate us much more than the Germans, and that they make us responsible for their misfortune. Why and by which motives remain secrets of the Jewish soul; notwithstanding this, it remains a fact proved time and again. ... We are not able to counteract the German murderers in an active way. ... Those of us who do not protest are not Catholic. ... We do not believe that the Poles gain some advantage from the German atrocities. The reverse is true. The persistent silence of the international Jewry together with ... the German propaganda prove ... a planned and inimical intention to divert the enormous hatred proliferated through the mass murders to the Lithuanians and the Poles. ... The forced participation of the Polish people in the bloody drama ..., in particular, leads to the terrible conviction that it is permitted to murder unpunished those who are nearest. The one who does not understand this ... is neither a Catholic nor a Pole.'

In the end, the interesting explanation of Blonski is not convincing. It is even strange that he did not comment on the obvious fear of the pamphleteers (there must have been more writers than one in an organisation which needed a *nihil*

---

62. For the following citations see J. Blonski, Der antisemitische Retter. Zu einem Aufruf polnischer Katholiken angesichts der Vernichtung im Warschauer Ghetto, in: *Transit. Europaische Revue*, 1-2 (1991), p. 36-47. For the present situation in Poland see M. Steinlauf, *Bondage to the Dead. Poland and the memory of the Holocaust* (New York: Syracuse University Press, 1997).

obstat for every step) that, after the war, the Poles should be blamed for their co-operation in this monstruous crime against humanity. This opportunism or cynicism explains the embarrassing combination of the shocking description of the Jewish destruction with the harsh condemnation of the Jews. In this case the message is: Jews do not interest us, but please protest, so that we can prove later how innocent we were. In the light of the present debate over the murder of Jewish inhabitants of Jedwabne by their Polish neighbours the following arguments are revealing.

Blonski comes up with an ideological explanation which could be relevant as well. The background for the alleged contradiction between antisemitic and pro-Jewish expressions he finds in the *Standesgesellschaft* in which a clear political, juridical, and, eventually, spatial-territorial division exists between groups who could come into conflict. The territorial division is again one between Western Poland and the East where most of the Jewish *stetl* were situated with their relative autonomy.

Blonski is not clear enough because he only refers to the classical oikoidal model of society which is, in a political sense, largely based on the maxim *divide et impera*. The Catholic Church, the monarchy and the Polish aristocracy used it for centuries, and Jews were allowed to have a place within the 'model' as long as the church, etc. did not intend to destroy this model and to change its inherent opportunistic tolerance for the *impera* alone, the absolute government.

From such a moment on, there was no place for non-conformist Jews in Poland, for comparable groups like gypsies or for every other minority. This was again the case in the pre-war Pilsudski-Catholic dictatorship. Therefore, anti-Judaism and anti-Jewish state measures as well as antisemitism since the end of the 19th century belong to the foundation of the Polish way of life. It is indeed with the very recent switch to a Western market society that Poland has for the first time an opportunity to abandon their stubborn oikoidal society. However, it is also still today that Polish writers like Jan Jozef Lipski express their deep regret about the general situation. He vehemently criticizes not only the usual antisemitism (although there are hardly any Jews left in the country), but also the traditional distaste of the Poles vis-à-vis the Czech, and the Polish megalomaniac superiority feelings against the Russians.[63]

If these attitudes should be explained as a result of the 'eternal' Polish position of being caught between the Russian and German 'eagles', for Jews who were mostly seen in Poland and Russia as too strongly German oriented, in the end, it

---

63. J.J. Lipski, *Wir müssen uns alles sagen* (Warschau: 1996). It seems to be a proof of the same intellectual backwardness when Lipski rather uncritically point to the 'same spiritual source of Germany, Poland and Europe', i.e. the ancient Greek culture and philosophy as well as Christianity. Catholicism in Poland has the worst record possible only comparable with Greek Orthodoxy in the Balkans and Russia. What Lipski learned from the ancient Greek culture had first to go through the Christian censorship.

does not make a difference. The following quotation undermines every illusion about German friendliness or about life in this triangle:

> 'No compromise is imaginable. In Russia and everywhere else Jews have shed costly German blood [litt.: Germanen blood; the racial meaning. H.D.]. That is the guilt of Jews all over the world, also of those living in Amsterdam. We are not sadistic ... We always respect the defeated enemy, but poison is not allowed to exist. We know how Jews did with us in the East. Revenge and hatred are their characteristics. Should one keep the Jew alive, he will revenge itself. If one leaves the Jew its own country, he will conspire against us. This war is a war of destruction and therefore, in God's name, the Jew must be destroyed and not we. We solve ... the Jewish problem once and for all. In nature every life lives at the cost of another. Man slaughters, therefore, calves, rabbits and chicken. The stronger one destroys the weak ... So the Creation wants it. In life of peoples [Volk] it is not different. If one replies that the Jews are anyway human beings, than one has to answer: the fate of the Jew is tragic, but ... if the Jew should win, a total destruction will be the consequence.'[64]

Also this terrible mixture of racism, biologism and religion confirms the earlier conclusion that along the West-East division a specific stream of prejudices ran which sometimes rose above the usual antipathies, but in many cases lay at the bottom of them. It also provides a confrontation between societies as diverse as the Dutch and the Polish, each located at another end of the West-East division. They share a terrible past of dumping their own citizens wholesale *as Jews*. In short: the former is Protestant oriented, where Jews are thrown out of the 'house' into the societal 'black hole', the empty space between the compartments; in Poland, Jews were simply treated like the waste of the 'Catholic house' itself.

JEWISH VICTIMS

Discussions about, in particular, 'Jewish Holocaust victims' in no time suffer from debating tricks like accusations of 'blaming the victims' until the chutzpah of the 'selfhating Jew' or of 'antisemite'. They are unavoidable but let's try to forget them a while as long as the following remarks are made.

From the above it could be concluded that a Jewish victim is difficult to define. Indeed, this is true. Rabbis of the various Jewish sects (or priests, etc.) can probably provide theologically sound definitions. However, I have never heard of nor read one helpful to people other than a certain small inner circle of theolo-

---

64. Quoted in M. Croes, P. Tammes (note 30), p. 535. Part of a speech of Kreisschulungsleiter Dr. Reibele (something like a regional instructor) at an Ortsgruppe of the NSDAP which is published in the paper *De Koerier*, 7-9-1942.

gians.[65] For historians or other scientists, the religious criteria for determining who is a Jew must be rather inappropriate, and they keep struggling with their secular problems and coping with the obvious disparities between the different perceptions. This apart from the fact that during the Shoah rabbis, priests, etc. played at best a role comparable to most Jewish Councils, a corrupting position as negotiator with the perpetrators. It is still debated whether their other roles in the tragedy were fully negligible or negative for the resistance of their flocks.[66] Anyway, the Jewish question was, is and will remain for a while a junction of many roads and a combination of sometimes contradictory developments.

For this reason, 'Jewish victims' have many faces connected to what I called the *triangle question* (Germans-Jews-Poles relationship) as well as a *perpetrator-victim-bystander question*; an *East-West question* as well as a *victim-victim question*. One can, furthermore, debate about many things but the German roots of the Shoah question cannot be found before 1871, the end of the French-German war and the start of the German Empire. The *three* sources of the Shoah problem came together somehow after these events. Its inherent antisemitism should be combined with the traditional anti-Judaism and with the authoritarian executive power of the state. The Jewish victims we discuss in the Holocaust context were born after 1871 and form the oldest generation in 'Auschwitz'.

In none of the following three or four periods after 1871 did the Jewish Question remain the same, which is equally true for its victims. The most crucial difference from earlier or later developments is that in 1933-1945 the state itself with all its terrible means of repression took over the initiative and incorporated *both* the new antisemitism and the old anti-Judaism within its legitimating ideology. All victim-perpetrator relationships became matters of life and death. To discover the profile of 'Jewish victims', all this is still too general and abstract. In the last part of this chapter , therefore, concrete problems concerning Shoah victims within the Holocaust will be discussed derived from the most puzzling and Western situation: in the absence of any relevant antisemitism in Dutch society and yet ....

---

65. Take, for example, the articles of E. Fackenheim and D. Hartman resp. 'Holocaust' and 'Suffering' in: A. Cohen, P. Mendes-Flohr (Ed.), *Contemporary Jewish Religious Thought* (New York: Free Press, 1987), p.399-409 and 939-946.

66. It is remarkable enough that in HH I did not found an article or a relevant remark about the role of rabbi's, priests, etc. also not in the part devoted to the role of (Jewish) leadership (pp. 585-647). After 1945 you did not hear anything from these branches, but after the Roaring Sixties when the sharp decline in religious allegiance was apparent they started their classical campaigns as fear producer in which a Holocaust horror story always did it well. See P. Novick, *The Holocaust and collective memory. The American experience* (London: Bloomsbury, 1999) which is published in the USA under the title *The Holocaust in American Life.*

How to become a Holocaust victim?

It is often (re)told that the 'principle of the Final Solution was neither persecution nor punishment but obliteration – the attempt to make the Jews vanish from the world.'[67] For many reasons this was from the beginning an immoral and, in particular, an unthinkable or irrealistic venture. The many Jews in, for instance, the UK, USA or Sovjetrussia could not be caught except wenn these countries were conquered. Even Stalin was not prepared to make a deal with Hitler with Jews as means of exchange: these already vanished in the UdSSR in their transformation into workers-citizens, who could not be alienated. In stead of with principles one can begin answering the given question from practice.

First comes the effect of what Arendt mentioned in the quotation opening this chapter: the totalitarian ruler *'persistently insults another ... until everybody knows that the latter is his enemy, so that he can, with some plausibility, go and kill* [the other.H.D] *in self-defense.'* By all means of modern state propaganda, the Nazis exploited the nonsensical stories told by religious, learned and antisemitic circles for decennia: thus 'the other' was created; 'they' attack 'us' and, therefore, 'we have to strike back by all means'. As Arendt had lived today, she had made a principal amendment to her statement: It is not only a highly popular game in despotic or totalitarian regimes but in 'western democracies' as well. This makes it clear that the creation of 'an inimical other' can or could never be enough to make Holocaust Jews.

An acquaintance, the now 83-year-old Arend L., lived in a small village in the northeast of the Netherlands. In 1942 he had a grandmother who was 81 year old, a widow who only talked the local dialect and always wore the local folkloristic costumes. One day, the mayor accompanied by the rural policeman came to her door and announced that according to his administration she must be 100% Jewish and that she immediately had to go to Westerbork (the camp from which the Dutch transports to Auschwitz, Treblinka, etc. were organized). She was brought to Westerbork but returned soon because in this camp they could not believe this peasant-woman was Jewish. The mayor, who was not a party member, protested against the Westerbork decision by means of letters to the Ministry in the Hague, but the old lady did not await the end of this bureaucratic battle and died at home. As a form of replacement, Arend himself was named 'a quarter Jew' and ordered to go to the provincial police-headquarters in order to be treated 'properly'. He refused, because he had never heard of any Jewish element in his family; he went into hiding and became an important man in the resistance, was caught several times but was never considered a Jew. Whatever the reason, the communication between the Dutch authorities and the Germans about Arend L.'s racial status must have been a failure.

---

67. Recently S. Buckler, The Curtailment of Memory: Hannah Arendt and Post-Holocaust Culture, in: *The European Legacy*, 6 (2001), p. 293.

This little story demonstrates what was also needed to become a Holocaust or Shoah victim. The perpetrator's racial definition decided who was a Jew, but the normal bourgeois registry and statistical offices sanctioned the decision and gave 'the other' a name and an address. Still the *local* power and bureaucracy had to acknowledge the result of the procedure while they had to be willing to obey a higher authority, which was normally the case. In all occupied countries, also in Germany and Austria, this was, I guess, the same.

The effect is, in the first instance, not different from the case of a US Minister of Foreign Affairs, Albright. Strangely enough, a short time *after* her nomination as Minister she publicly heard for the first time in her life that she could be or was Jewish according to some definition from somebody in Jerusalem: this could not concern religion, was it then a racial or ethnic definition? Whatever answer and for whatever reason, she was stigmatised at once and immediately her political image changed, which was apparently the purpose.

Before and during the last World War, probably millions of Europeans and Christians saw their religion and status changed by a stamp; like Albright much later, they heard for the first time in their life that they were Jewish, and they became stigmatised as if they were contaminated.[68] The Amsterdam registry office was extremely helpful and freely provided the perpetrators (including the willing Dutch police) even with excellent maps to find somebody who could be called 'Jewish' for whatever reason. This socialist city, therefore, could achieve the record of rounding up the most 'Jews' in the quickest and easiest way.

Time and again, at the moment of arrest, people were confronted for the first time with a Jewish past. In the Netherlands a large minority of all so-called 'Dutch Jews' was not religious at all and from the rest a substantial part was Christian and only a minority lived a life according to some Jewish religious customs and rules (see below). Besides this, the 'Jewish population' was known as very orangistic.[69] There was only one thing which they had in common: they all were Dutch citizens. So they were not only betrayed by the bureaucrats on different levels but also by the Christian churches (notwithstanding some protests from Christian peoples) and, as we saw already, by the Queen and her 'orange entourage'. The question

68. See, for instance, the autobiography of the psychoanalyst and historian Peter Gay, *My German question. Growing up in Nazi Berlin.*(New Haven: Yale University Press, 1998). His middle class parents were fully assimilated atheists who were even registered as '*konfessionslos*' ('without religion'). Peter did not attend a Jewish school, etc. In 1933 also the Fröhlich family was declared Jewish by law. Apparently, his parents accepted this and started to grow in the new identity: Peter now went to a Jewish boy scout group in 1934, etc. It took another four year and a *Kristallnacht* before the Fröhlichs wanted to flee, which happened whereupon they could become the Gay family in the USA.

69. N. van der Zee, p. 201. The 'extraordinary love for 'Orange' (= the Royal House) of Dutch Jews before the war can, in fact, only be connected with some journals, in particular the influential *Nieuw Israelitisch Weekblad,* and some rich Jewish personalities who used to speak for a non-existing 'Jewish community'. That, for instance, the important union with the largest 'jewish' membership, the 'diamant union', should have 'an extraordinary love for Orange' cannot be proved.

which must be explained further is why these followers nearly all listened to the orders from 'above' and started their walk into the death camps.

With the 'Gypsies' we meet the same problem of dealing with what is called an *Ordnungsbegriff*, an oikoidal or bureaucratic concept. All the rest was a matter of harsh intimidation at strategically well-chosen moments; of strong support of the governments of the *Wirtsländer* which received this name at the same time as some of their own citizens were illegally given overnight a guest status by their own bureaucrats; of strong support of the so-called 'Jewish Leadership' created by the Nazis but never chosen and only accepted for opportunistic reasons by a 'Jewish' elite; a matter also of an efficient organisation of a quick catch, transportation and destruction of the victims.

It is a most distressing problem when your identity is created by your worst enemy, but is this not the most crucial feature of the recent European 'Jewish history'? Still, it was never before like this: after Mai 1940 in most European countries a *foreign* enemy determined whether somebody was a 100 per cent Jew, or 50 or 25 per cent and the 'own enemy' accepted this racist nonsense. Even the first names one could bear were 'Nazi-allowed' from August 18, 1938 onwards: *Israel* and *Sarah* became at once the most common names. Yet, if Hitler personally was in a good mood, he could declare any Jew a 100 per cent Aryan: he did so several times as Brigitte Hamann discovered.[70]

In racial terms it is the same as if Hitler transformed a black man into a white one. Indeed, it is the ultimate proof of the absurdity of this dangerous racial game. Nevertheless, it is played anew if spiritual and political leaders have to struggle for mastery; scientists can be found to back their aspirations and followers can be recruited from the circles which, this time, have a narrow escape not to belong to 'the others'. With this our problem, how to become a Holocaust or Shoah victim, grows into a complex chain of causes and effects. The following part of the chain belongs to it as well.

In earlier times, at the level of daily life and death, only *specific* measures were taken *sometimes*; now after 1933 they became *routine* measures fixed in *general* laws and rules (backed by science) which could *always* be executed by the most minor bureaucrat. These were the large differences not only from pre-1871 periods but also from, for instance, the rather unexpected Stalinist purges as typical power-killings, expurgations of (alleged) competitors, and even the genuine racial genocide in Rwanda which was, first, a one-off raging act of revenge and, second, the eradication of a pastoral way of life by sedentaries. These differences are never well understood, not by Nolte or Bullock or whoever made the Hitler-Stalin

---

70. B. Hamann, *Hitlers Wien. Lehrjahre eines Diktators* (München: Piper, 1997) p.56, 498 ff.

comparisons[71] for political opportunist reasons, let alone by Goldhagen who intended to give us the solution of the Holocaust drama by means of cheap debating tricks.

I have never read a study in which the serious consequences of the arbitrary creation of the Holocaust Jew were studied. Not one of the 50 best researchers who tell us about the latest in Holocaust studies and contributed to *The Holocaust and History* even mentions this as a problem. Did they consider the possibility that a considerable part of the Shoah victims, were not Jews at all or never wanted to be a Jew or were simply killed for the wrong reasons?[72] Let's be clear, for the dead victims an answer does not matter; for our understanding of the Holocaust history, however, it is of the utmost importance. However, the problem raised cannot be solved here, but it seems possible to sketch some important elements.

As Dutch Jews?

Whatever is meant by a 'Jewish victim' and whoever has made the definition, it is a fact that there are between five and six million human beings killed *as Jews*. Why the German perpetrators were after them is explained before: they determined anyway the targets, guilt and punishment. Other obvious questions are always posed but not answered in a relevant way because 'after Auschwitz' it is difficult to express shame and guilt-feelings which surround these answers.

As I said, it concerns obvious questions like: Why on earth accepted the largest majority of these 'Jewish victims' all this? Why failed the largest possible majority to protest or to resist? Are they, therefore, also guilty in some way for what happened? Because from Jewish sides one sometimes stresses the existence of antisemitism from time immemorial, apparently relevant and very (if not too) difficult questions for these people to answer remain as well: If that should be true than there must be an original perpetrator from time immemorial? And: What was/were the sin(s) or accusation(s) in that very remote time? For a Christian period only, the shaky "the death of Christ" accusation and the like remain, but

---

71. Of course, this is not the last word about these Hitler-Stalin comparisons, a hot issue of the so-called *Historikerstreit* in which I participated in the Netherlands-'branche'. See G. Aalders, Der Historikerstreit in den Niederlanden. Eine vorläufige Bestandsaufnahme, in: *1999. Zeitschrift für Sozialgeschichte des 20. und 21. Jahrhunderts* 4 (1988), p. 112 ff. The end of the debate in the Netherlands arrived as one side did not want to understand the falseness of 'cleaning Hitler by means of Stalin', and the other side was fed up by the accusations of Stalinism when trying to reveal the historical 'facts' within the proper social-economic context.

72. Take also Saul Friedländer, *Nazi Germany and the Jews* (New York: HarperPerennial, 1998), Vol. 1, p. 27 ff. who made no remark whatsoever about the nonsensical character of racist laws, the problem of the creation *ex nihilo* of an identity by a definition which 'was the necessary initial basis of all the persecutions that were to follow.'(p.28). He does not see the problem of writing about Nazis who 'killed Jews on the assumption that they could somehow be identified as Jews' (id.). At least he should have written 'people' instead of the first 'Jews' and have explained the meaning of 'somehow'.

what for Roman, Greek or Egyptian periods from which is told that antisemitism should be raging? It is not wise to undermine your case by making it extra difficult or unnecessary mysterious, so let's keep to the 19th and 20th century and to the Dutch elements of the problem; they are complex enough.

Nearly the only question which leads to an unequivocal denial is: Did Jews in Europe or Holland, in particular in Amsterdam, have before 1940 something which made them vulnerable to extinction? Notwithstanding everybody's denial (then and now), it also happened in Holland and Amsterdam and must be explained.

My thesis for the pre-war situation is that from a non-Jewish Dutch point of view, the extermination of the small Jewish minority was *not a matter of biological (as for most Germans and some exceptionally clever Dutch scholars) or religious (as for most Christian theologians) but of social inferiority and displacement out of and/or non-acceptance in the "pillared society"*. From a Jewish Dutch point of view, there were also some preconditions fulfilled which gave social opportunities to act, like a rigorous urbanization, long-lasting poverty and nomadic job orientation. The Dutch case is so extreme that it is unlikely that it can deliver clear answers for other countries as well. So, what are the main characteristics of the later Jewish victims?

In 1940 serious antisemitism existed already for three-quarters of a century in *all* Western countries including the USA, but in the Netherlands it was not before 1938 that it was propagated in an aggressive, political way. Before that year, in which the radical right made her 'German move', not even this movement could be named antisemitic: it had not a few Jewish members, was fascistically and not nazistically oriented, etc. The reason for this is not that the Dutch people were very tolerant, but that the "pillared society" existed, in which political-ideological discussions were simply not done but 'solved' at the top where The Compromise ruled.[73] To create a profile of the later Jewish victims in the Netherlands, a comment on a few statistics about the period 1900 – 1940 seems necessary; in particular, about the situation in Amsterdam where most of the Dutch Jews lived.[74]

---

73. Symptomatic for this situation was how the protest of anti- nationalsocialist intellectuals around 1935, organized within the *Comite van Waakzaamheid* (Committee of Vigilance), occurred: right after the start the Roman-Catholic Archbishop De Jong first urged his representatives (priests) to leave and ordered next the two lay Catholic writers/professors, Anton van Duinkerken and Gerard Brom, to quit as well, which they did. Pretext was that in this dominant Protestant and rather left-wing company (with one Jewish Professor) also a Communist was accepted. Van Duinkerken wrote: 'Once I heard in an amicable way that according to the Archbishop our cooperation with infidel would be troublesome for Catholics, I communicated with the Archbishopric to say that under such circumstances I want to avoid more or less rightful misunderstandings with my co-religionists.' A. van Duinkerken, *Katholicisme en Nationaalsocialisme*. Assen, 1936, p. 24, 25.

74. For the period 1940 – 1945 now the excellent research from Marnix Croes and Peter Tammes is available (note 30) and my *Deutsche Westforschung*, chapter 4. The data mentioned below particularly come from J.P. Kruijt, Het Jodendom in de Nederlandse samenleving, in: H.J. Pos (Ed.), *Anti-Semitisme en Jodendom* (Arnhem: Van Loghum Slaterus, 1939), p. 190-231. Kruijt is a pupil of Sebald Steinmetz and he reproduces here more or less his masters 'Joden in het algemeen en in Nederland', in: Idem (Ed.), *De Rassen der Menschheid. Wording, strijd en toekomst*. Amsterdam, 1938, p. 344-374.

SUBJECTS	'JEWISH DISTRICT'	'RICHEST DISTRICT'
% tax-assessments above fl.2200.- in 1915/16	3.8	31.8
Cancer per 10,000 inh. 39 year and older	48.4	43.7
Tuberculosis per 100,000 inh. in 1920/21	120.6	69.8
Infant mortality per 100 births in 1919/21	6.14	3.07
Infant mortality from congenital defects per 100 births in 1919/21	1.2	0.4
Mortality per 1000 inhabitants 1908/11	12.3	8.1
Mortality per 1000 inhabitants 1920/21	10.9	8.4
Birth per 1000 inhabitants 1908/11	21.0	16.3
Birth per 1000 inhabitants 1920/21	22.8	14.7
Cellar dwellings 1909	374	11
Cellar dwellings 1916	218	10
Cellar dwellings 1919	193	4
Average people per dwelling 1909	14.8	8.78
Average people per dwelling 1920	15.3	9.1
Suicide per 100,000 inh. 1920	5.8	10.4
Total population around 1920	37,281	38,680
Density per hectare	469	128

In their hotchpotch of data, Blom/Cahen tell us also that in Amsterdam the rate of mortality among Jews was much lower than among Protestants and Catholics. They continue with: 'The numbers for infant mortality till 1910 show the same differences. For the period after 1910, these differences with the non-Jewish population cannot be found anymore. As an explanation for the relatively low death rate of the Jews, one points to the better care of the parents, the close family relations in general, a more hygienic way of life thanks to the Jewish dietary and other rules, the deviant structure of the working population (in particular commercial jobs and professions) and the living in large cities.'[75]

Both rely on studies of another Steinmetz pupil, E. Boekman (1924-1936). Still H. Daalder (note 34) relies heavily on Kruijt. Superficial and hagiographic is J. Blom, J. Cahen, Joodse Nederlanders, Nederlandse joden en joden in Nederland (1870-1940), in: J. Blom a.o. (Ed.), Geschiedenis van de Joden in Nederland (Amsterdam: Balans, 1995), p.247-313. They mention too many data and comment higly ambiguous on it as if they are themselves fully confused. For Steinmetz now see my essay 'Soziographie, Geographie und Kolonialismus in der holländischen Westforschung', in: Idem, Volk ohne Sprache (forthcoming), p. 63-184.
75. J. Blom, J. Cahen, p. 252. From earlier passages one could get the impression that these characteristics are still apparent in 1940/41.

Is this true, a clear matter of philosemitism, or does it show how myths around Dutch Jews are fostered? The answer to this question is given, first, through a comparison of health and living conditions between the Jewish and the richest parts of Amsterdam around 1920 with the following parameters.[76]

A comparison between religions with the available statistics is deeply flawed, which was remarked upon time and again by the Amsterdam statisticians in the 1920s, although they themselves provide the comparison. Apart from this, only extremely religious people and historians like Blom/Cahen presuppose that belief is able to change mortality rates, etc. But with the given comparison between the districts, we arrive again with two feet on the ground.

The Jewish district is nearly the poorest part in Amsterdam and for at least two generations the ugliest place to live in the whole of the Netherlands! Since about 1850 (since there were some reliable statistics there) at least half of the Jewish population was endowed with some subvention of the poor, which was at that time three times as much as other parts of the Amsterdam population. Although this percentage fell, Jewish people always needed much more poor-relief than others. During the diamond-boom around 1900, it was at its lowest point, but 25 years later when the diamond industry was collapsed, it again came near the 1850 mark.

The comparison with the richest district tells, first of all, that also after 1910, the health and living conditions in the Jewish part improve but are still serious; it remains the classic place of the (Jewish) *Lumpenproletariat*. And indeed a large part of them earned their meagre living with the gathering and selling of *Lumpen*, rags. Although a quarter of a century later it is still the same, now about half of the population are *not* known as Jews. In 1929, of the 345 ragsmerchants who had to rely on poor relief, 60% were of Jewish descent.[77] At this time they were spread further over the eastern city quarters, but remained mostly poor. Apparently, the fear for revolts had urged the socialist city government to take these measures instead of helping them.

The large number of cellar-dwellings here, the filthiest and most overcrowded holes, and the much higher density are in my opinion the most characteristic features (one has to know as well that the few cellar dwellings in the richest district are a paradise compared to those in the Jewish district; so figures do not tell

---

76. The figures come from *Statistiek der bevolking van Amsterdam tot 1921* (Amsterdam: Bureau van de Statistiek der Gemeente Amsterdam, 1923), passim. The richest district is the one called 'Tussen Vondelpark en Boerenwetering'. In the statistics it has the quarters CCii, AC, AJ – AM. The Jewish district is called *Jodenbuurt* (Jewish quarter) but I prefer 'district' because it has the city quarters C, N – S, Uii and Vi in which about 60 per cent of the Jewish population in Amsterdam live concentrated. In 1920 the other part is dispersed over several other 'districts'. In the richest district nearly no Jews dwell. All Jews ('Israelites' is the official name in the statistics) together occupy in 1920 about 10% of the total Amsterdam population of 647,427 peoples.

77. J. Blom, J. Cahen, p. 260.

everything). It is, therefore, utterly nonsense to credit 'a more hygienic way of Jewish life' or 'dietary rules' for their rate of mortality and so on.

No, Steinmetz and his pupils all rightly stressed the very quick and nearly absolute urbanization of the Dutch Jews and their concentration in the largest cities. This process was far ahead of those of all other and larger groups, but as soon as the latter urbanized as well, they quickly superseded the Jewish groups in 'good and evil' but the urban *starting* position of these newcomers was less poverty-stricken and less isolated from traditional bonds. Then Jewish groups entered the next phase of this urbanization process, involving the relative and absolute decline of birthrates, the more definite loosening of traditional religious bonds, the individualization. Their poverty made them marry much later than others, with fewer (official) children as a result, and so on.

This poverty, in my view, persisted much longer among Jews or "Israelites" because the newcomers arrived in fact "too early" and became, therefore, fierce competitors with much more social potential. In other words, we are confronted here with the classic migrants from rural areas who, attracted by the big city opportunities (diamonds), act as pioneers in the city-jungle. However, as soon as they want to receive a good reward for their sufferings, newcomers pour in (healthier, more savings, etc.) and this opportunity is gone: in this way they remain nonconformists and cannot incorporate (sufficiently) into the given society.

The over- used religious comparisons blur the problem the worst: comparable small religious groups in the Dutch population which strongly urbanized like the Jews showed the same and sometimes even extremer characteristics and developments over time. They prove, therefore, that the *relevant* differences have nothing to do with religious elements.[78] Religion as an effective means for group cohesion was, in my view, only important in the *starting position* of the urbanization process: the group with the strongest cohesion could make the most robust start. Judaism offered less of a dogmatic-ideological system than Calvinism or Catholicism and more of some shared tradition of commands and customs, which broke down too easily in this urbanization process.[79] But let's look at some general statistics as well.

In the period 1900 – 1940 the proprtion of Jews in the Dutch population decreased from 2% (105,000) to about 1.2% (107,000). In the 10-year census as well

---

78. See J. Kruijt, p. 208 and, in particular, S. Steinmetz, p. 368-370. H. Daalder (p.48-51), furthermore described how within the Jewish religious organizations as well numerous declining features could be seen. For instance: 'There were some five thousand seats in Amsterdam synagogues in 1880, and some three thousand in 1935, in either case sufficient for fewer than 10 percent of Amsterdam Jewry only.' (p. 49). This, however, would be an impossible announcement in not only Steinmetz' view, who rightly concluded: 'The christianized and the irreligous Jews did not belong here to the Jewry.'(p.367). How much people should be saved a few years later, if Steinmetz' definition was accepted relative to Daalders conclusion!
79. H. Daalder, p. 56,57.

as in the municipal statistics of Amsterdam (about 60% of the Dutch Jews lived here in 1930 or about 65,000 persons; 10% in Rotterdam, 10% in The Hague and the remainder spread over the country), respondents were asked about their membership of some church. A substantial rise of non-believers was recorded (in 1920 already a quarter of the Amsterdam population) and the widespread custom among "Israelites" to choose only one or two occasions like marriage or funeral to show their piety; also the fact is stressed, that mixed marriages among Jews (men and women) increased tremendously from 5% in 1906 to 41% in 1938, etc.[80]

The figures also show which kind of jobs these "Israelites" did: mostly with *nomadic work* along the streets and a small minority as diamond-polishers. Around 1900 Jewish working women did not show a different pattern to that of the general Amsterdam population except in the diamond industry; the Jewish men, however, were much more mobile.

Thus, we can conclude that whatever behaviour is shown by people called "Israelites" in Dutch society in the period 1900- 1940, it was largely determined by their overly rapid urbanization, severe and too long-lasting poverty, and their consequent drive to assimilate into a 'rich world' as quickly as possible which aggravated sharp, internal, class contradictions as new arguments to leave the Jewish milieu as soon as possible or to leave Amsterdam for Palestine or better places to live.

A "Dutch Jewish Society" – whatever its definition or meaning (in fact, it existed largely only for the outsiders and some rabbis) – was definitely on the brink of extinction in the period after 1930 due to a lack of external opportunities and internal decline (through assimilation, christianisation, zionism, mixed marriages, etc.). In the rural areas, it had already lost its Jewish identification by talking the local dialects, wearing the local costumes, accepting Christianity, living with the peasants. The only thing they did not do was to live a sedentary existence; they remained nomadic (*mediene soucher*) as merchants of everything, and if they were lucky, as cattle merchants.[81]

In the big city this process was largely reproduced, but there an excessively large proportion remained too poor for too long a period with too little *effective* support from in particular the socialist city governments and their bureaucrats. It is senseless to point to the few brilliant Jewish scholars or – for my part – Jewish city eldermen: apart from the fact that they were not scholar or eldermen because they were Jewish (in everything they had to be 200% assimilated); in particular, the

---

80. In, for instance, the introduction to *Statistiek der bevolking van Amsterdam tot 1921* , p. IV one finds the remarkable conclusion that the characteristics of the Catholic, Protestant or Israelite population are 'to a large extent racial characteristics'. This means that already in an early stage racist thinking was allowed in bureaucratic publications. See also Steinmetz, p. 349.
81. This rural life received its best and very popular writer in Herman de Man (*Het wassende water*, etc.), himself a christianized Jew and strong defender of Christianity and critic of Nationalsocialism around 1933 (See end of chapter 5).

sharpest contradictions between the succesful and the losers existed within this 'Dutch Jewish City Society'.

Certainly, here "in the West" there was never a widespread nor an effective antisemitism, but from the point of view of the very dominant sedentary 'pillar society', these people remained mostly "social scum", outsiders, nonconformists but did not belong *as Jews* to "the space in between the pillars". Not yet! *They were – whatever their image – not guests in an inimical country.* Not yet! Furthermore, it was very bad luck that for the few war years, the "roof on top of the pillar construction" was effectively reduced to a few Dutch Secretary Generals of the Ministeries with their many helpers in bureaucracy and police who demonstrated quite the same behaviour and think-models of the 200% assimilated Jewish elite of the *Judenrat.*

Therefore, as they stigmatized Dutch citizens *as Jews,* nearly nobody protested; as they robbed these citizens of their citizenship, nearly nobody protested; when they created "guests in an inimical country" and robbed the latter of all opportunities to live a big city life, nearly nobody protested: when pariahs were made and when these Dutch citizens ultimately had to disappear fully *as Jews,* nearly nobody protested, because ordinary Dutch people could not see these people in their "space in between the pillars".

Again: victims as Jews or Jewish victims?
The question of whether and how one became a victim *as Jew* or a Jewish victim is to be answered "in the East" and under other circumstances in a quite different way. Take the problem of the thousands of 'Jewish soldiers' in the SS and the Wehrmacht,[82] of the Rumkowskis, or in Holland the well organized group of Jewish women and men who betrayed hundreds of Jews and many non-Jews during the war, most of whom died in the camps. Most spectacular, there is Mr.

---

82. B.M.Rigg, Riggs Liste. Warum gehorchten Soldaten jüdischer Herkunft einem Regime, das ihre Familien umbrachte?, in: *Die Zeit,* 4-4-1997, p. 11-13. ('Why did Jewish soldiers join a regime which killed their families?'). It is not necessary to search for SS-Jews, because directly after Hitler came to power most religious Jews under the leadership of Leo Baeck strongly believed they could accomodate with Hitler c.s. The most 'nazifreundliche' among them founded organizations like *Vortrupp. Gefolgschaft deutscher Juden, Verband deutschnationaler Juden* or *Reichsbund jüdischen Frontsoldaten.* What was known at the time as *Hakenkreuz-Assimilation* was discussed lively. In fact the most 'nazifreundlich' were the German Zionists because, in the end, the latter thought in the same 'völkischen Kategorien' as the Nazis. For alle these developments see J. V.H. Dippel, *Bound upon a heel of fire: why so many German Jews made the tragic decision to remain in Nazi Germany* (New York: Basic Books, 1996). I used the German translation: *Die große Illusion. Warum deutsche Juden ...* (München: Econ Ullstein, 2001 with a preface by Alfred Grosser). Grosser zitiert, for instance, how German *deutschnational* Jews urged that without sentimentality the 'danger of the *Ostjuden*' should be eradicated with all possible means (*Berliner Tageblatt,* 4 June 1933). In oktober 1940 a representative of the old Jewish families in France asked Marshal Pétain to take strong measures against the invasion of foreigners because they stimulated '*une antisémitisme normal*' (p.16 ff.)

Fritz Haber, the Nobel Prize-winning chemist who created poison gas in full awareness of his action to kill the French and English in World War I or the nomads in Morocco in the 1920s; as co-creator of Zyklon B, in the end, he paved the way for the very death-machines of the Holocaust. As I understand, no one forced him to do this.

Was Haber still a 'Jewish victim'? Did he and the others commit their crimes against humanity *as Jews*?[83] If *Jew* is only a religious indication, as influential rabbis (Leibowitz for example) have stated, then these crimes seem to be either untenable or non-existent as Jewish problems. What is the meaning of '*as Jews*' if the enemy defines who is a Jew? Will it prove that Jews, like any other common group, are sinful and that the crimes are only related to 'people under specific circumstances'? Dutch Jewish women surrounding Ans van Dijk could betray so many people because *they operated as Jews within a Jewish environment*.[84] Are these circumstances determined by the degree of assimilation of Jewish people or by the internalization of the most extreme oikoidal norms? The problems discussed here were eloquently circumscribed by Primo Levi in the following way:

'If the interpretation of a Rumkowski intoxicated with power is valid, it must be admitted that the intoxication occurred not because of, but rather despite, the ghetto environment. ... In fact, in him as in his more famous models, the syndrome produced by protracted and undisputed power is clearly visible: a distorted view of the world, dogmatic arrogance, need for adulation, convulsive clinging to the levers of command, and contempt for the law. ... That a Rumkowski should have emerged from Lodz's affliction is painful and distressing. ... But there are extenuating circumstances: an infernal order such as National Socialism was exercises a frightful power of corruption, against which it is difficult to guard oneself. It degrades its victims and makes them similar to itself, because it needs both great and small complicities.'[85]

This unequivocal, but not definitive, answer to the above questions has far-reaching implications. In Levi's view the crimes were not committed *as Jews* but as (offshoots of) powerful oikoidal dictators who were able and willing to exploit

---

83. The first biography of the man, D. Stoltzenberg, *Fritz Haber*. (Weinheim/ New York: VCH, 1994) has the subtitle *Chemiker, Nobelpreisträger, Deutscher, Jude*. The author clearly knows that the Nazis 'eindeutig kein Unterschied gemacht [haben] zwischen Juden, die sich zum jüdischen Glauben bekannten, und solchen, die christlich getäuft oder atheistisch waren. Es ging um das ''jüdische Blut'', das das Deutsche verunreinige.' (p. 573). Fritz Haber understood this as well (p.576) but was confronted, first and foremost, with the difficulty of defining the Arier-concept (p. 579). As the Nazis already in April 1933 urged his departure he had to fill in forms with the question whether he was an Arier; for 'Arier' he could choose out of different official definitions which contradicted each other (two or four grandparents, etc.). Stoltzenberg does not mention Haber's solution of the problem.
84. K. Groen, *Als slachtoffers daders worden. De zaak van de joodse verraadster Ans van Dijk* (Baarn: Ambo, 1994); ('When victims become perpetrators').
85. P.Levi, *The drowned and the saved* (London: Abacus, 1988), p. 49.

this power to the ultimate limits. It is, therefore, inappropriate to use *as Jews*, but then *as Germans* is inappropriate as well, although for different reasons. 'German' and 'Jew' play antagonistic roles in the drama; both imply racial characterisations in this historical context. First, they are general qualifications and not specific, and second, they lead to exclusive accusations and to a confirmation of the usual anti-Judaism, antisemitism or anti-Germanism. See, for example, Goldhagen's 'exterminationist antisemitism'.

More important is the conclusion from the above discussion that victims and perpetrators cannot exist without each other, which is not only a semantic conclusion. Rumkowski's 'eternal power' rested on the huge eternal power of the German army and SS, while they needed the potentials of *Judenräte* or Rumkowskis to crush the opposition against their rules, to organize the solution of the Jewish Question effectively, to rob the victims of their last penny, and so on. Compared to this, it is a telling fact that for the past 20 years a steadily increasing number of (radical) Jews are now living in lands or places of their fiercest perpetrators like Poland, Germany or the Netherlands. In fact, they live there (temporarily) as 'eternal victims', at best talking and discussing the Shoah in public debates,[86] while youngsters often demonstrate an irrational neo-Zionism. This easily leads to isolation, pessimism and radicalization. It could be that the Rumkowskis play the *last phase* of this same process when the desperation becomes unbearable, and one looks for ultimate acts: 'Let's take a kalashnikov and kill all the bastards in this mosque!' This normal progression to the killing fields is, of course, not taken *as Jews* but as irresponsible idiots; Jewish idiots, indeed.

We come, however, closer to understanding the phenomenon when we see the Rumkowskis as those who successfully overcame the limitations of the 'eternal victim' by adapting to the role of *eternal evil* equal to that host of comparable Christian creations, the monsters of Frankenstein, constructed only for showing the *eternal power* of the religious leaders and their imitators like the Scientist as 'Master over the Powers of Nature'. If these creations can take over power, the not very innocent virtual reality transforms into a real nightmare because the corruption reaches total proportions: every alternative, opposition, chance has

---

86. In Poland orthodox Jews sponsored by USA sects came to live there; in Germany many intellectuals came because there was a good market for their products. Take, for instance, the Hungarian writer György Konrád who lives partly in Hungary and partly in Berlin, who is mostly effectively involved in numerous debates but cynically answers a journalist's question of whether it is difficult for him to live as victim in the land of the perpetrators: '*It is not necessary that they love me. It is already quite gentle if they do not kill me*'. (Michèle de Waard in: *NRC Handelsblad* 16-4-1999). In the same problem category one can locate those stringent Wagner-lovers like George Steiner or Hannah Arendt's love affaire with a notorious Nazi, Heidegger, which continued after 1945. In principle, one has to respect personal choices and one should not be eager to engage oneself in the usual psychoanalytical pep-talk. If, however, these people express their opinions publicly they have to expect critical reactions on these personal matters as well.

vanished while every neighbour has been transformed into a traitor, and only rumours reign.

In this way Levi's words: 'it degrades its victims and makes them similar to itself' are explained only partially. The still widespread antisemitism in a country with very few Jews (like Poland after 1945) is another clue.[87] It is too cheap to say that the anti-Zionism of the Communists replaced antisemitism. The power of the Polish Catholic Church was never seriously undermined, because they could accommodate too easily with the new Communist regime; their (and the Nazis) propaganda seem to be the truth: Communism and Judaism were of the same order now that a Jew like Gomulka could dominate post-war Poland for a long time. As shown earlier, this Catholic Church, like others, nurtures secular antisemitism by definition by the application of its immanent anti-Judaism, and this was/is always done where even the tiniest minority of the population could be defined as dangerous and 'Jewish'. That became clear from the first pogroms *after* the liberation in 1945 onwards (August 1945 in Cracow; July 1946 in Kielce, etc.) and before a full take-over of the Communists and the epidemic renewal of antisemitism *after* the take-over by the Catholic creation, Solidarity/Walensa.

This anti-Judaism, however, was part and parcel of a general theory of the perpetrator-victim relationship which was already implied in the paulinian and medieval uncompromising dualisms of the heathen, barbarian, heretic against the Christian, civilized, believer thoughts.[88] From the fifteenth century onwards, it was accepted as a practical guideline by the largest majority of the European elite, and it is not an accident that the most outspoken friend-foe theorist of the 20th century, the Catholic and Nazi Carl Schmitt, received the *imprimatur* of his church for the defence of their theory.[89] All this could be propagated under one major precondi

---

87. In this respect, the strangest example is Japan which never had any relationship with Jews; it is even difficult to prove whether 'a Jew' ever visited this country. Yet, at present, it seems as if Japan's foreign enemy is 'The Jew'. Many books 'prove' every possible world conspiracy. See S. Rosenman, Japanese Anti-Semitism: Conjuring Up Conspirational Jews in a Land Without Jews, in: *Journal of Psychohistory* 25 (1997), p. 2-32. The author is playing with neo-Freudian brainwaves. Happily, he also reveals some relevant facts which deserve more attention. The circles which after 1900 propagated Japanese hegemony in Asia still have many supporters who are vulnerable to the classical oikoidal ideology, a solid foundation for antisemitism. Before World War II Christian sects introduced (biological) philosemitism, claiming that there is a physiological identity of Japanese and Jews; the emperor descended from the Jews; etc.(p.5). At the same time Japan was flooded with German antisemitic propaganda. This material kept its 'value' after the lost war in widespread revanchistic circles. The virulent anti-Americanism found an outlet in supporting 'the enemy of the enemy', i.e. 'Arabs versus Israelis 'Jews''.

88. R. Koselleck, *Vergangene Zukunft. Zur Semantik geschichtlicher Zeiten* (Frankfurt a./M.: Suhrkamp, 1989), p. 211-260.

89. B. Rüthers, *Carl Schmitt im Dritten Reich* (München: Beck, 1990), p. 10. Notwithstanding the host of criticism Schmitt's writings rightly received, even today he has a circle of firm supporters. As one of the very few scholars, Schmitt (1888-1985) received for his 70th, 80th and 90th birthday a *Festschrift* with contributions from all over the world and many symposia discuss his thoughts. See D. Dyzenhaus, *Legality and Legitimacy. Carl Schmitt, Hans Kelsen and Hermann Heller in Weimar*

tion, namely, that an autocratically guided state machine could do the factual perpetration and killing work directed against *everybody* who did not want to be a follower of the autocratic Lords, secular or religious. That was the case in early modern Europe and is still implied in Levi's quotation, because the 19th century separation between state and church did not work very effectively in early 20th century Europe.[90] If one believes Stephen Feldman, who starts his book with 'I am Jewish', this is still the situation even in the USA today.[91]

For centuries, this strong distortion of the central power doctrines, the *creation mechanism* for 'eternal enemies', not only created something like 'Jews as eternal victims' but also 'Jews as obedient followers of the Lords'. This aim was achieved as well as the first. It is a myth created by Nazi and related propaganda that Jews generally belonged to left-wing political circles or to the opposition of established governments, which was already in variance with the other myth that they all belonged to the *crème de la crème* of the capitalist elite. Certainly, Karl Marx or Ferdinand Lasalle were left-wingers but not *as Jews* (not even 'assimilated Jews') although, historically, they both had some ties with the created 'obedient Jews'! The same is true for the Rothchilds or George Soros: they could not become top-capitalists *as Jews* but as clever and lucky people. Still, the Rothchilds seem to have direct ties with the 17th and 18th century *Hofjuden*. These, but also the poor majority of the 19th and 20th century *Ostjuden*, could not escape the primitive creation-mechanism: they were also victims in the sense that they always had to stay at the disposal of the Lords, had to do the dirty work for the Lords, and could replace the Lords as objects of *legitimate* protests against the Lords. The history of these effects of 'the syndrome produced by protracted and undisputed power' (Levi) still has to be written.

Whatever the crude characteristics of the mutual relationship of perpetrators and victims, it cannot be extended to abolish the perpetrators' guilt or identity, whatever the 'guilty actions' of the victims, or to overlook the large differences

---

(Oxford: Clarendon Press, 1997) who managed excellently to connect Schmitt's work with the modern discussions around Rawls, Dworkin, etc.

90. See the interesting text of the liberal professor of law J. Bluntschli 'Juden' in his famous *Deutsches Staats-Wörterbuch* (Stuttgart: Expedition des Staats-Wörterbuchs, 1860), Vol.5, p, 430-447.

91. S. Feldman, *Please don't wish me a Merry Christmas. A critical history of the separation of Church and State* (New York: New York University Press, 1997). O. Garschagen, Het hemelse huwelijk [The Celestial Marriage], in: *NRC-Handelsblad,* 24-04-2004 investigated into the power position of the so-called Evangelicals. According to recent research (he does not mention all his sources) conservative Christians, who have similar religious and political ideas as the Evangelicals, amount to at least 70 million. They do not accept a separation of Church and State: the State (i.e. President Bush) has to follow their interpretation of the Bible. The most radical part of them, for instance, the non-Jewish Christian Zionists (they say: 10 million of them exist) urge that the supposed dimension of the old biblical Palestine must be restored and, therefore, the total present Palestinian population driven out of that Holy Land (after which the present Jewish population must be converted to the Christian belief)!

between their positions as different as Judenräte and SS-Sonderkommandos. Hannah Arendt wrote a warning about this to Karl Jaspers (see beginning of this chapter) and Raul Hilberg rightly remarked: 'The crux of the matter for these people is the suffering of the victims – and that can't be found in the documents of the perpetrators'.[92]

Pointing to a common anti-Judaist or antisemitic language of victims and perpetrators is only one of the many preconditions of making a Holocaust or Shoah. If there is a common and deliberate policy to use these languages and their symbols, they can only be effective if *established* elements such as (university) theory building and educational systems, (religious) propaganda, (state) organizational work, the production of killing machines and so on are supportive. A same kind of list of *established* institutions must remain *neutral* and/or unwilling to counteract. The americanization of the Holocaust including its victim culture makes a mess of all these preconditions of good research and thinking about Shoah and Holocaust.

Questions remain in abundance. Who were historically more important (in ethics or juridically, more guilty): those who were acting or those who were refraining from necessary action? Formally, the latter could be victimized by the former, but the former did not have a chance unless the latter refrained. A related question which is not answered efficaciously, and certainly not by the post-war courts, is who is more responsible in the perpetrators' camp: the white-collar thinkers and bureaucrats or the blue-collar workers and hangmen in the fields? Although in the victims' camp, of course, no shred of guilt for the perpetrators' actions can exist, is it not so that its (quasi) leadership has to justify itself for the efficacy or neglect of reaction against the assaults and for the failure of protection?

One thing is certain: the large difference between a perpetrators' and a victims' victim cannot be found in the result, which was nearly always a cruel incarceration and/or death in some *Lager* or a fully alienated death in some self-dug mass grave

---

92. R. Hilberg commenting on the possible 'fraud' of the writer Binjamin Wilkomirski (*Time*, 14 June 1999, p. 146)in his *Fragments: Memories of a Childhood, 1939-1948*. Elena Lappin, The man with two heads, in: *Granta* 66 (1999), p. 7-67 tried valiantly to prove this 'fraud' and convince me at least to a large degree, because also Philip Gourevitch (see note 11) The Memory Thief, in: *The New Yorker* (14 june 1999) thinks of *Fragments* as victims-kitsch (see for this term Lappin, p. 22 as well). However, he also thinks that Wilkomirski gave a voice to the ca. 2000 Holocaust-children who survived and from whom we know almost nothing. He rightly uses the case to castigate the substantial commercialization of the Holocaust. His title made me think of Pierre Vidal-Naquet's famous book *Les assassins de la Mémoire* (Paris: Éditions la Découverte, 1987) which vehemently opposes the fallacious revisionists' claims. Even if Wilkomirski is a brilliant swindler, he cannot be a memory thief when he gives a voice to Holocaust-children! Apart from this, he never can be put in the corner of the revisionists who deny the gas-chambers and all the rest. Last but not least, I wonder why two clever researchers spend so much time and money, while so much serious work waits for good scholars. And if they want to do something relevant, they could investigate in the same energetic way the farreaching commercialization of the Holocaust before the revisionists do so!

in a remote wood. Another certainty is that a perpetrator in this story never belonged to the pariahs of society. It is also certain that most Holocaust victims, including the Shoah victims, were defined as such by the racial thoughts of the perpetrators, who were supported in this respect by a very broad stratum of 'Western' scientists and opinion makers. One resulting necessity, however, is that after Auschwitz, one has to look for a *non-racial definition of Jews* and a *non-racial definition of victims.*

So, in the history of the Holocaust, "perpetrators and victims as Jews" are human beings in some way or another created by Nazi, Fascist or, generally, antisemitic propaganda and specific biological research; "Jewish victims", on the other hand, are only partly created by the same sources if they are invented Jews, defined by Nazis, etc. as such without any relation to the persons in question. What is the proportion of real Jews among the latter should be discussed in another context. Again, this does not affect the current opinion that between 5 and 6 million Shoah victims are murdered during the years 1933-1945 because the Nazis believed they eliminated these people as Jews. As indicated, there are many more Holocaust victims about which very different stories should be told as detailed as those of Raul Hilberg for Shoah victims and their perpetrators. It is a shame, but such a comprehensive history does not exist at the moment (for instance, the whole Russian or Polish part of it – the largest part – is practically unknown). There is also the difficulty that new criteria should be developed for a history in which the Shoah history is incorporated. One thing they certainly all have in common: they became victims of "Western" racial thinking and policies guiding strong imperialistic state actions.

Jews as guests, as pariahs and as victims are discussed within the European context in which they belonged until 1948. Something fundamental seemed to happen in that year for more than just the subject of our study, the interrelations of the Jewish and Nomadic Questions: the Shoah problem slowly replaced the Holocaust problem, while it also migrated to a tiny spot on the world map. "Everybody" heaved a sigh of relief! Already twenty years later, the rebound caused a terrible political and cultural migraine which is asking for a definitive cure.

A PRESENT CONTEXT

'Because we were at first forced and afterwards, proficient at travelling from one foreign country to another, fortune favoured us. Unlike sedentary people, we lived out real experiences and did not remain stuck to narrow perspectives. In this way we became accustomed to the strangeness of the world [Fremdsein der Welt] *but not to the foreign worlds X or Y: it is this alleged contradiction which is the precondition to all thinking.*'

Günther Anders, *Ketzereien* (1982)[1]

---

1. G. Anders, *Ketzereien* (München: Beck, 1991), p. 280. Many of the famous aphorisms of my 'house-philosopher' point in the same direction. See, for instance, his *Philosophische Stenogramme* (München: Beck, 1965), p. 82-84, 92, 124-125, etc.

Source: Q. Sakamaki/Redux/HH

7. WHO IS A JEW?

'The Present Context' seems to have no other spatial boundary than the whole planet (and its adjacent galaxy!), like 'The World Historical Context' with which we began this book. The philosopher Günther Anders reminds us of nothing Else. It is also a warning because we are often concerned in this chapter with a tiny and, as such, unattractive spot on the map from which you get the impression, it is the centre of the world. That was never the case except sometimes at present for difficult reasons: most people there are not only 'stuck to narrow perspectives', but the chances are increasing rapidly that no perspectives at all remain for all of them.

From the moment I started working on this book a few years ago, the situation has grown from bad to worse in Israel. A 'simple' stone-throwing *intifadah* with practically only Palestinian victims was over; this spectacle ended with, at least, a moral and political victory for the Palestinians.[1] Expectations of peace were growing, and talk about some 'peace process' filled the columns of the media. New perspectives were needed, and this was one of the many reasons I decided to study a problem which became 'the relations between a Jewish and a Nomadic Question'. Optimism was the gist of my first texts, but this waned away with regard to the Israeli – Palestinian relations which are, by the way, *not* the subject of this book.

A scholar always has to pay a debt to everyday realities. However, if it is as high as that paid by the Dutch-Israeli historian, Martin van Creveld, writer of one of my favorite books, it will undermine every credibility of the profession. His *The Rise and Decline of the State* (1999) makes a convincing plea for the *retreat* of the state and perceives 'the shape of things' with the dictator Mao (!) peacefully and optimistically as follows:[2]

---

1. See M. Hoff, De Intifadah, in: H. Derks, *Kroniek van drie eeuwen revoluties*, p. 291-296.
2. M. van Creveld, *The Rise and Decline of the State* (Cambridge: Cambridge Univ. Press, 1999), p. 421. The author was (is?) during a long period adviser of the CIA and of many other (Israeli) military authorities; he is military historian at the Hebrew University in Jerusalem. Maybe, it is his long stay in the USA with its strong anti-state tradition which brought him to write his book. In the same year was published Garry Wills, *A Necessary Evil: A History of American Distrust of Government* (New York: Simon and Schuster, 1999) as an antidote to Van Creveld's theories.

'The sun will keep rising
trees will keep growing
and women
will keep having children'.

Today that same person is proposing on a Dutch radio that the state of Israel 'in a massive bloodshed must kill ten thousands of Palestinians and subsequently has to build an impenetrable wall between Israel and the Palestinian territories.'[3] A large part of this advice is being carried out by the Sharon government. He, furthermore, threatened directly European capitals with 'several hundred atomic warheads and rockets ... Most European capitals are targets for our air force, if Israel should have to suffer a defeat.'[4] Max Weber could see this as perfect proof of Jewish misanthropy and subsequently of the Jewish "voluntary" ghetto drive, which is done today with remarkable effects (see note 42 ch. 4). What is happening there, however, has nothing to do with a general racial or religious characteristic. It points to desperation and irrational panic, a fundamental loss of political and moral realism, reflecting the historical example of self-destruction through extreme isolation of a Marranos village.

Below, my comments on the present situation in Israel are reduced to the bare minimum. They have to serve the development of a long(er)-term perspective against the background of the given world and European historical analyses. The Jewish Question is historically nothing but an *internal European* Question, the combination with the Nomadic Question nothing but an *external European* Question. What the state of Israel is doing or refuses to do at the moment is a result of its choice and only an USA question. The whole of political, intellectual or ethical contradictions between a Jewish, a Zionist and an Israeli question, seems to be the best definition of 'present context' for this book; the unbridgeable gap between Zionist Van Creveld's 1999 and 2002 opinions is the first example of its dramatic outlook.

---

3. His shocking statements were made on the 15th of April 2002. See *NRC-Handelsblad*, 16-4-2002 which also reported that Van Creveld is directly accused of propagating massmurder. Van Creveld got the opportunity to repeat his apocalyptic message on the 23rd of March 2004 in the Dutch news-radioprogram 'Met het Oog op Morgen' discussing the murder of Sheich Yassin, 'spiritual leader of Hamas', by the Israeli. Also two left wingers support Creveld's view directly and indirectly. The well-known "new historian" Benny Morris, now justifies ethnic cleansing, while the darkest sides of Israeli history (the bloody terrorism of Irgun, Haganah, Stern group, Yabotinski, Begin, Shamir, etc.) receive benevolent comments from many sides. The big mistake of Ben Gurion is that he was not cruel enough; the horrible war crimes for which he still was responsible are sketched in all possible details; according to Morris, a future atomic war is, therefore, all in the Israeli game. See recently Ch. Glass, "It was necessary to uproot them", in: *London Review of Books*, 24 June 2004, p. 21 ff. Avishai Margalit, a highly attractive commentator, now uses his *New York Review of Books* platform to make dubious propaganda for the attack of "The West" on "Islam". See www.hderks.dds.nl/discussions.
4. In the Dutch weekly *Elsevier*, (20-01-2003) which was later quoted everywhere on internet: see, for example, www.spearhead.com (Ian Buckley), www.rense.com, www.jerusalemites.org etc.

The basic aim of this and the following chapters is, therefore, to discuss within this context the pariah concept in more detail because strangely enough, many respectable Jewish scholars did not discover the anti-Judaistic and antisemitic content of the *pariah* concept and, time and again, even stated that *they themselves or the Jews were pariahs*. So, why do perpetrators and victims use the same concept with such a dramatic content? Are we confronted with an immanent contradiction which can be solved only in a violent way? With their statements, these Jewish authors also take sides (*nolens volens?*) in a Weber versus Sombart debate which, in my view, represents two sides of the same coin. Hereafter, I shall only follow the Weberian argument, although Sombart was also criticized greatly by Jewish writers.[5]

Remember: Weber's explicit antisemitism was part and parcel of his general anti-market or oikoidal theory/ideology. Probably, this *pariah* analysis can help us to begin answering the most serious question of all: what are the consequences if it proves to be impossible to provide a satisfactory solution for the 'who/what is a Jew' problem? Who or what are 'secret gypsies' at present? (chapter 8)

The next aim of this and the following chapters is to slowly lift the veil covering *Hannah's choice* and discuss some of its consequences. These all concern the practical and theoretical implications of the *Jew as pariah* thesis and the *Nomadic Question*. Günther Anders, Hannah Arendt's first husband, reflects this more or less in his heretical aphorism quoted above. So far, most negative elements of the pariah complex have been sketched, to which must now be added positive elements, i.e. the affirmative use of the pariah concept within a more or less complicated context. Arendt's concept of a pariah (chapter 9) provides the ideal example, and her work certainly points to a highly differentiated context.[6]

---

5. See, for example, G. Mosse, *The Crisis of German Ideology. Intellectual Origins of the Third Reich* (New York: Shocken Books, 1981), p. 141 ff. Certainly, Mosse saw very well how Sombart with his *Die Juden* gave the economic prejudices academic respectability. He, however, refused to believe that Sombart condemned the Jews, as if it was not enough that S. used the economic 'argument' out of every proportion and created an abstract and dangerous Jewish world-money empire out of the blue. Sombart constantly made use of that 'organic language' which is typical for all German, French etc. racists. The way he treated the nomadic argument gave Jews characteristics which made them directly vulnerable to racist attacks because Sombart could locate them 'much better' in the usual black-white reasonings: agriculturalists against nomads; city against country; 'nordische Völker' against 'southern'; sedentarians versus wanderers; etc. all with their own bunch of pejorative thoughts. First he made the Jews *Händler* and in his next book he propagated a religious war of *Helden* against *Händler*! Constantly, Sombart used the most dangerous tactic of talking about The Jews which is in itself a proof of his racial way of thinking (see chapters 3 and 4). In addition, he made a mess of the argumentation we accept as a normal scientific one, that he had not the faintest idea of what nomads where doing and that he, time and again, tried to convince his readers of the '*unantastbare Objektivität meines Judenbuches*'. The philosemitic friendliness which sometimes comes out of his pen must make us even more suspicious about his hidden agenda.

6. Apart from the following notes, from the extensive new literature about her biography and thought I only mention here the well written overview of Amos Elon, The Case of Hannah Arendt, in: *New York Review of Books*, 6-11-1997, p. 25-30; E. Young-Bruehl, *Hannah Arendt. For Love of the World*

So, what is Jewish about the examples given in the previous chapters? The answer is quite simple: nearly nothing except, probably, some religious items. Every characteristic is to be found in other groups of people but apparently, the specificity of the combination is the point. Is it, for example, 'typically Jewish' to travel or migrate to many countries in the world, as Anders's quotation might suggest? Certainly, it is not just Jews who were/are desperate after experiencing the worst forms of persecution from people they knew/know well, who had/have the same political ideas, belonged/ belong to the same status group, or were/are neighbours.

One negative answer has already been given to the persistent difficult question, 'Who is a Jew?', namely one who does not belong to an ethnos. Apart from historical argumentation, one can point to the present impossibility of coming up with common ethnical characteristics of a Jew from Brooklyn, an Ethiopian Jew, a Chinese one, and so on. Other answers are needed. Could they be a People, a *Volk*?

The difficulty of this subject can be demonstrated by a discussion between Arendt and her (later) husband Heinrich Blücher directly before the war.[7] The latter, an ex-communist, speculated about the '*Volkwerdung*' of the Jews within the framework of a communist world revolution (i.e. an army of Jewish and Arab proletarians fighting the English). In a letter dated August 24th 1936, Hannah answers:

> 'The *Golem* makes a mistake if he thinks Jews are a People like other ones, or are busy becoming one. In the East [Eastern Europe] they are already a People but one without a territory. But in the West: God knows what they are there (me included!). Therefore, there is no need to force the first while it is impossible to force the other .... Some territory which could be gained some day in a world revolution is useless if we want to become a People ..'

(New Haven, London: Yale University Press, 1982); for the German reception of H.A. see B. Neumann, *Hannah Arendt und Heinrich Blücher. Ein deutsch-jüdisches Gespräch* (Berlin: Rowohlt, 1998); D. Ganzfried, S. Hefti (Ed.), *Hannah Arendt – Nach dem Totalitarismus* (Hamburg: Rotbuch, 1996); E. Ettinger, *Hannah Arendt Martin Heidegger. Eine Geschichte* (München: Piper, 1994); B. Baule (Ed.), *Hannah Arendt und die Berliner Republik. Fragen an das vereinigte Deutschland* (Berlin: Aufbau, 1996) in particular the contributions of Dan Diner, Wolfgang Heuer and Ernst Vollrath. For the USA-reception see L.J.Disch, *Hannah Arendt and the Limits of Philosophy* (Ithaca, London: Cornell University Press, 1994); R. Bernstein, *Hannah Arendt and the Jewish Question* (Cambridge: Polity Press, 1996); S. Benhabib, *The Reluctant Modernism of Hannah Arendt* (London: Sage, 1996); L.and S. Hinchmann (Ed.), *Hannah Arendt. Critical Essays* (New York: State University of New York Press, 1994). Remarkable are also the feministic reflections of J. Ring, *The Political Consequences of Thinking. Gender and Judaism in the Work of Hannah Arendt* (New York: State University of New York Press, 1997). For Israel the special issue of *History & Memory* is interesting (Tel Aviv University) 8-2-1996 (Ed. G.N.Arad) about the 'Eichmann in Jerusalem' controversy with articles of R. Wolin, S. Benhabib and others. For this row also see G. Smith (Ed.), *Hannah Arendt Revisited: "Eichmann in Jerusalem" und die Folgen* (Frankfurt a/M.: Suhrkamp, 2000) with good articles of Amos Elon, Anson Rabinbach or Richard Bernstein and S. Aschheim (Ed.), *Hannah Arendt in Jerusalem* (Berkeley, etc.: Un. of Chicago Press, 2001) with excellent articles of Agnes Heller, Moshe Zimmermann and others.
7. ABB, p. 14, 58.

So, let's make a new start.

WHO IS A JEW *IN ISRAEL* ?

This question can be answered in many ways. Throughout history a major element of characterizing Jews was the acceptance of the Jewish dietary laws of *kashrut* (lit., `fitness' or 'propriety'). It is said that until the end of the 18th century, they were kept by all Jews in the world. That is not easy to prove, but in any case, the Reform movement which started in the 19th century put an end to this 'universality' and declared that a Jew could be a Jew without practising *kashrut*. Currently, only 'Conservative Judaism' insists upon the acceptance of certain basic aspects of faith and worship, including the binding obligation of *halakhah*, circumcision or *kashrut*. Whoever insists on eating kosher food daily today in a 'Western' country not only has to pay more but will isolate him/herself from a rather large part of their (non) Jewish environment. Whether there is such a thing as 'Jewish food' is a question addressed in a beautiful book, Claudia Roden's *The Book of Jewish Food*.[8]

Roden was born in 1937 and raised in Cairo by Jewish parents who came from Aleppo; she received her education in Paris and London and stayed travelling the rest of her busy life. Her book is a mixture of autobiography, history of the peoples with their food customs, and comments on about 800 recipes from 'the Diaspora'. In 1981 she herself taught that what was familiar as Jewish food in Europe was totally unknown to Jews in Egypt, Morocco and India: 'Local regional food becomes Jewish when it travels with Jews to new homelands.' This means that not the food but only the eaters of the food could be Jewish. This conclusion is quite devastating for the acceptance of *kashrut*: which dietary 'law' from which country is the real one? Can one diet be called the 'universal model'? Are Egyptian or Indian Jews less Jewish than European or Israeli ones? Is Judaism incompatible with the eating of a specific food? What is especially Jewish about using oil instead of clarified butter when (olive) oil was and is *generally* consumed in the Mediterranean world? Indeed, long ago Reform Judaism realised these consequences and abandoned the dietary 'laws' altogether.

However, after many years of study and almost 15 years of travelling around the globe, Roden thinks it is possible to define 'Jewish Food' in 1997. First, she mentions the undeniable fact that there were and still are dietary 'laws', and their existence have and have had some influence on the form and quality of food, in particular, during the Sabbath and religious festivals. She also points to a 'touch of otherness' in Jewish cooking, a cosmopolitanism which broke even through ghetto walls:

---

8. C. Roden, *The Book of Jewish Food. An Odyssey from Samarkand to New York with more than 800 Ashkenazi and Sephardic recipes* (New York: Knopf, 1997). See for the following quotations p. 9-11.

'But the main influence on the development and shaping of their cuisine was their mobility – their propensity to move from one place to another. Jews moved to escape persecution or economic hardship, or for trade. Their history is one of migration and exile, of the disintegration and dispersion of communities and of the establishment of new ones. In their Diaspora ... Jews brought dishes from past homelands to new ones. The way these dishes changed and adopted new forms in a new environment created hybrids that were particular to them. It is the cooking of a nation within a nation, of a culture within a culture, the result of the interweaving of two or more cultures. The almost complete dispersion of the old communities has radiated their styles of cooking in different parts of the world ... but each dish represents a unique historical experience in a particular geographic location ... They are that part of an immigrant culture which survives the longest, kept up even when clothing, music, language, and religious observance have been abandoned.'

In my view, this statement proves nothing but the validity of her original opinion. The delusion becomes apparent thanks to the forced relationship between food and a religious universality. One can only think of individuals who cook in an unique, individual way under specific preconditions, namely, that *they all share the nomadic way of life*. Could this nomadic cooking/food also be called 'Jewish food' and could it be related, therefore, to something like a Jewish theory, a Jewish belief or a Jewish culture with their marked differences between Ashkenazi, Sephardi and many other views? That is the question.

In the first place it is 'minority food'. They brought with them food customs from their former homeland and mixed this with elements of the present homeland. *Therefore*, they always had 'strange' food relative to the present environment and 'foreign' food relative to another Jewish minority. Roden, furthermore, demonstrates not only the overriding importance of the exotic Sephardic kitchen. Her investigations resulted in an unique comparison between small minorities within many different cultures. The communication between these minorities in matters of food consumption and gastronomic knowledge is sustained again through mobile individuals: merchants (importers, middlemen, and wholesalers), peddlers, travelling rabbis, preachers and teachers, students and cantors, professional letter carriers, beggars (who were legion), and pilgrims 'on their way to and from the Holy Land'.

In short, we are dealing here with highly different and small minorities communicating through a loose but effective international network. Within this network of minorities, the Jewish *religious* elements can have only a minor influence. From them specific *meanings* are derived for certain food-elements which received a different or no meaning elsewhere in the so-called Diaspora or other corners of the world.

Within this fragile, global sphere of influence, tensions exist between this Diaspora and 'Jerusalem'. The following example is another Diaspora story from 'after 1492'.[9] In Turkey currently live 25,000 people called *dönmeler*. They are Moslem but also followers of the 17th century Jewish messiah, Sabbatai Sevi or Zwi (from Izmir, West Turkey). In fact, these *dönmeler* are descendants of Sephardic fugitives who had to leave Spain in 1492; after years of dangerous wanderings in Christian France and Italy, they were allowed to remain peacefully in several parts of the vast Ottoman Empire. In Thessaloniki they founded an important centre, which was much later transferred to Istanbul when the Greek Fascist movement began with the persecution of Jews (1924). Twenty years later, the rest of the Sephardic community which lived in Thessaloniki died in Auschwitz.[10]

However, the new modernist ruler in Turkey, Atatürk, welcomed the immigrants, and in their turn, the liberal *dönmeler* enthusiastically supported his reforms. Their nationalism became even stronger than their orthodox beliefs because their own progressive ideas about education, women's emancipation, and the necessary separation of state and religion perfectly fitted in the New Turkey. Therefore, they all converted to Islam. Today, radical Moslems still criticize the *dönmeler* for their modernism, while 'Jerusalem' tries to create a classical minority problem in the framework of its new 'Turkish policy'. The support for an Israeli case, let alone a mystical 'return to the Holy Land', is restricted to two *dönmeler*! In addition, one of them, Ilgaz Zorlu, is not considered a Jew by Israeli orthodox, while the other never challenged the Israeli wisdom in this matter. Anyway, in 'Jerusalem', somebody must know who or what is a Jew.

The most important Israeli theologian, Yeshayahu Leibowitz, has partly indicated what is implied in my reflections so far:

'The historical Jewish people is not defined as a race and not as the people of a particular land or of a specific political framework, nor even of a particular language, but as the people of the Torah and religious prescriptions ...' Boaz Evron, a journalist who is obliged to live from the 'empirical facts' and managed to become a sparring partner of Leibowitz, adds to this: 'If we give the state the operational definition of "the Jewish state", a state which has to be Jewish, we are immediately confronted with the question "Who is a Jew?" I do not want to, nor can, decide who is a Jew. Nobody is able to do that.' And again Leibowitz: 'Our problem cannot be "Where to go with the state of Israel?" ... but "The present Jewish people: what is this?" And again, it is a question which I cannot answer empirically; there is no human being and no institution allowed to pose this question from a normative point of view and to answer it.'[11]

9. For the following example see G. Scholem, *Sabbatai Sevi. The Mythical Messiah 1626-1676* (Princeton: Princeton University Press, 1973); F. Santing, Waar zijn de volgelingen van de messias? in: *NRC Handelsblad*, 6-12-1997.

10. H. Derks, *De Koe van Troje*, p. 102-108.

11. The quotations are from Y. Leibowitz, *Het geweten van Israel* (Amsterdam: Arena,1993), p. 25, 117, and 171 respectively. This booklet is the translation of the important discussion between Leibowitz, Zimmermann, Galnor, Burg, Evron and Naor (mostly from the Hebrew University of Jerusalem). It

Indeed, a historian or sociologist like me does not take such a normative point of view. With Evron's reservation in mind, is it then 'empirically' and sociologically safest to perceive *Jew* only as the name of a member of 'the people of the Torah', and a 'Jewish state' as a contradiction in terms? Of course, this is not a commonly held opinion among Jews or Israelis. What, however, is common opinion in this case? A secular Israeli prime minister accuses left-wing Israelis that they are 'not Jews'; a Sephardic rabbi announces that liberal rabbis do not stick to the Torah; most orthodox Jews in Israel think that most American Jews cannot be acknowledged in Israel because of their far-reaching extensive alienation of 'real Judaism'. The Israeli orthodoxy started a crusade in order to convert American Jews from their assimilation (50-60% of the American Jews are in 'mixed' marriages, etc.).[12] Radical right-wing American Jews are responsible for serious destabilizing activities in Israel, ranging from sharp economic provocations to mass killings including a prime minister.

We conclude that even for Jewish insiders it is very uncertain what or who is a Jew,[13] and it is, therefore, wise to look step by step for an alternative. One has to

---

was originally published as *Am, Erets, Medina* (Jerusalem: Shorashim Institute, 1992). If one is looking for strange definitions of Jews, compare a Protestant view in P. Achtemeier (Ed.), *Bible Dictionary*, p. 525 with a Catholic one in X.Leon-Dufour (Ed.), *Vocabulaire de Theologie Biblique* (Paris, 1962), p. 512 ff. It is selfevident that Leibowitz denies the importance of race in this respect. It is, however, a shocking experience to read how the one who gave me and many other people many pleasant hours with her anthologies of Yiddish *Witze* defends anew the Jewish Race concept in the full conscience of the Nazi use of it: Salcia Landmann, *Der ewige Jude* (München: Piper, 1974), p. 38-65. It goes without saying that Landmann as well provides us with the usual mix of most non-sensical reasonings, half-truths, so called scientific facts and approved opinions. Three typical 19th century authorities (Disraeli, Marx and Freud) are enough for her to believe that '*die Rassenlehre sei überhaupt der Schlüssel zur gesamten Weltgeschichte*' (p. 64). It remains interesting that Landmann time and again relies on nomadic-bedouinic analyses to make her point.

12. *NRC Handelsblad*, 28-10-1997, p. 4. A former ambassador of Israel, Shimson Arad, wrote in this paper (22-1-1998) about the increase of mixed marriages, the decrease in antisemitism and the conversion of Jews not to Christianity but to the 'American Culture': 'If this trend of integration, assimilation and prosperity continues ... this success could lead to the decline as a community with a special heritage and value.' Half of this article is devoted to the usual listing of how intelligent Jews are, how many of the most eminent Americans are 100% Jewish, etc. Also, Arad thinks in a 19th century racist way that the people are intelligent because they are Jews, who are the product of 'a mysterious combination of genes, heritage and environment' which settled in 'a fundamental humanistic American tradition'!

13. Other examples of this game of the deaf and dumb is N. Solomon, *Judaism* (Oxford: Oxford University Press, 1996) who begins his book with the chapter 'Who are the Jews?' (p. 6-17) but manages not to answer this question. Instead he start yoking: 'Is the tomato a fruit or a vegetable? To the botanist it is undoubtedly a fruit, to the chef a vegetable, but what would the tomato itself say? If it thought about the matter at all, it would probably have the same sort of identity crisis Jews are apt to get when people try to strait-jacket them as a race, an ethnic group, or a religion. Neither tomatoes nor Jews are particularly complicated or obscure when left to themselves ...' (p. 6). In this way you can say anything you like, right or wrong: the only thing you get, however, is ketchup, many kilos squeezed tomatoes in a German marked bottle. Compare also the introduction of F.Bautz (Ed.), *Geschichte der Juden*, p.7: 'Wer Jude ist, das läßt sich auf keine der Weisen ausmachen, mit denen in

realize, for instance, that without an answer it is impossible to talk about antisemitism at all! The direction in which to go is already indicated by Anders, Roden and Arendt.

In Arendt's strongly worded answer to Gershom Scholem's dubious attack during the 'Eichmann row', she wrote about a meeting with Golda Meir

> 'who was defending the – in my opinion disastrous – non-separation of religion and state in Israel ... 'You will understand that, as a Socialist, I, of course, do not believe in God; I believe in the Jewish people.' I found this a shocking statement ... the greatness of this people was once that it believed in God, and believed in Him in such a way that its trust and love towards Him was greater than its fear. And now this people believes only in itself? What good can come out of that? Well, in this sense I do not 'love' the Jews, nor do I 'believe' in them; I merely belong to them as a matter of course, beyond dispute or argument.' [14]

For Arendt, a *Jewish* state in/of Israel would be a nightmare and, probably, a contradiction in terms as well. For her, a *Zionist* state cannot secure a separation between ideology and state. This separation is an important precondition for accepting a state as only an imperfect means to an end, which is the view of Leibowitz as well.

Now, however, about 50 years later, *every* Israeli government nearly always depends on (support for) theological considerations of some Torah sect, on some interpretation of *halakhah* rules. Sects use any means available to expand their already powerful position. In addition, the very legitimation for this state comes to rely more than ever upon a highly questionable theological theory about Old Testament Settlement myths and a Shoah myth as well. This comes close to a definition of a 'Jewish state'.[15] Every year the dependence on fundamentalist

---

der Regel die Zugehörigkeit zu einem Volk bestimmt wird ..' No common territory, language, culture, or religion; no common juridical system and no specific race or whatever '*einheitlichen, unverwechselbaren Merkmale*'. I consider this as too meagre! What Solomon did, joking in stead of answering the question, is repeated in the otherwise interesting book of E. Beck-Gernsheim, *Juden, Deutsche und andere Erinnerungslandschaften. Im Dschungel der ethnischen Kategorien* (Frankfurt a.M.: Suhrkamp, 1999), p. 146-165.

14. JP, p. 247. The information about Golda Meir comes from the reprint of this letter in EK, I, p. 73. Arendt could have mentioned here another notorious exclamation from Meir: 'We shall never forgive the Arabs for having forced our children to kill them.' Quoted in Avishai Margalit, The Kitsch of Israel, in: *The New York Review of Books*, nov. 24 (1988), p. 23.

15. See M. Rosenak's article: State of Israel, in: A. Cohen, P. Mendes-Flohr (Ed.), p. 909-917. It was written in 1983 and ended with: 'The State of Israel is seen as giving Judaism a new lease on life; it is the embodiment of Judaism as a historical reality, mysteriously endowed with more than mere historical meaning.' It was not meant as a reassuring remark as R. informs us that 'many Jews never think about the State of Israel in theological terms' (his own article proves the opposite). No, according to him, it is this alleged fact which 'reveals the crisis of present-day Judaism – both in Israel and in the Diaspora.' (p. 916). This case is complicated by the fact that one of the largest Jewish groups, The Haredim, it is highly anti-Zionistic and anti the state of Israel.

religious powers grows, and therefore, the day seems not very far away that Israel will be wholly transformed into a 'Jewish state' with very pious and very aggressive inhabitants. There seems to be even a mathematical certainty in this case relative to the considerable population growth of the fundamentalists. Indeed, is this not a contradiction in terms: dwarfs carrying atomic bombs on their little backs embarking on a Masada scenario?[16]

A clear separation of state and religion is necessary because 98% of all countries in the world accepts no other rules and religion is historically definitely (?) outdated, a process which is enhanced as well in a sociological and political sense by making fundamentalist claims. (It is more than symbolic that the two Islamic theocracies, Iran and Saudi Arabia, are the arch-enemies of the Jewish theocracy and *vice versa*.). A man like Van Creveld should have given another cynical advice: Although most religious people are highly intolerant, belligerent, and talks about a *'peace process'* too often function as the hypocritical legitimation for a new war, energies should not be wasted in an Israeli civil war; thus, separate state and religion as soon as possible in order to win a new war with neighbours. There are, however, better explanations of why it would be wise to separate state and religion in Israel; the following is one of them.

Time and again Israel has legitimated its very existence with reference to the Holocaust (not even just the Shoah) which seems to be in a large measure an immature, imprudent and historically false legitimation. Arendt rightly protested against it in the Eichmann trial context. In her correspondence, her motivations are described in the following understatement and it is here that one can read, for instance in a letter to Karl Jaspers (Feb. 5, 1961), not only 'how rotten this state' must be and what a dangerous 'idealist' this Mr. Gurion is, but also that the

> 'concept of *hostis humani generis* ... crime against humanity ... is more or less indispensable to the trial. The crucial point is that although the crime at issue was committed primarily against the Jews, it is in no way limited to the Jews or the Jewish question.' [17]

Of course, the juridical implications would have been far-reaching if the Israeli government at the time had prescribed to this principle. Still, at present, the case

---

16. Another *contradiction in terms*. The most German-oriented Israeli writer, Yoram Kaniuk, refuses to speak German ('still I am very fond of staying in Germany')! For polemical purposes he proposed splitting Israel up into a secular and a religious part. As a 'German' Zionist, he hates the ultra-orthodox and ultra-nationalist Jews and calls them 'our own Hamas', 'the largest obstacle to peace'. The orthodox 'do not want to give up cities like Hebron because there are some stones which are considered as holy.' For this reason they cooperate with ultra-nationalists. 'At the moment the government of Netanyahu is fully under their control.' 'Zionism was a struggle against religion as well as against antisemitism.' Interview in: *De Groene Amsterdammer*, December 3, 1997, p. 33.
17. AJC, p. 423.

is not fixed historically as precisely as needed.[18] Apart from the obvious idea that it is fully impossible for any country to make whatever claims on a phenomenon like this even if it should correctly separate the Holocaust from the Shoah, the clear conclusions which can be drawn from the previous chapters should make those claims rather ridiculous.

... AND IN A WORLD(HISTORICAL) CONTEXT?

First, Jews 'as the people of the Torah' were *not* the target of the Nazi or Fascist perpetrators. For centuries *these* peoples have had to cope with Protestant, Catholic and Greek-Orthodox persecutors for anti-Judaistic reasons and with state-*Realpolitik*. They were not a Nazi target either because of their adherence to another belief, i.e. a Christian or political belief. The latter, eventually, could only result in an additional sin as was, for instance, the case with the so-called Bolsheviks, while the former, the so-called Jewish Christians or Christian Jews, were not saved because of this quality.

In 1933-1945 quite a different definition was used, although we still hesitate to accept its consequences. The Nazis (all confessed Christians) were not after members of a specific belief: they *(re)invented a tradition* by naming as 'Jews' those who were socially, economically and culturally unacceptable on specific *biological criteria*. The making-enemy mechanism was well-known, but the result was the creation of a virtual reality of fully new victim-species. These, furthermore, had to be instrumental within the *Lebensraum* policies and practices of the most extreme and *aggressive oikoidal state*. The one could not be effective (in the sense of committing a Holocaust) without the other. Traditional sentiments, from anti-

---

18. Even after 30 years, Richard Wolin cannot stop hitting hard under the belt by insinuating an evil banality in Hannah Arendt without seeing the point of the problem at hand. He, first, thinks that Arendt emphasized 'the "Universal " constituents of the Final Solution at the expense of their specifically German qualities, she also managed to avoid implicating her country of origin – and thereby, in an act of narcistic selfprotection, herself.' According to Wolin, it was this attitude which brought Arendt to talk about 'a crime against humanity' instead of against Jews. For Wolin it is still a necessity to recognize 'the Holocaust as a "Judeocide"'. See: *History & Memory*, p. 28, 29. In this way, thirty years of research in these matters was not spend for Wolin. Even worse is editor G. Smith in his introduction to the interesting reader *Hannah Arendt Revisited: 'Eichmann in Jerusalem' und die Folgen* (Frankfurt a.M.: Suhrkamp, 2000), p.7 ff. He falsely accuses Arendt of 'plundering' Raul Hilberg's *Destruction* without acknowledgement, while Hilberg's autobiography explicitly tells how Arendt several times in the most clear way honours him telling about her use of *Destruction*! See Hilberg, *Unerbetene Erinnerung*, p. 128 ('In der zweiten Folge ihres Berichts vom 16. Februar 1963 stieß ich auf eine schmeichelhafte Äusserung über mich ...', p. 130). Here Hilberg reminds how Arendt called his *Destruction* a 'grundlegendes Buch', etc. That 'mehrere Kommentatoren' told their audience that Arendt and Hilberg had the same views, cannot be Arendt's mistake. That Arendt did not liked Hilberg's introduction to *Destruction* had, apparently, no influence on her general flattering judgement. Mr. Smith's other opinions about Arendt demonstrate an (unsubstantiated) biblical hate against her which is met nowadays only in radical orthodox circles. But it exists and can creep into publications of serious publishers!

(big) city feelings to anti-Judaism, from xenophobia to the lost World War I sentiments, had an *accelerating* effect and *removed all sources of criticism* of the biological arguments and policies (even in the spirit of people like Weber: 'personally I agree, but scientifically ...') and of the *Lebensraum* state.[19]

This is, in my opinion, the *basic* mechanism which led specifically in Germany to the planning, decision-making and execution of a Holocaust and not only a Shoah; it was a very specific *combination* of mostly existing or traditional elements; a combination which could not be made at an earlier time or elsewhere. There is nothing mysterious, let alone religious about it. Not even when Hitler or one of his ideologues made metaphysical statements in this respect like: 'the Jew is the anti-man, the creature of another god ... He is a creature outside nature and alien to nature.'[20]

This lunatic definition is simply adapted from the old Christian discourse of the Jew as 'eternal enemy' and is a traditional element of many 19th and early 20th century antisemitic tracts. Germans, including German Jews, were traditionally highly discriminating against Poles and *Ostjuden* and often placed these outside human nature by calling them 'animals' or 'beasts' as did even a scientific saint like Weber around 1900 and the Nazi-ideologue Rosenberg 30 years later. For the nomadic gypsies or the homosexuals, the same story can be told. These pejorative languages were combined within the biologically based *Lebensraum* policies and put into practice in several ways by the army, police forces and the bureaucracies: that is the remarkable thing.

All this resulted, therefore, in artificial constructions derived from a purely bio-utopian and extreme oikoidal model of society, the combined characteristics of which could be applied to many kinds of 'types'. Even within their own National Socialist discourses, fundamental differences appeared among ideologues who labelled as 'Jews' those who were biologically unacceptable on social, economic and cultural criteria. For one, 'Jews' were an internal sickness caused by 'house-parasites'; for another, they were a sickness coming from abroad brought by alien pariahs; again others saw the dangers from both sides, while some connected both dangers by considering that the pariahs of today could become the parasites of

---

19. These conclusions also form a criticism of Steven Katz's article: The Holocaust. A very particular racism, in: HH, p.56-64. Katz is probably the most lucid interpreter of the Shoah as a phenomenon in European history, but when he comes to the period in which it 'all' happened, he switches again to at present untenable, particularistic Jewish opinions.

20. Quoted in J.Connelly, Nazis and Slavs: From Racial Theory to Racist Practice, in: *Central European History*, 32 (1999), p.33, an article which is interesting for the bibliographical data and some quotations. Apart from the fact that the figures he uses are nearly all wrong, his conclusions about the 'unique' position of Jews relative to Polish, Russian and other victims are hardly supported by his own findings. Besides this, although he extensively refers to the writings of Götz Aly or Wippermann, the principles and implications of the *Lebensraum* policies are not considered adequately.

tomorrow. For some, 'Jews' were of a pure race, and for others, as for instance the top-ideologue Hans K. Günther,[21] they were already as mixed as possible.

Within the framework of the aggressive state, all these became arguments for boosting one's own superiority and eliminating as far as possible all 'non- and sub-humans' but led, practically, to different measures. Elimination could be done quickly (gassing) or slowly (*Vernichtung durch Arbeit*), well organized or opportunistic, in a sedentary (*Lager*) or a 'nomadic' way (from slaughter-raids to transferring large groups to distant places) depending not only on available logistics, phase of the war, etc. but to a large extent on who was executing the elimination.

But 'non- or sub-humans' were humans who did not confirm to the strict standards set by all militant bourgeois and other supporters of classical oikoidal ideals from the political right as well as the left.[22] Therefore, the Holocaust was the ultimate attempt to eradicate *all non-conformists* of this biologically fixed standard set of values which had and has, alas, strong ties with mainstreams in 'Western' thoughts and civilization: to the ca. 60-70 million victims of the *Holocaust* also belonged the other (invented) Jews and many other types deviating from the Nazi model of a decent, orderly, healthy, authoritarian, patriotic, pure, militant, heroic, hygienic, Christian, hierarchical, etc. society.[23]

---

21. For Günther see J. Connelly, p. 12 and 26. See also the large quotation from present Polish scholars, Borejsza or Szarota, p. 25

22. It is essential to stress that also in left-wing circles often quite the same ideas and practices were available at the time (and sometimes long after) as in the extreme right-wing corner. See my article: Social Sciences in Germany, 1933-1945, in: *German History* 17 (1999), p. 177-220 in which I showed, among others, how Theodor Geiger (1891-1952), famous sociologist and main ideologue of the socialists (SPD), propagated more extreme racist and euthanasia ideas than the Nazis while he supported them from 1933 to ca. 1938. For Ralf Dahrendorf Geiger was 'one of the most important German sociologists' in this century. The main practical problem is the overriding role of the state bureaucracy in matters of population control, health, etc. which is stil being taken for granted by most Christian parties and conservative pressure-groups (the classical supporters of euthanasia practices) but also by the socialists and social-democrats who supported the strong state to 'counter-balance' capitalism. It is, however, a shame that the editor of HH, p. 101, could accept the opinion about the existing situation: 'if one leaves genetics to forces of the market place .... this can become an essential component of mass murder'. It was exactly because of the combination of state power + eradication ideology that mass murder was organized: the 'market place' was the location which was detested the most by the oikoidal powers! Max Weber knew all about it as he wrote about the '*Oikos gegen Market*' principle. For these reasons I disagree as well with Isaac Deutscher in this respect, who points to Marx, Engels, Luxemburg and Trotsky to find alternatives for the European barbarism of the Holocaust: 'They could not, however, foresee to what depths of barbarism mankind, failing to embrace socialism, would sink' and 'Nazism was nothing but the self-defence of the old order against communism.' Idem, *The Non-Jewish Jew*, p. 49.

23. In my view, the bookkeeping of the Holocaust is not the most important part of the problem but, still, a necessary undertaking. The 'at least 12 million' are constituted as follows: 5-6 million (invented) Jews, 3 million Soviet Russian war prisoners, 2-3 million Polish citizens, 2 million 'others' (gypsies, euthanasia victims, homosexuals, Jehovas Witnesses, political prisoners, etc.). These are the murdered camp or *sedentary victims*, and the number must be on the conservative side. Then, there

Historically, it was the outcome not of an act of self-defence of the old order against communism, the usual Cold War explication. No, in my view, the Holocaust was the last desperate attempt of that 'old order' (aristocracy, churches, state bureaucracies) to restore the loss of power in the bourgeois, capitalist, anti-religious and liberal 19th century. The increasing and, at last, overwhelming support for fascist ideas and practices, state interventions and authoritarian policies from about 1890 onwards in nearly all 'Western' countries created the climate to 'exorcise all evil' and to restrain criticism if one of the radical regimes started to eliminate and kill their non-conformists at home or in their colonies at a large scale.

Isaac Deutscher's 'Communism' as it demonstrated itself after 1900 was not a competitor of Fascism because it supported and established strong authoritarian centralized states. Competition existed because the basis of the former state was an egalitarian mass of workers-comrades whereas the basis of the Fascist states was the aristocratic hierarchical order: the 'factory-organization' against the 'palace-organization'[24]; the 'Machine' against the 'Body'; mechanism against organicism; the prime duty of work against the prime duty of obeying orders; etc.

---

are the *nomadic victims* to which belong the 1-1.5 million victims murdered by the hunter squads, the *Einsatzgruppen* etc., the x-millions of the German 'Black Earth' policy in Soviet Russia (mainly village and town inhabitants killed wholesale in concerted actions as 'tactic measures', revenge, intimidation and always as elimination of a barbarian race). This last category has to be seen as a 'foretaste' of the 30-40 million 'Slaves' to be eliminated in the framework of the so-called *Generalplan Ost*. Historically and according to bookkeepers rules, this last plan should be incorporated within a new history of the Holocaust together with other plans. There seems to be a *Denkschrift zur Aussiedlung aller Polen* (March 1941) which prescribed – as the title indicates – the transportation of all Poles far into Soviet Russia. The meaning and effects of *Aussiedlung* are well known, the details of this plan, however, are not. The problem remains of the distinction between religious and non-religious victims who cannot be Jews. An *indication* of the content is given by checking the untenable assumption that the entire European Jewry (whatever that may be) was religious and orthodox. Two examples: the majority of the transported Dutch 'Jews' was not religious; in 1938/39 the Polish 'Jews' comprised 3.3 million people. Of these, the Zionists and their sympathizers outnumbered the combined numerical strength of those orthodox from the Bund and Agudat Israel (= ca. 20% of Polish 'Jewry'). See D. Porat, *Amalek's Accomplices. Blaming Zionism for the Holocaust ...,* in: *Journal of Contemporary History,* 27 (1992), p. 712. A last and quite serious omission is the systematical neglect of the many millions of mentally and physically disabled as a consequence of all these Holocaust-actions: it is utterly non-sense to practise only body counts as is done so far and neglect, for instance, the first generation children in all categories. Therefore, in my perception, the Shoah victims should be amount 'at least 12 million' (twice the usual 5-6 million death) and the Holocaust victims (including the Shoah) 60 to 70 million. In recent non-Israeli studies the much more differentiated view on the real perpetrator – victim relationships in the Holocaust (including the Shoah) is demonstrated as in, for instance, Christian Gerlach, *Kalkulierte Morde. Die deutsche Wirtschafts- und Vernichtungspolitik in Weißrußland, 1941 bis 1944* (Hamburg: Hamburger Edition, 1999) or Karel Berkhoff, *Harvest of Death. Life and Death in the Ukraine under Nazi Rule* (Cambridge: Harvard University Press, 2004).

24. At the moment they mixed all this up in Soviet Russia by making 'workers-palaces', one knew that a *contradiction in terminus* had been organized

The *common* enemy of these two oikoidal Molochs was and is 'The Market', the network of free and uncontrollable streams of money, goods, messages, ideas but also the extensive graveyard of factories, states, bureaucracies or kings who tried to organize from time immemorial a monopoly, autarky or large-scale theft, and failed inevitably sooner or later. A new *'triangular hate relation'* was established in this way. (For a present image of 'The Market', look at the *Internet* under the constant attack of oikoidal institutions like the military, the police and monopoly players to capture or eliminate it). 'The Market' was erroneously called 'capitalism' by the other two as if it was/is an ideology formulated by some personal leadership comparable to their own positions which relied so heavily on all sorts of (learned) propaganda and personal cults of leadership. They were overly simplistic reasonings mainly for propaganda purposes, but that does not concern us here.

In a very sketchy way, the situation can be described as follows. Originating in principle as several variants of Oikos-Market contradictions in Europe and its outer world from about 1500,[25] in the original 'two-sided hate affair' *functional roles* were filled by all kinds of sedentary and nomadic peoples. In 'The Market' mostly nomadic functional peoples acted as their own masters connected through a large network of commercial and industrial cities and countries. The sedentary ones received their roles thanks to the aristocracy, monarchs and churches. The financial, organizational, information or ideological problems of the basic oikoidal institutions had to be solved, and the executors of the functional roles had to bear the fate and the hate of their masters.

Among, in particular, the sedentary functional roles, some real ('people of the Torah') and mostly invented Jews (' stigmatized by the churches as 'eternal enemy' and further criminalized) were doing oikoidal services. The latter remained non-conformists as long as they could not assimilate or abandon their roles as *conversos* and become 'normal' members of sedentary society. In the market the invented Jews did not play any role as such, while the few 'people of the Torah' could not be merchants, etc. because they were sedentary 'people of the Torah' with the banker at the top, too often caught in the usual oikoidal tensions within their hierarchy and always worrying about compromising with or assimilating into Christian society. Only in times of oikoidal crisis did all non-conformists in sedentary societies have a great chance to be persecuted, especially the invented Jews because of their specific functional roles. Therefore, the general *Jewish*

---

25. In the medieval world things were much more fluid, which gave invented Jews and 'people of the Torah', in fact, many more possibilities. Besides this, the sources on which one can rely to uncover the realities of Jewish life are scarce and highly suspect. Ariel Toaff's study (note 126 chapter 3) about Jewish life in Medieval Umbria (1996) is one of the first to alter this situation. Immediately a much more shadowy world emerges compared to the situation after – say- 1492: it should be good to study the possibility that – in my terminology – there must be much more room for non-conformism in the medieval world than afterwards.

Question can never be about the guilt, responsibility, etc. of Jews, whatever their definition, but is a problem of established oikoidal European elites and governments and the way they managed their own crises.

In the end of the 19th and early 20th centuries, this constellation became seriously complicated by the rise of the competing 'workers-Oikos', the international division of labour, the 'industrial revolution', and several other reasons: the 'triangular hate affair' was born. Each part had and got 'its *functional* Jews', which all became politically emancipated after the middle of the 19th century. In any case, they are to be defined as *Staatsbürger* who remain non-conformistic peoples in the cultural, social and economical sense and who, therefore, still do not belong to the groups or institutions which they served: the old stigmas still exercised their influence and new ones, scientifically underpinned, were invented (see chapter 4).

Historically, the most important one was *Oikos I*, which provided the framework for the Holocaust in all countries west of the Soviet Union. The most famous of the 'functional Jews' were the modern successors of the *Hofjuden*. They were not only the more spectacular examples like the Rothchilds, Bleichröders and so on who exclusively served the aristocrats, monarchs, state bureaucrats and Christian churches as before. Just as important were people like the Italian Momiglianos who helped to modernize these institutions and supported their imperialistic adventures. Politically, they became 'conversos' (extra-assimilated, patriotic, etc.), and culturally, this was often also the case. It was their Oikos which principally was transformed into the many fascist dictatorships in Europe; it was in this Oikos only that several forms of racism could develop and be supported, providing positive and negative selection criteria for a place in or outside the oikoidal status hierarchy.

The competing Workers-Oikos had its functional 'Jews' as well serving in established trade unions, political organizations, etc. They never worked 'as Jews', not even as 'conversos'[26] but as people who could deliver a useful piece of work. Soon they were part and parcel of the middle and higher echelons in the socialist bureaucracies, concentrated in Russia and Germany. The 'non-Jewish Jew' (Isaac Deutscher) may be their model, but for instance, in the Stalinist Oikos, Tsarist racism (which belonged to Oikos 1) could survive including its main source, the Greek Orthodox Church. For the victims it does not matter, but generally, one could be eliminated only on utilitarian grounds. The cruelties of the Gulag system were partly mitigated by the educational expectation that people could again be useful in the 'workers' palace'.

The third corner, 'The Market', in the personalized form, consists of all 'mobile' institutions, 'mobile' persons, 'mobile' groups acting together or against

---

26. Against Salo Baron, *The Russian Jew under Tsars and Soviets* (New York: Schocken, 1987) who often (p. 243 ff.,339 ff.) uses the expression in a pejorative sense because he is a believer but it is not appropriate in a sociological sense as well.

each other with money, (small) production, communication, intellectual (not necessarily scientific) work, entertainment, etc. A meltingpot of non-state-guided work and activities in which, at least, nobody is interesting for his religion or ideology but for his skills. One of Arendt's profound enemies in the USA, Norman Podhoretz, could be symptomatic for the 'functional Jew' of 'The Market' as he recently wrote that the piety he felt toward Jewish tradition 'did not extend to belief in the Jewish religion or in the observance of its laws.'[27] Podhoretz is, in this respect, a 'Non-Jewish Jew', like comrade Isaac Deutscher.

Later this triangle will be discussed in a bit more detail with the help of Arendt's pariah theory. Here, I provide a loose framework to finish this part of the chapter by discussing the question: What about the interrelationships between the Shoah, the Holocaust and the Jewish victims?

Yehuda Bauer tells us: 'There is simply no way of comprehending the Holocaust (read: 'Shoah'. D.) unless one realizes who the Jews were and are, and why they became the chosen victim of an ideology that wanted to rebel against what we call 'Western civilization' ....'[28] The ideologues of Nazism and Fascism saw (and see) themselves as the first *defenders* of 'Western Civilization against the Red Threat' and also against the Slavs, Avars, Magyars, Mongols with their *Unkultur* who for centuries threatened Christian Europe. Indeed, all *elements* of their thoughts and deeds were very well-known before they created their unique mixture in 1933. In the given triangle its representatives defended, therefore, Oikos 1 against Oikos 2 and 'The Market' or – to avoid Cold War jargon – they attacked with the aim to eradicate Oikos 2 and 'The Market'. But if it is impossible to understand who Jews were and are (in the established ways of reasoning), is it then impossible as well to comprehend the Holocaust? Not at all! However, a very peculiar problem arises in this respect.

In the *Shoah* itself, about 6 million (invented) Jews died who were only partly (probably 20%) and, for the Nazis *by chance*, 'peoples of the Torah'. I have already concluded that, formally, 'the people of the Torah' were not victims of the Shoah, as generally, all other religious peoples were 'safe' no matter how widespread anti-clericalism was at the time. For Nazis the way people were religiously stigmatized was as unimportant as their Catholicism, Protestantism, etc. was for many victims: the victims were mostly caught on racial grounds.

In addition, Bauer's thesis should be replaced by one of real importance: if it is impossible for perpetrators as well as victims to define 'Jews', who then were the real Shoah victims?[29] Only for Zionists is this an easy question, as we shall see

---

27. N. Podhoretz, *Ex-Friends* (New York: Free Press, 1999), p. 157.
28. In HH, p. 20. See also Michael Marrus response to Bauer's contribution in idem, p. 32 ff.
29. Of course, somebody with a suspicious mind will protest already against this question, reminding his readers of the neo-nazistic attempts to minimize the number of Jewish victims. Apart from context etc., there is, first, nothing minimized in the number of the ca. 6 million victims which concern us here and, second, the great forebears of the neo-Nazis defined them as Jews.

below. However, there is an additional question to pose: if the *Jewish Question* is simply created or invented by non-Jewish governing and dominant elites in the crisis of, what is called, 'Oikos 1' and nobody can tell who are the *Jewish* victims, then the Holocaust drama must be seen in a fully different historical context? This leads automatically to another question for the researcher: is it allowed to accept without any qualification directly or by implication the Nazi's racist definition of 'Jews'? In my view, it is the growing consciousness of these background problems which made historians of a new generation after Bauer start to rebel.

Several answers to these questions have already been given above, which must be put to the test in the confrontation with Arendt's political philosophy. Briefly, however, I have to give due attention to the Zionists and their claims to be the true representatives of the Shoah and Holocaust victims and the real defenders of their material interests. Although there is the danger that I may get entangled in the day-to-day political skirmishes,[30] it may also be possible to discover basic elements of the diaspora – 'Jerusalem'/ 'Tel Aviv' contradictions. These could give us a clear insight into the relevancy of my leading concepts. One symptomatic example must be enough to demonstrate the antagonism between 'Diaspora' and 'Jerusalem', which is nothing but a variant of the general 'nomads' versus 'sedentarians'.

The Israeli historian Tevet demonstrates a Zionist solution of the problem. After a visit to Auschwitz where he was confronted with a suitcase and the text: '*Peter Eisler, Kind, geboren am 20.3.1942*' written on it, he could exclaim: 'It lay on

---

30. This happens certainly through the many questions surrounding what is called 'Jewish gold' which does not concern us here. The papers often report about nervous people quarreling about a lot of money which comes from many and pours down on a few (*NRC Handelsblad* 7-7-1999). A real insiders' view which is certainly of interest is the following. The subject is, of course, the money which is rightly being paid by banks and government institutions in many countries to the survivors of the Holocaust. Now, again, definitions are very important; not anymore a matter of life and death, but still ... H. Knoop, the former chief editor of the Dutch *New Israelite Weekly* and author of a critical book about the Dutch *Judenrat*, accuses several Jewish organisations of unlawful appropriation of this bank and government money. He rightly points to the fact that the money was robbed from individual account holders and not from Jewish organisations. 'Not because [these account holders] were member of some Jewish church ... but because they were subject to the Neurenberg racial laws. Also they who turned one's back upon institutionalised Dutch Judaism were subject of these laws. They too were robbed and deported ..' Knoop proposes to divide the money among individual surviving account holders and if they are dead, then the money must be given to all available individual survivors, but never to Jewish organisations. These have no moral nor juridical rights and are unable to represent survivors. In the same paper, however, the report is given of a government commission established to divide nearly 200 million Dutch guilders compensation among '*survivors of the Holocaust*': 95% of the money went to Jewish organisations and only 5% to Roma and Sinti, Jehovah's Witnesses, etc. Knoop: '... in every respect it seems that today for the second time the concept "receiving" is appropriate.' In the meantime the conflict recieved absurd proportions because there is about 800 million Dutch guilders to divide. See now N. Finkelstein, *The Holocaust Industry. Reflections on the Exploitation of Jewish Suffering* (London: Verso, 2000) and his critics like, for instance, P. Steinberger (Ed.), *Die Finkelstein Debatte* (München: Piper, 2001), R. Surmann (Ed.), *Das Finkelstein Alibi ....* (Köln: PapyRossa, 2001) or Finkelstein's website www.normanfinkelstein.com.

the mountain of suitcases ... without any indication of whether it concerns a Jewish child. I am not prepared to renounce Peter Eisler, not on behalf of mankind nor of the Poles. He belongs to us and must remain with us. There is no power in the world which can tear him away from us. Like all Holocaust victims, also the 1.5 million dead Auschwitz Jews and their memory belong to *our* national heritage ...' (T.'s italics).[31] Tevet's problem, however, could be that the power to 'hold him' is largely vanishing or even gone, and 'Peter Eisler' will simply slip out of his hands. Which possibility must be chosen?

If we do not consider Tevet's own discriminating attitude against the Polish victims, it is his colleague, Moshe Zuckermann, who effectively undermines Tevet's point of view: the Zionist state of Israel has established for the past 30 years 'a brutal occupation' in which it is, among others, responsible for the killing of little children as well. The direct motive for his reaction was the barbarious killing of a Palestinian child, Chilmi Shousha, by an Israeli and Jewish soldier, which was an accident symptomatic of the present climate in Israel.

Zuckermann, in fact, points to the large differences between the perpetrators' and the victims' views as discussed earlier. Only in the former view can one stipulate the direct relationship between a military imperialism and the capture of non-Jewish Holocaust victims and their memory (Zuckermann: it is now impossible 'to ask the little Peter Eisler ... how he wanted to be remembered ..'). But Tevet's indirect[32]occupation of a general historical phenomenon like the Holocaust for particular nationalistic purposes provides us again with another definition of 'Jews': all victims of the Holocaust are 'Jews'. This *nearly* coincides with one result of my study so far: a substantial proportion of all victims of the Shoah are invented Jews and a smaller proportion 'people of the Torah'.

Zuckermann, furthermore, rightly concludes that Zionism and the Holocaust were utterly incompatible because this 'worldhistorical catastrophe ... does *not* refer to Israel; Israel 'appropriated' the Holocaust' (Z.'s italics); Israels 'national ethos' avoided an understanding of the universal lesson to be learned from the Holocaust; the Holocaust could be only used 'as an ultimate proof for the right ... to negate the Diaspora.'

This historian reminds me of Arendt, who was, indeed, one of the first who became suspicious about the policy of making the Shoah or Holocaust an incomprehensible historical phenomenon and subject to Zionist policies.[33] So, in

---

31. Quoted by M. Zuckermann, Über soldatische Gewaltmenschen und Kinder. In memoriam Peter Eisler und Chilmi Shousha, in: M.Brumlik (Ed.), *Mein Israel. 21 Erbetene Interventionen* (Frankfurt a./M.: Fischer, 1998), p. 144, 145. The other quotations are from p.146,147.
32. Supposing Tevet does not make the necessary differentiation between Holocaust and Shoah.
33. How appropriate this is for the present situation can be learned from Hannah Arendt, Albert Einstein, etc. who protested in an open letter to *The New York Times* (Dec 2, 1948) against the visit of Menahem Begin to 'conservative Zionist groups in the USA'. The letter accused Begin's party of being 'in their organisation, methods, philosophy and social attraction similar to a National Socialist and Fascist party. It contains members and supporters of the former Irgun Zvai Leumi, a terrorist,

one stroke many painful historical, political-philosophical or moral problems could be swept under the carpet, and many organisations started fishing in troubled waters. People like Arendt, however, remained 'homeless' from a Zionist point of view. What does this mean and do we touch here at the other side of a well-known coin?

---

radical-right and chauvinistic organisation in Palestine.' The letter also accused Begin et al. of the wholesale murder of an unarmed village, Deir Yassin – 240 men, women and children killed – of actions as strike-breakers and destroyers of free trade unions, of harsh intimidation and the murder of schoolteachers and adults who opposed their aims, of terror against Jews, Arabs and English alike. This letter is reproduced in H. Arendt, EK, II, p. 113-117. About the present influence of this radical right, P. Vidal-Naquet, *The Jews,* made an appropriate remark: 'Look at the hierarchy of bank notes ... Herzl is worth only ten shekels, Ben-Gurion fifty and Jabotinsky one hundred.' (p.220). The latter is the ideologue of the Israeli radical right. See also A. Margalit, The Violent Life of Yitzhak Shamir, in: *The New York Review of Books,* 14-5-1992, p. 18-24. The most recent assault on the Zionist theft of the Holocaust is from the German-Dutch Auschwitz-victim, Hajo Meyer, *Het einde van het Jodendom*(Amsterdam: Vassallucci, 2003) in particular chapter 6. It is a book that should be published soon in the USA.

8. SECRET GYPSIES

The strong antagonisms between oikoidal Zionism and the Exile-Diaspora sides reproduce in many realistic details the social and political contradictions between the sedentary and mobile ways of life of people who are, at least theologically, *homeless*. If it is characteristic that they have to pay the highest price in the market of well-being and happiness, then it is reasonable that they come, subjectively, to a much fuller understanding of the Holocaust.[1] Their experiences can be easily related to 'universal types' such as the wholesale slaughter of people of all ages, tortured prisoners or frightened fugitives who are looking for survival and who, first, have to decide between a nomadic or sedentary existence somewhere.

This last attitude is, practically speaking, the same as choosing between 'taking your fate in your own hands' and 'dependence on the powerful other'. Many orthodox people, in particular, demonstrate the entire spectrum of human reactions to extreme and highly institutionalised violence. Sedentary rabbis soon told the world: it has to be seen as a special punishment of God; it is the same kind of cliché as that used when some Jew criticizes other Jews too strongly: this must be a special case of '*Jewish Selbsthass*' (always in German!). However, the spectrum

---

1. See, for example, D. Porat, Amalek, p.712-715. Porat's attempt to undermine the Orthodox Holocaust experience by pointing to the role of their rabbis (some or many of them knew quite well how to leave their flocks in time for Palestine) is contrasted to the behaviour of a Zionist leader who had a son as *kapo* in Buchenwald. The latter was attacked by Orthodox exploiting this fact. The example demonstrates the low level of argumentation. Margalit complains that Segev did not touch on the role and position of the Orthodox in *The Seventh Million*. This must lead to the schoolboy's-casuistic about who suffered the most, which is only comparable to Menaham Begin's manipulation with 'Holocaust Day', the usual competition between memorial sites, etc. See T. Segev, p. 440 note and chapter 24, entitled 'Holocaust and Heroism'. What is urgently needed, however, is research on the general role of religion and its (official) representatives in the Holocaust which is, I think, not the most heroic part of the whole story to say the least. To be confronted always with the stories about brave Italian nuns, etc. without a word about their bosses who were (in)directly involved in the worst perpetration in Croatia (see also Goldhagen in HH, p.305), or with stories about the always absent rabbis, without an analysis of their general role of mitigating protests, etc. is not worth consuming anymore. See now also D. Goldhagen, *Die katholische Kirche und der Holocaust. Eine Untersuchung über Schuld und Sühne* (Berlin: Siedler, 2002), passim for the Kroatian adventures of the Catholic Church, in particular p. 90 ff.

of these traumatic experiences is not or insufficiently digested into a new 'exilic behaviour'. In addition, there is an awareness that an 'exilic life' is, ultimately, the normal way of life and incompatible with sedentary life. But there is, in my view at least, an even more important question: how real is this state of *homelessness,* which is not necessarily fixed to a short period of time?

By staying mobile, gypsies never took the risk of being caught in a 'Diaspora trap' and of having to choose between some nebulous centre and periphery, while Chinese minorities outside China (the *yellow Jews*) did not want to be involved in State or Church matters or even the culture of their 'guest-lands', while often only their remains must be buried in Chinese soil. Both gypsies and Chinese minorities were the first to establish successful international networks which could operate more or less independently of national repression. The differences between these networks are large, and both have their share of dramatic persecution, but in qualitatively and quantitatively different ways than the European sedentary or mobile 'Jews' or real 'peoples of the Torah'. It is certain one of the main differences that at least a substantial part of the Jewish 'elite' wanted to penetrate into the heart of the (Western) sedentary society in which, however, their strongest enemies were situated.

In addition, gypsy behaviour contains all modalities from total wanderer to temporary sedentary which, of course, also produce different reactions from their environments. The Antwerp orthodox diamond market seems a relevant example of how to deal with the world in which the 'law of supply and demand' rules, and some monopolizing oikoidal power fundamentally threatens these rules.

'Pariahs', 'parasites' or 'outcasts' were names given to these people by all sorts of perpetrators as well as sedentaries; Zionists formed no exception. This happened partly on realistic grounds and shaped to some extent their proper place in history. This history, however, drastically altered 'after Auschwitz'. One has to reflect anew on the whole spectrum of victim-perpetrator relations as discussed in previous chapters while perceiving the Holocaust (and not only the Shoah) as the most concerted action of a Super-Oikos to eradicate all its non-conformists and basic internal and external 'market enemies' labelled as such through its biologically induced ideology. Thus, it is 'after Auschwitz' a matter of urgency to pose and answer the pariah question with a large degree of objectivity and not too much 'metaphysical prejudice'. We have reached a phase in which the *preconditions* for a religious debate have to be redefined.

A preliminary conclusion from the discussion so far is that it is rather difficult to solve the question of *the Jew as pariah* because the definition of a 'Jew' remains too unclear. There are no persons or institutions able to decide who is a Jew. As a sociologist I can easily suggest abandoning this name and referring henceforth only to 'men/women/peoples of the Torah' or 'Hebrews' by which one addresses specific groups all over the world. These people belong to a series of nomadic minorities or 'secret gypsies' all over the world which can have a different status according to the quality of their relationship with sedentary peoples, states, or institutions. The meaning of 'Jew' nowadays is largely connected to the question of what to do with the Israeli Super-Oikos and its ultra-sedentary Zionist ideology and practices (see Leibowitz). Again as a sociologist, I would suggest making as great a separation as possible between this state and 'the people of the Torah'.

As a historian, however, one cannot change at will the names and concepts of the past and present, and I am in principle obliged to show the three sides of the coin. It is not by accident that often on the smallest side of this 'market means of production' *par excellence* is engraved 'God is with us'. It seems, therefore, perfectly appropriate to (oddly) redefine the question we have to address as the relational problem of the homelessness of 'Jews' as 'peoples of the Torah' and as pariahs as defined by Zionists and other sedentary ideological institutions.

Within this problem definition and this field of many tensions, therefore, we have to ask now who is a pariah. Above several examples were given of recent 'pro-pariah' writers from Maccoby to Lazare. Below, we take the last steps before discussing Arendt's position to discover why she accepted Weber's pariah concept.

Among her many qualities is her ability to make a connection between the modern American and the anti-modern European culture. In fact, Arendt is the best representative of those who support an 'external' pariah concept. We learned, however, to look as well into its counter-concept, the 'internal' pariah concept, discussed earlier as the 'incast'. This 'incast' as pariah is used by Allan Bloom, to whom I shall turn first before discussing Arendt's position. Through Bloom we are not only confronted with Arendt's American environment but also with a mutual relationship between the two main antagonistic positions of 'Jews' vis-à-vis (ultra)-sedentary ideology and practices.

The second example demonstrates this relationship in a most subtle way. However, it is located in the present European context and is directly related to Arendt's biography. Today's best-known Dutch writer, Harry Mulisch, accompanied her during the Eichmann trial and also wrote an interesting book about this event. This is not the subject here. An analysis of his peculiar place within the 'dangerously hypocritical Dutch society' supplements Bloom's treatment of the pariah problem. In addition, Mulisch' and Arendt's much criticized position as intellectuals is comparable. Through both examples, we shall discover something of the 'class-bound' context which must be connected with the internal-external relationship in order to clarify which preconditions must be fulfilled to solve our redefined question.

Also in her book on the Eichmann trial Arendt hinted to her version of the Jewish history as one in which one has the choice between parvenu and pariah only. In particular the Jewish so-called 'New York intellectuals', the milieu to which she herself belonged, criticized her in a horrific way which led to much speculation about the 'real background' of this outburst. Samuel Heilman offers this interesting dialectical answer which is a good introduction to the following analysis: 'While European Jews in the past were confronted with a situation in which they could not be Jews or something else, American Jews discovered in the sixties that they, from then on, could identify themselves as Jews although they became in the mean time something else.'[2] The Hannah Arendt row, anyway, made these 'American gypsies' a bit less secret.

A 'GRUMPY GURU OF CHICAGO'

In the American context the connection between class and internal-external relations can best be called the *Woody Allen Bloom complex*.[3] The philosopher Allan Bloom (now styled 'Ravelstein' by Saul Bellow) used the pariah concept to elucidate the general thesis that 'the herd is modern, the hive ancient'. These metaphors support his plea for a back to some good life (hive) and his criticism of the relativistic lifestyle (herd) for which 'Woody Allen' seems to be the protagonist.

Strangely enough, Bloom, 'the grumpy guru of Chicago', did not hesitate to adhere to Weber's pariah concept, although he detested Weber wholeheartedly as one of the alleged architects of value-relativism. First, let me present a long quotation from Bloom's *Closing of the American Mind* (1987) to show how several aspects of our discussion come together:

'A value-creating man is a plausible substitute for a good man ... The respectable and accessible nobility of man is [nowadays] to be found not in the quest for or discovery of the good life, but in creating one's own 'lifestyle', of which there is not just one but many possible, none comparable to another ... All this has become everyday fare in the United States ... Woody Allen's comedy is nothing but a set of variations on the theme of the man who does not have a real 'self' or 'identity' ... Zelig .. is the story of an 'other-directed' man, as opposed to an 'inner-directed' ... terms popularized in the 1950s by David Riesman ... borrowed by him from his analyst, Erich Fromm, who himself absorbed them ... from a really serious thinker, Nietzsche's heir, Martin Heidegger ... One of the links between Germany and the United States, the psychologist Bruno Bettelheim, actually plays a cameo role in Zelig. Zelig is a man who literally becomes whoever or whatever is expected of him – a Republican when with the rich; a gangster when with Mafiosi; black, Chinese or female, when with blacks, Chinese or females. He is nothing in himself, just a collection of roles prescribed by others ... he was once 'tradition-directed', i.e., from a family of silly, dancing rabbinic

2. Quoted by A.G. Rabinbach, Hannah Arendt und die New Yorker Intellekuellen, in: G. Smith (Ed.), *Hannah Arendt Revisited: "Eichmann in Jerusalem" und die Folgen* (Frankfurt a/M.: Suhrkamp, 2000), p. 51, 52.

3. That the following represents a 'complex' can be seen in A. Dershowitz, *The Vanishing American Jew*, p. 34; this book could be perfectly used as a soap version of Bloom's discussion. This is certainly not meant in a pejorative sense because Allan Bloom's proposed solution equals Dershowitz' seven-step program 'how to make sure your child marries a Jew' (p. 171).

Jews ... guided by old values ... usually religious ... One is supposed to laugh at the dancing Jew, although it is not clear whether from the point of view of alienation or health. It is sure that the Jew is a pariah, Max Weber's category given special notoriety by Hannah Arendt, here meaning interesting only as an outsider who has a special insight into the insider, but whose Jewishness has no merit in itself ... His health is restored when he becomes 'inner-directed', when he follows his real instincts and sets his own values ... Allen is tasteless and superficial in playing with his Jewishness, which apparently has no inner dignity for him ... Allen's inner-directed man is simply empty or nonexistent ... Allen helps to make us feel comfortable with nihilism, to Americanize it. I'm O.K., thou are O.K. too, if we agree to be a bit haunted together. ... We have here the peculiarly American way of digesting Continental despair ... a Disneyland version of the Weimar Republic for the whole family.'[4] Whether one agrees with Bloom or not, he created a modern American context for the use of the pariah concept. My first interpretation of his rather ambiguous reasoning is as follows. In Bloom's perception of Allen, a pariah is defined as a typical, empty-headed, Jewish family man who can socially act as a chameleon, reacting directly to authoritative impulses from his environment. This pariah has to be *the ultimate outsider* in the sense of *nowhere an insider*, but he must be highly manageable by the insiders.

However, Bloom hates the way Allen caricatures the petty bourgeois who is or must be no pariah but, instead, the cornerstone for all conservative oikoidal thinking and policies. Therefore, Bloom sees the beehive, among others, as a metaphor for his ideal, the classical Greek family. Without any doubt Bloom thinks in terms of the usual patriarchal Roman-Christian model of this Greek family – father is hero and farmer, while the docile mother rears children, cooks and cleans the house (so, everything against which *Portnoy complained* and for which Italian mafiosi commit their crimes as Godfathers always announce) – which has nothing to do with Greek realities in classical, let alone present times. The classical Greek father nearly always had at least one other woman, man or boys for fun, which is forbidden in the USA, while American men still make love in Hollywood fashion: commit adultery twice between your 25th and 35th birthday in a learning process to become the best husband ever; and do not have fun but a hang-over.

It seems, at first, rather difficult to discover Weber's pariah concept in Bloom's characterization and, therefore, 'Woody Allen's pariah' as well. Even more rigid than Weber, Bloom connects the concept not to Jews as 'people of the Torah' but to a social stratum and context more or less alien to Weber's analysis and aims. Originally, Weber bound the concept to groups which come from outside-abroad

---

4. A. Bloom, *The Closing of the American Mind. How Higher Education Has Failed Democracy and Impoverished the Souls of Today's Students* (New York: Simon & Schuster, 1988), p. 144-147. It should be a revelation if not Saul Bellow but the author of *Portnoy's Complaint* had written 'a Ravelstein'.

to inside society. Bloom relates the word to the next phase, in which these pariahs become, as I have named it, *incast* with a fair chance to be called *parasite* if they do not fit into the plans of the real insiders. These, however, seem to be superficial differences for a philosopher.

He demonstrates a profound criticism of the Weimar-German Jewish intellectuals from Adorno, Bettelheim down to 'Zelig' and back. They are the really bad guys who all moved to the States to poison the minds even of the common people. The Woody Allen Bloom complex is portrayed by Bloom's taxi-driver who chats about his *Gestalt* treatment during his stay in prison. It seems that Bloom's ideal taxi-driver must receive daily lashes with the whip in his prison. In short, he repeatedly refers to the well-known *mésalliance* between German high culture and American low taste and confronts both with the excitements of the (christianized) heroes Socrates/Plato and Aristotle. He, therefore, reproduces within an American context the European antagonism between Western (German) and Eastern Jews.

Next, we come to understand why Bloom connects the herd with the pariah-outsider and the hive with his oikoidal alternative, the pariah-incast. In the herd the animals form a democratic (here reduced to 'everybody is equal') mass which run empty-headed after their nose in all directions where food can be found. The beehive is the metaphor of the so-called ordered hierarchical life in which everybody knows his place and task and the petty work-drones, including the small Jewish shopkeepers and labourers, work and die without any protest against their always honourable queens and kings. Indeed, he could have named them pariah-incasts. Here, value-relativism is forbidden, for which he substitutes his Socrates, etc.

His first point is, therefore, that the herd has to be transformed into a hive. Second, intellectuals, apparently all highly influenced by the writings of German-Jewish sociologists and philosophers (most of whom strongly criticized Weber) have to leave and be shipped to an inhabitable destination as soon as possible.

Bloom, herewith, also reproduces the age-old antagonisms between mobile and sedentary life while touching on rather typical antisemitic and xenophobic themes. In this sense as well, he did not understand that he shared Weber's basic philosophy to a large extent. Like Weber, he did not intend to use pariah as outcast but as incast, which can easily become a *parasite* and expelled from 'the house – the beehive'. Although one cannot expect to make Bloom into a supporter of the ultimate cleansing measures, again the road to this kind of solution has been taken.

In European eyes, Bloom's right-wing criticism of a right-wing theoretician like Weber is difficult to understand if one persists in thinking in abstract right-left categories outside any sociocultural context. At present, many honourable conservative European Christian politicians would still be abused as 'communists' in most American states. But doesn't this difference in political valuation equals the large gap between a European and USA treatment of – say – a Clinton-Lewinsky affair? In Europe there was a remarkably widespread shame on behalf of the Americans who *en masse* bathed themselves in pornography made public by the same people, who are the most stringent crusaders against indecent behaviour, abortion, women emancipation and whatsoever is deemed non-conformism.

One starts understanding these different discourses when an American love for apocalyptic Old Testament descriptions of mass rapes, genocide or murder are compared with the hypocritical and quiet European New Testament description of the torture and murder of only one man: realistic against abstract sin which deserve, respectively, strong direct hate and the ambiguous all-embracing reassuring language of the clergy for a cure. In any case, Bloom's middle-class expressionism and criticism of the apathy and emptiness of modern lifestyles often provide good reading, but they leave the same bitter taste as the petty-bourgeois Israeli onslaught on the German *yekkes* like Arendt.

Bloom helps to give old socio-economical class-categories flesh and bones. However, this picture is in need of some improvement because socio-cultural elements of the pariah position are still missing. Bloom's anti-Adorno and Zionist anti-*yekkes* attitudes, for example, return to a certain extent in specific Dutch attacks on the novelist Harry Mulisch, who developed from an interesting local literary talent into an international bestselling writer. For several reasons, this example is highly appropriate for our discussion. Of course, the following remarks do not criticize any literary quality of Mulisch's many novels and other writings. They are intended to demonstrate mechanisms responsible for the creation of pariahs-outsiders in civilized Western environments. With the novelist Mulisch we turn again closer to Arendt's position.

A Dutch 'Touareg homme de lettres'

During the Eichmann trial, Arendt realised that Mulisch was one of the few who really understood her own intention in studying the Eichmann case.[5] In hindsight,

---

5. H. Arendt, *Eichmann in Jerusalem. Ein Bericht von der Banalität des Bösen* (München: Piper, 1964), p. 11. See also p. 50, 55 ff. and note 17 ch. 7. This intention and, therefore, Mulisch support was and is aggressively misunderstood everywhere. How long this aggression can last is proved, for example, in a letter to the *New York Review of Books* (11-5-1995) from the elderly Lionel Abel. He protests against the way Tony Judt recapitulates the onslaught on Arendt in the USA 30 years (!) ago. Abel now regrets his participation in the *Dissent* crusade against Arendt at the time, but still persists in his very negative opinion about Arend's book as an attack on The Jews. As E. Young-Bruehl, p. 355 ff. informs us, it was Abel who coined the terrible and much repeated insinuation that in Arendt's book Eichmann '*comes off much better .. than do his victims.*' In his reply, Tony Judt rightly stressed another background of the anti-Arendt crusade: 'One of the "life-sustaining lies" is the fiction that "Israel and the Jews" form a single bloc and that to criticize any part of one is to perpetrate an unacceptable attack on both. The role of a certain narrative of the Holocaust in Israeli pedagogy and in the national foundation myth was prominent and remains so. Arendt was quite right to place it at the center of her analysis of the trial ..' Recently Goldhagen started anew to accuse Arendt in the Abel-way (see his *Die katholische Kirche*, p. 18 ff., 30 ff.).

I see this as a remarkable proof of Mulisch's independence and insight. Both the philosopher and the novelist attended the trial as journalists; both wrote important books about it[6] and defended the view that Eichmann was the faithful, punctual, impersonal bureaucrat and loyal executioner of orders. For Mulisch, Eichmann was the metaphor of the modern, amoral technocrat. Arendt, supported by Mulisch, stressed the fact that Eichmann as a perpetrator discriminated between his victims, i.e. between the Western and Eastern Jews. Eichmann acknowledged that he knew of the killing orders for *Ostjuden* but doubted the existence of such orders for German Jews, especially ones who had received the Iron Cross in World War I. In short, it was permitted to eliminate *Ostjuden,* but not Jews who knew Goethe and Schiller by heart and who served the German side with their lives.[7]

Elsewhere, we discovered many other aspects of the East-West antagonism as, for instance, the similar discriminatory practices among the victims themselves. Here we can conclude that the Eastern Jews were eliminated as pariahs-parasites, while the German Jews had the honour of being eliminated as pariahs-outsiders. Below, I will comment further on this contradiction, which was sharpened by Mulisch. Arendt quoted the novelist with approval where he was irritated about the testimony of the Bible scholar, Salo W. Baron (a friend of Arendt), concerning the alleged fabulous cultural Jewish performance:

----

6. H. Mulisch, *De zaak 40/61. Een reportage* (Amsterdam: Bezige Bij, 1962). The title refers to the number of the case on the cause-list. Is it strange that in a recent review of this book (*NRC Handelsblad,* 11-4-1997) the Abel insinuation (previous note) also appears? Mulisch argues that it is impossible to understand crimes of this magnitude; therefore, a man like Eichmann cannot have all his wits about him and act accordingly: 'To a certain extent, he even did not know that he acted at all.' The reviewer, R. Havenaar, thinks of it as a tricky explanation 'which avoids all the usual concepts of guilt and responsibility.' This reviewer did not understand Mulisch's treatment of the trial nor its subject, Eichmann and the Shoah. Who are looking for guilt and a proportionate punishment have to talk in a very different way as people who try to understand and explain a phenomenon before coming to a conclusion and, eventually, a moral declaration: the former act as tricky theologians and lawyers restricted by fixed rules of the game; the latter argue, weigh pros and cons together with people with different experiences and knowledge, discuss alternatives, etc. It must be clear which 'party' I have to choose from my profession as scholar.

7. One of the most remarkable books about German Jewish life before 1935 is the *Philo-Lexikon. Handbuch des Jüdischen Wissens* (Berlin: Philo Verlag, 1935). All well-known *yekkes* cooperated in this condensed last testimony of their German achievements knowing that the new National Socialist Movement (see lemma, p. 485!) had come into power to start a serious Jew hunt. For *Ostjuden* see headword p.515 (these are conservative, mystifying, zionistic, culturally isolated). The statistics and maps form a large contribution (in July 1933 there were 499,682 Jews in Germany, etc.); the *Kriegsstatistik* and the *Kriegsopferversorgung* (p. 387) are most remarkable. According to these headwords, in 1914-1918 ca. 100,000 German Jews joined the army, which is an improbable number of nearly one in every five Jews or nearly *all* men. Anyway, from these 80,000 went to the front and 12,000 died; 35,000 received an Iron Cross; 23,000 were promoted, of which 2000 became officer. From these officers 322 were killed in combat '*also 16,1%. Von den Offizieren der gleichen Kategorie in der deutschen Wehrmacht fielen 14,74% ..*' German Jews in everything the best Germans! The picture of their *Kriegsgefallenen-Denkmal in Köln* should have been publicised at the time Germans were quarreling about the next *Denkmal* in Berlin nowadays.

'If Jews were a tribe without a high culture as, for instance, the Gypsies who are exterminated as well, would their death be less regrettable? Eichmann, why is he sentenced: for being a mass murderer or a destroyer of culture? Is a mass murderer more guilty if through his acts a culture is destroyed as well?'[8]

Mulisch confronted the general prosecutor Hausner with these fundamental questions and concluded: 'He agreed, but not me!' To emphasize Mulisch's opinion, Arendt referred to the Dr. Strangelove film with its peculiar lover of atomic bombs who proposed sparing 100,000 highly intelligent people by protecting them in special bunkers before dropping his bombs and triggering the destruction of mankind.

Mulisch's and Arendt's questions could be put into perspective by the following examples. During the war, the president of the Dutch Jewish Council, Asscher, persuaded the representative of the Dutch gypsies, Lau Mazirel, to have confidence in his leadership because it was his aim 'to keep the best part of the Jewish people in Holland'.[9] Another side of the same coin and a future perspective are given when a German reviewer of a book about American Jewish gangsters questions whether such a book can be published in Germany in 1999.[10] Two years before his Eichmann book, Mulisch addressed the same question from another angle in his novel *Het stenen bruidsbed* (1959). Here, the war crimes of the victorious allied armies (bombardment of Dresden) are criticized, which was, in the midst of the Cold War, a precarious venture.

In all examples we are confronted with that difficult and dangerous symmetry in thought and culture between the victims and their perpetrator and/or between victims and other victims. This can lead to nothing but the disenchanting conclusion that it is the power(less) position you occupy in a critical situation which is decisive for the outcome and not thought or culture. It is difficult to decide whether to cry or to laugh about the article of C.K. Williams, a poet, professor for English Literature in Princeton and Pulitzer prizewinner, who wrote in the German weekly *Die Zeit* (7. 11.2002) about '*das symbolische Volk der Täter*', which was directly followed by the text: 'In vain, the Germans are longing for normality. Since the Holocaust, they represent Evil for the whole world. It is impossible for them to determine their own identity anymore. They became a symbolic people – like the Jews earlier.'[11] A near total symmetry between perpetrator and victim is created by this 'American poet'.

8. H. Arendt, *Eichmann*, p. 132; H. Mulisch, p. 72-75.

9. Op cit. J. Rogier, Het Koninkrijk ..aflevering 7, in: *Vrij Nederland*, 20-11-1976, p. 11.

10. Wilfried Weinke in *Die Zeit*, July 15, 1999 about R. Rockaway's book *Meyer Lansky, Bugsy Siegel & Co* (1998).

11. My translation (H.D.) from: 'Vergeblich sehnen sich die Deutschen nach Normalität. Seit dem Holocaust verkörpern sie für die Welt das Böse. Sie können ihre Identität nicht mehr selbst bestimmen. Sie sind ein symbolisches Volk geworden – wie einst die Juden.'

Both Arendt and Mulisch are 'world intellectuals',[12] always reacting according to where and how the world political and cultural storms rage. This constitutes many of their strengths and weaknesses, whatever their mutual differences. It is good, for instance, that Mulisch also pointed here to the useless boasting about one's own culture which only leads to highly disappointing experiences (see the Momigliano case in the first chapter). However, for them also, the relation to their home or homelessness is of crucial importance. For Arendt's case, see next chapters. A biographer's remark will do here:

> 'In Hannah Arendt's personal lexicon, *wirkliche Menschen*, real people, were 'pariahs'. Her friends were not outcasts, but outsiders, sometimes by choice and sometimes by destiny. In the broadest sense, they were unassimilated.'[13]

Let us examine how we can clarify opinions like these. Is Harry Mulisch a pariah or unassimilated as well? To answer this question, I make use of the recent and ambiguous attention paid to him on the occasion of his 70th birthday,[14] with the earlier analysis of the 'pillar structure' of Dutch society (see chapter 6) serving as a background.

During the 1960s, the best-known Dutch novelists (Mulisch, Hermans, Reve, Nooteboom, Komrij, Wolkers, etc.) could only operate within the 'free space between the pillars'. Most of them gained their popularity by rebelling against their 'birth pillar' and contributed in this way to what became known as the 'Dutch cultural revolution'.[15] During the following decades, the 'pillars' modernized, and in particular, the novelists with a petty bourgeois background (most of those mentioned above) underwent a substantial transformation. Once their material position flourished, they often decided to leave the country for tax reasons. In every other country, these people would lose contact with 'home', but this was not the case in Holland. On the contrary.

---

12. For their mutual context see also BF, p. 184 ff.

13. E. Young-Bruehl, p. XV.

14. In particular, I used an interesting review of A. Heumakers, Harry Mulisch en de compositie van Nederland, in: *NRC-Handelsblad*, 17-10-1997 concerning the publication of Mulisch's collected works and a satirical novel about Mulisch's flamboyant lifestyle from the journalist M. Pam. Furthermore, there were commentaries of R. Kousbroek and A. Heumakers in *idem*, 24-10-1997 and 31-10-1997, respectively. Kousbroek and Pam belong to the anti-Mulisch group. They demonstrate a typical European hate mechanism well-known from petty bourgeois drop-outs with their many (often radical right-wing) resentments. Kousbroek, for instance, defends the view that the victims of the Japanese concentration camps should not complain because their sufferings were much less than the victims of the German camps. They could better tell us that the Japanese emperor Hirohito was just a good fellow! He, furthermore, thinks it appropriate that Chomsky defended in a preface to his book the radical right-wing Robert Faurisson who denied the existence of the Holocaust. Still, in Holland Kousbroek is glorified as a one-eyed king in the land of the blind.

15. See H. Derks, De Nederlandse culturele revolutie 1963-1973. in: idem, *Kroniek van drie eeuwen revoluties*, p. 215-224.

First, tax dodging is a national sport, and the one who is doing this as openly as these famous writers could be sure of a heroic reception. More important was the transformation of their criticism. Now that they had drastically changed their geographical location, their criticism became transformed into empty formalities, *ad hominem* attacks or silly jokes, while at the same time, it gained the status of national masochistic entertainment in the modernizing 'pillars'. These 'counter-revolutionary' novelists (Hermans, Reve, etc.) now only met blind adoration, supported by the usual Dutch glorification of everything coming from abroad. It is, furthermore, not unimportant that the Dutch religiously oriented way of thinking and arguing has remained nearly undisturbed or even supported (Reve).[16] One has to keep in mind that there are marked differences in this respect between the 'Protestant North' of the Netherlands and the 'Catholic South'.

From the start of his highly successful career, Harry Mulisch did not fit into this picture. He was and is not interested in the typical Dutch oikoidal novels (inner-house problems of kids and their petty bourgeois parents about sex, religion and provoking house friends or neighbours). Like a proud or arrogant 'Touareg',[17] he looked at this sedentary quarreling and concluded: 'I am sur

---

16. Nowadays, theological faculties in some Dutch universities are being abandoned. This is an economical matter and not due to a weakening of *institutionalized* religious influence. An interesting case in this respect is made by J.W. McAllister, Philosophy of Science in the Netherlands, in: *Int. Studies in the Philosophy of Science*, 11 (1997), p. 191-204. From the 150 university professors in philosophy, only 1 calls himself an atheist. This in a country in which officially 80% of the population does not attend religious services and 60% does not belong to some church. The dominant attitude among the professional thinkers remains the exegetic one (no discussions, let alone research, about problems but about the right or wrong of persons), every philosophical department in every university has more or less strong religious affiliations; theologians and philosophers together decide about the distribution of the available money; if somebody wants to criticize the attitudes, etc. of the 'pillars' and their 'pillar-saints' (priests, rabbis, pastors and their secular clones), he can be sure of losing his job, as happened in 1997 with Prof. Dorling from the University of Amsterdam. Other areas of education are analysed by A. Dijkstra et al.(Eds.), *Verzuiling in het onderwijs* (Groningen: Wolters-Noordhoff, 1997) in which the substantial power-*increase* of the religious institutions within an irreligious society is sketched.

17. To my great surprise, in his report of the Eichmann trial Harry Mulisch had a secret agenda. In the first pages he acted as sightseer in Israel and arrived in the Negev desert, the Old Testament Edom or the 'land of Amalek', Ishmael, etc. He reacted highly emotionally to the sight of the Bedouin: 'While the guide scornfully talks about their laziness, dirtiness, polygamy, I nearly cannot withhold my tears of emotion. Perhaps, one can divide men into those who drive their tractors trying to make a job of it, and those who only like to wander lonely through the desert.' Elsewhere (p. 44) he already talks about 'my Bedouins' and after he became seriously annoyed with the Baron testimony, Mulisch fled 'back' to the desert (pp. 76-81). All this cannot be accidental. It is not an accident either that he was following in the desert a kind of fata morgana because at that time already, and certainly now that we are celebrating the 50th anniversary of Israel, the nomadic Bedu belonged to the most strongly discriminated people in the extremely sedentary Israel. For decades, it has been common practice to bulldoze under the tents and simple houses (often tarned as tents) of the 160,000 Bedouin. Only for the Eilat tourists, as I could see, some 'original black tents' are erected for photographing and as a backdrop for belly dancers. Talking with a Negev Bedu, a journalist noted: 'On the question of whether he feels himself a second-hand inhabitant, the sjeich brought his hands as low as possible to

rounded by the desert of a non-existent literature!' and started creating his own literary universe. There remains a certain bond with a Dutch environment but only as the place of rest for his imagination; it is a location which receives his intellectual attention only if something happens relevant on a 'world scale' like the German occupation and the Provo-movement in the 1960s. The world (of his imagination) was and is his home, which makes, he once remarked, Holland like a foreign country for him.

In other words, Holland/Amsterdam is one of the oases in his desert, and from a Dutch point of view, he has chosen to live as a guest in his own country. Concerning this last opportunity, he may gratefully repeat Arendt's words: in the USA she could have 'the freedom of becoming a citizen without having to pay the price of assimilation.'[18] In this context, *homelessness* is related to the world and not to Holland, let alone an urban village like Amsterdam. In the 'Touareg way', he told his audience that Holland depends on him and not the reverse and that he himself was a god (and, therefore, independent of the Dutch 'pillar' saints and peasant gods).

In analogy to this social foundation of his art, Mulisch makes an art of his social life fully antagonistic to most of his oikoidal colleagues. He dwells in Holland but does not bother much with the local religious customs, nor with the peasant wars between the 'pillars' and, seen from a Dutch context, he consequently remains in the 'free space between the pillars'. Nor did he, therefore, exploit in some way or another his Jewish antecedents. In other words, similar to the world traveller, the author Cees Nooteboom, he did not develop his writer's identity in a constant struggle with Dutch oikoidal problems. He is, however, a much more political writer and, therefore, highly interested in Dutch political affairs *as part of world political developments.* Mulisch's political and artistic engagement is occupied by problems in Cuba, old and new Germany, Egypt or Israel, etc. and, only by chance, by problems in his Dutch birthplace, Haarlem. Certainly, it is not insignificant that his father was Austrian and his mother Belgian, from which he developed a reasonable hatred of nationalities.

From the very start of his career, it was this lifestyle and engagement which aroused among Dutch (or better: Amsterdam?) urban villagers a remarkable aggression and even hatred. The criticisms only partly derive from the usual *jalousie de métier,* although the anti-Mulisch campaigns certainly come from unsuccessful or small literati who are successful only thanks to some power position in one of the two relevant 'pillar' newspapers or other media. While Jewish antecedents are also at stake, anti-Jewish sentiments play their tricky role,

---

the ground. He is a pariah. The Israeli want us to disappear, even when we are citizens of this country, pay our taxes and send our sons to the army.' Theo Koelé in: *De Volkskrant,* Feb. 2, 1998. See also Els van Diggelen in: *NRC Handelsblad,* Oct. 18, 1997.
18. E. Young-Bruehl, p. XIV.

too. The main thrust, however, comes from the typical petty bourgeois attitudes against pariahs-outsiders.

After Mulisch gained a fully independent position, the kafkaesque situation arose that he was *accused* of being an outsider. This means, of course, that being an outsider is a sin in itself and that the *definition* is imposed only by (oikoidal) insiders. It could also mean that the accusers are of the opinion that Mulisch ought to be an insider, part of an oikoidal 'pillar', subject to the usual mediocrity of sedentary life or 'one of us'. 'They', however, do not favour a coercive 'conversion to assimilation' any longer but some sort of elimination.

Mulisch is *accused*, furthermore, of making a gentlemen's club, a conspiratorial undertaking, an isolated activity out of the control of the oikoidal conscience-police. Next, Mulisch has to act as if he is a victim. The accusers wrote:

> 'To arm himself against the evil of the outside world, he [Mulisch] had surrounded himself with a little group of intimates. The members were carefully selected, and they all occupied important positions in social life.' Another added: 'If this is true, Mulisch succeeded in creating his own establishment. No wonder that conflicts could be avoided and that it was not necessary for him to flee abroad.' [19]

When reading this, be aware that it is written in a 'quality newspaper' at the end of 1997 in, they say, the most democratic country of the world by, I presume, intelligent writers. Without any form of relativism and as if it is self-evident, one writes about '*a necessity to flee*'. From whom or for what? If you are not considered a criminal, in peacetime you need only flee from the taxman or from people who want to eliminate you in some way or another. Mulisch left the former option to his colleagues and is threatened, indeed, by the latter: here the mechanism is exposed of how to create an enemy-outsider out of thin air and, at the same time, the alleged legitimation to eliminate him. One of the paradoxes is that the one who is writing about Mulisch's flight is trying to defend him against 'the real villains'.[20] This shows how important is the manner in which one is defended (if it is the wrong way, it can be as disastrous or more so than a 'good attack') as well as the

---

19. The first citation is quoted by A. Heumakers ; the next one is from Heumakers himself.
20. There is no room for studying these paradoxes further. One of the major ones is the following: Heumakers is a defender or, at least, an 'unwilling executioner' of Heideggger's and Ernst Jünger's dubious heritage. He simply reproduces a highly ambiguous intellectual position of the Weimar period (*NRC-Handelsblad* 23-1-1998 and 30-1-1998). Furthermore, it is well-known that Hannah Arendt did not come to terms with her typical Heidegger relationship. I could not find any anti-Jünger statements like those of her husband (Blücher wrote about the post-war Jünger as 'versaute Sprengstoff-Literat', 'Elitegesindel', etc. See HAB, p.15.) In his Eichmann book Mulisch referred to both Heidegger and Jünger (Id., p.130 ff.) because they understood something essential of Nazism, its drive to self-destruction, and of the overriding influence of the technology. Contrary to Heumakers, Mulisch argued in a political sense about both.

relationship between attack and defense. In the 1930s numerous Christian, socialist or communist peoples and groups attacked antisemitism or National Socialism; most of them, however, used *race* as a self-evident concept or were organized nearly in the same way as the SA, Hitlerjugend, and what have you.

For every oikoidal accuser and perpetrator, the 'outside world' is a place of sin and evil as a matter of fact. However, for the one, in this case Harry Mulisch, who (like every Touareg) is accustomed to a life in a 'free space', this same 'outside world' is his home and, in principle, never associated with evil.[21] This world-home was called already by the more peaceful oikoidalists in Holland 'something apart .. too strange, too bizarre to become threatening or dangerous; one is surprised at it but, after a while, it leads to an astonishing fascination.'[22] The very words to create an evil place are already being used. It is true that Mulisch's 'world-home' is haunted by the *Jinns* who are able to attack people but are rarely harmful. Some foundation for a highly superficial criticism could be found in these facts.

The malicious oikoidalists who attack Mulisch, however, are accustomed to a more sophisticated use of weaponry against *their* outside world. In this case, they discovered that 'the enemy' had fortified himself behind the broad backs of 'carefully selected' and experienced body-builders. Implicitly, Mulisch is *accused* of sabotaging the judgement and of defending himself or securing his position. The typical oikoidal arrogance is related to the conviction that the one who is attacked by them must accept this as his fate. If he wants to defend himself, he is perceived as a spoil-sport or an unfair person. Now that Mulisch has surrounded himself by 'an establishment', the perpetrators might fear some sort of revenge because in *their own* petty bourgeois minds and oikos, they are always afraid of *their own* *establishment*. If in these aggressive oikoidal actions oikoidal fear-mechanisms become introduced, alleged outsiders could really fall on hard times, and start being hated. A new pariah is created.

Mulisch's group, however, is quite similar to Arendt's 'peer group' and 'tribe'.[23] The former contained people who together formed her 'thinking space' (Jaspers, Benjamin, Blumenfeld, Heidegger, Blücher and a few others). The latter was the name for her closest friends with whom she acted together in (public) debates, publications, etc. and who helped each other with large and small pro-blems. Everybody who is busy 'in the desert' has to rely on friends, who replace in several respects the (oikoidal) family, otherwise he/she will soon become dis-

---

21. It could be the 'space' about which Hannah Arendt wrote shortly before the Eichmann trial when she tried to locate the 'world' that was denied her as a Jew and as a woman: '...The world lies between people, and this in-between ... is today the object of the greatest concern and the most obvious upheaval in almost all the countries of the globe. Even where the world is still halfway in order, or is kept halfway in order, the public realm has lost the power of illumination which was originally part of its very nature'. Quoted by S. Benhabib, p. 13. See further below.
22. A. Heumakers, idem.
23. E. Young-Bruehl, p. X-XVI and *passim.*

oriented and helpless. 'Guest-friendship' is a holy law along with loyalty to friends (see chapter 2 and 3).

All this has a totally different impact than an establishment. This is an oikoidal institution which manipulates fears and conflicts, and rules and conspires in order to keep power over its subjects and make them fear the next punishment. Indeed, the establishment 'decides' who will be expelled from the country. Mulisch, I suppose, did not or does not need any protection from or against the authorities simply because he was not involved in any Dutch oikoidal, authoritative (authoritarian) undertaking.

Last but not least, one can ask which sin Mulisch has to commit to make him flee from Holland? In short, an image is created of an outside enemy by using the usual well-known terms of inside the oikos. In other words, Mulisch dwells in 'a space' neighbouring a 'house' with which he only deals in friendly neutral attitudes, but now people from this 'house' have started to shoot with the aim of killing him (in this case, happily, without any possibility of succeeding).

What motives could have inspired Mulisch's perpetrators? Apart from those mentioned above (jealousy, etc.), one could think of the following. On the same (low) level, one can find anger because a *money*-generating Mulisch disappeared from the oikos and with him opportunities for dividing spoils. This must be called an uncommercial motive: whether the 'product Mulisch' sells depends wholly on an 'outer-oikoidal' constellation in an artistic as well as a political or cultural sense. More irritating must be a *successful* Mulisch who is *uninterested in and not engaged in* internal oikoidal problems or with persons. This will ridicule those people simply through the expressed lack of interest. Why? Because *inside* the oikos hierarchy, neglected persons lose their status and oikoidal importance, whereupon eventually the entire 'pillar' or oikos can diminish in importance. Aggressively expressed neglect, therefore, can easily have the same status as an attack from outside. Against this, one has to 'defend' oneself, e.g. organize revenge.

Next, there is explicit *anti-intellectualism*. Thanks to the 'pillar' structure of society, there is no tradition whatsoever of factual discussions about *problems,* but there exists a whole gamut of rules and attitudes in talking and thinking about *persons* according to their positions in the oikoidal hierarchy. Real social, cultural, etc. problems are reduced to persons or derived from personal circumstances but nearly never treated in their own right. A major characteristic of intellectuals is that they are *talking and writing* first and foremost about *problems*. Therefore, *they* are seen as the problem-*makers*, and if they are Dutch recidivists, they will be gradually pushed outside the 'pillar'' into the 'empty space between the pillars', which is the meeting-place of all pariahs. The problems at stake (environment, production, energy, democracy, etc.) remain largely unsolved.

The one who is trying to meet compatriots in the inbetween space becomes more dangerous for the suspicious oikoidalists. Conspiratory activities come very quickly to mind as they are well-known from their experienced in-fighting tactics into some oikoidal hierarchy. These are supported by a highly selective hear-both-sides practice in the public media. Only 'pillar' authorities and VIPs have these opportunities, others by chance or, mostly, never. Already in his Eichmann book Mulisch reminds us of the cowardly behaviour of most Dutch people during the war; it is reproduced in the attitudes of what are called 'intellectuals' in this country. An excellent example, Menno Ter Braak, not only wrote in a burst of self-criticism about 'the minimum value of the intellect in [Dutch] intellectuals', but he also advised the European intellectuals to follow the Dutch variant of the English *muddling through,* namely, the 'give and take as a unity of opportunism'. He committed suicide on the first day of the German occupation.[24]

A beloved weapon against problem-'making' intellectuals is *keeping silent* if the 'enemy' lives its intellectual life only in the space inbetween the 'pillars'. The *Rufmord* is chosen if *cases* are too well founded to be beaten or personalities rather 'big'. Apart from this, several forms of deprivation of income are always available. They are all mixed with (oral or written) *accusations* of being an outsider of the cosy oikoidal world of the 'pillars'. Even a Mulisch is, in the end, defenceless against concerted attacks from inside the 'pillars' which will, first, result in the gradually reduction of his 'free space between the pillars' in which his Dutch house is erected. We must expect, however, that the present accusers are not strong enough to succeed or that Harry Mulisch is a bit too 'big' for them.[25]

---

24. H. Mulisch, *De zaak 40/61,* p. 171-173.
25. The relevance and validity of this Mulisch analysis (written in November 1997 and nothing altered), is proved in a most dramatic way in March 2000. Mulisch was threatened in a higly symbolic and disturbing way by means of a call to burn publicly his last book (800,000 copies!). This apocalyptic call came from a rather famous Dutch cabaret performer, Freek de Jonge, and received international press attention, not the least because Mulisch immediately referred to Goebbels campaigns. De Jonge falsely understood Mulisch's book as a defence of a well-known player, the (invented Jew) Jules Croiset. During the Dutch row (1987) about Rainer Werner Fassbinder's provocative play, *Der Müll, die Stadt und der Tod,* this Croiset had written several threatening letters to himself and famous friends (including Freek de Jonge!), and organized his own kidnapping to alarm the public for an antisemitic conspiracy or something like that. Now, in March 2000 Mulisch used this story for his booklet *Het theater, de brief en de waarheid* [The Theatre, the Letter, and the Truth] (Amsterdam: De Bezige Bij, 2000). The urban village comic De Jonge, son of a reformed Protestant clergyman and typical middle class moralist, aggressively misunderstood the clue of Mulisch's highly dialectical story. He even was blinded for Mulisch's explicit explanation at the end that the story has 'nearly nothing to do with his [Croiset's] adventures' (p. 85) *in combination with* the denial at the very start: 'Who wants to be understood, does not provide an explanation.' It was sad that after all protests De Jonge insisted to burn symbolically a copy of Mulisch's book during all his performances. Kousbroek again commented: 'Long live Freek de Jonge, but he is yet a son of a clergyman.' He also attacks Heumakers on his catholic background (*NRC Handelsblad* March,17, 2000) whereupon Heumakers reacts as prescribed in the pillar-competition: he starts *defending* Mulisch (idem, March 10, 2000) and this time unequivocal.

*

The *Woody Allen Bloom complex* shows the intricacies of internal contradictions in which arguments from elsewhere are implemented to create and attack insider-pariahs, 'incasts' or parasites. This complex demonstrates the possibilities and difficulties with which, for example, a Jewish immigrant is confronted in the USA. They still refer to the deep racial antipathies of the white oikoidal and privileged domains with the 'Woody Allen-mobile 'lifestyle' or the 'Allan Bloom-petty bourgeois' variants. Arendt, indeed, described it in one of the *Leitmotive* of my book: 'it is possible to assimilate only by assimilating to antisemitism also'.

It is Bloom's one-sidedness which prevented him from seeing how his 'herd-model' also referred to the classical American scene of the cowboy culture, its typical macho and individualistic market behaviour, which in itself referred to the highly popular gangster and entertainment culture as well. He, furthermore, failed to discuss the very important *practical* absence of one ideological framework to which the immigrating ideologies must be subdued. It is one main reason why the American ideological scene is so anachronistic and rigid compared with the original European. At the same time it is this loose structure of ideological back-yards which gives the opportunities of 'a space in-between' as in the Dutch case. That famous 'entrance ticket to American civilization' provides, therefore, for the immigrating and assimilating Jewish European a harder in-fight but more opportunities than in Old Europe. From where they came, shopkeepers' ideals and not Rothchilds' values prevailed; the American rigidity drove most of them into the same environment of a Hollywood-*shtetl* life (Anatevka) or worse, but quite a few took advantage of the opportunities of the 'space in-between'.[26]

The Mulisch case demonstrates a quite different phase in the process: how and why outsider-pariahs are created and attacked. Above, the question was posed of

---

26. See as a typical representative N. Podhoretz (note 27 ch. 7). In J. Melnick, *A right to sing the blues. African Americans, Jews, and American popular song* (Harvard: Harvard University Press, 1999) the 'Black-Jewish relationship' is strongly critized for its many racial preconditions. It seems that from 1900 onwards Jews in the entertainment business 'reorganize Jewishness as a species of whiteness'; it is thought that their 'hazy racial status' gave them special closeness to blacks (Jews became America's predominant 'blackface' performers!). Melnick states however: 'While leading African Americans seemed most interested in achieving basic civil rights gains through cultural productions, Jews looked to culture as a vehicle to enter the privileged domains of whiteness, American style'. Quoted in J. Cobb, Whose Promised Land? in: *TLS*, August 6 (1999), p.35. At present this 'Black-Jewish relationship' has become totally absurd now blacks claim a much larger 'Holocaust' than the Jews in the centuries-long slavery. They also discovered that many slave plantations were run by Jews! Isaac Deutscher p. 43 pointed long ago to 'the other Negro, a white-skinned one ... in the Southern States more often than not it is the Jew who is one of the most fanatical upholders of white supremacy.' It is another fact illustrating the *Hofjuden complex* and the problem of the fanaticism of *conversos/ Marranos*. See also A. Dershowitz, p. 118-135.

281

whether Mulisch himself could be called a pariah. I have to deny this on several grounds which form part of my criticism of Arendt's pariah theory and pariah practice, but now we obtain our first glimpse of what Adorno called 'the secret Gypsy of world history'.

My thesis is that Mulisch is not a pariah because he is in a socio-artistical sense fully unassimilated and in a socio-cultural and political sense sufficiently un-assimilated; he, therefore, succeeded in creating his own space as an intellectual nomad independent of a national Oikos. Mulisch also demonstrates an important variant of Anders's thesis quoted at the beginning of this part of the study, inasmuch as his case elucidates the difficult understanding of some *necessary* relation between a 'nomadic' and an oikoidal constellation.

From a theoretical point of view, the outsider-pariah is to be considered as a 'device' for diverting the internal contradictions and dilemmas of the Oikos externally, whereas the insider-pariah (parasite) has everything to do with 'cleaning up' the own 'House-Oikos' (to get rid of the 'garbage').[27] Together, they also form two sides of antisemitism as developed from about 1870 onwards; its biologism provides criteria for racially cleaning up the *persons* (parasites as well as outsiders) and, subsequently, does not solve the real problems.

The following chapter will explain these thoughts further. In the discussion so far, I have already elaborated on many elements of Arendt's position and its context. Her exploitation of Weber's pariah concept can now be described without further digression.

---

27. The most intrigueing affair in which this is demonstrated is what now must be called 'the first phase of the Shoah with all possibilities to become a Holocaust' namely, the long-term *international* (and not only German) efforts to transport all Jews to Madagascar. Several writers, in particular Götz Aly, have written about the German side of the Plan. H. Jansen, however, could analyse for the first time in all possible detail this whole process of planning and non-execution of the Madagascar Plan from English, German, Polish, French, etc. sides. H. Jansen, *Het Madagascar Plan. De voorgenomen deportatie van Europese joden naar Madagascar* (Den Haag: SDU, 1996). Hannah Arendt, *Eichmann*, p. 108 ff. and many others erroneously thought that this plan was a smoke screen for the real '*Endlösung*' but that is not the case. Most researchers did not see the importance of the plan, like Yehuda Bauer or Eberhard Jäckel in HH, p. 21, 25; see also Charles Sydnor in HH, p.169 ff. If there should be a connection between '1492' and the Shoah, then one can find it here: now many masters wanted to get rid of their obedient servants and quarrelled so long among each other that the time was over. A Madagascar Plan makes it crystal clear why it is necessary, as I proposed, to study the internal European history from ca. 1870 onwards on the subject: why and how 'one' wanted to get rid of the non-conformists.

9. CONFESSIONS OF A PRUSSIAN JEWESS

The theory of the pariah complex, thus, is part and parcel of a 19th century French, English and German (*Bildungsbürger*) theory about the place of Jews in world history. In turn, this theory belongs to a more general theory of non-conformist behaviour of social or cultural groups who are internally or externally 'on the move'; the criteria used in these theories are derived from European sedentary elite ideologies about the way society should be organized.

Weber was the first to develop the pariah concept properly (in his view at least) and apply it in a rather universal way. It cannot be seen as a regrettable aberration of Weber's vast oeuvre. Nowadays, it is used by sociologists and related sciences as a general concept;[1] philosophers and historians also celebrate it as an adequate concept with world historical dimensions or even as suitable to characterize local American class relations.

Weber may be the theoretician of the concept, but it is Hannah Arendt who made it popular, politicized it to the utmost, and gave it flesh and bone in a literal sense by stating in several ways: '*I am a pariah!*' In addition, likewise, other people

---

1. For instance G. Hartfiel, K-H. Hillmann, *Wörterbuch der Soziologie* (Stuttgart: Kröner, 1982) p. 567. In the newest edition of the *Lexikon zur Soziologie* edited by W. Fuchs-Heinritz et al. (Opladen: Westdeutscher Verlag, 1995) there are entries on *Paria, Paria-Intellektualismus* and *Pariareligion* (p. 487) as developed by Weber. And in, for instance, the weekly *Die Zeit* (6-9-1996 p. 8) you can read about P*aria-Staaten* and *Paria-Regimes*, i.e. pejorative expressions for countries like Iran, Iraq and Libya which are seen as fundamentalist killer states (see also chapter 1). A. Giddens in his *Sociology* (London: Polity, 1995), p. 212 referred to Weber, Jewish pariahs and a new universal concept 'pariah group'. He first defined Jews as pariahs only for medieval Europe; on p. 746 they were already pariahs 'throughout much of European history'! Strange is Tim Ingold's excellent *Companion Encyclopedia of Anthropology* (London: Routledge, 1997), p. 715: '.. many *ethnie*, ... have survived for long periods under foreign rule, notably as "pariah castes" like the Jews in medieval Europe ..' Another relevant reference book is *The Dictionary of Anthropology* , Ed. T. Barfield (Oxford: Blackwell, 1997); it is the strangest one at issue. Under 'Pariah groups' (p. 348) appears only the cross-reference 'See middleman minorities'. Under this lemma you can find the following definition: 'Middleman minorities are ethnic groups recruited to a country by those in power to fill a gap in the economic or labor structure. The term describes the economic and social position these groups occupy in society ... In early anthropology and sociology such groups were referred to as "pariahs" and "guest peoples" (M. Weber 1952: 3) or "strangers" (Simmel 1950: 402). Historic examples of this phenomenon include the Jews and Gypsies in Europe .. '! Here everything is wrong or misunderstood.

judged Arendt as 'a self-conscious pariah in the Jewish community.'[2] In the latter case, her Jewishness also became problematic.

Pariah and Parvenu

Arendt is one of the most interesting mediators between the leading 19th century ideas and ours due to her profound 'German fixation', her large influence on American political philosophy, and critical interventions into matters of the utmost importance for 20th century people. The present Arendt hype was triggered by the publication of her highly interesting correspondence with Karl Jaspers, Kurt Blumenfeld, Mary McCarthy, Herman Broch, Martin Heidegger, etc. She is a woman who not only can match the best political writers in our time but also express herself in a 'womanly' manner. It is refreshing how she time and again broke through those barriers academic men always erect to save their status and mediocrity.[3]

However, I do not intend to elaborate here on her biography, philosophical works with which I am not familiar, her love affair with Heidegger, or the tragic *Eichmann in Jerusalem* row.[4] They reveal how *Rufmord* mechanisms work on an international scale and how Arendt's 'space in-between' shrank considerably. These questions are all more or less well covered in the existing literature. Here we will only deal with the origin, meaning and use of her pariah concept. After what has been mentioned so far, we can reduce even this treatment to the bare essentials.[5] The first question is how Arendt defined the pariah.

---

2. S. Benhabib, p. 39.

3. It is Jennifer Ring who addresses the gender theme in Arendt's biography and writings in her *The Political Consequences of Thinking* (note 6 ch. 7) in a critical sense: Arendt shows a 'flight from femininity' in her scholarly work which should correspond with a 'denial of a major part of her identity': Judaism; Arendt was looking for a 'parvenu legitimacy' (p.237); etc. Reason for all this should lie in the 'fact' that 'the model of scholarly legitimacy for Arendt was male and Christian' (p. 284). I disagree with Ring in all respects, but I do not want a direct confrontation with her interesting argumentation. What follows must be good enough.

4. For the Eichmann row see *AJC*, p. 402-479; *BF*, p. 81-155; *ABB*, p. 513-541; J. Ring chapters 2 and 4; R. Bernstein, chapters 7 and 8; E. Young-Bruehl, chapter 8. See notes 18 ch. 7 and 5 ch. 8 above. Concerning the Heidegger affair I only pose my thesis here: In her long (love) relation with Heidegger Hannah Arendt found her liberation in the understanding and criticism of his concept of *Heimatlosigkeit*. See next chapter.

5. Up to the present the impact and background of Arendt's concept are always underestimated and ill treated. The best analyses of the subject so far come from R. Bernstein, p. 14-46 and L.J.Disch, p. 172-204. Even these two knew next to nothing about the Weber connexion, which partly explains why they are sometimes perplexed and troubled by Arendt's texts.

She had used the term before, but in April 1944 it was fully developed for the first time in an article in *Jewish Social Studies* entitled *The Jew as Pariah: A Hidden Tradition*. She says:[6]

'That the status of the Jews in Europe has been not only that of an oppressed people but also of what Max Weber has called a 'pariah people' is a fact ... It is therefore not surprising that ... Jewish poets, writers and artists should have been able to evolve the concept of the pariah as a human type – a concept of supreme importance for the evaluation of mankind in our day and one which has exerted upon the gentile world an influence in strange contrast to the spiritual and political ineffectiveness which has been the fate of these men among their own brethren. Indeed, the concept of the pariah has become traditional, even though the tradition be but tacit and latent, and its continuance automatic and unconscious. Nor need we wonder why: for over a hundred years the same basic conditions have obtained and evoked the same basic reaction.'[7]

Thus, Arendt ascribes the concept to Weber and states that its status is one of supreme importance for mankind. She must have gained the information about Weber's concept from his *Ancient Judaism*, and she may have been led to it by one of her spiritual fathers, Karl Jaspers, who was a fanatic Weber adept (see below), and/or Kurt Blumenfeld,[8] a German Zionist leader. However, she also cited historical sources which formed 'the basis out of which the concept was created and out of which it was progressively developed'. This tradition is traced back to Salomon Maimon in the 18th century and endured until Franz Kafka in the early 20th century. Arendt did not provide more information about the origin of 'her' concept and did not inform the reader about the contradictions between the two sources. Let us now look at it in more detail.

In her sociological and historical understanding, Arendt used the concept together with *parvenu* which, therefore, became a real counter-concept. The best description of this 'type' is found in Arendt's study about Rahel Varnhagen. The Jewish Rahel (1771-1833) married a Prussian aristocrat Varnhagen and 'arrived' in this way, leaving 'no trace of her infamous birth': she became a parvenu. Arendt defined this situation as follows.

6. Reprinted in *JP*. p. 67-91. After writing and publishing this article in 1944, Hannah Arendt reprinted it in the journal *Reconstructionist* (1959). The development of her thinking up to this article of 1944 can be reconstructed thanks to the recent publication of her AUFBAU-articles. AUFBAU was an emigrant journal written in German and published in New York during the World War. See H. Arendt, *Vor Antisemitismus ist man nur noch auf dem Monde sicher. Beiträge für die deutsch-jüdische Emigrantenzeitung 'Aufbau', 1941-45.* Ed. Marie Luise Knott (München: Piper, 2000).
7. *JP*, p. 68.
8. See for Kurt Blumenfeld (1884-1963) E. Young-Bruehl, p. 70-74, 121ff.

'All parvenus are familiar with Varnhagen's impulse, all those who must climb by fraud into a society, a rank, a class, not theirs by birthright. Making a strenuous effort to love, where there is no alternative but obedience, is more productive of good results than simple and undisguised servility. In "tracking down the good qualities" of superiors they hope to purge themselves of inevitable but intolerable resentment. Those who are resolutely determined to rise, to "arrive", must early accustom themselves to anticipating the stage they hope to attain by simulating voluntary appreciation; must early set their sights higher than the blind obedience ... as if they were performing freely .. the things that are in any case expected of hirelings and subordinates. ... By this fraud the pariah prepares society to accept his career as a parvenu.'[9]

The classic parvenu seems to be the freedman Trimalchio in Petronius' *Satyricon* (better: *Satyrica*, ca. AD 60). This ex-slave displays vast wealth in a vulgar and tasteless ostentation. The satirist Petronius reminds us through Trimalchio's affectation of culture, his superstition, and his maudlin lapses into his natural vulgarity of the Roman petty bourgeois roots of this *nouveau riche*. Shakespeare's Fallstaff is another famous example of the parvenu. In the 19th century the real bourgeois parvenus came into existence. In my view we have analysed many acts of parvenus in chapter 5 and thoughts and, probably, attitudes of a brilliant parvenu in the first chapter. The reasons given for Momigliano's tragic and ambiguous opposition to Weber's pariah concept could, in the end, be understood from the angle of this parvenu-fraud.

Within the framework of my analysis, the parvenu position is a *rite de passage* for becoming, among others, acceptable and trustworthy for the oikoidal power. From this it follows that the pariah still can follow an alternative path, and at least lives in an *in-between situation*. Rahel Varnhagen was well aware of her parvenu duties after she received rank, title and acknowledgement: to do, for everybody to see, the sort of thing she could not in any case bear to give up doing, acting 'as a Prussian woman; and I was modest, helpful, good, gentle – and popular – and that was credited to all Prussian women ... And I had the absolutely infinite satisfaction

9. *Rahel Varnhagen. The Life of a Jewess.* (Leo Baeck Institute), London 1957 p. 162. The expanded German translation titled *Rahel Varnhagen. Lebensgeschichte einer deutschen Jüdin aus der Romantik*. München, 1959 p. 186. A new English edition, RV, has just been published and announced as 'the first complete edition'. Arendt's book was written around 1933 (except the last two chapters) but could not be published before the war. Earlier drafts of the manuscript were strongly criticised by Karl Jaspers (AJC, p. 10, 192-196) in a letter of 23-8-1952 as well as by Hermann Broch in a letter of 14-12-1947 (HAB, p.65 ff.). Both, in the end, applauded publication of the book. Their criticism must have hampered the publication. The following quotations come from the 1997 edition (p. 237 ff.) which is annotated and introduced well. Hannah Arendt nor her present editor, Liliane Weissberg, discovered the Nazi reception of the Varnhagen history within the context of the highly antisemitic Christlich-Deutsche Tischgesellschaft in the dissertation H.K. Krüger, *Berliner Romantik und Berliner Judentum* (Bonn: Röhrscheid Verlag, 1939). K. compared Rahel not only with Brentano but with Heinrich von Kleist as well.

that at last I stood on such a pedestal that the good I did also counted for some-thing."[10] In nothing and 'not for a single minute' did the parvenu dare to be himself any longer.

The parvenu phase is not the only assimilatory element and is certainly not confined to Jews but is a rather *general* way of assimilating to and climbing into an oikoidal hierarchy. It belongs to the daily experiences of the many new immigrants and minorities within American and European societies. Like many other climbers, Jews must shed their history or religion like a snake does his skin. As long as they do not succeed, the memory of their (recent) past remains clear and unsublimated.

Modern sociologists already know that assimilation is not a unitary process and that it has to be studied on the individual and group level, including their full political and social context.[11] However, they are in need of more sophisticated thoughts about this subject, which can be found through Arendt's pariah concept. She disclosed, for instance, that it is possible for a Jew to assimilate only by assimilating antisemitism as well. In other words, one comes from 'abroad' attracted by the oikoidal glamour and gold which could be reached only when accepting the oikoidal iron and garbage as well. Many or most of the climbers in the oikoidal hierarchy found only the latter, and compared with the world they had left, their confrontation was lost by definition (see the *Woody Allen Bloom Complex*).

The pariah is, generally, formed due to his starting situation: one can become a pariah after one is thrown out of the 'environment of origin'; one can remain a pariah thanks to certain characteristics of the 'environment of origin'; or one can still be a pariah because one is not yet properly accepted in a 'new environment'. In these cases the pariah's identity must be negative as it is defined by the loss of the old without yet arriving at a new 'house'. I am afraid that a pariah must be always defined, at very least, as someone who has an anti-identity from the standpoint of the several 'houses' or competing groups of pariahs.

Through Arendt's eyes, Rahel Varnhagen provides us with a good demonstra-tion of this. Her non-Jewish pen-friend, Pauline Wiesel, was a rather famous

---

10. *RV*, p. 241. The historical background for the fate of RV and many of her later 'companions in distress' (men and women) is sketched in the excellent M. Kaplan, *Jüdisches Bürgertum. Frau, Familie und Identität im Kaiserreich* (Hamburg: Dölling und Galitz, 1997) which sketches, by the way, the direct background of Hannah Arendt's own education as a Prussian Jewess. Kaplan concludes that this Jewish bourgeoisie eagerly looked for respectability of and inroads into the German bourgeoisie avoiding all acts and thoughts which could provoke antisemitic reactions. From earlier writings (Jacob Katz for instance) a more farreaching relationship between an original religious Jewish family ideology and the German one is demonstrated. For both "The House" (Oikos) symbolized not only showplace of status and identity, but also the continuity in the positions of men and women. Therefore, as Hermann Glaser puts it, they all were 'besonders wertkonservativ'. (*Die Zeit*, 6-6-1997). Which one is the real original House-ideology remains to be seen. See my: Über die Faszination des ''Haus-Konzeptes'' in: *Geschichte und Gesellschaft*, 22 (1996), p. 221-242.

11. E. Cashmore (Ed.), *Dictionary of Race and Ethnic relations*, p. 37 ff.

courtisan in the highest aristocratic circles, a person of the worst reputation, but with an outspoken *non-conformistic* behaviour. Pauline was the only woman Rahel had ever thought her equal: 'One who knows nature and the world as do we ..., who knows everything in advance as do we ... who is surprised at nothing unusual and who is eternally preoccupied with the mysteriousness of the usual ...'[12] With 'we' she undoubtedly meant 'the Jews'. Rahel accepted Pauline even when she tried to seduce her husband because Rahel believed they belonged together. Like herself, Pauline was 'bankrupt, although in an opposite way and with the greatest courage.' At the very moment Rahel 'arrived over the hill', she contacted Pauline anew so that her parvenu 'status' oscillated towards the pariah-rebel position. Arendt comments that

> 'Pauline exercised utter freedom in placing herself outside the pale of respectable society because her temperamental and untamable nature would submit to no conventions. Her courage was her naturalness, which was supported and strengthened by all those who fled from society to her, and made a free life possible for her.'[13]

Here Arendt makes clear that 'pariah' and 'parvenu' are not at all 'Jewish concepts' as most commentators think: temporarily or permanently, Jews and non-Jews, men and women, all can become parvenus as well as pariahs. In my view, it is of crucial importance that Arendt also sketches conditions of a liberation through the *locus operandi* ('outside the pale'l) and qualities of Pauline. Indeed, 'freedom' is the keyword here. This meant for Rahel Varnhagen rebellion against her social obligation of making a fraudulent self-identification and a search for an opportunity of saying wholeheartedly, 'I consider myself Rahel and nothing else.' This was a false hope because Rahel

> 'had had to sacrifice the freer life of the pariah ... If one had freedom one was, in the eyes of that society, always in "wretched situations". ... After all, the much-praised freedom of the outcast against society was rarely more than complete

---

12. *RV*, p. 242. Seyla Benhabib (p. 17) mentions Pauline Wiesel only in passing. Like me, R.Bernstein (p.29) sees Rahel's identification with Pauline Wiesel as crucial for the understanding of Arendt's aims. He, however, is disappointed because Arendt 'has very little to say about (Jewishness and Judaism), and what she does say is hardly convincing.' His feminist colleague, Jennifer Ring, even has 'an unfashionable disinterest' (p.2) in Arendt's *Rahel Varnhagen*. This is curious since Ring focuses upon 'Arendt's central Jewish concepts ... the pariah and parvenu, the outsider and the assimilationist' (p.3). Ring intends to find their meaning in Arendt's *The Human Condition* and, in particular, in *Thinking*, the first volume of *The Life of the Mind*. This seems to me an act of scholarly sado masochism because in these writings you can hardly find even the concepts. In my view, they deal with the *consequences* for public political discourse of overcoming the pariah constellation. Ring as well as Bernstein did not see how Arendt was struggling with a specific freedom problem.
13. *RV*, p. 244.

freedom to feel despair over being "nothing ... not a sister, not a sweetheart, not a wife, not even a citizen.""[14]

Gratitude helped hold everything in check; gratitude, excessive attachment, is the typical vice of the pariah. This longing would become a fault if it were not accompanied by another characteristic of a pariah. In an oikoidal society based upon privilege, pride of birth and arrogance of title, 'the pariah instinctively discovers human dignity in general long before Reason has made it the foundation of morality.'[15] Parvenu Rahel Varnhagen's pariah qualities opened up a loophole for her: it was the 'very loophole through which the pariah, precisely because he is an outcast, can see life as a whole and ... can attain to his '*great* love for free existence'. This must be the perspective Arendt opens up when confessing '*I am a pariah*', but it also brings in other dimensions of pariah life which have to be considered next.

HANNAH ARENDT, PARIAH

In her 1944 article Arendt first described several phases within the pariah tradition:

> 'As long as the Jews of Western Europe were pariahs only in a social sense, they could find salvation, to a large extent by becoming parvenus. Insecure as their position may have been, they could nevertheless achieve a modus vivendi by combining ... "inner slavery" with "outward freedom". Moreover, those who deemed the price too high could still remain mere pariahs, calmly enjoying the freedom and untouchability of outcasts. .... The life of the pariah ... was by no means senseless. But today it is. Today, the bottom has dropped out of the old ideology. The pariah Jew and the parvenu Jew are in the same boat ... Both are branded with the same mark; both alike are outlaws.'[16]

In fact, Arendt points to the following situation arising from the Holocaust and Shoah. In the dictatorial oikoidal regime, the pressure on non-conformistic behaviour is heightened to the extreme so that, as much as possible, everything and everybody have to become uniform (*gleichgeschaltet*) within a hierarchical order. All sorts of older social, economic or cultural diversifications must be eradicated under the new rules of biological-organic dictatorship which defines and creates its *own non-conformistic behaviour* fit to be eliminated wholesale. That is the reason why even the relevant differences between (Jewish) parvenu and pariah disappeared, while the content or intention of these concepts was replaced by the biologically oriented *parasite* (harmful animals which everybody is allowed to exterminate).

---

14. Idem, p. 247, 248.
15. Idem, p. 248.
16. JP, p. 89, 90.

However, after the dictatorial oikoidal social and political pressure vanished, pariah-parvenu reappeared as a general connotation, and Arendt asked herself whether this was appropriate, for example, within the framework of settled and aggressive Zionism. The pariah and parvenu, indeed, were forced into the same boat by the Nazis, but why couldn't 'Auschwitz' lead to alternative thinking and practice? In her eyes the (Jewish) pariahs she met in the USA were not liberated but had only moved from the one parvenu or *schnorrer* place into the other.

Within the framework of her criticism of Zionism, she could have hypothesised: after 'Auschwitz' it is senseless to start thinking again of a pariah Zion and act accordingly; not only because the Nazis had sunk the pariah/parvenu boat from which only a few had been rescued, but in particular because the idea and practice of a pariah-Zion were highly compromised. In addition, for a new pariah country there is only a future as a parvenu state, i.e. a state which always has to live under the umbrella of another and gentile oikoidal power, 'the pseudo-sovereignty of a Jewish state'.[17] After Auschwitz, Arendt as a rescued European Jew could only think of trying to rescue her mind and that of her rescued fellows within a worldwide and organized communication in order to recuperate and find a new identity.

A real help for this search is Arendt's remarkable differentiation of the pariah concept. She characterised four forms which the pariah concept had assumed. In each, an alternative portrayal of the Jewish people is expressed: Heinrich Heine's *schlemihl* and 'lord of dreams' (*Traumweltherrscher*); Bernard-Lazare's 'conscious pariah'; Charlie Chaplin's grotesque portrayal of the suspect; and Franz Kafka's poetic vision of the fate of the man of goodwill. Together they define the concept as well as the pariah.

Among these, Bernard-Lazare undoubtedly exercised the most profound influence on Arendt's political stand. About Chaplin, for example, Arendt's editor remarked: 'Chaplin has recently declared that he is of Irish and Gipsy descent, but he has been selected for discussion because, even if not himself a Jew, he has epitomized in an artistic form a character born of the Jewish pariah mentality.'[18]

---

17. JP, p. 192. No one can deny that Arendt predicted the future of Israel remarkably well as one read on p. 187 ff. her analysis starting with 'There is very little doubt about the final outcome of an allout war between Arabs and Jews ...'

18. Idem, p. 69, note 1. Another editor remarked: 'It is not in the last resort thanks to the Nazi publication *Juden sehen dich an* (1933) and the film *Der ewige Jude* that Charlie Chaplin is defined a Jew. ... Chaplin himself never told that he was not a Jew, because during the NS-period this could be perceived as a contribution to antisemitism. ... Later, Hannah Arendt did not stop thinking of Chaplin as a Jew. In a letter to [the publisher] Klaus Wagenbach (16th of July 1964) she complains that "Chaplin obstinately refuses to be a Jew" (Arendt inheritance, Library of Congress, Container 32)'. See H. Arendt, *Vor Antisemitismus*, p. 27, note 17. This is a good example of how a 'Jew' was invented by the Nazis and how this was accepted as a truth even by people like Arendt. It could be a good example as well of how the boosting practices ('the best intellectuals, musicians, filmmakers, etc., etc. are Jews'), so familiar to all people busy to make up arrears, are internalized. Recently JP was translated in German and published as H. Arendt, *Die verborgene Tradition. Essays* (Frankfurt a.M.:

The example is a significant proof of the effectiveness of Nazi propaganda, and in its typical boosting-element it is an interesting illustration of the *Woody Allen Bloom Complex* in the USA as well.

It would be worthwhile to deal extensively with Heine's and Kafka's contributions to the pariah concept, but this would take too much room and can be skipped in our fundamental exploration of the problems in question.

Bernard-Lazare,[19] then, taught Arendt to differentiate between parvenus and pariahs; to hate the former (with the Rothchilds as prototype) and to situate him/her in a 'social realm'; to accept the latter as a good metaphor for her own identity and to place him/her in a 'political realm' as the basis for a possible revolutionary change. According to Bernard-Lazare, every Jew should come out openly as a rebellious or 'conscious' pariah since it is his duty to resist oppression. As such he has not only to fight the 'gentilic' oppression but also the organized opposition of the rich, privileged Jews, called by Arendt and many others the 'nabobs and philantropists'. 'Nabob', like 'pariah', is derived from Mogul-Indian society (a nabob was a high government official), and around 1800 its meaning had already changed into 'one who has returned from India with a large fortune' (OED) earned in many cases with tax-fraud, repression of indigenous work forces, exploitation of resources, etc.

She may have first learned about pariahs/parvenus as acting persons through Bernard-Lazare, but Weber must have added the confrontation with Arendt's German culture, its antisemitism and anti-Judaism. Most likely, the way Arendt treated Weber's views is symptomatic of her treatment of the contemporary main antagonists of German culture like Nietzsche, Heidegger, Mannheim or Jaspers.

What, in fact, is Arendt's relationship to Weber and his concept? Part of the answer is quite simple. There is no indication whatsoever that Arendt played with the Weberian concept as she must have learned to do in her philosophical studies. In addition, it is not likely that she discovered in Weber's *Ancient Judaism* the many indications of a more differentiated usage, let alone its antisemitic orientation (see chapter 3). Weber himself, however, and specific other writings received Arendt's attention, but her Weber reception remained highly ambiguous. In particular, in her correspondence with Karl Jaspers (1883-1969), we are struck by a long and profound discussion about Weber. Let us follow this debate in some detail, to uncover Jasper's impact on Arendt.

Already in his youth, Jaspers was a romantic Weber admirer, and his awe remained unshakeable. The first confrontation with this philosophically boundless

Jüdischer Verlag, 2000). Its editor, in his wisdom, censored this note 1 on p. 69 of JP away!
19. See also Arendt's article from 1942, Herzl and Lazare, in: JP, p. 125-131, p. 76 ff. Already in 1945 she wanted to publish an English anthology of his writings which appeared in 1948 as *Job's Dungheap*. See ABK, p. 25; E. Young-Bruehl, p. 121 ff.; R. Bernstein, *passim*. For Lazare and his context see also chapter 1 above.

Heldenverehrung was shocking for Arendt. On the first day of 1933, she wrote to the professor after he had sent her his book, *Max Weber. Deutsches Wesen,*[20] published by a National Socialist publisher:

> 'It does not bother me that you portray Max Weber as the great German but, rather, that you find the "German essence" in him and identify that essence with "rationality and humanity originating in passion". I have the same difficulty with that as I do with Max Weber's imposing patriotism itself.'[21]

As if frightened of her own words, Hannah continued:

> 'You will understand that I as a Jew ... do not have to keep my distance as long as you are talking about "the meaning of the German world power" and its mission for the "culture of the future". I can identify with this German mission, though I do not feel myself unquestioningly identical with it. For me, Germany means my mother tongue, philosophy, and literature...'

Jaspers had written about Weber's real belief in the German *Volk* and his ability to develop 'German political thinking' (something different from 'nationalistic talk', he assumed), and quoted the following Weber text:

> 'For the resurrection of Germany in all its old mastery, without doubt, I should be prepared to form an alliance with every power in the world including the devil himself, except the power of stupidity [*Macht der Dummheit*].'[22]

Hannah Arendt commented on this exclamation:

> 'I am obliged to keep my distance, I can neither be for nor against when I read Max Weber's wonderful sentence where he says that to put Germany back on her

---

20. K. Jaspers, *Max Weber. Deutsches Wesen im politischen Denken, im Forschen und Philosophieren* (Oldenburg i.O.: Stalling, 1932). It was reprinted directly after the war in 1946 with a different subtitle and remained unchanged also in later reprints (München: Piper, 1958). This hagiography must be the reason why after 1945 Weber could become Saint Max in Germany and the USA. In 1958 he could still start this reprint with a new preface beginning with: 'Max Weber (1863-1920) was the greatest German of our time'! Whether one (dis)likes these sentimental exclamations, one knows for sure that something not arguable reasonably to be consumed has to follow: sheer demagogy after Hannah Arendt already had protested against it 25 years earlier.

21. AJC, p.16.

22. K. Jaspers, *Max Weber*, (1932) p.35 and (1958), p. 40. Jaspers gave as the ultimate conclusion of Weber's thought: 'Der Adel des Menschen und die weltpolitische Geltung der Nation – nicht eines ohne das andere – bedeutet ihm den Willen: daß die späteren Menschen uns als ihre Ahnen kennen; nicht notwendig im Sinne von Rasse und Abstammung, sondern so, wie wir die Griechen kennen, denen wir unser Sein verdanken.' Later, Jaspers knew how to incorporate Weber in the harshest forms of Cold War ideology in idem, *Lebensfragen der deutschen Politik* (München: DTV, 1963) p.282-293.

feet he would form an alliance with the devil himself. And it is this sentence which seems to me to reveal the critical point here.'

Just two days later, Jaspers, who with many others seriously considered his whole life long the question 'was wäre geworden, wenn Max Weber Deutschland geführt hätte?'[23] ('what would have happened if Max Weber had led Germany?') castigated the 25 years' younger student:

> 'How tricky this business with the German character is! I find it odd that you as a Jew want to set yourself apart from what is German.' And: 'I made the attempt ... to give (the word "German") ethical content through the figure of Max Weber. That attempt (is) successful only if you, too, could say: That's the way it is. I want to be a German.'[24]

As a German, in the end, Hannah Arendt did not make much trouble. She continued her Weber letter and her last quotation with

> 'I wanted to convey this reservation to you, although it faded as I read further. ... I hardly need tell you that this book prompts the reader to read Weber himself ... it vividly conveys his intellectual power.'

That was precisely what Jaspers wanted. He apologized for choosing the odd formulation (which was criticized) with the intention of following a particular pedagogical impulse: he wanted to make the German nationalistic youth aware of the responsibilities inherent in being German while, at the same time, acknowledging their need to feel pride in being German. It was for this reason that Jaspers had selected a typical nationalistic publisher and a man like Weber to give the concept 'German' an ethical content. In 1933 they needed this opportunism and help in Germany.

> 'That's the way it is. I want to be a German. When you speak of mother tongue, philosophy, and literature, all you need add is historical-political destiny, and there is no difference left at all.' And: 'This destiny today is that Germany can exist only in a unified Europe ... the devil with whom we will inevitably have to make our pact is the egoistic, bourgeois anxiety of the French.'

23. K. Jaspers, *Max Weber (1932)*, p. 27 ff., (1958), p. 32 ff. See for this W. Mommsen, *Max Weber und die deutsche Politik 1890-1920* (Tübingen: Mohr, 1974), p.354. See also K. Jaspers, *Lebensfragen*, p. 291 ff. Here not only the pathological drive for leaders is apparent but also the fundamentally wrong idea that a society will be well organized and 'good' only when a good leader is available. That was never a bad idea of the lowest classes but of the oikoidal elite. See also R. Baum, *The Holocaust and the German Elite* (London: Croom Helm, 1981), p. 109 ff.

24. AJC, p. 17, 18.

Arendt did not wait too long with her answer. On January 6, she informed Jaspers of the impossibility of adding a German historical and political destiny to her own German profile. The reason is obvious:

> 'I know only too well how late and how fragmentary the Jews' participation in that destiny has been, how much by chance they entered into what was then a foreign history. ... When we speak of Jews, we cannot really mean the few families that have been in Germany for generations now, but only the immigrant stream from the east for whom the process of assimilation keeps going on. Germany in its old glory is your past. What my Germany is can hardly be expressed in one phrase ... whether it is that of the Zionists, the assimilationists, or the anti-Semites ...'

Here Arendt's case becomes complicated by introducing the well-known contradiction between Western and Eastern Jews, the disappearance of the Western Jews through the assimilation process or emigration to Palestine following the Zionist creed. In an original Faustian way Jaspers closed the debate (January 10, 1933):

> '...what [is it] you are really after. We cannot live solely from negations, problems, and ambiguities. All these things need to be informed by something positive. How that is to be accomplished in the totality of human society without the devil is the question I would ask you, or with what other devil would you prefer to make your pact.'

It did not take long before even Jaspers knew who could be chosen as the best candidate for his devil's role. Compared to Heidegger's active contributions to the Nazi case, Jasper's opportunism seems rather childish, but both Arendt and her second famous philosopher-teacher showed their teeth in a symptomatic way.

Four letters later a world war was over, and gradually, life resumed its course. It took 14 years, but Jaspers renewed the debate.[25] He had just reprinted his Weber booklet to provide the post-war youth also with a good German hero. In fact, he made Weber a man and his own books publications for all seasons. In 1946 Jaspers also published a moral-theological bestseller, *Die Schuldfrage*. Indeed, he was one of the few more or less 'politically correct' well-known Germans at that time who tried to estimate the German guilt. Thanks to its abstractness and formality, the booklet could have functioned as a (quasi-) official German answer to the Nuremberg Trial, but it did not receive the overwhelming attention Jaspers expected. Thanks to the *Die Schuldfrage*, philosophers and theologians could monopolize the guilt question of the Germans who were too busy clearing up the

---

25. AJC, p. 87 ff. letter of May 16, 1947.

rubble and rebuilding the country. Now, in May 1947, Jaspers wrote this astonishing text to Arendt from behind the German ruins:

> 'I affirmed with Max Weber the idea of a German political greatness, and at the same time regarded Switzerland and Holland as German entities that fortunately lay beyond political risk and kept German qualities viable that were threatened in the German Reich ... That this German Reich .. has .. by its criminal actions brought about the demise of what is best in Germany does not destroy that other possibility, which retains its place among our noble memories (from .. Stein to Max Weber). Our only failing has been to grossly overestimate that possibility.'

In her answer Arendt again made clear that she was not prepared to accept a Weberian political profile because she did not reply to this strong statement at all. In correspondence or other works,[26] she and her husband vehemently criticized *Die Schuldfrage,* but Jaspers hardly reacted. She tried to redefine the German-Jew relation because Jaspers insisted on his ridiculous opinion that she always remained a German.

For Arendt this is the key point: if German Jews do not want to be German anymore, she answered, it means that they have no intention of sharing any political responsibility for Germany. With this she *ipso facto* argues that 'Jew' has nothing to do with (any) nationality. Including Israel? Although she declares her intention never to go to Palestine, convinced as she is 'that things will not work out there', it is a matter of course to follow 'things' there on a daily basis. It is at this juncture that she formulates for the first time her ideal way of life (see below). Before elaborating on 'Hannah's choice' the following question must be dealt with.

If there was no political affinity with Weber, what then fascinated Arendt? With her new husband, Heinrich Blücher, she made jokes about Jaspers' hero: 'It should be more effective to tell the students first that Weber was a boozer because of his annoyance with his country, while afterwards informing them about

---

26. H. Arendt, *Men in Dark Times* (San Diego, New York: Harvest Books, 1995) in which there are two articles about Jaspers (p.71-95) from 1957/58. In a letter to Jaspers (17-8-1946) Arendt wrote: 'Well, then, we are very much in agreement with you in all the major points ..' (AJC, p.52) which was fully in variance with the truth. Her husband had given a devastating review of the *Schuldfrage* (see ABB, p. 146 ff.) and, in fact, Hannah herself diplomatically launched only critical remarks. Jaspers showed his true cowardly nature by reacting arrogantly to her mild, submissive remarks (AJC, p.62) and silence regarding a highly critical review by Ben Halpern in *Jewish Frontier* (AJC, p. 121) with the 'argument': 'Speak your piece once and then keep your silence ..' (AJC, p. 162)! The Zionist Kurt Blumenfeld, one of Arendt's beloved pen-friends, concluded after reading the *Schuldfrage* (5-11-1954): ' that he [Jaspers] understood the German people as badly as he did the problem of the structure of world history.' (ABK, p.114). That is an understatement: one who, after this war, is able to talk about Switzerland and Holland as 'German entities', still accepts Weber's highly aggressive plans with these countries (see GPS, p. 136) and has nothing learnt from the last war. See also H. Derks, *Deutsche Westforschung,* p. 13 ff.

"politics as a vocation", than cramming them with the methylalcohol of the ideal types schemes with which Weber boozes himself into the grave.'[27] This does not mean that she detested Weber.

Jaspers is always looking over her shoulder and urging her time and again to consult Weber. He even dreamed of a situation in which Arendt and he 'were together at Max Weber's. You, Hannah, arrived late, were warmly welcomed. The stairway led through a ravine. The apartment was Weber's old one. He had just returned from a world trip, had brought back political documents and artworks, particularly of the Far East. He gave us some of them, you the best ones because you understood more of politics than I.'[28] If dreams mean something, the dantesque 'latecoming' or the 'ravine' must have impressed Arendt as well as the biblical connotation that 'the last will be the first' in getting precious presents from the Godfather himself.

All this turned Arendt into a real Weber adept, who could think that after Weber's *Agrarverhältnisse im Altertum* or *Die protestantische Ethik*, there could be 'nothing in the literature after it that begins to approach it'.[29] The only place, however, where I could see a real Weberian influence in her work is in *The Human Condition*, where her false analysis of the Greek oikos-polis relationship is directly derived from Weber's erroneous theory of the consumer city.[30]

It was not until the 1960s that people surrounding her discovered the ultra-nationalistic passages in Jasper's Max Weber book and Weber's own writings about Poland.[31] Arendt and Jaspers did not know how to react other than with cosmetic alterations (Arendt: 'phrasing it in a slightly different way'; Jaspers: 'replace a paragraph in the foreword with a new one'; etc.). Here, Arendt was confronted again with Weber's political profile, as usual related to 'Germany's Mission in World History'. Her 'German Zionist conscience', Kurt Blumenfeld, wrote very critically about Jaspers. However, he also remarked about Arendt's key concept:

'Max Weber's assertion: 'The Jews are a Pariah-people', may be witty [geistreich] but not as correct as I assumed once; the differences are much greater than the

27. ABB, p.126 Letter to Arendt 2-8-1941.

28. AJC, p.148 Letter to Arendt 20-4-1950.

29. AJC, p.282 Letter to Jaspers 17-2-1956. It is highly artificial how Arendt behaved here as the obedient pupil, whereas her *Origins of Totalitarianism* is five years old and *The Human Condition* is nearly ready. To both, Jasper's (nor Heidegger's) thinking did not contribute much.

30. *The Human Condition* (Chicago: University of Chicago Press, 1989) p. 37, 65 note 69 or p. 119. See H. Derks, *De Koe van Troje*, p. 8, 11, 14 and in particular, p. 193-197. For background and analysis of Weber's and others views on Greek society see my, The Ancient Economy: the problem and the fraud, in: *The European Legacy* 7 (2002), pp. 597 – 620.

31. AJC, p.546 Letter to Jaspers 19-2-1964. See also Idem, p. 548-549. For Weber's racism concerning Poles, see p. 118 above and K. Tribe, Prussian agriculture – German politics: Max Weber 1892-7, in: *Economy and Society*, 12 (1983), p. 181-226, in particular p. 211; W. Mommsen, p. 24 ff.

analogies. It is, in any case, much better to describe the single event than to produce new mistakes even if the terminology seems highly appropriate.'[32]

As we now know, qualifying Weber's pariah analysis as 'witty' is the last thing to do and if Blumenberg suggested not using the concept anymore then he failed: four years later Arendt published the Rahel Varnhagen study, which is the most extensive and subtle analysis of the pariah concept and practice to date.[33]

Therefore, one could go a step further and conclude that Arendt's pariah analysis is a much more modern and scientific way of analysis compared with Weber's classical ideological way of treating the concept. In a technical sense, her conceptualization falls behind Weber's or – better – is of a different, a socio-historical, political and non-ideological order. Weber designed a concept to be used at an universal historical level and not only for Jews of Western Europe. Instead, she created an entirely new origin of the concept in 18th century Western Europe (Maimon's writings), while Weber harked back to ancient patriarchal times and extended his search geographically into the Indian subcontinent and incorporated the hard-core of Christian theological discourse. For her purpose, Arendt did not revise the historical context of Weber's concept, nor the sociological or theological. In fact, she did not give any indication whatsoever of having read Weber's relevant writings! How then to perceive her choice?

Thanks to Jasper's outright Weber propaganda[34] *and* Blumenberg's Zionist fascination for the concept in pre-war times, Arendt came to the conclusion that she had to come up with a *victim's* conceptualization, whereas Weber represented the *view of the traditional oikoidal perpetrator* and Blumenberg that of the *modern oikoidal perpetrator*. Arendt was well aware of this deadly triangle, sometimes as a result of philosophical reflection which did not help her much; mostly through universalistic historical analysis as in *The Origins of Totalitarianism* or a fine social milieu reflection as in *Rahel Varnhagen*. For her, however, her many face-to-face relations as reproduced in her large correspondence certainly are a substantial source of inspiration of how to make her choice.

Of course, somebody living so energetically and conscious in such a terrible time could make several errors of judgement in her personal relations as well as in her works. These errors, however, are highly illustrative of the personal and intellectual struggle to find a road out of the serious mess the governing elites had made before, during and after World War II, and out of the farce Zionists/ 'people of the Torah'/the State of Israel made of the reflections of the Holocaust and Shoah.

---

32. ABK, p.117 (5-11-1954).
33. See ABK, p.240 ff. (10-8-1959).
34. For other aspects of Jasper's influence see L.& S.Hinchman, Existentialism Politicized: Arendt's Debt to Jaspers, in: Idem (Ed.), p. 143-179.

At least my fascination with her person and work rests not only on the remarkable qualities of her work but on her largely independent judgements as well: they are given *sine ira et studio;* they are, in principle, worth studying today and exposed her to hate from many fundamentalists, which is a quality in its own right.

A FUTURE WORLD HISTORICAL CONTEXT

'What I would like to see and what cannot be achieved today would be such a change in circumstances that everyone could freely choose where he would like to exercise his political rights and responsibilities and in which cultural tradition he feels most comfortable. So that there will finally be an end to genealogical investigations both here and in Europe ... (At) the moment ... we would do best not to settle down too permanently anywhere, not really to depend on any nation, for it can change overnight into a mob and a blind instrument of ruin.'

Hannah Arendt, June 30, 1947

10. TOWARDS A LIBERATION OF THE PARIAHS

Once upon a time there was a writer, Essad Bey or Kurban Said (1905-1942), who apparently happened to be a son of German-Jewish parents and was born in Baku, Azerbaijan. As a young man he converted to Islam, presented himself in Berlin as a Caucasian warrior, a strong anti-communist flirting with monarchism, and – in particular – as an inspired romancier. In any respects, today two of his novels are world bestsellers and one tells the national epos of Azerbaijan. This rather mysterious Said exploited a theory of world history in his books which runs as follows:

> 'Maybe there is only one proper division of mankind, the one between wood people and desert people. The dry drunkeness of the Orient comes from the desert, where hot winds and hot sand intoxicate men: the world becomes simple and uncomplicated. The wood, however, is full of questions. The desert never asks, gives and promises anything. But the fire of the soul comes from the wood. The desert man – I can see – possesses only one feeling and knows only one truth which both fulfill him completely. Wood man has many faces. The fanatic comes from the desert, the creator from the wood. Maybe, these are the main differences between Orient and Occident.'[1]

---

1. Kurban Said, *Ali and Nino* (New York: Anchor Books, 2000), p. 51; also quoted without source by Hafid Bouazza in his bookreview of Kurban Said's newly translated novel, *The Girl of the Golden Horn*, in: *Vrij Nederland*, 3/10 August 2002, p. 108. My translation is not quite the same as in the Anchor Book. It was helpful that Said's life is shrouded in mystery. His father could be the German-Jewish merchant Leo Nussimbaum (or Noussembaum); his mother a German governess; both lived in Baku as son Lev was born; the mother mysteriously disappeared from the picture; father and son lived later in Istanbul where son Lev converted to Islam and took the name of Essad Bey. At the moment one believes that his *The Girl of the Golden Horn* (1938) was written in German under the name of the Austrian Elfriede Ehrenfels. Kurban Said's other novel, *Ali and Nino* was issued a year earlier by a small Jewish publisher in Vienna. He also wrote biographies of Stalin, Nicholas II, the Shah of Persia, Mussolini. Both books at issue were discovered in the 1970s in the UK, rediscovered in the USA 1999 and now translated in many languages and probably filmed. Kurban Said died in 1941 or 1942 in Italy of a blood poisoning disease, alone and penniless while fleeing the Nazis. In short: his life and writings are a metaphor for non-conformistic life between the two world wars in South Eastern Europe. See the article from S. May in: www. kultur.orf.at; R. Shea's bookreview from *The Girl from the Golden Horn* in: bookreporter. com; W. Steavenson, *Ali and Nino* in: www.tbilisipastimes.com. So far the present information which is fully in variance with the *Vorwort* Werner Schendell wrote to Essad-Bey's first book, *Öl und Blut im Orient* (Berlin/ Leipzig: DVA, 1930) and with its chapter one. In this most topical book about the oil rush in Baku (1900-1930) the author tells also about the slow infiltration of the communists in these nomadic, freedom-loving Caucasian tribes (including the 'wild Jews', the Kipta, who hated in particular the sedentary Russian Jews!), about many legends of desert- and citylife in the Near-East. Here Essad Bey is the son of a Samarkand

It does not matter here whether Said's 'theory' is sound or not. It is easy to perceive his bestsellers as proof of Kipling's much quoted adage: *East is East and West is West, but never the twain shall meet.* In the present times of strained relations between Muslims and Christians, his dramatic love stories and docu-dramas will announce a pessimistic message underscoring, for example, Hunting-ton's superficial and dangerous so-called 'clash of civilizations'. It is easy to connect Said's work and Its immanent thoughts to our discussion of Max Weber's and Werner Sombart's strongly related but much more shaded theories which originated in the same historical period.

However, in a scholarly sense one has to stress *relations between phenomena* as is done in this book throughout; this must be more realistic and probably gives more reasons to political optimism as the usual dangerous exploitation of stub-born dichotomies. Also Jewish scholars discovered its advantage like, for instance, the sociologist Werner Cahnman who remarked

'When I came to understand that the trader and the peasant live in symbiosis and conflict, I was relieved ... The Jewish people dwells among the nations, whether in Israel or in the Diaspora, and the tensions between intimate symbiosis and bitter conflict remains a guiding theme of Jewish history.'[2]

But to end my book with a Hollywood happy ending at the moment 'elephants' in the USA, bravely assisted by 'ants' of Israel, unilaterally started a war against everybody and everything else under the heading 'terrorism' and 'world domination' would be a bit too much. We have to leave thoughts about a happy end of history to Fukuyama. However, it is necessary to come to some conclusion in this chapter, and again, I will do this with the critical help of Hannah Arendt. Some optimism can be gained from her writings anyway.

HANNAH'S CHOICE

As shown in chapter 3, with the backing of the Old Testament teachings, Weber issued a 'biblical ordeal' over the Jewish pariah who was identified fully with an 'eternal enemy', the nomadic Bedouin, Amalek, and so on; an ordeal that was repeated later in Zionist Israel.[3] In turn, Arendt developed within the heart of her political philosophical thinking an anti-Weberian concept of power which must receive our attention first.

Weber defined power as the possibility of forcing one's own will on the behaviour of others, while Arendt, long before Habermas, 'understands power as

---

based feudal lord and oil-tycoon and an intellectual Russian revolutionary mother. Anyway, this seems to be the only personal note about his background.

2. Quoted in J. Marcus, Z. Tarr, 'Recalling Werner Cahnman: on the history of Jews and Gentiles' in www.logosjournal.com/cahnman.htm which is the introduction to W. Cahnman, *Jews and Gentiles: A Historical Sociology of Their Relations* (New Brunswick: Transaction, 2004).

3. Hajo Meyer, *Het einde van het Jodendom*, p. 70.

the ability to agree upon a common course of action in unconstrained communication.'[4] Here we are confronted once again with the differences between an authoritarian oikoidal (concept of) political power and the *market* form of it. In the latter, power is generally not the property of an individual, which means it loses its fascination rather soon. It belongs to a group and remains true only as long as this group stays together and communicates with each other. Some political leader can be accepted only during a course of action and related to a certain job, and therefore, some political hierarchical ordering is or should be only temporary.

With this concept, pariahs have a chance, because it is directly connected to the conviction that 'no political leadership can with impunity replace power through force; and it can gain power only from a nondeformed public realm.' This fits more or less with the Madisonian dictum that 'all government rests on opinion'. In an oikoidal setting, however, *this* kind of public realm is to be found only as an *in-between space* as we discussed above (chapter 6 and 8).

The real oikoidal public realm is occupied by the military and police, heroic-political and religious symbols of power, their memory, glorification and so on. Where Arendt looks at *her* public realm as a space which can produce legitimate power, this is rather relevant only in existing market societies like the USA. In large parts of Europe and in most countries elsewhere, it is still associated with *illegitimate* power, because of the (often highly false) claims of legitimacy by the neighbouring oikoidal 'houses'. In abstract terms: the relations between the Oikos and the Market are very different under European, American or – say – Chinese conditions and, *ipso facto*, the non-conformist tendencies (pariah/parvenu and other developments).

Historically, this seems also the most realistic option, because time and again revolutionaries had and have to seize power at street level from where new *institutionalized* public spaces originate as well as new illegitimate (always from the oikoidal point of view) ones. Historians who take their profession seriously enough to study the many conflicting sides of problems are methodologically confronted with the need always to consider *mutual relationships* between antagonistic societies, groups with their public/private realms as dialectical and not as highly ideologically oriented dichotomic relations. Marxism paid only lip service to this demand.

Now, Arendt, in her central pariah/parvenu analysis or communication/public power analyses could, contrary to Weber and Habermas, carve inroads into a liberation of the pariahs, in the first place the Jewish ones. She ends her analysis in *The Jew as Pariah* with the following perspective:

4. See for the following citations the interesting comparison between Weber and Arendt in J. Habermas, Hannah Arendt's Communications Concept of Power, in: L.& S. Hinchman (Ed.), p. 211-231.

'Social isolation is no longer possible. You cannot stand aloof from society, whether as a *schlemihl* or as a lord of dreams. The old escape-mechanisms have broken down, and a man can no longer come to terms with a world in which the Jew cannot be a human being either as a *parvenu* using his elbows or as a *pariah* voluntarily spurning its gifts. Both the realism of the one and the idealism of the other are today utopian.'[5]

The horrors of war transformed millions of peoples into non-believers in whatever idea, ideology or belief system; they had, first and foremost, to look for food, a job and shelter. Also, Hannah Arendt had to digest many disillusions about her earlier life and aspirations of a German parvenu (she was even '*Hofjude*' for a while at a Rothchilds-Oikos); her work for the 'reconstruction' of 'Jewish culture' (1938-1952) made her a pariah desperately seeking for liberation; it also made her a gradually much better equipped political animal. For the first time, in 1944, she not only denied a pariah/parvenu existence but also the Kafka suggestion of foregoing all claims to individual freedom and inviolability and contenting oneself with a simple, decent life. At this juncture, the only alternative for her was the Zionist one, which came close to a flight into a dark future. All these flight movements made her much more willing to accept the kind of world view and consequently its practice indicated by her first husband, Günther Anders.

After 1945, as normal life regained its course, Arendt became gradually enmeshed between a *Jewish* and a *German sedentarianism*. The former contained the variants: the German enlightened Zionism of Blumenfeld; the Mapai Socialist Nationalism; and Begin et al.'s National Socialism.[6] The 'German sedentarianism' was differentiated into the German enlightened pragmatism of her husband Heinrich Blücher; the political metaphysics of Jaspers; the Weberian Nationalism; and the Heideggerian *Blut und Boden* metaphysics. It remains a remarkable achievement of Hannah Arendt how she managed to formulate a pragmatic alternative with an utopian element by degrees by provoking a lifelong debate with these ideal typical sparring partners.

The tensions and suspense of these debates always threatened her with capitulation to these 'big men' who could and were allowed to enter into her dreams, her bed and, eventually, her breakfast. When she was fully awake, however, and could travel[7] around outside their orbits, she resisted all longings and

---

5. JP, p. 90.
6. A good political analysis of these alternatives is Z. Sternhell, *The Founding Myths of Israel* (Princeton: Princeton University Press, 1998). See *TLS* 6-3-1998 p. 3 ff. See also my *Who is afraid of Zionism? Answers and alternatives* (forthcoming, 2005).
7. Her correspondence with Heinrich Blücher is symptomatically followed by a list of Arendt's travels (ABB, p. 586 ff.), while he was a prototypical introvert 'house-builder' trying to form a patriarchal family with his students and friends. '*Ich brauche die vier Wände mit Dir viel, viel mehr, als Du sie brauchst.*' (id., p. 227).

temptations of becoming this bed-and-breakfast parvenu. Apart from an article in 1930,[8] I could not discover any *serious* Heideggerian influence, and she never copied his typical archaic, uncommunicative way of expression and conceptualization. Even from the correspondence with Blücher, it is not clear what kind of philosophy her second husband propagates, let alone how much Arendt accepted of it. How she treated Weber is demonstrated above, and therefore, the obtrusive Weberian Jaspers is roughly put into his place.

Now, the first part of Hannah's choice consists of the following. After the cultural European ruin, after the destruction of Jews and after the serious disappointment about the Israeli Zionism which had learned nothing but to flee from the world by encapsulating itself while repressing and 'transferring' an indigenous population, Hannah choose for direct confrontation with the best representatives of the 'German Spirit' to get her questions answered. In my view, she permanently 'used' these strong representatives of her own German tradition, first, to remain conscious of her own history and, second, to be able to depart from this history as best as possible, i.e. to improve understanding of her own place little by little.

The second part of her choice was that she did not want to 'assimilate, taking all the consequences of denial of one's own origin and cutting herself off from those who have not or have not yet done it' while she refused to become 'a scoundrel' (see Arendt's quotation above this study).[9] Of course, this non-engagement vis-á-vis her closest oikoidalists could have resulted in a purely dichotomic reaction: the acceptance of Marxism was a quite realistic alternative as, for instance, with Isaac Deutscher; she was already a non-Jewish Jew.

---

8. Philosophie und Soziologie, in: *Die Gesellschaft*, 7-1-1930, p. 163-176, in particular, p. 166 ff. Of course, her dissertation on the love-concept in Augustine's work (1929) is fully inspired by Heidegger and Jaspers. From what E. Young-Bruehl, (p.490-501) tells us about its content, Arendt made a wise decision not to republish it. Already here Arendt was looking for counter-solutions as she started to think about the 'natality' problem, while Heidegger was occupied with 'mortality'. For that matter, 'natality' remained Arendt's most banal concept. Her main objective, however, was clear enough: to get rid of these dangerous metaphysical constructors of her youth in order to land properly on earth, and to walk around learning to understand this new world. She also wanted to be liberated from the abstract, typical oikoidal way of thinking of the professionals. See J.Taminiaux, Nothingness and the Professional Thinker: Arendt and Heidegger, in: R. Lilly (Ed.), *The Ancients and the Moderns* (Bloomington: Indiana University Press, 1996), p. 196-211.

9. Her anyway highly controversial relationship with Heidegger *after the war* must be seen in this perspective. The most stupid aspect of it is that she did not leave it as the personal confrontation she described, but that she became a staunch exporter of Heidegger's (and Jasper's) ambiguous *Gedankengut* in the USA, making this superoikoidal thinker (and his mediocre offshoot) world famous. However, looking for an explanation, I would say that she gradually became convinced that her personal commitment had to be a general lesson for everybody who is looking for the answer to the question: Why the Holocaust? Cynically, one could say: if this was Arendt's aim, it is a new variant of the '*am deutschen Wesen soll die Welt genesen*'. I think, there is no room for this suspicion and certainly in hindsight, now many new dirty facts about Heidegger's Nazi past are available.

However, Arendt made a dialectical jump, taking the chances for carving out her own place in the world through communication with these people. The next part of her choice was accepting/finding a new *locus operandi,* indeed:

> 'What I would like to see and what cannot be achieved today would be such a change in circumstances that everyone could freely choose where he would like to exercise his political rights and responsibilities and in which cultural tradition he feels most comfortable. So that there will finally be an end to genealogical investigations both here and in Europe ... (At) the moment ... we would do best not to settle down too permanently anywhere, not really to depend on any nation, for it can change overnight into a mob and a blind instrument of ruin.'[10]

Arendt wrote this in 1947 in a letter in which she, politely, knocked Jaspers down on 'his silence in 1933' and in which she returned to their disagreement on the Jewish question. To get rid of this problem, Arendt came up with her alternative, which is nothing other than a true *nomadic confession.*

The first aim is to realize the demand for political and cultural freedom which was yet a classical aim of 'Western' democratic politics but which from the end of the 19th century was undermined by the sheer dominance of a degenerating and barbaric Superoikos/ State. Furthermore, it is to perceive as a wish, idea or policy relative to the possibilities of living more or less peacefully with neighbours everywhere in this world as an extra safeguard for the own life, thought or 'home'.

Arendt stressed, therefore, the *homelessness* concept perceived as an anti-oikoidal concept *par excellence* and as a quality of life in its own right.[11] It is a nomadic way of thinking which says here:

---

10. AJC, p. 91.

11. H. Arendt, *The Life of the Mind (Thinking)* (New York, London: Harcourt Brace & Co, 1981), p. 199. See L.J. Disch, chapter 6 in particular p.176 ff.; S. Benhabib, p.49, 62 and 213 for the antagonistic, oikoidal interpretation of 'home', 'private' and 'homeless'. After I had finished this chapter, I discovered by accident the dissertation of J. Hermsen, *Nomadisch Narcisme* (Kampen: Kok, 1993). This is a comparative analysis of the (sex)lifes and writings of 'emancipated women' like Lou Andreas-Salomé, Belle van Zuylen and Ingeborg Bachmann. Hermsen is highly influenced by modern French philosophers like Deleuze (*La pensée nomade,* 1973) and Guattari or R. Braidotti with her thesis about 'the nomadic subject' (1993). It is not appropriate to discuss here Hermsen's book but found on her last page (p. 308) the quotation given from Hannah Arendt's *The Life of the Mind.* I was astonished that my historical and sociological analyses could be supported by Arendt's philosophical thinking as well. I also discovered another stunning parallel: at exactly the same time (1974-75) as Arendt formulated her thoughts about 'thinking' and 'willing', shortly before her death, I published for the first time an outline of my 'theory of hands and feet' in *De Armoede van het Ekologisme* [The Poverty of Ecologism] (Utrecht: University of Utrecht, 1974-75 second printing), p.32-64; for a further extention see also my *Stad en Land, Markt en Oikos,* p. 101-155. Arendt's thoughts about 'the mental activities in a world of appearances' perfectly fit with my thoughts about the effects of standing still (hands) and moving (feet) on thinking. Another publication will elaborate on these relationships.

'Generalization is inherent in every thought, even though that thought is insisting on the universal primacy of the particular. In other words, the 'essential' is what is applicable everywhere, and this 'everywhere' that bestows on thought its specific weight is spatially speaking a 'nowhere'. The thinking ego, moving among universals, among invisible essences, is, strictly speaking nowhere; it is homeless in an emphatic sense – which may explain the early rise of a cosmopolitan spirit among the philosophers. The only great thinker I know of who was explicitly aware of this condition of homelessness as being natural to the thinking activity was Aristotle ...'

She points, furthermore, to the *space* in which this homelessness has to be explained and further developed. It is the *world as communication network*, free from national boundaries and nationalistic pecularities, but as political as the old Greek *polis*. Here, she discovered *in practice* what remained closed to her in theory, namely that the main quality of this *polis* life was not the oikoidal autarchy and autarky but the market-related independence (autarkeia).[12] Already, she subjectively sympathized with Socrates, the 'thinker of the agora-market', and was on the brink of rejecting the Christian oikoidal Aristotle in favour of the Greek one, who is much more market oriented.

Arendt was a Jewess 'beyond dispute or argument' as she expressed it once; she refused, however, to give this any substance and, therefore, did not fit in any definition except, of course, that of the Nazis; in short: a non-Jewish Jew. She refused, in particular, to have some bond with a Zionist Israel and could not fit into any definition of Jew made in Israel. Eventually, Arendt and the nomadic principle and practice were deemed not in variance with some Diaspora theology.

Concerning the Jewishness of the unsettled, she could have elaborated on new sociological or theological meanings of 'The Diaspora'. Again, seen in their complex relationship, they are historically coupled to some 'Jerusalem' and, mostly, negatively appreciated. But if 'Jerusalem' only remains the metaphor for 'the end of our worldly journey' or the 'home where one will be buried' instead of a specific place which has to be violently conquered, it will be difficult to object to it: there comes an end to every voyage. The nomadic Jew as the liberated pariah, however, has to be seen as fully assimilated to and settled in the world as market.

---

12. H. Derks, Autarkeia in Greek theory and practice, in: *The European Legacy*, 1 (1996), p.1915-1933. Autarky was/ is a main economic objective of every oikoidal economy including the Nazi one. In this article, however, I argued that the 20th century supporters of this idea wrongly relied on Aristotle's political philosophy which said exactly the opposite: It is not an oikoidal but a market concept; the Greek *autarkeia* referred to freedom and independence and not to a closed circuit and a stubborn self-sufficiency as, for instance, also Martha Nussbaum argued.

They have nothing to do with any religious construction but find, eventually, their opponents in the typically assimilated Jews in the 'Western World', those who suffer from the 'Woody Allen Complex'. For both categories the name 'Jew' as 'people of the Torah' can be dropped; they have to be understood and explained in socio-political terms (see also below). For them Arendt's characterization of the *classically* assimilated European Jew must be an interesting eye-opener:

> 'instead of being defined by nationality or religion, Jews were being transformed into a social group whose members shared certain psychological attributes and reactions, the sum total of which was supposed to constitute 'Jewishness'. In other words, Judaism became a psychological quality, and the Jewish Question became an involved personal problem for every individual Jew.'[13]

Although they may share group qualities, there are substantial differences between the 'nomadic world Jew' and the earlier species of the 'assimilated Western Jew'. It is obvious that the former moves in a quite different spatial scale, and the latter, by definition, reproduces the 'other's identity' instead of nurturing its own. The 'nomadic world Jew' has a quite different socio-economic position which, in many respects, depends on the world market situation in the broadest sense of the word. The 'assimilated Western Jew' went through the whole transformation of pariah and parvenu right into the oikoidal bulwarks. He/she cannot ignore the alien present nor its past and has to assimilate antisemitism also; he/she is often possessed by the zealous drive of the convert and can easily become a 'scoundrel'.

Now, two last aspects require further comment: first, the relationship between the nomadic world Jew and the (Super)oikoidal powers, and second, the question of the nomadic identity.

FALLACIES OF THE NATIONAL STATE

Concerning the counter-power, the (Super)Oikos, Arendt insists that the overwhelming might of the national state-machines must be broken down in all corners of the world. Time and again she rightly fulminates against the largely unbridled power of bureaucracies, police forces and armies. These state-machines are the real menace of our era. They brought us right from the start of the 20th century with the Armenian or Herero genocide and Mexican revolution to today's severe losses in lives and capital in *all* parts of the world; they were the 'houses' of

---

13. Quoted in JP, p. 43. See also TOT, p. 66. An example at issue is Michael Kustow's short essay: Perplexities of a PNJJ. Modern Jewish identity and the unresolved questions about Zionism, in: *TLS*, April 6, 2001 p. 14, 15. After Deutscher's concept of a NJJ or Non-Jewish Jew (which is certainly not self-cancelling as a practising Jew told K.) Kustow now coined the PNJJ, the Post-Non-Jewish Jew as an ambiguous concept since he explains, for instance,: 'The unwieldy bagage of the PNJJ may be all that is left for a mental nomad like me'. It is still a good demonstration of our discussion.

the most terrifying regimes; also after 1945 they destroyed the best technical, social and democratic opportunities for alleviating life in large parts of the world. Their fascination created the Super-parvenu, the *Hofjude*; their Christian-inspired drive to 'clean up' the Oikos and to conquer an allegedly 'barbarian-bestial outside world' created the Holocaust. It must be the deep mistrust against the European superoikoidal national state-power which brought Arendt to criticize the Ben-Gurions and Begins with their 'Jewish State' and which inspired her together with Judah Magnes et al.[14] to seek cooperation with the Arabs/Palestinians from the start.

These opinions were directly derived from her pariah-analysis. To prove this, Arendt's recently published AUFBAU contributions are highly interesting. They, first, learn how Arendt's 'Jew as Pariah' article from 1944 developed from 1940 onwards in an increasing pessimistic mood: the rumours about a Holocaust and Shoah started to spread in 1943 and became a near certainty in 1944. In november 1941 she already wrote, for instance, that the Jewish people only was the first 'Paria-Volk':

> 'Today all European peoples are outlawed. Therefore, the refugees from all countries who are chased to all countries raised to the *avantgarde* of their peoples. *The world citizens of the 19th century became world travellers against their will in the 20th century.* This tradition one has to keep in mind. ... All European nations became pariah-peoples; all are forced to fight for *freedom and equal rights* ... for the first time, our struggle became identical with the battle for European freedom.'[15]

Apparently, an extensive letter to Erich Cohn-Bendit (january 1940) is the basis of this opinion.[16] Here Arendt addresses the minority-question and the serious shortcomings of the Jewish and Zionist organizations. She is still optimistic about the possibilities of changing the course of history within some of the given political frameworks which only needed some reforms. A summary of her highly topical argument in this letter is the following.

From about 1920 onwards Jews form a minority *par excellence*: they constitute the only fully de-politicized minority because of the failure of a *Mutterland*. The Jewish leadership, which has no relationship with a Jewish people whatsoever, cannot provide an *Ersatz* for this omission in the form of Palestine or of 'the so-called

---

14. See her articles: Zionism Reconsidered (1945) or To Save the Jewish Homeland (1948) in: *JP*, p. 131-164 and 178-193 for her still highly relevant opinion about Israel. For Judah Magnes see *JP*, p. 193-225 the article: Peace or Armistice in the Near East? (1950); E.Young-Bruehl, p. 225 ff.; AJC, p.126; R.Bernstein, p. 109 ff., 119 ff.

15. H. Arendt, *Vor Antisemitismus* (note 6 ch. 9), p. 28 (my italics).

16. Idem, p. 225-235 .

Weltjudenheit'. The latter is still non-existent and for the former there is no Diaspora-policy: Zionism 'will perish thanks to this failure'. The masses of stateless people, the modern pariahs, are 'the most important product of contemporary history'. The impossibility to absorb these masses is a practical reason why one must be very critical about assimilation policies:

> 'In Europe, there is no assimilation anymore: the nations are too developed and too old. For Jews as well there is no assimilation whatsoever. ... Yes, you can even see quite the opposite development: the repulsion of large masses of people and their deprivation to pariahs. Although Europeans, these pariahs are separated from all specific national interests, but interested first in a total European policy. ... If everything runs very good, they could be the forerunners of a new Europe.'[17]

However, the national states oppose for very opportunistic reasons any all-European solution of the refugee question[18] and pave the way for several kinds of 'final solutions', in particular for unprotected people like Gypsies, Jews, etc. So-called 're-importation plans' [like the Madagascar Plan] are popular. For Jews these

> 'are only related to deportation. This kind of projects existed before the war and since the Evian Conference they are multiplied. It is one of the most evil omens that the Zionist Organisation did not protested against these plans ... and most quarters of the Jewish territorialists ... participated in this project-misery. One cannot undersign its own death sentence.'[19]

Later she talked about deportation with compulsory labour. The alternative Arendt proposes is as follows:

> 'Our only chance ... lies in Europe as a new federal system. ... It would be an utopia – and not a very attractive one – to believe in one single European nation. This could exist only in America ... But it seems to me no utopia to long for an [European] union of nations with an European parliament. ... With this 'solution' of the Jewish Question the puzzlegame of 'the People without Land,

---

17. Idem, p. 229.
18. The most dishonest gathering of worldleaders, on the initiative of Roosevelt, met in Evian-les-Bains in July 1938 in order to come up with a solution for the refugee problem and, in particular, for the Jewish question. Nobody condemned Germany as one of the most responsible at the time, while nearly all (including the USA) closed their borders for Jews and other refugees. Here also projects like the Madagascar Plan were propagated. See H. Jansen (note 27 ch. 8), p. 203-229; S. Heim, T. Schmid, Wir sind kein Einwanderungsland, in: *Die Zeit* 2-7-1998, p. 78; now also M. Burleigh, *The Third Reich. A New History* (London: Macmillan, 2000), p. 317-322, p. 590-597.
19. H. Arendt, *Vor Antisemitismus,*, p. 230.

looking for a Land without a People' (so practically on the moon or through the disappearance of politics into folklore) should have been non-sense at last.'[20]

It is clear that Arendt's AUFBAU columns support my general 'pariah-argument' and they are still of topical interest. As is well known two models of the New Europe fight for recognition: the centralized French and the federal German Europe. Since Mitterand's death the French influence lost momentum and, therefore, the federal model could receive more support. Hannah Arendt's europeanism is anyway one of the first political pro-European stands (as usual combined with a certain anti-americanism).

Her criticism of the Zionists and the failure of a Diaspora-policy, furthermore, is still appropriate for the present Israel: in the end the highly ambiguous settlement activities are the result of the pernicious *People Without Land* creed, while a Diaspora-policy is still confined to a rather opportunistic oneway traffic of people from every corner available and to money from the USA, whereas the religious folklore of orthodox Jerusalem has been turned into sheer ukases for everybody. The dominance of Jewish-USA 'big guns', Arendt regrets so much, is still a major element in the USA-Israeli relations. Indeed, to a large degree the selfdetermination of the latter is undermined: no Israeli leader, and certainly nobody recruited from the army, is able to gain power without USA- money and USA-political support, including Ariel Sharon. It is all part of the classical *Hofjuden*-complex.

However, her suspicion is not very realistic because there is no such thing as a 'Jewish community' or 'Volk', speaking with one voice, etc., and because Arendt could not predict the post-war countervailing political influence of stubborn religious leaders. Besides this, one can ask whether the 19th century position of the European Rothchilds was so different from the present Jewish-USA 'big guns'.

The real eye-opener of these texts is her analysis of the topical minority-question and her valuation of the stateless worldtravellers as a new political force. In it she dialectically incorporated the Jewish Question into the Nomadic Question so that the latter could be enriched with her pariah differentiations as given in the 1944 article. The present discussion about quite new forms of nomadism will loose its psychological and philosophical partiality if the (adjusted) Arendt arguments could be discussed as well.

Furthermore, participants in this discussion have to be realistic. They cannot forget how the position of Arendt's worldtravellers paralleled that of the real tribal nomads all over the world. These have been (and still are) severely threatened since the end of the 19th century. They, too, have their peculiar and structural drive to

---

20. Idem, p. 231, 232.

cooperate with their settled environment. The need to do this is also economically motivated. The political economic basis of a nomadic economy is the practice of a *democratic market of products and ideas*. (Arendt started playing with the same thoughts.[21]) To its main quality belongs the pragmatism of all nomadism. Therefore, the specific relationship between the actual place of the nomadic settlement and its socio-economic and political environment is of the utmost importance. This environment is mostly nothing but the settlement of the (oikoidal) sedentary majority.

In other words: old and new nomads are highly interested in forms of structural cooperation with oikoidal interests, which are directed to several forms of structural *suppression* of their environment. Due to this fundamental antagonism, therefore, the main political aim of the classical as well as the new nomadism has to be the democratization of societies in East and West, North and South. Or, better, the democratization of the societies with which they have to deal on a more or less permanent basis. This democratization will be enhanced with the gradual disappearance of the national states.

Within the political philosophy of this long term process also Arendt's 'nomadic confession' and analysis of the European minority-problem could receive a new basis. If, however, we confine ourselves to the subject of this book, the Jewish Question vis à vis the (new and old) Nomadic Question, a last element must be discussed.

NOMADS WITH A COMMON BACKGROUND

This element, not surprisingly, concerns the identity of the 'nomadic world Jew'. How could an identity be formed in such a historically, sociologically or culturally complex case as this?

Right at the beginning of this book, I quoted rabbi Joachim Prinz (1902-1988), a popular Berlin rabbi before the war who is called today 'a counterpoint to his staid conservative colleagues'.[22] A sentence was left out of this quote, namely: 'The

---

21. Idem, p. 227 and 234.
22. See introduction note 3 and www.joachimprinz.com. page 1 of this website. Here one learns that rabbi Prinz could go to the USA in 1937 (expelled 'for reasons that he would never know'), stayed there until his death and became one of the ' big shots' in the American and World Jewish Congress, sometimes a Director of the famous Claims Conference Against Germany and even a President of the Presidents (sic) of all American Jewish organizations. Peter Novick, *The Holocaust and collective memory* tells some remarkable things about the American Prinz. First that he belongs to the earliest critics of Hannah Arendt's *Eichmann in Jerusalem* (p. 135) which was, according to Novick 'not just false but the reverse of the truth' ! In 1961 he declared as president of the American Jewish Congress (AJC): 'Zionism is – for all practical purposes – dead.' But see below! Five years later Prinz told this AJC that young Jews' unwillingness to consider 'Jewish identification and solidarity' was largely attributable to their ignorance of the Holocaust which triggered a specific American Holocaust-policy (p. 187). See also p. 323 note 9 and compare this with the given website in which Prinz is sketched as

ghetto is not a geographically limited district anymore as was the case in the Middle Ages. Now "the World" is the ghetto...' That is not the illogical and also pessimistic answer which could be expected at the end of my study. Anyway, It is interesting to stay a while with this sharp alternative to my conclusions.

We now know, first, that the medieval situation was quite different, as suggested here (see chapters 4 and 5). Notwithstanding Evian, a declaration that the whole world was closed, a prison for Jews, reminds us of irrationalities like the existential fear of the poor and/or helpless Jews and *marranos* or the calculating opportunism of a Jewish leadership. The latter seems to be the case, because a few months earlier Prinz published his most acclaimed book, *Wir Juden* ('We Jews'), which is indeed important to discover the reactions of leading Jews in Germany and the Zionist drive among a small minority of them.[23]

In this book time and again, Prinz declared Jews and himself to be of Bedouin descent; they were not only 'Händler' as Sombart already wrote but 'Helden' as well (see chapter 4).[24] It is very clear what rabbi Prinz's message was: at last we Jews must sedentarize after being nomads for three thousand years and that must happen in Palestine/Israel. How did he support this remarkable message?

In his *Jüdische Geschichte* he regrets the increasing antisemitism in Europe not so much for Jews but for 'culture and civilization' in general. For Jews, however, it provides the stick to make them a really strong community which cannot be affected anymore by Christian baptizing – the *marranos* complex – nor by non-

---

more active in the civil rights movement as Martin Luther King himself. Notwithstanding this exaggerations, in Prinz we are confronted with a highly assimilated American Jew.
23. J. Prinz, *Wir Juden* (Berlin: Erich Reiss, 1934). I quote only a few sentences from the original which sounds: 'WIR JUDEN wandern mehr als drei Jahrtausende über die Welt. Stolze, wilde Beduinen, braun und stark, kämpften gegen Wüste und Gefahr. Helden rangen mit Riesen ... WIR JUDEN zogen durch alle Länder der Erde. Von den Inseln Kleinasiens nach Spanien, Afrika, Griechenland, Italien, in die deutschen Rheingaue, in die russischen Steppen, in die Täler der Champagne und weit nach Indien und China ... in und lebte noch die männliche Entschlossenheit der Urväter-Beduinen, die Stärke der Helden, der Mut der Abenteuer ... WIR JUDEN wurden durch das harte Schicksal unserer Geschichte Kleinbürger, Händler, Schacherer, Gelehrte ... In allen Dingen unseres Leben zerbrachen wir – wenn wir unserer Art vergaßen. Unser Leben wir unsere Geschichte verrieten. ... WIR JUDEN, Beduinen, Helden, Könige .. von einst vergaßen uns selbst, unsere Art und unseren Glauben, zerbrachen an diesem Vergessen ... WIR JUDEN suchen die eigene Freiheit.' (p. 13 ff.). These exclamations are continued on p. 173 ff. with, for instance,: 'WIR JUDEN suchen die eigene Freiheit die auch die Freiheit der Völker ist. Wir finden sie nur im eigenen Land .. Es wird den Völkern ein neues, schöneres Bild des neuen Juden zeigen .. eines zum Boden zurückgekehrten Juden weisen. ... WIR JUDEN weisen so der Welt, der ganzen Welt, den Weg zur Lösung unserer Frage ...'
24. In fact, Prinz was strongly influenced by Sombart as can be proved not only by his ridiculous Beduin-story but also by his *Jüdische Geschichte* (Berlin: Verlag für Kulturpolitik, 1931) p. 129 for his view on the Sephardim, by his erroneous view on the relationship between Jews and 'money' and 'commerce' (Sombart's *Händler* interpretation!), etc. For Prinz' racist and inimical views on the *marranos* see p. 136 ff.

Jewish marriages – the crux of the *assimilation* complex.[25] He welcomed anti-semitism, therefore, as the lesser evil because the pressure from outside made them stronger inside. He wrote this at the moment 'that 107 members of parliament [Reichstag] were nominated to crush the "*Vormachtstellung des Judentums*" with all means and that the incited mob splintered the shop-windows of the large Jewish firms in the middle of the capital Berlin.'[26] Still, the last sentence of this history written by a young popular rabbi in this city was:

> 'There is one word that you can write above the whole Jewish history: *Wait*. For thousands of years we have been waiting for the Saviour ... but He did not come. Therefore, we are still waiting. We are not disappointed ... *We wait.*'[27]

With *Wir Juden* Prinz probably realized that this advice was not best suited to the given German circumstances, to say the least. After again criticizing at length many kinds of assimilation practices and – in particular – the *marranos* anti-Judaism (defined as 'Jewish *Selbsthass*' which he found, for instance, in the writings of Marx, the 'baptized Jew'), and after stating that Jews had fully internalized the German culture or that in the new Germany all Jews have happily lost their anonymity, Prinz now wrote:

> 'The assimilation theory broke down. There is no hiding place to hide us. Instead of assimilation we demand the new: *the belief in a Jewish nation and in a Jewish race*. A state built on the Principle of the Purity of Nation and Race can respect and accept only Jews who believe in their own kind. [....] Because only they who respect their *own* kind and *own* blood can have respect for the *national will of other nations*. [...] Whatever the place we have to live ... it is also in our own land that the German Jew will profess to the German culture. This is part of our being. [...] The energy (Kräfte) of Jews begins to fade (versanden und verdorren). .. its society has degenerated to one of merchants, medical doctors and lawyers. What is yet to be expected from this community? ... Where in the world do you find creative processes (Entfaltungen) which come to a dead end in intellectualism (im Intellekt) and do not derive their power from the soil? How can she understand the love of the peasant for his land, if she is divorced from the peasants' piece of land, home (Scholle) and labour? How long will this people

---

25. He literally wrote about 'eine sehr festgeschlossene jüdische Gesellschaftsschicht aus deren Fangarmen weder Taufe noch Mischehen führen können.' ('a very closed Jewish social stratum with tentacles which can avoid the effects of baptizing and mixed marriages'), p. 268. See note 84 ch. 4 for the same exclamations of a Chief Rabbi of Israel, Baksi-Doron today.
26. Idem, p. 268.
27. Idem, p. 268, 269. Prinz italics. For other reactions of Prinz see S. Friedländer, *Nazi Germany and the Jews. The Years of Persecution, 1933-1939.* (New York: HarperCollins, 1997), passim.

have to satisfy itself with the asphalt of the Big City? ... *It is for these reasons that the world suffers from the Jews* (leidet die Welt am Juden).'[28]

In this way one can quote many passages which will give the clear impression that Prinz preached exactly the same ideological language in 1934 as the supporters of the regime which he and his followers wanted to leave behind as soon as possible. Here he also exaggerated the already strongly overdone Sombartian elements in his history (that is to say from Sombart II); antisemitism is not only welcomed as an argument to go to Palestine but also to criticize specific behaviour of other Jews; in Prinz's view liberalism and liberal reforms undermine not only the *Volkskraft* and a *Jüdische Rasse* but were also 'entangled with a process of de-judaization (*Entjudungsprozeß*)' in which Judaism only became a religion; he combined the current anti-urbanism with anti-intellectualism and praised, therefore, the purity of peasant muscles to plough land in an anti-democratic society with a '*volkhafte jüdische Religiosität*'.

Thus, all this refers to the harshest forms of sedentarization, and Prinz, indeed, preached a counter-revolution (as, for instance, the rural alternative of Sombart I) to people who were 'Bedouins for thousands of years'. But he did not understand what a forced sedentarization of nomads means in modern times or what original nomadic life looks like (see chapter 2). That was already the case with Sombart. His study, in fact, did not go beyond current orientalisms mixed with well-known elements of the German Ideology. The same is even true of Max Weber who could combine this with a reasonable theoretical framework. Prinz was not a scholar but a preacher apt to reduce complex matters into consumerable bites for demagogic purposes. The problem is that these people were and still are much more influential in difficult times than scholars, whatever their own reductionist writings.

If we remember now how Hannah Arendt warned that 'it is possible to assimilate only by assimilating to antisemitism also', a new dimension is given to opinions like those of Prinz: in several ways Prinz assimilated the language of antisemitism and denied in the harshest way the *oldest Jewish traditions of the nomadic Patriarchs* by the sedentarizing and peasantization of Jews. In other words, in *Wir Juden* he only reproduced the *newly invented Bedouin tradition* of Max Weber and Werner Sombart with its many antisemitic traits and reacted accordingly as prescribed by the given German political model in which a very specific religiosity replaced the given German ideology of the New Man.[29]

---

28. J. Prinz, *Wir Juden*. The first part of the quotation comes from p. 154, the second from p. 157, the third from p. 161 and 162. Italics from J. Prinz.

29. This is probably the reason why the theocracy erected in 1948 by Jews and non-Jews in Palestine was also at that time such a strange and archaic relict from European 'soil'.

Anyway, this kind of Zionism has nothing to do with a Jewish answer, but it is one of the answers given by Jews in this highly critical time.[30] The Nazis who at this stage tried by all possible means to get rid of Jews by supporting Madagascar, Palestine and many other plans, must have been delighted with Prinz's books, speeches and Zionism. When he tells us that for Jews 'the world is a ghetto', several explanations are possible: 1. this must be a variant on: there is no way out so we Jews have to *wait*; 2. although this world is a ghetto, we Jews must stop irritating everybody else and retire to a remote corner of this ghetto doing simple, pious and inconspicious peasant labour; 3. as the combination of the preceding two: 'the world' is only a 'vale of tears' in which you are dependent on all kinds of institutions mediating between you and the coming Saviour. Whatever their (very Christian) meanings, all these choices are pessimistic in nature and consolidate the pariah ('incast', parasite, outcast) position of Jews, always taken as an undifferentiated group vulnerable to all sorts of repression like all minorities are. In addition, of course, there is the fact that from the beginning one is practically fully dependent on some *foreign* power in its broad meaning, in particular a state and church/religion.

From my book also other harsh lessons can be learned. The fundamental inability of what is called the 'Jewish community' to provide any relevant and satisfactory answer to the question of 'who is a Jew' is a *function of the oikoidal Christian creation of the negative Jewish identity*. Seen from a 'Jewish' side, also Prinz documents that 'Jew' is an alien and inimical concept. It does not represent a race, a people, an ethnos, and one can even doubt if it refers to a religion. Its representatives, certainly, belong to the non-conformists relative only to a Christian, European and oikoidal value system (Sephardim to the Catholic and Askenazim to the Lutheran Protestant variant); their rich or powerful representatives have to act within a 'Hofjuden complex' and its several variants prescribe: little and big obedient servants of masters; little and big payments; no rights, no security except some empty juridical rules for quiet times.

If this system is jeopardized and a reshuffling of the *foreign* (from a minority point of view) political, cultural and economic map has to be forced, which was the case at a European level in 1492 and in a very different way as in the period 1870-1945, all non-conformists of this kind have to be eliminated just because they had a behaviour and customs (not so much a value system) which perishes. Later, when the relative peace returns, new non-conformists of this kind were necessary,

---

30. For the reactions within the several Jewish communities and personalities see J.Dippel, *Bound Upon a Wheel of Fire* (New York: Basic Books, 1996). Generally one can see three answers: a liberal one, a Zionist one and an ultra-German one represented by Hans-Joachim Schoeps who published in 1934 also a booklet with the title *Wir deutsche Juden*. See Idem, p. 265 ff. and passim. Dippel mentions Prinz only in the bibliography.

recruitable and available. And so on? Do we describe here the 'present future' of, for instance, Israel, the Jewish state ?

By answering also questions like these It is helpful that we discovered thanks to Arendt's choice a clearer understanding of the problems at hand and of the people who claim a certain Jewish background. We have to consider political-philosophically that we are dealing with *nomadic non-conformists who have only two directions in their way of life:* towards the pariah/outcast, parvenu and so on until the assimilation into the/an alien Oikos, or towards the metaphorical or historically real nomad and adaptation to the homelessness in the 'desert of the world'. Of course, practically, these two directions can be interconnected by several semi-permanent arrangements, but that is evident and not very interesting here.

Therefore, the identity (knowledge about a common background) of, originally, 'non-Jewish Jews' only concerns these facts of nomadic life. My study suggests that four historical and other sources for this identity are available, which were all discussed in the previous chapters, apart from elements arising from specific locations in the world (see, for instance, Claudia Roden's story about the different kinds of food). These four sources can be summarized as follows:

1.   Knowledge about the Old Palestinian constellation from urbanizing nomadic societies with spiritual characteristics of a highly individual, non-authoritarian spiritual life, etc. (see Abraham-Ishmael nomads).
2.   Knowledge arising from the election as eternal enemy of the Christians (see Amalek nomads).
3.   Knowledge derived from a life as a (very) small minority of refugees within European societies which look for some security and cohesion in rather closed oikoidal settlements (see *marranos* villages, *shtetl*).
4.   Knowledge of the Shoah within a Holocaust context.

This 'knowing about a common background' guarantees that these are the true elements and the binding factors between past, present and future. Together, they transcend every notion of ethnos, race or religion and are strongly based in a realistic and not a metaphysical history. Furthermore, they demonstrate the changeability of the identity in the sense of a growing complexity in time. It is not an apolitical life to do global business, visiting friends with whom these ex-Jews share a common history, but one with active involvement in world and local politics stimulating conflict prevention and a solution in the oikoidal bulwarks to establish lively democracies.[31]

---

31. A good example of someone who recently demonstrated the constellation as envisaged here is the politically very active Hajo Meyer (now 81 years). Asked how he as non-religious Jew should define 'the Jewish identity', he first agreed with the thesis that too often some identification with Israel is a replacement for such an identity; he answered further: ' ... To be honest, without Hitler I probably

What about the cohesion among and between these nomads, apart from the modern facilities like *Internet*? In the last quotation from Arendt in the former paragraph, she talked about a social group. How could we view such a social group? Is it not strange to describe this by means of socio-psychological attributes? In my view, we come nearer to a basic characteristic through what is called 'group-feeling', nurtured by a combination of specific customs (the way of eating, clothing and the like), a common history (the Holocaust, some spiritual ideas) and common experiences (specific skills exercised in a non-permanent way at a non-permanently settled place).

Here the historical theory of the *Nomadic Challenge* from Ibn Khaldûn[32] can be consulted for a relevant way of looking at the social groups Jews have formed in history as a consequence of nomadic life or oikoidal repression. 'Group feeling' (*asabiyya*) is a most important keyword in Ibn Khaldûn's theory. It produces the ability to defend oneself, to offer opposition, to protect oneself, to press one's claims and so on.[33] The prestige and nobility of a 'house' is in direct proportion to the different degrees of group feeling.[34] Ibn Khaldûn sketches this relationship as follows.

'Isolated (that is, belonging to no tribe) inhabitants of cities can have a 'house' only in a metaphorical sense. The assumption that they possess one is a specious claim. ... A 'house' possesses an original nobility through group feeling and (personal) qualities. Later on, the people (who have a 'house') divest themselves of that nobility when group feeling disappears as the result of sedentary life. ... A certain delusion as to their former prestige remains in their souls ... They are, however, far from that (status), because their group feeling has completely disappeared. ... The Israelites are the most firmly misled in this delusion. They

was not jewish at all. Before Hitler religion and Judaism did not play any roll in our family [a lawyers family from Bielefeld, Germany. H.D.]. Because I was an Auschwitz inmate, I cannot say I have nothing to do with Judaism. [Later] I started to read a lot about Judaism and I realized that it has positive and negative elements ... Jews often do as if they have a monopoly on suffering in history ... At the moment the growth of antisemitism is highly exaggerated...' This he told the interviewer, Arthur Bruls, in www.grenzeloos.org (Mai-June, 2003). In his book, *Het einde van het jodendom* (p. 289), he also tells about his pre-Hitler youth: 'In that time, you was a Jew whether you liked it or not, because your (antisemitic) environment perceived you as such. The freedom to get rid of your jewish identity nearly did not existed.' That is very different as people now decide for themselves whether they become or remain jewish: 'They do not have any externally imposed obligation to their jewish heritage.' (p. 290). Meyer does not believe anymore in an attractiveness of Judaism now Israel can be accused of serious crimes (id.).
32. See my *Stad en Land, Markt en Oikos*, p.99, 546 ff., 555 ff.
33. Ibn Khaldûn, *The Muqaddimah. An Introduction to History* Franz Rosenthal edition (Princeton: Princeton University Press, 1967), Vol. 1, p. lxxxviii ff., 264 ff., 289 and many other places.
34. Idem, p. 274, 275.

originally had one of the greatest 'houses' in the world, first, because of the great number of prophets and messengers born among their ancestors, extending from Abraham to Moses ... and next, because of their group feeling ... Then, they were divested of all that, and they suffered humiliation and indigence. They were destined to live as exiles on earth. For thousands of years, they knew only enslavement and unbelief. Still, the delusion of (nobility) has not left them. They can be found saying: 'He is an Aaronite' ... 'He is from the tribe of Judah'. This in spite of the fact that their group feeling has disappeared and that for many long years they have been exposed to humiliation. Many other inhabitants of cities who hold (noble) pedigrees but no longer share in any group feeling are inclined to (utter) similar nonsense.'

So, according to him, for sedentary people (almost identical to urban dwellers), it is too difficult to sustain group feelings. Luxury, 'civilization', poor leadership and other evils cause the loss of group feeling. Nowadays, one could say, the urban individualization spreads so quickly that some form of overall solidarity to a case is difficult to establish. In Ibn Khaldûn's eyes, nomads have the strongest *asabiyya*, and they, time and again, will re-establish group feeling where it is lost. Repression and sedentarisation also lead to a loss of group feeling.

How Ibn Khaldûn judges this situation is demonstrated also by his opposition to severe punishment in the course of instruction of students: 'Students, slaves, and servants who are brought up with injustice and (tyrannical) force are overcome by it. It makes them feel oppressed and causes them to lose their energy. It makes them lazy and induces them to lie and be insincere.'[35] He extends this opinion to all individuals and nations who suffer under the yoke of tyranny. Again, Jews are given as an example for people who acquired 'bad character' because of their repression. At the time they were nomads, they had one of the greatest 'houses' of the world. Once they became sedentary, e.g. urban dwellers and repressed, they lost their identity.

From Ibn Khaldûn's writings one may derive a message which is crystal clear: fight oppression, stay free, live a moderate life, sustain your group feeling and – if you have to live a sedentary existence temporarily – keep closely in touch with mobile life from which – in the end – must come 'all the good'. In his theory of history, however, he also showed how sooner or later some *relationship* with the inimical Oikos must be (re)established: this can be one of victim versus perpetrator, of rebel against oppression, or in commercial or cultural exchange.

Is there much difference from the themes and intention of Arendt's studies? In many respects, she added her study and engagement of the individual's action in searching for freedom. Once combined with Ibn Khaldûn's insights or the results of my studies, we are able to see the thorny road to liberation from a pariah

---

35. Idem, Vol. III, p. 305.

position of outcasts. With their great chance of becoming a parvenu and further caught in the darkrooms of oikoidal houses, they cannot be optimistic about whether these houses will ever become their homes instead of places for 'incasts'.[36] The location where the liberation takes place is elsewhere, on the other side of the 'pariah-line', in the (world)market, 'home' of the ex-pariahs. Once consciously arrived, one will become strong enough to survive the inevitable confrontations with the oikoidal powers, which can only be humanized by real democracy. Will this be the theme and, hopefully, the practice of this still new century?

---

36. It is difficult to see it as an accident that the Israeli/Jewish Avishai Margalit and Ian Buruma recently refered to Ibn Khaldûn as an Arabian precursor of the Nazi *Blut und Boden* theory in their irresponsible and over-excited attempt to mobilize something like "The West" against something like "The Islam". See their 'Seeds of Revolution', in: *The New York Review of Books*, 11.03.2004. My short protest against this mystification (01.03. 2004) was not accepted by this paper (see www.hderks.dds.nl under "Discussions"). Another criticism of Margalit's aim and support for my thesis unintentionally comes from the present Lebanese novelist Hanan al-Shaykh who wept 'because we Arabs have no connection with the Arabs of Andalucia, with those who, having borrowed the pens and chisels of angels, have carved and embellished to such melodious perfection. Why is it that we didn't complete our cultural journey, and how is it that we have ended up today in the very worst of times. ... It is enough for us to mention the works of al-Farabi, Avicenna, Ibn Khaldun, Ibn Rushd, Ziryab, Ibn Hazm Ibn Zeydoun and countless others.' Quoted by William Dalrymple, 'An inhabitable book', in: *Times Literary Supplement*, 16.07.2004, p.5. .

INDEX